The COMMUNIST PARTY of POLAND

Russian Research Center Studies

32

The COMMUNIST PARTY of POLAND

An Outline of History

Second Edition

M. K. Dziewanowski

HARVARD UNIVERSITY PRESS

Cambridge, Massachusetts, and London, England
1976

Library of Congress Catalog Card Number: 75–18050
ISBN: 0–674–15055–4
Printed in the United States of America

To Professor Michael M. Karpovich

Preface to the Second Edition

The first edition of this book, published in 1959 under the sponsorship of the Russian Research Center of Harvard University, was an extension of an introductory study of the Communist movement in Poland. The volume traced the evolution of leftist Marxist groups to the formation of the Communist Party of Poland in December 1918; the first edition covered the history of Polish Communism until the return of Gomułka to power, in October 1956, and the Sejm elections of January 20, 1957. This new edition is an expanded version of the first; it covers the entire era of Gomułka (October 1956–December 1970), and tries as well to cope with the first four years of Gierek's leadership of the Polish United Workers' Party.

The subtitle of the book stresses that it is merely a beginning, an outline, and not a definitive work. No final treatment of the Communist movement in Poland can be possible until the archives of the party, and those of the Comintern and Cominform, are made accessible to independent scholars. My work is merely an attempt to gather and analyze the quintessential material available in the West, and to draw a preliminary sketch that can serve as a point of departure for further investigation of the subject.

Circumstances made the rewriting of the book in the light of newly discovered sources and recent monographs impossible; nevertheless, the old text has been corrected of printing mistakes and factual errors. Otherwise the book remains unchanged, except for a few additions warranted by available space. I have tried to approach the origin and history of the Communist Party of Poland and its later transformations, the Polish Workers' Party and the Polish United Workers' Party, from the aspect of its effects on East European history, emphasizing cultural and even religious aspects when essential. Thus the book continues to focus on the Communist movement as a social and political force, and not upon the internal functioning of the party machinery as such.

I did not feel qualified, nor did I have sufficient material, to cover either the Communist parties of Western Byelorussia and of the Western Ukraine, both active in the territory of the Polish Republic during the 1920's and 1930's, or the Jewish leftist groups. Each of these deserves a special treatment by an historian.

I wish to take this opportunity to express my gratitude to the Russian Research Center of Harvard University, with which I have been associated since 1949, for generously financing the first edition of my book, and for providing a stimulating environment and human contacts necessary for my continuous investigation of the East European Communism, with special emphasis on Poland. I would also like to thank the American Philosophical Society for the grant that enabled me to do research at the Hoover Library in 1974.

I am much obliged to Princeton University Press for permission to quote R. V. Burk's *The Dynamics of Communism in Eastern Europe,* and to David S. Mason for use of a table from his yet un-published doctoral thesis, prepared at Indiana University. I would also like to thank all those persons too numerous to mention by name who have contributed their information on various aspects of history of the Polish Communist movement during my trips to Poland in 1958, 1969, 1972, and 1973.

M. K. Dziewanowski

Contents

revolt of the intellectuals. The Polish youth in
revolt. The economic crisis and the Poznań uprising.

The elections. Search for a middle way. The
emergence of the "Partisans." Retreat from
October. The "Zionist problem" in its political context. The Arab-Israeli war and its
consequences. The "Prague Spring" and the
Sino-Soviet split. The mounting crisis. The December revolt and Gomułka's fall. The era of
Gomułka in perspective.

Potential problems. Church-state relations.
Gierek consolidates his power base. Reshaping
the party. Opening windows to the West. A
contemporary profile of the party.

Part I

The ORIGINS

The BEGINNINGS
of SOCIALISM in
POLAND, 1832-1892

1

Polish socialism was born in exile, spawned by the *émigré* groups who had fled from the Congress Kingdom of Poland to the West, mainly to France and England, after the unsuccessful insurrection against Russia in 1830–31. A new wave of *émigrés* fled the Polish frontier after another abortive uprising in 1863–64. Poland itself had undergone a three-fold partition by Russia, Prussia, and Austria, first in the eighteenth century and later on following the Congress of Vienna in 1815; nowhere were conditions favorable for open political activity. It was dangerous to speak out in favor of radical ideas and, unlike the social climate in the West, an industrial proletariat was in only the earliest stages of development.

For many years the Polish socialist movement was to remain outside the country, gravitating about several small groups, all of which were overwhelmingly intellectual in character. The first of these was the Democratic Society, founded in 1832. Although not strictly socialist in character, this group proclaimed for workers the exclusive right to own land or other means of production. Strongly influenced by the contemporary French utopian socialism, the Democratic Society gained a large following among Polish émigrés, who were attracted by its slogan "Everything for the people and by the people." In 1846, through its emissaries in Galicia, the society raised the banner of agrarian revolution, gaining the support of Marx and Engels. "The Communists," the two wrote, "fight for the attainment of the immediate aims . . . In Poland they support the party that insists on an agrarian revolution as the prime condition for national emancipation . . ." [1]

Simultaneously with the Democratic Society, a more radical view was developing. In 1835 a group of former soldiers of the 1830 Insurrection, mostly of peasant origin, was dissatisfied with the moderate social program of the society and seceded from it. They formed a separate organization called the Polish People. This was the first organized group to be led by Stanisław Worcell, the first Polish socialist thinker. The Polish People aimed at abolishing all political as well as social privileges and it preached an equalitarian society based on public ownership of all means of production. "Levelling of social condition" and "Everything for the people and by the people," were the principal slogans.[2]

Outside the organized socialist groups stood two great leaders of the emigration: Joachim Lelewel and Adam Mickiewicz. Lelewel, a prominent historian, tried to legitimize agrarian communism by tracing its origin back to the ancient Slavonic institution of the commune (*gmina*) which, he supposed, owned the land originally. He wanted to build the entire social and political system of *sui generis* communism (*gminowładztwo*) on the foundation of the commune. Lelewel was in close touch with the Communist League for which Karl Marx and Friedrich Engels produced their historic *Manifesto*. Certain elements of agrarian socialism are to be found in the political and social program written in biblical language by the great poet Mickiewicz in 1848, for his Polish Legion which was to aid the Italian revolution against Austria. The Democratic Society, the Polish People, Lelewel, and Mickiewicz, unlike their Russian counterparts, were all chiefly interested in politics and intensely nationalistic. For them the social upheaval had to be, if not preceded, at least accompanied by the rebuilding of a free Poland.

Thus, between 1830 and 1850 Polish socialist thought in general was characterized by two distinctive features: first, it was patriotic with certain religious and even mystical overtones; second, since an urban proletariat hardly existed in its native country, it was primarily agrarian. Their mystical inclinations prevented the socialists of those days from expressing their ideas concretely, either in well-defined programs or in definite acts, such as the founding of settlements of communist colonies overseas — those "Pocket editions of the New Jerusalem," as Marx and Engels branded them, "still dreams of experimental realization of . . . social utopias . . ."[3] Father Ściegienny, a radical Catholic priest of the Lublin region who preached redistribution of land among peasants and formation of village cooperatives was, perhaps, the best representative of this sort of socialism.

Among the émigrés who settled in the West after the insurrection of 1863–64 were members of a more radical party than had previously appeared, the "Reds." Some members of the Reds' left wing, displaying strong socialist leanings, founded an organization in

London called the International Workers' Association. Their social and national aspirations were similar to those of the groups founded earlier, but there was greater stress on the association's working-class character and on international solidarity with other workers. Religious emphasis had disappeared. The Paris Commune had many Poles among its leading participants, among them two generals, Jarosław Dąbrowski and Walery Wróblewski, the latter a prominent leader of the uprising of 1863–64. Wróblewski managed to escape to London where he became an intimate friend of Marx and Engels and there, in 1872, he founded a Polish socialist group which continued the tradition of the Polish People. Wróblewski later became a Polish delegate to the General Council of the First International and at its Hague meeting in 1872 supported Marx against Bakunin.

The appeal of socialism to the Poles was considerably enhanced by the frequent positive statements of Marx and Engels, which stressed the necessity for rebuilding a free Polish state as an indispensable segment of a free and democratic European community of nations. In a memorandum to the First Congress of the International Marx explained why the workers of Europe should occupy themselves with the Polish question:

In the first instance, because middle-class writers and agitators conspire to suppress it, although they patronize all sorts of other nationalities, even Ireland. Whence this reticence? Because both aristocrats and bourgeois look upon the dark Asiatic power in the background as a last resource against the advancing tide of working-class ascendancy. That power can effectually be put down only by the restoration of Poland upon a democratic basis. In the present changed state of Central Europe, and especially Germany, it is more than ever necessary to have a democratic Poland . . . The working-class movement will continually be interrupted, checked, and retarded until the great European question is set at rest.[4]

This statement of Marx, as well as many others of a similar kind, deeply impressed the early socialists of Poland.

POLAND AFTER 1864

The growth of "scientific" socialism in Poland was pushed forward by two factors. First, large-scale industry, which employed a considerable number of workers, was developing and this produced social conditions similar to those in Western Europe. Second, Marxist theories were penetrating into Polish soil. Both forces started operating first in the Russian part of Poland (Congress Poland). This was not accidental. Russian Poland was the most important and the largest part of the national territory. Out of the fifteen million Poles that lived within the historic area of Poland at the end of the nineteenth century, nearly nine million were in Russian Poland; the Prussian part numbered at that time only three and one-half million Poles, and the Austrian segment slightly over two and one-half million.[5] Also, except for Upper Silesia, the industries of Russian Poland were growing faster than those in other parts of the country. Moreover, this rapid growth, added to the lack of a social policy on the part of St. Petersburg, made the fate of the worker in Warsaw, Łódź, or in the Dąbrowa coal basin worse than that of his compatriots in the Silesian mines (Prussian Poland) or even in the Galician oil fields (Austrian Poland). Even as late as the beginning of the twentieth century, when conditions had already improved somewhat, the average wage of an industrial worker in Russian Poland was still at least 25 per cent lower than that of a Silesian miner, the lowest paid worker in Germany.[6]

During the eighteen-seventies, when the working-class movement started to develop, Russian Poland was the most handicapped part of the country, both politically and nationally. Galicia was already beginning to enjoy the first fruits of its autonomous existence and the Prussian part had not yet begun suffering from the policies of the *Kulturkampf* and the Prussian Colonization Commission, but in Warsaw it was a time of ruthless Russification, following the unsuccessful rebellion of 1863–64. In Upper Silesia, with its great accumulation of men and capital and its foreign oppression and economic exploitation, conditions might have seemed more favorable for the development of a large-scale working-class movement, but there were several reasons why the workers of Western Poland never did play a leading role in Polish socialism. First, they lacked the leadership of a native intelligentsia, which was, at that time, largely Germanized; second, the powerful and long-organized German Social Democratic Party and its trade-unions drew many Polish workers into their orbit and thus considerably delayed the growth of the native working-class parties. When the national revival took place the workers of Western Poland turned not to socialism but to more moderate Christian labor groups. Socialism in Western Poland always remained a more or less feeble branch of the general socialist movement; socialists from the Russian-controlled part of the country, and especially those of Warsaw, took the lead from the very beginning and retained it, almost without interruption. For this reason we have to focus our attention mainly on the conditions prevailing in the major part of Poland.

The defeat of the insurrection in 1863–64 marked a milestone in the history of the country. In 1864 the last remnant of the country's autonomy was abolished. In the same year the so-called "Committee of Reconstruction" set to work reshaping the administrative structure of the country. Civilian and military power were united in the hands of a governor general, which virtually amounted to the establishment of martial law. Huge garrisons numbering up to 300,000 soldiers were quartered in a country of about 7 million people. The very name of Poland was erased and replaced by the new term "Vistula Land." Russian was made the official language of the country. The existing system of law courts and schools, still overwhelmingly Polish until 1864, was supplanted by the Russian system and crowded with officials from distant parts of the Tsarist Empire. In 1869 the Polish University of Warsaw was closed down. The Uniate Church was abolished in 1874. In 1886 the Polish Bank was made into a branch of the St. Petersburg State Bank. This trend continued until the time of the October Manifesto, in 1905.

Intellectual changes, which had been ripening for several years, were increasingly evident in the temper of the educated classes. The romantic conception of life imposed on the nation during the last generation by the genius of the great poets was rapidly being discarded and even ridiculed. The insurrections of 1830–31 and of 1863–64 were products of a spirit which was dying harder in Poland than elsewhere in Europe. Work and the acquisition of knowledge as well as of wealth were the virtues needed for the survival of the battered nation, argued the young generation of Poles. This new temper, which had prevailed in Western Poland half a generation earlier (after the events of 1846–1848), now spread from Warsaw to Galicia, where recent political autonomy gave new scope to the latent national energies.

Attempts to regain political independence exhausted and financially ruined a large proportion of the gentry. This class, which had formed the backbone of the partisan movement, was bled white for eighteen months and had to bear the brunt of the reprisals of the tsarist vengeance. Numerous estates were confiscated and several thousand members of the gentry were deported to Siberia. Many members of that ruined and decimated stratum flocked to the towns in search of employment. In most cases they swelled the ranks of the urban middle class and especially those of the intelligentsia. This new middle class was to provide, together with the members of the ascendant Jewish intelligentsia, the leadership of the revolutionary movement of the later years. Both Polish and Jewish intellectuals, barred from public offices, restless and frustrated, became important factors in shaping the revolutionary ideology of the socialist movement and supplied it with a considerable proportion of its leaders.

But not all the ruined members of the nobility, especially of the numerous petty gentry, were able to find employment in the ranks of the middle classes. Many of them, or their children, could not find suitable jobs and eventually had to join the proletarian mass of workers and artisans. In most cases it was possible to identify rapidly with the new social groups and to take a leading part in the fight for social advancement, as well as for national liberation. The newcomers brought with them a strong patriotic and revolutionary tradition, a higher level of education, and a longing to regain their lost standard of living. It was the large group of educated and alert Warsaw workers and craftsmen which so impressed a Russian visitor, the well-known revolutionist Stepniak (S. Kravchinskii) in 1879:

When all had assembled [he writes in one of his essays describing a Polish socialist meeting] there were altogether some fifteen to eighteen people. It was a meeting of delegates or organizers, each of whom represented a circle of fifteen to twenty persons. Thus at that moment there must have been about 150 to 200 workmen united in one organization — a number that surprised me, indeed; for I know that all this had been done in a few months, and that eighteen months before there was not a single socialist circle among the Warsaw workmen. I remembered that when we Russian revolutionists began our propaganda in St. Petersburg in 1871, at the end of the first two years we could hardly contrive to impart to a dozen workmen the notions of socialism. Only in 1879, after nine years' exertion, the first strong and serious workmen's organization, called the Northern League, was founded. The difference in the results seemed still more surprising when one compared the respective forces that began the movement in the two countries. At St. Petersburg the number of propagandists belonging to the instructed classes — let us say of students, although the term is not quite exact — was so great, that in the first four or five years of propaganda we may reckon without exaggeration at least three propagandist students who have spent their forces to gain over one socialist of the working classes. In Warsaw it was quite the reverse. The 150 to 200 socialists, united in a few months into one association, were the result of the work of only three agitators of the educated classes. All these three propagandists I knew. They were very devoted, energetic persons; but they were not at all superior to those of St. Petersburg, among whom there were many people of longer experience.

Their wonderfully quick success was, therefore, only an illustration and a measure of the great difference in the material on which they had to work.[7]

Such a group, led by a mobile and determined intellectual elite, gave the socialism of Russian Poland a great deal of dynamic control over the movement in other parts of the country. Neither better educated Galicia nor economically more highly developed Western Poland could upset that initial superiority, and both had to accept the leadership of Warsaw.

ECONOMIC DEVELOPMENT OF RUSSIAN POLAND AFTER 1864

The catastrophe of 1863–64 had other far-reaching economic and social consequences for the Congress Kingdom. Foreign oppression increasingly affected the political and cultural life of the nation. It channeled the energies of the people toward economic life, the so-called "organic work." General conditions for that work were fairly favorable. The revolutionary authorities had promised the peasants the land on which they worked. In order to counteract that scheme of agrarian reform and to woo the rural masses of the rebellious land, the tsarist government carried out land settlement in the ten Polish provinces more speedily than in other parts of the empire. This was done in a manner much more advantageous to the Polish peasants, who received more land than their Russian counterparts. Hence, the Polish villages during the first years after the rebellion were fairly prosperous. This fact had a favorable influence on industrial development, which had begun to make rapid progress.[8]

Between 1870 and 1885 an industrial revolution took place in "Vistula Land." The advantageous land settlement increased the purchasing power of the peasants. The introduction of machinery, especially in the major industry of the country, textiles, created a relative abundance of goods. The removal of the custom frontier, which had separated Congress Poland from the rest of the empire until 1851, opened the vast markets of European and Asiatic Russia. The construction of railways connecting Poland with these markets put the products of the growing Polish industry within the reach of hitherto inaccessible consumers.

In 1877 (after a short break), Russia adopted a high tariff, especially on industrial products and primarily on textiles. "In 1884 a high, almost prohibitive tariff . . . was placed on coal, iron, and steel, which meant that now all the important Polish industries were heavily protected."[9] Behind this wall of tariffs the young industries could expand safely. The results were striking, especially until the end of the nineteenth century. From 1873 to 1891 the output of mines, foundries, and factories increased tenfold. The industrial center of Łódź grew from an insignificant small town to a "Polish

Manchester," the "promised land" of capitalism. Agriculture pros-
pered with the rapidly expanding markets in towns. But only half
of the industrial output was locally consumed; the other half was
exported, mainly to Russia.[10] Although in 1890 the population of
Congress Poland numbered only 7.3 per cent of the whole empire,
her industrial output amounted to 25 per cent of the empire's
production.[11] This expansion of economic life in the Congress Kingdom, originally favored by the St. Petersburg government, soon
became the headache of the Russian industrialist, who feared the
growing competition of Warsaw, Łódź, and Białystok. These fears
were reflected in government policies which, by manipulating custom
duties and railway fares, consistently favored the Russian industries
over those of the Congress Kingdom. Moreover, the protectionist
policy of the empire, beneficial to the industries of the Congress
Kingdom during their infancy, hampered their development in the
more advanced stages, especially after 1906. High import tariffs
imposed on foreign iron ore, for instance, compelled the manufacturers of Russian Poland to use almost exclusively the much
more expensive ores of the Ukraine, and thus increased the production cost of iron and steel. The considerable commercial success of
the Congress Kingdom industries in Asiatic Russia gave rise to an
exaggerated theory which emphasized the decisive importance of the
so-called "eastern markets" for the very existence of those industries.
This theory, widely publicized by Rosa Luxemburg's book "Industrial Development of Poland," provided the economic basis for
the theory of organic incorporation of Russian Poland into the
Tsarist Empire.

The rapid growth of Polish industries greatly favored the enterprising elements, "the sober and the strong." They took very seriously
the slogan "enrichissez-vous" and reaped enormous profits: at that
time an annual dividend of 40–50 per cent was not considered un-
usual. On the other hand, the conditions of the working class,
although better than in Russia, were unsatisfactory. Lack of social
legislation left wide scope for abuse and gave the industrialists
numerous advantages. As in the rest of the empire, the workers were
not allowed either to form trade-unions or to strike.

At the end of the nineteenth century, when the future Madame
Piłsudska came to Warsaw to work as a secretary in a leather goods
factory, she was appalled by factory conditions, although they were
well above average since the manager was a liberal and considerate
man and very popular with his employees.[12] Nevertheless, she wrote:
"Both men and women worked from 7 A.M. till 7 P.M. for wages which

ranged from the equivalent of six to fifteen shillings a week. But they were at least allowed an hour for dinner in the middle of the day, which was exceptional, for in the majority of factories there was only a fifteen-minutes break, and the workers took their parcels of food which they ate standing by their machines." Substantial changes in the position of the industrial proletariat did not come until the constitutional period that followed the revolution of 1905.[13] In 1864 the number of industrial workers in Russian Poland was only 78,000, less than the number of craftsmen, which exceeded 90,000. In 1900 the industrial proletariat already numbered about 300,000; if one adds to it slightly over 140,000 craftsmen and artisans, who by then played a very important role in the economy of the country, one gets the figure around 440,000. Except for a small group of the more prosperous ones, these craftsmen and artisans should be considered as urban proletariat. Subsequent events proved that impoverished craftsmen were often better recruiting grounds for radical socialist ideas than were industrial workers. The concentration of both capital and labor in the Congress Kingdom was very high. In 1897 the number of workers in factories employing over 50 people amounted to nearly 290,000, and together with their families they numbered well over one million. Factories with over 50 workers numbered one half of all industrial establishments.[14] Wages were low, approximately as low as in Galicia and about 25 per cent lower than in Silesia. Until the beginning of the twentieth century security as well as hygienic conditions were, in most cases, rather primitive. In spite of these conditions the working masses, especially outside Warsaw, were politically passive until the late eighteen-seventies.

THE FIRST SOCIALIST GROUPS

The first socialist circles on Polish soil came into being in Galicia, which enjoyed more political freedom than the other parts of the country. The first trade-union, composed of printers, was set up in 1870 at Lwów, and the first regular strikes were organized in 1871 and in 1872, at Poznań. But it was Warsaw that can lay claim to having produced the first socialist party of some consequence. By this time socialist theory had begun to have some acceptance, a fact that was acknowledged by a memorandum of the Third Section of the Imperial Chancellery on August 24, 1873: "Of all lands belonging to His Imperial Majesty [we read in that memorandum] the Kingdom of Poland more than any other constitutes a favorable ground for the International." The Third Section then recommended setting up a mixed commission composed of factory owners and of Russian officials, "to investigate to what extent there is at present any agitation among the workers in the Kingdom of Poland and what measures are advisable on the part of the government as well as private owners in order to preserve our land from being penetrated by the International and similar associations." [15]

The measures taken proved singularly ineffective. Students returning from the West, especially from Switzerland, France, and Germany, as well as those from the Russian universities,[16] brought home books and ideas that helped to disseminate the doctrine of Marx, Engels, and Ferdinand Lassalle. Lassalle, with his fiery eloquence and flowery style, had a particular appeal to the imagination of many young Poles. His "Program of the Workers" was by far the most popular book among the first generation of Polish socialists.

The first socialist organizations in Warsaw were simple debating clubs, composed almost entirely of students. This state of affairs lasted until the appearance in 1876 of a dynamic leader named Ludwik Waryński. The son of Polish petty gentry, Waryński came from the Ukraine. Expelled from the Technological Institute of St. Petersburg in 1875, he went to Warsaw to satisfy his urge for social work among his proletarian countrymen. Waryński was a good organizer, a gifted writer, and a magnetic orator. Well acquainted with the socialist writing of the time, he came with the idea of transforming the disconnected students' circles into a mass movement. He was a born tribune, a natural leader, and was determined to gain the adherence of the workers. One of his first moves was to get books from abroad and have them translated into Polish. Then, in order to be close to the people, he engaged himself as a simple worker in one of the factories of Warsaw. Soon he became the idol of the city workers. His ideas spread. Around the so-called "Resistance Funds," a kind of conspiratorial trade-union, he managed to organize some 300 to 400 workers. The ideas Waryński propagated at that time were formulated in what is known as the "Brussels Program," so called in order to mislead the police. Actually written in Warsaw, in September 1878, and printed in Geneva, the program was a mixture of Marxism and anarchism. This sort of activity, however, lasted less than two years. Arrests crippled the beginnings of the movement. In 1878 Waryński and a few other leaders had to escape to Galicia, while another member, Stanisław Mendelson, eventually landed at Poznań (Prussian Poland). Thus, the first seeds of socialism were sown in all three parts of Poland. The fact that they produced different results can be explained by the different political, economic, and social conditions prevailing in each part of the country.

Waryński went first to Eastern Galicia. There, at Lwów, he started his work anew, mainly among the printers, who were the leading proletarian group. The Austrian police were soon on his track and Waryński moved to Cracow. There he was finally caught and tried. The jury acquitted him but the Austrian authorities ordered his expulsion as an alien without proper visa. He left Galicia and went to Geneva to join a group of his comrades. But his trial and his short stay in Galicia gave impetus to the socialist cause in that part of the country. It is characteristic of the expansion of the movement that among the accused were not only twenty-three intellectuals but also twenty-one workers. Soon afterwards a few arrests took place at Poznań which, by means of another public trial, made propaganda for the socialists. From Galicia Waryński went to Geneva, Switzerland, where he considerably influenced George Plekhanov. Soon, however, he decided to return to his country and to organize a genuine socialist mass party.

THE FIRST "PROLETARIAT" AND THE "POLISH PEOPLE"

The return of Waryński from Geneva to Warsaw in 1881 marks the beginning of a brief but momentous period in the annals of the socialist movement of Poland. In 1882, Waryński's activity brought about the formation of the first regular socialist party, the Proletariat.[17] It was composed of remnants of debating and self-help groups, already in existence, gathered about a "Resistance Funds" nucleus. The efforts of Waryński and his friends unified and expanded those groups into a fairly strong organization.

Like the earlier debating circles, the members of the Proletariat believed, almost religiously, that a social upheaval was imminent. They emphasized the priority, and even the superiority, of economic over national problems. The latter, according to the party, would be solved as a matter of course in an approaching socialist revolution. The need for unified action with Russian revolutionaries was underscored. The problem of Poland's independence was shelved, if not completely disregarded, although within the party there were numerous patriotic individuals. However, Waryński, who dominated the movement, and other leaders as well, considered this problem to be of secondary importance and thought that it should not be permitted to interfere with the social and economic issues. The well-to-do classes of Poland, argued Waryński, were not revolutionary;

they aimed at conciliation with the autocracy. It was only the urban proletariat which was truly revolutionary. With Lassalle, he said that "the workers are the rock on which the church of the present age will be built." On the one hand, the proletariat of Poland suffered as much from native exploitation as from foreign oppression; on the other hand, Russia was ceasing to be the mainstay of the old order because she was pregnant with a revolution that was being prepared by her socialists.

Terror was not an original part of the Proletariat program. It came later on, partly as a result of governmental reprisals and partly as a consequence of the powerful example set by the Russian revolutionary party known as "People's Will."

Many workers and large groups of intellectuals considered the cosmopolitan emphasis of the Proletariat Party to be unpatriotic. In 1881 some of these dissenters established another organization in Geneva, the Polish People, led by Bolesław Limanowski. It will be recalled that the name "Polish People" had previously been used by Poland's first socialist organization, in 1835. This organization did not want to break away from the democratic objectives of the insurrections but to enrich these with socialist doctrine, and to adapt them to the current conditions and specific needs of the country. Limanowski, also a son of the "Eastern Marches" (*Kresy*) and of a social origin similar to Waryński, was a noble and selfless person, a devoted social worker and a conscientious scholar. Lacking some of the brilliant and dynamic qualities of his antagonist, he was less imaginative but more realistic. Limanowski believed that an independent Poland was as necessary to the proletariat as to the upper middle classes, because national oppression, unavoidable in a conquered country, was degrading to any human being. Moreover, the oppression was obviously hampering the social and economic development of the whole nation. He was as much in favor of international solidarity of the proletariat as was Waryński, but Limanowski thought that international cooperation of any kind should take place between nations acting as sovereign entities. To reject the right of self-determination would mean to confirm those existing injustices which had resulted from imperialistic conquests.

The failure of Russian populism made a deep impression on Limanowski. He believed that the main cause of its defeat lay in the very abstractness of its formulae. Limanowski considered the socialism of the Russian populist writer Lavrov, as much too abstract, too intellectual, and therefore unsuitable for the broad masses of people. In order to succeed, socialists must be practical and concrete; they must choose slogans and methods understandable to workers and to peasants in agrarian countries. The concrete grievances and demands of working people, especially those of his own country, mattered more to Limanowski than distant Utopias. He wanted to treat workers and peasants with equal consideration, and for most of them emotional patriotism was a matter of course while cosmopolitan solidarity remained a suspect and empty abstraction. These ideas were discussed in a pamphlet entitled "Patriotism and Socialism." [18] As previously stated, Limanowski did not oppose collaboration with the Russian revolutionary organization but insisted that it ought to be carried out on the basis of complete equality between separate entities.

Thus, the whole pattern of future development was already taking shape by 1882. On the one hand, the more patriotic position, represented by Limanowski, stressed an amalgamation of socialism with national sentiment; on the other hand, the cosmopolitan branch tended to project the interests of a social international revolution over everything else, and was determined to establish close ties with Russian comrades. This second view was embodied in the person of Waryński. Waryński gave expression to his cosmopolitan feelings by saying "There is a nation more unfortunate than the Polish nation: it is the nation of proletarians."

One incident is especially characteristic of the intensity of the cosmopolitan feelings of a group of Polish exiles, many of whom two years afterwards became the leading members of the Proletariat. On November 29, 1880, they organized a large public meeting to commemorate the fiftieth anniversary of the Rising of 1830–31, but with an avowed purpose of manifesting that they did not care any more for patriotic programs. Their two chief slogans were "For an international social revolution" and "For the universal socialist republic of workers." In the invitations which they sent all over Europe they wrote, among other things, "The old motto — *Vive la Pologne* — has now disappeared completely in the class struggle, in the struggle of labor with capital . . ." In reply to that invitation the former members of the General Council of the International, Marx, Engels, and others, stressed the great service of Polish democracy to the cause of revolution in Europe and ended with the words: ". . . so let us repeat the old motto — *Vive la Pologne!*" In spite of this snub the organizers of the meeting changed neither their slogans nor their speeches. Moreover, when they returned to Poland they tried to stick to the new line in spite of a certain patriotic undercurrent that was being definitely felt even within the Proletariat. There is no doubt that at the beginning of the movement, during the seventies and eighties, the cosmopolitan trend had a far larger following and a much greater dynamic power.

The lack of interest in the national question on the part of the followers of Waryński can be seen in the agreement, signed in 1884, between the Proletariat and the Russian revolutionary group, People's Will. Originally most of the leading Polish revolutionaries sympathized with the Black Partition, a Russian populist group bent on division of the land among peasants. Many members of the Black Partition were personal friends of the Poles from student days in Switzerland. Later on, however, the People's Will captured the Poles' imagination and their feelings underwent considerable change. Several Polish revolutionaries went over to the People's Will, attracted by its reckless courage and grim determination. When the future assassin of Tsar Alexander II, a Pole, Ignacy Hryniewiecki, was reproached for his participation in a Russian conspiracy, he answered "When you start partisan fighting I will be with you. But for the moment, when you do nothing, I shall work for Russia's freedom . . ."[19] Some, like Stanisław Kunicki, acted in both Polish and Russian organizations. There were also several Russians who were members of the Proletariat.

The idea of an alliance with the People's Will was conceived by Kunicki, who, after the arrest of Waryński in 1883, took over the leadership of the Proletariat. At that time the Polish revolutionaries recognized the seniority of their Russian colleagues, admired them somewhat uncritically, and greatly overestimated their real strength. The agreement, signed in Paris in 1884, between the Proletariat and the already declining People's Will, provided for close cooperation of the two autonomous parties for the ultimate purpose of overthrowing the tsarist autocracy. The chief means of the struggle was to be "economic as well as political terror in various forms." Thus the Russian organization managed to impose its terroristic program on the Proletariat, who were dazzled by the daring "liberals with bombs." The vagueness of the agreement on this matter seems to indicate that the authors did not attach very much importance to this point. Each party, however, preserved complete autonomy of action within the borders of its own country, though both parties were to continue their activity under the leadership of the Russian group, since it was functioning primarily in the important capital of Russia.[20]

The Proletariat-People's Will agreement, assassinations of several police agents, publication of a clandestine paper also entitled *Prole-*

tariat, and a series of strikes organized by the party in Warsaw, Łódź, and Żyrardów alarmed St. Petersburg and made the government act swiftly. The strike which took place in April 1883, at the textile factory of Żyrardów, near Warsaw, was the first mass strike in Poland. Several thousand workers participated, and to cope with them the government had to use troops. Three workers were killed and fifteen wounded. Systematic arrests followed; during 1884 and 1885 about two hundred persons were taken in custody. Among them were twenty-nine leading party members, or about half the active membership. After almost two years of imprisonment the twenty-nine leaders were tried and condemned while the rest were punished by executive order. All of the accused received their harsh sentences with courage. Four men were condemned to death. Two others, including Waryński, were sentenced to long-term imprisonment in the Schlusselburg fortress.[21] Twenty men, among them Feliks Kon, a future leader of the Communist Party, were sentenced to long terms of penal servitude. Three others were exiled without being condemned to penal servitude.[22] On January 28, 1886, the first gallows since 1864 were erected on the slope of the Warsaw citadel and the first socialist martyrs were hung.

The program and the tendencies of the Proletariat were a mixture of Marxist theories, Blanquist and Bakuninist traditions, and practices of the People's Will. The Proletariat believed that a revolution was around the corner and would be achieved by a small handful of fighters, provided that they were supported at a crucial moment by the working masses.[23] The Proletariat was more than a conspiratorial group and less than a mass party — over the years 1882–86 it had over 700 members. The aims of the Polish group were stated by Waryński, when defending himself before the tribunal against the charge of organizing "a conspiracy aimed at the violent extirpation of the present political, economic, and social order."

Our aim [said Waryński] has been to beget a worker's movement and to organize a workers' party in Poland . . . We have organized the working class in its fight against the present order. We have not organized a revolution, but we have organized *for* a revolution. We know that the ever mounting social antagonism and the ever spreading wounds in the social organism will inevitably lead to cataclysm. And we know the terror and the devastation that follow when the masses, driven by poverty and to the last limits of despair, burst their shackles and turn on the existing order. It is precisely for that reason that we consider it our duty to prepare the workers for the revolution, to make their rise a conscious one, tempered and disciplined by organization, and to give them a clear programme of ends and means.[24]

The many arrests of 1883–1886 and the trial of the Proletariat leaders were severe blows to the socialist movement. During the next four years the movement was smaller in scope and slower in tempo. The broad masses of the working people were hardly touched by socialist ideas and still less by any organization. For that another twenty years would be needed.

FROM THE DESTRUCTION OF THE "PROLETARIAT" TO THE FOUNDATION OF THE POLISH SOCIALIST PARTY (1886–1892)

Immediately after the destruction of the Proletariat, the socialist movement was at a very low ebb. Between 1888 and 1892 three small socialist parties engaged in some activity inside Russian Poland: an organization usually called the Second Proletariat, the Union of Polish Workers (UPW), and a still smaller and less active party called the Association of Workers — a group that had seceded from the Proletariat in 1891 in protest against a terrorist philosophy. This so-called Second Proletariat tried to maintain the political traditions of Waryński and his comrades but ceased to believe in the possibility of a quick upheaval. The Union of Polish Workers (1888–1893) founded and led principally by Julian Marchlewski (Jan Karski), Adolf Warszawski (Warski), and Bronisław Wesołowski (Smutny) later became the nucleus of the Social Democratic Party of Poland and Lithuania. Originally the Union of Polish Workers emphasized purely economic action, concentrating on the daily struggle for betterment of working conditions. Toward the end of its activity, however, in 1892, the Union of Polish Workers shifted its emphasis more to political matters and advanced as its platform the fight against autocracy.[25] On May 1, 1892, a fresh wave of strikes swept Warsaw and the provinces. By that time the celebration of May Day, established three years earlier, was becoming a regular custom with the Polish workers. The workers demanded an eight-hour day and a 15 per cent rise in wages. Although the factory owners were willing to make concessions and tried to influence the government authorities in this direction, the latter were adamant. "Shoot and do not spare the cartridges," telegraphed the governor general of "Vistula Land" to the chief of the local gendarmes. The police organized anti-Jewish riots and used these as a pretext for sending troops against the striking workers. This led to bloody clashes. There were numerous casualties; forty-six were killed and about two hundred wounded.[26] These events speeded up the crystallization of new ideas within the UPW, but they came too late to find any practical expression. The wave of arrests following these strikes crippled the Union of Polish Workers and almost completely liquidated the Second Proletariat. The Marxist movement of "Vistula Land" reached another low point.

Simultaneous with these events in Russian Poland there was a constantly growing ferment initiated by Waryński, Stanisław Mendelson, and their companions from the Proletariat, both in Galicia and in the western, German-controlled part of the country. In Western Poland the Bismarckian "special laws" greatly hampered the development of a clandestine movement. As soon as these laws were removed, at the end of 1890, a Society of Polish Socialists was founded openly in Berlin, with several branches in Prussian Poland. In 1891 this society started issuing a weekly called *The Workers' Journal* edited by Ignacy Daszyński, among others. Soon socialist ideas took deep root among the Polish workers of Silesia, but because of the lack of a native educated class, the workers at first fell under the influence of the German Social Democrats. The next year, in 1892, Galician comrades united with the Poles in Silesia and founded the Polish Social Democratic Party of Galicia and Silesia at Lwów.[27]

Meanwhile groups of patriotic socialists, at that time often called National Socialists, remained disorganized and scattered. However, defeat of the cosmopolitan and terroristic Proletariat, which based its hopes on the theory of quick revolution, caused reflection on the part of all the socialist groups. That the strength of the Russian revolutionary movement had been overestimated, as the National Socialists charged, became obvious to everyone. The small and scattered pockets of opposition to autocracy which existed in Russia at that time tended to limit both their demands and their expectations to a gradual transformation from an autocratic regime to a constitutional monarchy. This did not satisfy even the more moderate socialists of Poland, who wished for complete destruction of tsardom and for a republican government. According to the National Socialists, the cosmopolitan approach of the Proletariat had been largely responsible for the movement's failure to reach the broad masses of the people.

THE FOUNDATION OF THE POLISH SOCIALIST PARTY (PPS) (1892–1893)

A new trend toward nationalism took hold both in Poland and among the émigrés living abroad in Paris and London. The unification of scattered socialist groups and the creation of a single socialist party received fresh impetus from the efforts of Limanowski, his National Socialist associates, and Stanisław Mendelson. A congress of Polish socialists was summoned to Paris on November 17, 1892.

Only those who did not openly oppose the idea of a unified socialist party were invited. Altogether, eighteen persons took part in the congress, unofficially representing four leading organizations from the Russian-controlled part of Poland: (1) the second Proletariat; (2) the Union of Polish Workers; (3) the National Socialist Commune; (4) the Union of Workers. These four organizations proceeded, first, to found the Association of Polish Socialists Abroad as a cornerstone of a new party. Next, the association was entrusted with drawing up a program for the party.[28] Limanowski was elected chairman of the congress, and after three days of lively discussions the program was ready.

The new Polish Socialist Party proclaimed itself the political organization of the Polish working class, struggling not only for liberation from capitalist exploitation, but also for freedom from political subjugation. Utilizing the power of the proletariat, the party aimed to establish an independent democratic republic as a stepping stone to a socialist state. The program also provided for gradual nationalization of land, instruments of production, and means of communication. There was disassociation from "Econo-monism" by acceptance of terror, under certain circumstances, as a necessary means of attaining important objectives.

In addition to this program, the Paris Congress passed several resolutions concerning party tactics. The new party issued a special declaration to the Russian socialists expressing readiness to work side by side with them against tsarist autocracy, but only as separate and equal partners. The Polish Socialist Party opposed a unified socialist movement covering the whole of the Russian Empire. This attitude was explained by two arguments: first, the social structure of Poland, being more advanced, required a different program as well as a different and autonomous organization; second, in case of a successful revolution and an overthrow of autocracy, Russia would have to be satisfied for a considerable period of time with a constitutional monarch, while Poland would be a democratic republic "quickly marching toward socialism." [29] In 1893, soon after the congress, the Polish Socialist Party formulated more concretely two conditions on which its cooperation with Russian socialists would be based: (1) the Russian socialists would "support actively the political demands" of the party; (2) all activity in the territory covered by the Polish Socialist Party, the PPS, would be directed by that party.[30]

The program was largely an adaptation to Polish conditions of the Erfurt program of the German Social Democratic Party. The platform represented a blend of socialism and nationalism, as well as political, social, and economic objectives. It implied that the growth of class consciousness should go hand-in-hand with the spread of national consciousness. The party bypassed the problem of a dictatorship of the proletariat and limited the use of terror to "special circumstances." The points of gradual socialization and a democratic, possibly federal, republic were part of the party's immediate, minimum program. Generally speaking, the program accorded with moderate, democratic, views which stressed the necessity of proceeding gradually to achieve full socialism.

The Polish Socialist Party was the first political movement of importance in Poland's history which directly connected the problem of social justice with that of national liberation, and it decided to fight with equal determination for both at the same time. The split in the socialist labor movement was to be healed by fusing Marxist doctrine with Poland's national aspirations. Here lies, perhaps, the secret of the party's initial successes. But even while the PPS was still being organized, opposition to its program of independence arose in many places. This was soon to crystallize into a separate political party named the Social Democracy of the Kingdom of Poland (SDKP). The history of the Polish labor movement after this time was largely the story of the fight between these two rival groups.

SOCIAL DEMOCRATS
Versus
2   "SOCIAL PATRIOTS"

A longing for unity among the working class was strong, and at the beginning the new party seemed to be an unqualified success. The cosmopolitan position had suffered a major defeat in the liquidation of the Proletariat Party (1884–1886); it had been in steady decline since 1886 and was greatly weakened by the growth of a new nationalist generation that did not remember the previous catastrophes of the uprising. Nevertheless, cosmopolitan principles were far from being completely abandoned. Some believed it was hopeless to embark on a new national insurrection after three successive failures. Partisans of the cosmopolitan approach argued that only a concerted effort by the international proletariat could bring about social revolution. After such a revolution all manner of exploitation and national oppression would automatically be ended. A second argument against nationalism was based on a literal interpretation of a slogan found in the *Communist Manifesto:* "Workers have no country." While the PPS interpreted this slogan as a statement of deplorable reality, the cosmopolitan extremists thought it expressed the desire that workers *should* have no country.

Even if it were possible to regain political independence, argued the cosmopolitans, what would be the point of trying? Native exploitation would be as bad as foreign. Polish workers should not, therefore, shed their blood in order to exchange one yoke for another. "We have nothing to lose but our chains," the leaders of the cosmopolitan groups repeated, after the *Communist Manifesto*. "We would gain only from a social and not a national upheaval. For this purpose we should unite our efforts not with the nonproletarian elements of the country, our main exploiters, but with the proletariat of all other countries, and especially with those of other provinces of the Russian state."

Some extremists belonging to the Union of Polish Workers and to the Second Proletariat either refused to join the newly founded PPS or seceded from it in March and July of 1893, shortly after its establishment. These schisms were deepened by quarrels which occurred at the International Socialist Congress held at Zurich in August 1893. During that congress the all-Polish Socialist delegation, headed by Ignacy Daszyński from Galicia, successfully opposed the secessionists led by Julian Marchlewski (Karski) and a brilliant young girl, Rosa Luxemburg. Those favoring secession were eventually excluded from the congress for attending it under false pretences without proper mandate. This bitter struggle, humiliating for the expelled delegation, widened the gap still further between the two antagonistic groups competing for the leadership of the working-class movement. The split, which had actually taken place in the spring of 1893, was further consolidated with the lapse of time.

A second new party was formed. It included the bulk of the Union of Polish Workers and absorbed some remnants of the group which claimed to be a successor to the Proletariat. This new party was called the Social Democracy of the Kingdom of Poland (SDKP). The very name was, to a certain extent, a political platform. The Polish Socialist Party used its first adjective to underline its aspiration for an all-Polish character, transcending partition frontiers. The use of the term "Kingdom of Poland," however, meant that the Social Democrats were determined to limit their activities to the Russian-controlled part of the country known, since the Congress of Vienna, as the Kingdom of Poland, or the Congress Kingdom. The Social Democrats applied the spiteful name "social-patriots" to the members of the PPS. On the other hand, the PPS looked upon the Social Democrats as traitors whose attitude toward their native country was often less friendly than many of the Russian, German, or Austrian socialists, and who sometimes fought against the PPS more fiercely than against tsardom. The PPS considered the Social Democrats to be twofold traitors: first, because they betrayed the national cause by advocating an immediate unconditional surrender to the three partitioning powers; second, because they were heretics to the creed of Marx and Engels, whose doctrine they pretended to worship but whose opinions concerning Poland and her right to free and independent existence they ignored.

THE PROGRAM OF THE SDKP

The program of the SDKP was to be found in three separate statements: (1) in an editorial published in the first issue of "The Work-

ers' Cause," at that time the main press organ of the new party; (2)
in the report on the Zurich International Congress of 1893; (3) in
the minutes of the First Congress of the SDKP, which took place in
1894.[1] From the very beginning the SDKP stressed close collaboration with Russian comrades while rejecting the goal of Polish independence.[2]

An all-Russian constitution, with territorial autonomy for Poland,
was accepted as the minimum aim of the Social Democratic Party.
An independent Poland was branded a utopian objective, harmful to
the workers' cause. First, independence diverted attention to aims
that had nothing to do with class struggle and proletarian internationalism; second, it spelled the loss of Russian markets, which were
essential to the very existence of Polish industry and therefore essential to the working class also. Polish socialists in the parts of the
country controlled by Germany and Austria were advised to follow
the example of the SDKP and to integrate their activities with their
respective social-democratic movements. Soon Rosa Luxemburg was
to formulate her theory of the "organic incorporation" of the Congress Kingdom of Poland into the Russian state, and to expand the
economic foundations of this thesis in her doctoral dissertation, entitled *Die industrielle Entwicklung Polens*, published in Leipzig in
1898.

Thus, from the very beginnings, the differences between the two
parties centered on the national problem. On one side were the Social
Democrats, who claimed that national cultural autonomy, following
Russia's transformation into a constitutional state, would sufficiently
safeguard the legitimate national interests of the Polish proletariat
and would prevent further national oppression. On the other side
stood the PPS, who would be satisfied with nothing short of full
political independence and severance of all ties with the Russian
Empire, whatever its future political structure. For the SDKP the
international solidarity of the proletariat was a primary and decisive
factor, overruling national allegiance. Such allegiance was held to be
only a remnant of a receding barbarous past, to be discarded as
quickly as possible in order to reach a higher stage of social development. The Social Democratic Party rejected the idea of an all-
Polish socialist movement, and instead advocated a separate group
for each of the three partitioned sections of Poland. Activity of each
group would be limited to the partition frontiers, and there would be
encouragement to merge or at least federate with their respective
Russian, Austrian, and Prussian comrades. As for the SDKP, it declared itself for a common fight with Russian labor groups against

the existing social patterns. The SDKP regretted that there was as yet no single social-democratic group in Russia with which to negotiate a merger.

The Social Democrats pushed the promotion of a mass movement which, by means of strikes and by insistence on an eight-hour workday, would satisfy the concrete demands of the laboring classes. Strong political slogans accompanied this program and it was urged that as many deputies as possible be elected to a constituent assembly which would gather in the future.

THE CONTROVERSY: PPS–SDKP

All competent sources agree that between 1896 and 1905 the PPS still overwhelmingly dominated the labor movement of Russian Poland, especially industrial workers. The Social Democrats retained a narrow foothold in Lithuania and enjoyed some popularity among craftsmen, particularly the cobblers of Warsaw, who remained throughout their history the stronghold of this movement.

The International Socialist Congress of London in 1896 was the scene of a second clash between the two antagonistic parties, the PPS and the SDKP, represented in this instance by Józef Piłsudski and Rosa Luxemburg respectively. Here again, the national problem was at the center of the dispute. The PPS scored a limited success by persuading the congress to reject a motion by Luxemburg which attempted to ignore the problem of freedom for subjugated nations. Instead, the PPS persuaded the congress to adopt another resolution which, though not identical to its own, nevertheless recognized the right of full self-determination for each nation. This was another bitter defeat that was neither accepted nor forgotten by so ambitious a person as Rosa Luxemburg.[3]

During this period the PPS continued to expand in membership. Its program, which intermingled social and national objectives, appealed to the patriotism of large numbers of workers who found satisfaction for both their economic and their emotional aspirations. The doctrinaire Marxism of the Social Democrats seemed not only in large part incomprehensible to these workers but it also offended their sense of nationalism. The fact that the PPS proclaimed its all-Polish character, irrespective of the partition frontiers, gave that party added strength. There were helpful allies in Galicia as well as in Posnania and Silesia. The Polish socialists of Galicia were headed by Ignacy Daszyński, a prominent leader, great orator, and parliamentarian, and were never affected by the ideological split that occurred in Russian Poland in 1893. The socialists of Galicia gave

united support to the PPS, both moral and material. Also all of the
small socialist circles of Western Poland allied with the PPS. Thus
money and shelter, as well as all sorts of organizational and publishing facilities, were put at the disposal of the PPS by its comrades
over the border, in areas where milder political regimes gave wider
scope to public activities. In addition, a well organized net of cells,
frontier and liaison posts, and fighting squads provided opportunities
for activity that no other Polish party could equal at the end of the
nineteenth and the beginning of the twentieth century. Led by a
brilliant vanguard of revolutionaries, the PPS managed to capture
the imagination and attract the support of a considerable section of
youth who were eager for action.

This was the time when Józef Piłsudski appeared on the scene as
a figure of importance, first as the editor of "The Worker," then as
one of the leaders of the patriotic stream within the Polish socialist
movement. Along with Witold Jodko-Narkiewicz, Kazimierz Kelles-
Krauz, Feliks Perl (Res), and Leon Wasilewski, Józef Piłsudski
quickly became one of the central figures among those in the PPS
who favored continuing the traditions of the insurrections which had
occurred in 1794, 1830–31, and 1863–64. These men believed in
training cadres within the party for a future uprising that would,
at a favorable moment, overthrow the rule of the three partitioning
powers. They considered Russia to be Poland's main enemy and
stressed the fact that the cause of Poland's independence and that of
freedom for the country's working class were complementary.

FROM SDKP TO SDKPiL

The program of the PPS, which combined demands for national as
well as social justice, proved to be so attractive to workers and to
radical intellectuals that some of the SDKP leaders who had escaped
arrest and remained in Poland hesitated in their cosmopolitanism. A
group which formed around former Proletariat member Stanisław
Trusiewicz (K. Zalewski), besides showing a tendency to abandon
the uncompromising, unpatriotic attitude of Luxemburg, reflected
also a general "reformist" trend common to all European socialism
of the time.[4] This drift was strongly opposed by Luxemburg and suppressed by the cosmopolitan majority, but it continued to have some
influence on the rank and file of the party between 1896 and 1902,
and the seeds of this "nationalist deviation" were to remain. However, in 1901 Trusiewicz was arrested.

Two years earlier, in 1899, Feliks Dzierżyński, an energetic and
able organizer, had escaped from exile. With his return to political

activity came an expansion of the small and scattered social-democratic groups. Dzierżyński proceeded first to Lithuania, where he had begun his political career. Lithuania, like Poland, had two socialist groups at this time. One was called the Lithuanian Social Democratic Party and was concerned chiefly with Lithuanian-speaking workers. The other, founded in 1896 by Trusiewicz (Zalewski), was called the Union of Workers in Lithuania and was composed of Polish-speaking workers. The program of the first group, in spite of its name, was closer to the ideology of the PPS, adapted to Lithuanian conditions, than it was to the program of the SDKP. It preached national independence as a first step towards a socialist Lithuanian Republic, possibly federated with its neighbors. The Union of Workers in Lithuania was more influenced by the SDKP. Persuaded by Dzierżyński, with the help of Trusiewicz, this group decided to end its separate existence and to federate with the SDKP. The merger took place in December 1899, and the united party took the name Social Democracy of the Kingdom of Poland and of Lithuania (SDKPiL).[5]

The next step for Dzierżyński was to rebuild the almost nonexistent social-democratic organization in Warsaw. This was achieved within a few months. Although Dzierżyński was soon arrested again, the push he gave to the organization outlasted his physical presence. During 1900 several new branches of the SDKPiL arose in Łódź, Częstochowa, Radom, Białystok, Płock, Kowno, and in the Dąbrowa industrial basin. In spite of this expansion, which took place mainly among artisans, the PPS still remained by far the largest socialist party.

Meanwhile, in spite of PPS pessimism, the Russian Social Democratic movement was growing. A wave of strikes swept Russia, and in 1898 a Russian Social Democratic Workers Party was formed, giving some encouragement to the non-Russian groups who had tied their fate to the destinies of the Russian movement. Moreover, the creation of a third group, a separate Jewish socialist movement, known as the *Bund*, further weakened the commanding position of the PPS among socialists in Russian Poland. The PPS however, remained the leading Polish socialist organization of the country until 1906, but after 1901 it had to reckon with at least two dangerous antagonists, the SDKPiL and the Bund.[6]

THE SOCIAL DEMOCRATIC ELITE: ROSA LUXEMBURG

The SDKPiL was headed by a mobile and versatile elite, roughly divided into two groups. One group resided mostly in the country and was preoccupied with the practical activities of organization and agitation. The other part of the team lived chiefly in exile, in Germany, Switzerland, and, after 1902, in Galicia. The émigré group was busy writing, discussing ideological problems, and representing the party at international congresses. There was nothing prearranged in this rather spontaneous division of labor. The two groups were interconnected and exchanged their members according to the necessities of their struggle. Both teams were strongly under the influence of Russian revolutionaries, not only ideologically but also in regard to their mode of life. The leading role within this elite should undoubtedly be assigned to Rosa Luxemburg, perhaps the most remarkable woman thus far produced by any socialist movement.

Rosa Luxemburg's nervous, dynamic, highly intellectual and emotional personality lent a great deal of color to the whole movement and largely determined its development. She was born in 1871, in central Poland, of a prosperous Jewish family.[7] From childhood she was afflicted by a hip ailment, which by keeping her permanently handicapped channelled most of her energies toward intellectual activities and tended to make her both sensitive and ambitious. When still in a Warsaw high school she joined the revolutionary circles of the Proletariat. In 1886, to avoid imprisonment, Luxemburg escaped to Zurich, which at that time was a rallying point for Russian socialists. While in exile she participated in Polish revolutionary activities and in 1893, with her friends Leon Jogiches (Tyszko), J. Marchlewski (Karski), and Adolf Warszawski (Warski), she helped to engineer the split which ended the newly achieved unity of the Polish socialist movement and resulted in the foundation of the Social Democracy of the Kingdom of Poland.

In Zurich Rosa Luxemburg studied economics and wrote a doctoral dissertation, "Industrial Development of Poland." When her studies were completed, in 1897, the Polish Social Democratic Party appointed her its representative on the Inter-Socialist Bureau of the Second International. Luxemburg moved to Berlin, where her apartment became the headquarters of the movement abroad; she contributed often to the organ of the German Social Democrats, *Die Neue Zeit*, edited by Karl Kautsky, and soon became its associate editor. From the beginning Rosa Luxemburg considered the Kingdom of Poland too small a field of activity for her. Consequently she, as well as many of her close companions in exile, joined the German Social Democratic Party and almost all of this band achieved considerable prominence in the German ranks. Luxemburg also worked with socialist groups in Posnania and Silesia, as well as in Saxony.

Luxemburg decided at the outset of her activity, that the Polish Marxist movement should reject the idea of national independence. This step meant breaking with the policy of Marx and Engels, which they had long supported and which old Engels was still upholding at the time Rosa Luxemburg was beginning her political career. This policy was also dogma for Western European socialism. Rosa Luxemburg decided to fight against the objective of political independence and much of her writing is devoted to this task.[8]

How could the proletariat of Poland, Luxemburg argued, create a bourgeois national state? The rebirth of such a state would contradict both the workers' own vital economic interests and the interest of the Polish bourgeoisie who gained so many economic advantages from the fact that the industries of the Congress Kingdom served Russian markets. On the other hand, if the Polish working class had sufficient strength to overthrow the power of the three strongest governments in Europe, then it would also have enough drive to achieve social revolution. For it was only *social* revolution that could offer the hope of better conditions for the Polish proletariat. Not even the fantasy of a café politician, she repeatedly said, could conceive of an independent Poland emerging from its present subjugation. This attitude made her unpopular not only with the Polish Socialist Party but also with many contemporary Western European comrades who generally subscribed to the traditional Marxist doctrine.

In 1895, while still at Zurich, Rosa Luxemburg wrote a pamphlet, "Independent Poland and the Workers' Cause." [9] When Marx supported Polish independence, the pamphlet argued, Poland was one of the revolutionary centers of Europe, a highly explosive force that could have upset the Holy Alliance of the reactionary powers. Now, it was stressed, Russia was gradually ceasing to be the mainstay of reaction and beginning instead to be the chief revolutionary force, the hope of world socialism. For this reason the national aspirations of the Poles had to be subordinated to the socialist objective of world revolution.

THE SOCIAL DEMOCRATIC ELITE: THE REST OF THE TEAM

The most intimate friend of Rosa Luxemburg was Leon Jogiches (Tyszka or Tyszko). Jogiches (Tyszko) was born in Wilno, in 1867, of a wealthy Jewish family. His grandfather was a well-known Talmud scholar; his father was already Russianized and the family spoke Russian as their native language. Jogiches soon devoted himself entirely to the socialist cause and for some time belonged to the

Jewish labor circles from which the Bund, an organization Jogiches helped to create, eventually emerged. Forced to emigrate, Jogiches landed at Zurich where he met Rosa Luxemburg, started working with her, and began learning Polish. Soon he became her lifelong friend and political companion. Though he was a skilled editor, Jogiches was devoid of any gift or taste for writing. Strong willed, domineering, and versatile, he was the originator of many of the ideas that were later on associated mainly with Luxemburg, who was the brains of the party as well as its principal organizer. Together with Luxemburg, Jogiches was to play a prominent role in the revolutionary events in Poland in 1905–06. After that revolution both Jogiches and Luxemburg entered more and more into the activities of the Bolshevik as well as the German Social Democratic Party. In the latter they headed the left wing, opposing Kautsky's center. From the beginning of his activities in the SDKPiL Jogiches revealed strong dictatorial tendencies. During World War I, with other colleagues from Poland like Marchlewski (Karski) and Karol Radek, Jogiches organized the first illegal communist-inclined Spartacus groups and led their revolt in 1919. He was assassinated in prison in 1919, soon after the deaths of Rosa Luxemburg and Karl Liebknecht.

The background of Adolf Warszawski (Warski) was very similar to that of Luxemburg and Jogiches, but his destiny was somewhat different. A gifted propagandist and a good speaker, he became, with Luxemburg and Radek, one of the main publicists of the party and the chief popularizer of its ideas. He outlived his comrades to become one of the founders of the Polish Communist Workers' Party, a leader of its right wing, and a deputy to the Polish Diet (*Sejm*). Sentenced by a Polish tribunal for subversive activities to a few years of imprisonment, he fled to seek refuge in the Soviet Union. There he was soon accused of Trotskyism and finally liquidated together with most of the "old guard" of Polish communism. Marcin Kasprzak was a simple worker from Poznań, the only authentic proletarian among the leaders of the SDKPiL. Kasprzak gained wide popularity among his fellow workers, with whom he always remained in close touch, because of his reckless courage and ability as an organizer. After being arrested and escaping several times, he was eventually captured in Warsaw in April 1904, while printing May Day proclamations, and hanged for having killed two tsarist gendarmes.

In discussing the elite of the SDKPiL one should also mention Karol Sobelson (Radek), Józef Unszlicht (Jurowski), and Jakób Firstenberg (Hanecki), all of whom, after a relatively short but active period in the ranks of their native party, were eventually drawn into the orbit of the Bolsheviks and came to play a prominent role in the Soviet set-up. Firstenberg (Hanecki) occupied several high administrative posts and Unszlicht was for some time, after Dzierżyński's death, the acting chief of the GPU; then the head of the Intelligence Service of the Comintern, and, for a period, even the nominal commander of Soviet aviation. The most gifted propagandist of the party was Karol Sobelson, known as Radek. Born in a Galician ghetto and fed a mixed diet of the Talmud, Lessing, and Mickiewicz, he revealed great gifts as a dialectician and propagandist from the very beginning of his swift career in revolution. After playing a considerable role in the Polish and German social-democratic movements, Radek climbed to an influential position in international communism. Radek's writing ability soon made him a leading publicist and pamphleteer of the Communists.

One should also remember two other prominent leaders, Julian Marchlewski (Karski) and Feliks Dzierżyński. Marchlewski, born in Western Poland of a German mother, was one of the leaders of the Union of Polish Workers, the parent organization of the SDKP. He was an economist, educated with Luxemburg, Tyszko, and Warski at Zurich University, and an expert in the problems of rural economy. A Marxist missionary urge, and perhaps also a kind of inverted socialist snobbishness, made him follow the example of Proletariat leader Waryński in "going to the people." Several times during his revolutionary career, Marchlewski sought employment as a simple worker in Warsaw and Łódź, as well as in Germany. An industrious student of agrarian problems, he preached the need for transferring the socialist revolution to the village and making Marxist doctrine digestible to the peasants. In 1901, when in Munich, Marchlewski helped Lenin to organize the paper, *Iskra,* drawing on his own close relations with the Bavarian workers' movement. After 1915 he organized the Spartacus Association with Luxemburg, Liebknecht, and Klara Zetkin, edited the "Letters of Spartacus," and was instrumental in founding the German Communist Party.[10] In 1919 Marchlewski acted as a go between for Lenin and Piłsudski in the negotiations that brought about a temporary truce between their two countries. With Dzierżyński and Feliks Kon, Marchlewski, Unszlicht, and Próchniak made up the team that the Red Army was to establish as a revolutionary government in Poland in the summer of 1920. Marchlewski ended his days in 1925 as a high official of the Soviet Union.

Feliks Dzierżyński (Józef), like Jogiches (Tyszko), started his revolutionary career very early in life in Wilno. Arrested and deported, he soon escaped and returned to his former task. In 1889, he achieved a merger between the Union of Lithuanian Workers and the Social Democracy of the Kingdom of Poland and Lithuania. Impatient and intolerant, ruthless and idealistic, he was one of the first members of the SDKPiL to identify himself, without reservation, with the Bolsheviks. His devotion to Lenin and Lenin's cause and his hatred of political opponents had no equal among his party comrades. National sentiment had no place in the mind of this ascetic, with his deathly pale face and the thin bloodless lips of a terrorist fanatic. He regarded himself as consecrated to his task, with no personal interests, no emotions, and with only one passion — the revolution. To this objective all other interests and aspirations had to be subordinated. His role of the grand inquisitor of bolshevism suited him perfectly. He devoted himself to this task with a cruel and merciless integrity. After 1924 his devotion to Lenin was transferred to Stalin, for he was one of the first among Soviet leaders to support Stalin without reservation in all fields of activities, including the Comintern. Dzierżyński eventually worked himself to death in this task of extermination. He died in 1926.

Such was the leadership of the SDKPiL. It was perhaps the most remarkable elite of dedicated professional revolutionaries next to that of the Bolsheviks. But these leaders differed from the Bolsheviks in many respects, one of them being a dislike for central control and rigid discipline. The SDKPiL social composition was not very different from that of other contemporary leftist parties in Poland: a mixture of Jewish intelligentsia and descendants of the ruined nobility. All of them were truly devoted to their cause. However, despite their efforts, hard work, courage, and personal sacrifice; despite even some successes at international forums, such as the International Socialist Congress of Paris in 1900, the SDKPiL leadership remained a self-styled vanguard of a hardly existing mass movement. The proletariat either remained passive or followed the PPS.[11]

THE REBIRTH OF THE SDKPiL (1902) AND THE FIRST ATTEMPT AT UNION WITH THE RSDWP (1903)

The growth of Russian social-democratic groups, at the beginning of the twentieth century, and the rapid rebirth of social democracy in the Congress Kingdom, once more emphasized the problem of unifying both movements. This idea, which was fundamental to the program of the SDKPiL, was recurring constantly at party discussions and in the clandestine press. Some practical attempts to realize these fundamental aspirations took place soon after the rebirth of the party at the turn of the century.

As early as February 1901, the Central Committee of the party sent four letters proposing the unification of the two movements on the basis of a loose federation, with wide autonomy for the Polish group within the combined movement. These letters were addressed to the foreign section of the Russian Social Democratic Workers' Party and to the editors of *Iskra,* as well as to the Central Committee of the Bund and to the Lettish Social Democratic parties. The idea of a loose federation did not appeal to Lenin, who was just preparing his pamphlet "What is to be Done?" and who was already strong enough to frustrate the scheme by his veto.[12] Lenin was already fully determined to create a centralized and monolithic party.

The arrest of Trusiewicz (Zalewski) in 1902 and Dzierżyński's second flight from deportation marked a definite recession of the revisionist trend within the SDKPiL, a trend that had tended towards cooperation with the PPS.[13] Toward the end of 1902 Dzierżyński established the general headquarters of the party in Cracow. Energetic preparations were made for merging with the Russian movement. The creation of a popular paper, "Red Flag," was a part of the policy to march along parallel lines with the Russian Social Democratic Workers' Party (RSDWP), so long as a straight merger proved impractical. The new paper was to have the same editorial policy and to play the same role as *Iskra.* In his policy of unification Dzierżyński, now the driving force of the group, encountered numerous difficulties. One was the attitude of Luxemburg and Jogiches (Tyszko), who were reluctant to subordinate themselves completely to the Russian party. This opposition to the idea of a monolithic party with a dictatorial central committee, as represented by Lenin, has often been cited as the main obstacle to unity. This is, however, incorrect. It was another problem, national in character, which again provoked major disagreements, as it had previously between the PPS and SDKPiL. The prolonged correspondence between the two parties testifies to the persistence of Lenin and the *Iskra* group in trying to achieve unification and underscores the elusive attitude of the SDKPiL.[14] Rosa Luxemburg was not present at the RSDWP Congress of 1903, which was memorable for the split between the Bolsheviks and the Mensheviks, factions of the Russian movement. Acting behind the scenes, by means of daily telegrams and letters, she kept in touch with Warski and Hanecki and insisted on autonomy for her party, which she considered older and more advanced than

the Russian one. But she particularly emphasized the "proper interpretation" of point 7 of the *Iskra* program. This point granted the
right of self-determination, including the right of secession, to each
and every nationality of the Russian Empire. To the right of secession she objected. Luxemburg made revision of this point the unal-
terable condition for joining the RSDWP. The RSDWP, however,
categorically refused to accept the conditions put forward by the
SDKPiL, especially the one pertaining to self-determination. Thus
ended the first debate on the national problem within the Russian
social-democratic movement, as well as the attempt to turn the
RSDWP into a loose federation of autonomous national groups.

THE CONTROVERSY: LUXEMBURG-LENIN

After the 1903 Congress Rosa Luxemburg often stressed her differences with Lenin, not so much on the national question as on the
matter of party structure. She expressed fear of the dictatorial tendencies of Lenin and his group in several articles, the most famous one
being "Organisation Fragen der russischen Sozialdemokratie." [15] In
these articles, not unlike Trotsky, she attacked the Leninist conception of a party headed by a leadership invested with absolute power.
According to Luxemburg this would imply a complete denial of "proletarian democracy," Lenin, in his "One Step Forward, Two Steps
Back," directed as much against Luxemburg as against the Mensheviks, scornfully rejected the idea that the working class alone, without proper leadership, could be the active and conscious agent of
revolutionary change. Luxemburg condemned this attitude as "bourgeois" and branded as conspiratorial Lenin's idea of a small elite,
imposing socialism on the working class. When the Mensheviks captured *Iskra,* Luxemburg supported their point of view on the organization of the party. She argued that the centralist trend of Lenin's
group was a result of underdevelopment of the Russian movement,
which had grown up under the abnormal conditions of tsarist terror.
Luxemburg rejected Leninist tactics, understood as a conscious plan,
and offered hers instead, which she interpreted as a spontaneous process. Like Bakunin she trusted the "healthy revolutionary instinct of
the masses" and considered meticulous plans to be "out of touch
with the spontaneous class struggle." According to her the social-
democratic dynamics "should derive from spontaneous class action."

Despite a seemingly democratic attitude, as compared with Lenin,
Luxemburg was strongly opposed to "bourgeois democracy" and
preached the necessity of replacing it with "proletarian" or "revolu-

tionary democracy." She did not harbor any illusions that workers could ever achieve socialism by a majority vote in parliament. "The use of violence will always remain the *ultima ratio* for the working class, the supreme law of the class struggle, always present, sometimes in a latent, sometimes in an active form." Luxemburg believed that the paramount task of social democracy was to give workers a consciousness of their mission and to prepare them for their task as champions of all toiling masses in their political struggle. She subscribed to the basic view that a revolutionary party must be the vanguard of the proletariat, meaning primarily the urban proletariat, and that such a party must be centrally organized. But, and here again she clashed with Lenin and his followers, Luxemburg thought that an all-powerful central committee could become a hindrance to the future development of the class struggle. She was, therefore, in favor of subjecting "his Majesty the Central Committee" to an effective control on behalf of the party membership. She defended the freedom to criticize, insisting that it was indispensable to the development and to the very existence of a social-democratic party. Luxemburg often stressed that revolutionary movements could not be "manufactured," that they could not come as a result of party decisions, but could grow only spontaneously and under certain objective historical conditions. Here, also, she differed from the Bolsheviks who, later on, were to brand her numerous "deviations" from the Leninist line with the inclusive term "Luxemburgism."

This "heresy" consisted of three main points, according to the criticism of Leninist-Stalinist commentators like O. B. Szmidt. First, it implied a depreciation in the role of the party as leader in the class struggle. This meant, according to the commentators, an uncritical worship of the masses as such and an overestimation of impersonal, objective, socio-economic factors of development. It implied, as well, a denial of the importance of the subjective factors of human will and planning and submission to the mechanical fatalism of historical process. In short, it was allegedly equal to a passive attitude, which resulted from negation of the importance of conscious and organized action of the party, and to emphasis on "spontaneity" and the "automatic process of history." Second, "Luxemburgism" underestimated the revolutionary role of the peasants, especially poor and middle-class farmers, as allies of the urban proletariat. It tended to look at all peasantry with suspicion and distrust, regarding them as property-minded, backward, and greedy petty-bourgeois. Third, Luxemburg and her followers misunderstood the potentialities of the national problem as a revolutionary factor that could be turned not only against tsarist autocracy but also against all kinds of imperialism.

As bitter as their polemics might have seemed to their contemporaries, from a historical point of view it appears that Lenin and Luxemburg disagreed not on the ultimate goal but on the tactics. Theoretically they both fully accepted one of the basic premises of Marxism: that nations are transient capitalistic phenomena and should disappear with the overturn of the capitalist system. Exclusively in the sphere of theory Lenin certainly would have agreed with Luxemburg that nations should be regarded as remnants of the barbarous past. But as a practical politician he knew that these remnants were still forceful factors on the political scene. Lenin's shrewd, practical sense made him reject any idea that national aspirations and national frontiers could be obliterated overnight. Both Lenin and Luxemburg believed in the ultimate disappearance of nations but differed on the method of bringing this about. According to Lenin nationalism was to be outlived and gradually overcome by internationalism. According to Luxemburg it was to be destroyed straight away. Lenin wanted to take the fortress of nationalism by subterfuge; Luxemburg wanted to capture it by storm.[16]

THE PPS AND THE SDKPiL ON THE EVE OF THE REVOLUTION OF 1904–05

Meanwhile, in 1903 and 1904, the revolutionary wave was rising. It was expressed largely in the form of strikes and public manifestations that were taking place both in Russia and Poland. During this period the SDKPiL made some progress among the industrial workers of Warsaw, Łódź, and Białystok. In 1902 the party established its headquarters in Galicia. The PPS began to emphasize the slogan of independence and, in spite of the strong opposition of its left wing, was preparing for a national rising should the opportunity arise. Attempts made by both rival groups to coordinate the activities of the two major proletarian parties failed. The differences not only in program but in psychological make-up were too great.

There was, first of all, the central theme of Poland's independence. The PPS considered it a cornerstone of its minimum program and wanted to achieve it by means of an armed insurrection. The SDKPiL stuck to its original "proletarian internationalism." It claimed only some vague autonomy within a reformed, constitutional, Russian state, an objective it wanted to achieve by means of economic as well as political mass action concerted with their Russian comrades.

The PPS was in favor of close ties with the socialists of Galicia and of Western Poland, treating them as separate Polish political parties; the SDKPiL, on the other hand, regarded them merely as sections of the Austrian and German movements, and recommended if not merger at least federation. Following this principle the SDKPiL aimed at a federation with the Russian Social Democratic Workers Party, reserving for itself full autonomy in local matters, a proper representation on the editorial board of the all-party paper and in the central committee, and a free hand in interpreting point 7 of the *Iskra* program.

The PPS regarded the non-Russian nationalities of the empire, irrespective of class divisions, as the main allies of the Poles in their fight against the tsarist rule. The SDKPiL favored a close collaboration with the working masses of the whole state, mainly, however, with its strongest segment, the Russian proletariat. During the negotiations for the merger with the RSDWP, the SDKPiL was determined to preserve the integrity of the Russian state, which it regarded as a potential revolutionary base that should be kept intact. The PPS always jealously guarded its independence from the Russian socialist movement and cultivated closer relations only with the social revolutionaries. As a matter of fact, there were both temperamental and programmatic similarities between the two parties. Both parties had a predilection for terror, and emphasized federalism as a possible solution for national problems.

The Jewish problem, a slippery question in a country where a large Jewish minority formed a high percentage of the urban proletariat, also separated the PPS and the SDKPiL. They agreed on one point: both parties condemned anti-Semitism. While SDKPiL refused to recognize Jews as a separate national group with distinct proletarian interests, the PPS had a different point of view. The SDKPiL would have been perfectly satisfied with the Jewish workers' losing their national identity and merging with the rest of the local proletariat, while the PPS insisted on their cultural assimilation in the Polish community. The SDKPiL supported the Bund's rejection of Polish independence as an objective, while the PPS decried it as one more proof of the unfriendly attitude of the so-called "Litwaks," or Jews from Lithuania, Byelorussia, and the Ukraine, who were considered by the PPS as instruments of Russification. The Bund was a member of an all-Russian Social Democratic Party, to which the SDKPiL wanted to belong from the very beginning, while the PPS criticized and opposed that party.

The same Fourth Congress of the PPS that put forward conditions of collaboration with the Russians also formulated its platform regarding the Jewish problem. The PPS, which had organized a special Jewish section of the party and published some propaganda material in Yiddish, condemned the Bund as a separatist attempt aimed at breaking the unity of the proletarian movement in Poland, and thus, though unwillingly, facilitated the government's anti-Semitic policy. According to the PPS, the Jewish proletariat could not possibly have interests separate from those of the country in which it lived and worked. The Bund reciprocated and at its third (1899) and fourth (1900) congresses refused its support for the idea of Poland's independence.[17]

As for the SDKPiL, its attitude toward the Bund, in spite of the latter's "opportunistic and nationalistic tendencies," was much more conciliatory. For its part the Fourth Congress of the Bund regarded the SDKPiL "as one of the social-democratic parties of a nationality belonging to the Russian state" and expressed the hope of "establishing a federal link" with that party.[18] In spite of fierce ideological battles fought sometimes between the press organs of the Bund and those of the SDKPiL, the actual relations between the two groups were never as strained as between the SDKPiL and the PPS.

As for the organizational structure of the PPS and the SDKPiL, its main feature was its looseness. It was partly determined by security conditions and partly adapted to effective agitation in order to maintain the widest possible contact with the masses. The parties were not sharply divided from the masses, and this in itself facilitated the spread of ideas and printed matter. The second characteristic common feature was the small size of these underground groups. Here all sources agree on one point: in 1904 the PPS was the largest and the most influential among them, numbering several thousand active members. Nevertheless, even the position of the PPS in an overwhelmingly agricultural, Catholic, and traditionalist society was rather precarious. The events of 1905–1907 were to prove it in a striking way.

Thus on the eve of the revolution of 1904–05, the organizational structure of the two main socialist parties of the country was similar, while the ideological differences were deep, touching practically every major point of their programs. To these programmatic controversies must be added differences in temperament and mentality. The leadership of the SDKPiL was composed chiefly of intellectuals given to theoretical speculations. People who swore by Marx, Engels, and historic materialism, looked down on national traditions and underestimated the elemental emotional force of a subject nation. Most of them were convinced cosmopolitans, feeling as much at home in St. Petersburg, Berlin, or Zurich, as in Warsaw, Wilno, or Łódź. Many of them felt more at home among Russian revolutionaries than among their countrymen. Luxemburg, Jogiches, Radek, and Marchlewski played simultaneously a considerable role in three national parties (Polish, German, and Russian) while most of the others, with Dzierżyński at the head, belonged to two such parties (Polish and Russian).

In the leadership of the PPS the dominant type was a man to whom Marxism was primarily a rationalization of his own moral revolt against social as well as national injustice. But abstract, doctrinaire Marxism had for him little appeal unless adopted to the realities of the country and integrated with the native revolutionary tradition. For the PPS, revolution meant as much a *national* liberation as a social overturn, while for the SDKPiL, the word had exclusively a *social* content.

With such programs and such mental attitudes the two rival parties came to face the Russian-Japanese war of 1904–05. The events of those fateful years widened the gap between the two trends of the socialist movement and opened a new chapter in their respective history.

The REVOLUTION
of 1904-05 and
3   Its AFTERMATH

The economic recession which the Russian Empire experienced in 1903 laid the groundwork for the revolutionary events of 1904–05. After July of 1903 a wave of strikes swept the whole country, paralyzing most of the larger industrial centers. The Congress Kingdom was no exception. When the Russo-Japanese war broke out in February 1904, the working classes were already in a state of ferment. The war, by disrupting communication on the trans-Siberian line and by closing a part of the eastern market, profoundly affected the whole economy of Russian Poland, geared as it was to that very market. Unemployment spread rapidly. The initial Japanese successes helped to reawaken the patriotism of the middle classes, to galvanize the politically conscious into a state of expectation, and to reactivate latent political discontent. The endemic social and political unrest was skillfully exploited by both major rivals for the leadership of the revolutionary movement: the Polish Socialist Party and the Social Democracy of Poland and Lithuania.

In one respect the attitude of the PPS and the SDKPiL toward the war was similar. Like the other revolutionary parties of Russian Poland, they both hoped for defeat and were convinced that it would give them a unique chance for action. They differed, however, over what kind of action should be taken and with which social group they should ally. Although strongly defeatist, the Social Democrats never publicized their pro-Japanese sentiments. They emphasized that in this conflict of rival imperialism they hoped for a *tsarist* and not a Russian defeat; they objected to all pro-Japanese manifestations and preached unity with the Russian socialist movement.[1]

The bulk of the PPS, however, especially its right wing led by Piłsudski, was enthusiatically pro-Japanese. The PPS believed that the Russian Empire was bound to be defeated and could be weakened by internal dissension. Were the party to conduct an armed action in the Congress Kingdom, concerted with diversionary moves by other subjected nationalities and supported by Japan, the eventual result would be the creation of an independent Polish Republic. Accordingly, soon after the war's outbreak, Piłsudski was dispatched by the PPS to Tokyo to enlist Japanese assistance for an uprising in Russian Poland. These plans were frustrated by the leader of the newly founded conservative and conciliatory National Democratic Party, Roman Dmowski, who went to Tokyo to persuade the Japanese not to accept Piłsudski's offer because it was useless for the Japanese and harmful for Poland. Dmowski expected to gain basic concessions for the Congress Kingdom, including political autonomy, by offering to St. Petersburg his party's limited cooperation. The autonomy, he hoped, would put an end to the process of systematic Russification, and might possibly turn this part of the country into another Galicia, if not another Piedmont. Although deprived of any hope of support from abroad, Piłsudski, after his return from Japan, resumed execution of his original plan. With PPS approval, he immediately started to organize military detachments of the party. Piłsudski considered the formation of these fighting squads the first step toward establishing cadres of a future national army.[2]

The SDKPiL. and the Jewish Bund emphatically stressed unity of the revolutionary movement in all the empire. Both these groups insisted, therefore, upon the necessity for supporting what they considered to be the strongest element of discontent — the Russian socialist movement. Both these parties were convinced that an internal upheaval would inevitably follow a military defeat, and that unrest should be exploited by means of mass strikes in order to wring some fundamental concessions from the autocracy, if it were not to be abolished altogether. There was hope that the empire would first be transformed into a democratic structure, with a constitution and guarantees of universal suffrage, and eventually into a socialist federation. Then some sort of autonomy for the non-Russian provinces would have to be granted.[3]

Around this dilemma of insurrection and independence, or mass strike action and autonomy, revolved the endless debates that went on in revolutionary circles. To this was added another tactical problem: with whom should one form an alliance? From the beginning the Social Democrats took an aggressive position against two fronts, the autocracy and the native bourgeoisie, with their alleged ally — the PPS.[4]

THE GROWTH OF REVOLUTIONARY FERMENT

All over Russian Poland, and especially in Warsaw and Łódź, revolutionary ferment was mounting. Already on February 21, 1904, anti-war demonstrations took place in Warsaw. The government replied by arresting several hundred persons. Numerous strikes and demonstrations followed throughout the country. Many of the SDKPiL leaders, who had previously been compelled to stay abroad, started to take an active part in the struggle they had been planning for ten years. The May Day proclamation of the SDKPiL condemned the war for its imperialistic character. They appealed to the toiling masses to sabotage the tsarist war effort and to fight in close collaboration with their Russian comrades for peace. The abolition of absolutism and the establishment of a democratic republic was demanded.[5] The May Day demonstration in Warsaw was jointly organized by the SDKPiL and the Bund.

The PPS instructed its members and sympathizers to sabotage the war effort by all possible means and appealed to the soldiers to desert and form guerilla bands, or, if sent to the front, to desert to the Japanese. At the same time the party was feverishly preparing for an armed insurrection. The PPS hoped to construct a broad, multinational front from a variety of revolutionary, if not necessarily socialist, parties, all of which were dedicated to the overthrow of the autocracy.

In the fall of 1904, a group of revolutionary organizations which were active within the Russian Empire held a conference in Paris for the purpose of coordinating their efforts. The conference was attended by seven major groups, including the PPS. Although the SDKPiL and the Bund were also invited, they refused (following the example of the RSDWP) on the ground that, being class parties, they could not cooperate with bourgeois groups.[6] This meeting, usually referred to as the Paris Conference, formulated a common minimum program in terms general enough to satisfy all the participants. It may be summed up in three main points: abolition of autocracy, introduction of a free democratic system of government based on universal suffrage, and recognition of the national rights of the people of the empire, including the right of self-determination. The Paris Conference, while initiating a series of similar meetings during the years to follow, failed to bring about any concrete results other than a general *rapprochement* among the various revolutionary parties of the Tsarist Empire. The SDKPiL was, of course, highly critical of the PPS position. It accused the PPS of fraternizing with nonproletarian elements and of being carried away by the tide of a bourgeois revolutionary stream. The PPS, argued the Social Democrats, had erroneously concluded that the aim of the coming upheaval would be a democratic and bourgeois Polish Republic and, therefore, leadership of the struggle and the fruits of an eventual victory should be shared with the bourgeoisie. In reality, said the Social Democrats, the revolution had a double character: it was indeed a democratic and a bourgeois revolution so far as its avowed objective was concerned, but a proletarian one in respect to its methods and its leadership. Moreover, by neglecting strikes and emphasizing terroristic activities and bloody demonstrations, the PPS was actually denying the fundamental principle of a socialist mass movement.[7] Such a movement could not rely solely upon terrorists but had to permeate the masses and ultimately penetrate the ranks of the opponent's armed forces and police — those "proletarians in uniforms." Terror, inherently bad and never effective, was declared to be suicidal under the circumstances, since it tended to alienate the very persons whom the Social Democrats hoped to win to their side — the Russian armed forces.

Events soon afterward pressed even the SDKPiL into armed activity. The bloody demonstrations of November 13, 1904, at Grzybowski Square in Warsaw, as well as May Day manifestations of 1905, had been followed by bloody repressions; pogroms were encouraged by the government, and armed groups of rightists made their appearance. The Social Democrats, however, restricted terror to individual acts, and large-scale armed uprising, preached by Lenin, was never seriously contemplated. Thus the Social Democrats, who bitterly criticized the "social-patriots" for too much armed activity, were soon, in turn condemned by the Bolsheviks for not doing enough. The SDKPiL also took issue with the Bolsheviks on the Leninist "revolutionary-democratic dictatorship of the proletariat and the peasantry." Without denying in theory the necessity for cooperation with the peasantry in order to bring about the revolution, the Social Democrats prophesied that the peasants, especially the more prosperous ones, would join the camp of reaction as soon as they secured some land from the bourgeois government. Thus, the SDKPiL refused to cooperate either with the peasantry or with the bourgeoisie.

THE REVOLUTION IN POLAND AND RUSSIA

Simultaneously with the military defeats in the Far East, revolutionary discontent was smouldering all over the Tsarist Empire. The St. Petersburg demonstration of January 22, 1905, led by the priest Gapon, resulted in a massacre of hundreds of innocent people by the troops. The news of a general strike by Russian workers found a warm reception throughout Poland; the success of the strike surprised the country. This managed to shake the distrust of the PPS leadership toward the potentialities of the Russian movement. It also strengthened the hand of the left or the "Young" wing of the party, which began to protest more openly against the insurrectionist and separatist tactics of the "Old" wing. Since that time a revolt of the "Young" was gathering momentum. Under the impact of the bloody Sunday of January 22, 1905, or the so-called Gaponade, all the revolutionary parties of Russian Poland, while never burying the hatchet formally, decided to support the struggle initiated by the Russian workers.[8] Accordingly, a general strike was called in the Congress Kingdom by all the socialist groups. The strike began January 27, 1905, accompanied by slogans against autocracy and for both a democratic republic and an eight-hour work day. Like the Russian strike, this too was successful. From Warsaw the strike spread to almost all the major industrial centers. Demonstrations inevitably led to violent clashes with the police and army and numerous lives were lost on both sides. The civil administration almost collapsed and a state of siege was proclaimed. In spite of bloody repressions, the wave of strikes unleashed in January continued through most of the year. May Day 1905 claimed about one hundred victims when a large demonstration in Warsaw, organized by the SDKPiL, turned into a bloody riot with police.[9] The climax of this almost continuous series of clashes and demonstrations was reached between June 22 and 23, 1905, during a three-day street fight which broke out in Łódź. Barricades were erected and fierce skirmishes between workers and police ensued. Again several hundred were killed and wounded.

A Constitutional Manifesto, which promised a bill of rights and a legislative assembly (*Duma*), was acclaimed by street demonstrations in Warsaw November 5, 1905, when loyalist elements of the city organized a street procession and the next day submitted a petition to the governor general demanding autonomy for the Congress Kingdom. On November 11 a reply came in the form of a decree instituting martial law. The press organ of the PPS, "The Worker," already directed by the left wing of the party, or the "Young," published a dramatic proclamation on December 26, 1905. It appealed to the working masses of Poland to support the Moscow uprising by a general strike, to refuse to pay taxes, and to establish a revolutionary self-government. This appeal had little response.

There was no general strike; only in the industrial cities of Warsaw, Łódź, Sosnowiec, and Radom were there some local demonstrations. Poland was exhausted by months of revolutionary fervor and torn between resignation and hope for the benefits promised by the Constitutional Manifesto. The Military Organization of the PPS, the only serious fighting group in the country, had already been broken by arrests and decimated by skirmishes. The SDKPiL had no comparable force ready to act. Workers were tired and apathetic, and the rest of the nation was frightened by the "red specter."

The introduction of martial law did not unite the nation in opposition but, on the contrary, divided it even more deeply. Those who cherished hope for improvement in the country's position were more anxious than ever not to jeopardize those concessions which Tsar Nicolas promised in his Manifesto. Those few who wanted to continue to fight were overwhelmed and paralyzed by the growing conflict between the SDKPiL and the PPS on the one hand, and the deepening cleavage within the PPS on the other.

THE CHANGING MOOD OF THE COUNTRY

The Constitutional Manifesto had a dramatic impact on Poland. Although the Manifesto's provisions did not satisfy even the more moderate in the nation, it was widely regarded as a valuable step in the right direction, a chance worth trying, a ray of hope. As a result, the socialist parties lost the support of nonsocialists, who had previously joined in the struggle against tsarist troops and a tsarist administration. Parties of every political coloration had joined in a successful strike to force Russian liberalization of the Polish school system, but the middle classes feared an economic duel between workers and industrialists and began to view the revolutionary movement as leading toward complete anarchy. Leadership of the country was assumed by the strongest political group, the National Democrats, headed by Dmowski. This group became ascendant by stressing the growing danger of German intervention in the event of conflict between Poles and Russians.

The unsuccessful aftermath of the revolution and the mistakes committed by socialist groups gave the National Democrats[10] their first chance to venture into the devastated field of labor politics. The new party opened their fight "against socialism and anarchy" by demanding a fair trial for the new constitutional regime, supporting the state Duma election, and hoping for Congress Kingdom autonomy.

It soon became obvious that socialism as a whole was rapidly losing whatever popularity it had managed to acquire among workers and the more radical intelligentsia, and that the National Democrats remained masters of the situation. The socialist parties had never had any serious influence on the bulk of the nation — the peasant masses. The Social Democrats, contemptuous of the peasants, never even seriously tried to win them over. Such attempts as were made by the PPS during the early period of the revolution failed. The Peasant Union, organized in the autumn of 1904, played a less significant role in Poland than in Russia. There were some strikes by agricultural workers but the peasant masses lacked leadership and organization.

Toward the middle of 1905 the National Workers' Association emerged as an instrument of the National Democratic Party in its life-and-death struggle against the socialists.[11] After that time it became a factor to be reckoned with in the labor movement. The association organized fighting squads to oppose those of the PPS and SDKPiL. To the boycott of the first Duma election, which had been advocated by the socialists, the association responded with a "counter-boycott." [12] Fratricidal fights ensued; numerous acts of banditry were perpetrated in the name of every party under cover of the general confusion. The country was on the verge of civil war. By June 1906, even the Social Democrats, who had once urged boycotts and violence, became frightened and advised their supporters to return to reason.[13] The influence of all socialist groups was shrinking rapidly as internal tensions and dissensions increased. Discord was most apparent in the PPS, whose forces had spearheaded the long socialist struggle.

THE CLEAVAGE WITHIN THE PPS

The prolonged fight against the superior forces of the tsarist police, the army, and the administration, as well as the unexpected dynamism shown by the revolutionary movement in Russia, weakened the position of the PPS leadership. The party had repeatedly denied the potentialities of that movement, as well as the possibility of a constitutional evolution of the Tsarist Empire, and staked all its force on a successful insurrection. When, momentarily, the Russian movement surprised the world by its elemental strength, the PPS had to suffer the consequences of its tactics.

At first, impressed by the events in Russia, many left-wing members of the party believed that a democratic republic was about to be established. This republic, they argued, would surely grant a wide autonomy to the Congress Kingdom and, therefore, make it unnecessary to separate Poland from the rest of the state in order to carry out a program of "democracy first and socialism next." This was not very different from the platform advocated by the SDKPiL. The apparent triumph of the Social Democrats caused a considerable shift within the socialist camp. When, however, both groups proved to be mistaken, the revolution failed and no democratic republic was established, a severe crisis developed among the socialists. Since the PPS position was more deeply committed, it was also more vulnerable to defection than the other groups. The disillusioned workers who did not abandon Marxism altogether in favor of the rising National Workers' Association now followed the lead of the SDKPiL or of the PPS left wing.

In order to understand this development within the PPS it is necessary to glance backward to the revolutionary effort in 1905. The general strike of January 1905 was organized largely by the PPS and had enhanced the party's prestige. On the other hand, the initial success of the revolution in other parts of the empire, especially in St. Petersburg and in Moscow, strengthened the position of the PPS left wing. Why risk an isolated uprising, asked the left wing, when almost as much could be gained by joining forces with Russian comrades? Piłsudski's reckless guerilla warfare, for a seemingly utopian aim, alienated him from all but a few followers. For months Piłsudski's band defied an armed force of nearly three hundred thousand men and suffered great hardships and sacrifices. They were decimated both by the fighting and by the inevitable reprisals that followed establishment of martial law.[14]

At the Seventh Party Congress in March 1905, the left wing of the PPS, the "Young," took over political leadership. Reluctantly the "Old Guard" was left in control of the Military Organization, although it was accused of being a "fighting aristocracy" and a potential danger to the party. The "Young" were largely supported by Feliks Kon and Tadeusz Rechniewski, two founding members of the first Proletariat, who had returned from exile and had again begun to play a considerable role within the party. Thus two distinct factions took shape within the PPS. At the beginning the real differences between them were camouflaged by their common desire for a separate constituent assembly or Sejm, to meet in Warsaw. The right wing thought of such an assembly as an instrument of separation from Russia, while the left wing saw in it a stepping stone toward a wider autonomy, which in the future might or might not lead towards complete separation. However, in accordance with the forebodings expressed by Piłsudski, the future development of events was to cause the left faction to interpret separate parliamentary institutions in an ever narrower sense, and eventually they came to mean no more than some kind of local autonomy. This was, in practice, not very distant from the autonomy espoused by the SDKPiL. The Social Democrats, however, unlike the left wing of the PPS were, more often than not, inclined to support the idea of a single parliament for the whole Russian state, in accordance with the centralist ideas professed by Luxemburg. The right wing of the PPS conceded that whatever liberties might be granted by Russia should be accepted, but they should be regarded merely as a step toward complete independence eventually.[15]

In order to compel Russia to concede as much as possible, Piłsudski advocated continuance of armed opposition. This policy of "permanent insurrection" gradually found less support among the rank and file. They were drawn toward the opportunistic program of the PPS left wing, which wanted to seize instantly whatever was offered and make the best of it. Autonomy and an eight-hour work day became immediate objectives. Thus, the differences of opinion between the right and the left wings of the PPS were widening. Under the circumstances, a congress became a necessity.

THE PPS SPLITS (1906)

The PPS held its Eighth Congress during February 1906, in Lwów. The left wing had an overwhelming majority and carried the day. The congress passed a declaration that spelled a major revolution within the party — it condemned the idea of an uprising, in the sense of a war leading to separation from Russia, and proclaimed social revolution as the main objective of the party. The congress resolution stated that revolutionary proletarian tactics had nothing to do with the idea of a national rising. Thus it shelved, if it did not drop altogether, the independence plank of the party which had been formulated in Paris in 1892. The congress also declared that in the event of a revolutionary victory in Russia the empire should become a federal and democratic republic, with wide autonomy for Poland. Terror was condemned once more and the general strike was accepted as the principal, though not exclusive, means of achieving the party objectives.

The right wing of the PPS had, from the beginning, opposed the resolutions of the Eighth Congress and continued to object to them. Despite orders of the Central Committee, Piłsudski and the Military Organization went their own way without, however, formally leaving the party. They carried out a series of bold raids or "fighting actions"

as they were then called. It soon became obvious that the Eighth
Congress had settled nothing, and another congress was badly
needed. It occurred in November 1906, in Vienna. The Ninth Congress again condemned the fighting activities of the Military
Organization and now excluded it from the party altogether. Moreover, the congress emphatically reaffirmed that it was, for the present,
replacing its platform of independence with a demand for autonomy.
Although the party never finally abandoned the idea of separate
Polish statehood, this was declared impractical and subordinate to
the issue of an all-Russian social revolution. Again only the
majority of PPS members followed the new line and only a small
group sided with Piłsudski.

From that moment an evolution began which was gradually to
carry Piłsudski away from socialism. When the international crisis
of 1908 came, he formed the Union of Active Resistance. This organization was to cooperate with the Military Organization and to
prepare cadres for a future government and armed forces of Poland.

AFTER THE SPLIT

Thus the two PPS factions were severed. The PPS-Left attempted
to narrow the gap between it and SDKPiL. Both groups repudiated
independence as a policy objective and armed insurrection as a
tactical method, and both proclaimed the general strike to be their
main instrument. But the tendency of the PPS-Left toward collaboration with bourgeois groups, its legalism and gradualism, as
well as a definite emphasis on the political separateness of Poland,
prevented a closer *rapprochement*.

Aided by skillfully phrased slogans that gained popularity among
workers, the PPS-Left managed to acquire a considerable following
among those inclined toward socialism. The party was led by
intellectuals, including Feliks Kon, Tadeusz Rechniewski,[16] Paweł
Lewinson (Łapiński), Maksymilian Horwitz (Walecki), and Maria
Koszucka (Kostrzewa). In its attempts to establish some kind of
collaboration with non-Marxist parties, in its efforts to create broad,
nonparty trade-unions and, generally speaking, in its preference
for legal and parliamentary action, the PPS-Left resembled the
Mensheviks. Indeed, the PPS-Left collaborated with the Mensheviks
without, however, formally joining the Russian party.

In the Spring of 1906 the SDKPiL and both the Left and Right
PPS boycotted the election of the first Duma. The socialists had
little chance of electing their deputies anyway, since the indirect
election and the curial system did not favor the worker.[17] Owing to

socialist abstention, and to Dmowski's growing influence throughout
the country, the National Democrats elected all thirty-six deputies,
thus achieving a complete victory. However, despite their loyalty,
the National Democrats did not obtain the expected concession of
autonomy for the Congress Kingdom.

Consequently, even after 1905 Poland had to live largely under
the disadvantageous conditions of martial law and did not enjoy
many of the limited benefits which were granted to the rest of the
empire by the Constitutional Manifesto. Nevertheless, the law of
March 17, 1906, for the first time permitted chartering of legal
trade-unions. Moreover, a relatively free press left some scope for
discussion. The PPS-Left, following the example of the Mensheviks,
used these opportunities to the utmost.

THE SDKPiL, THE PPS-LEFT, AND THE RUSSIAN SOCIAL DEMOCRATIC MOVEMENT

Even before the welcome split within the camp of the "social-
patriots" came the long-awaited closing of ranks of the all-Russian
social-democratic movement. The impact of the 1905 revolution in
Russia, its apparent potentialities, and the reconciliation of two
rival factions of the RSDWP, the Bolsheviks and the Mensheviks,
all made a profound impression upon the leadership of the SDKPiL.
The Russian party now could appear as a single bloc. On the other
hand, Luxemburg and Jogiches realized that a temporary paralysis
of the socialist movement in Poland had been a fact to reckon with
for some time, and felt that they themselves had lost whatever touch
they had had with the masses. Joining the Russian Social Democracy
was reconsidered, despite avowed ideological differences. The current
Menshevik control of the Russian party, with its more indefinite
position toward the national problem, and a milder attitude toward
centralized leadership, tended to minimize the gap in ideology.

A delegation of the SDKPiL, composed of Warski, Firstenberg,
and Dzierżyński, was invited to a Unity Congress at Stockholm in
a consultive capacity. Anxious to achieve the merger, the Polish
delegates readily accepted the *Iskra* program, as interpreted by the
Menshevik majority, and declared their adherency to the all-Russian
movement.[18] The SDKPiL was granted representation on the Central
Committee of the party and on its press organ. It was guaranteed
that no other Polish socialist group would be allowed to join the all-
Russian movement without prior approval of the SDKPiL.[19] Communist historian O. B. Szmidt admitted that this merger was undertaken by the SDKPiL "without accepting at heart" the principle of

national self-determination. Complete unification was never achieved, prevented by factionalism within both the Russian and Polish parties and among the various émigré groups.

The Fifth Congress of the RSDWP, held in London in 1907, proved to be the last congress before 1917 in which all major factions participated.[20] Out of 305 representatives of the all-Russian movement, the SDKPiL had a delegation of 40 persons who claimed to speak on behalf of no less than 25,000 organized members. Thanks to the support of Jogiches and Warski, who were elected members of the Central Committee, the Bolsheviks gained a majority. The new Central Committee was composed of five Bolsheviks and four Mensheviks; the SDKPiL, the Bund, and the Lettish Social Democrats were represented by two members each. With SDKPiL and Lettish support, the Bolsheviks could in most instances count on being in the majority. However, the SDKPiL sometimes shifted its support to the Mensheviks, incurring the occasional hostility of both Russian factions. It was hoped that a balance of power could be achieved between the two groups; and Leon Trotsky, also a variable supporter of the Bolsheviks, became the most frequent contributor to the "Social Democratic Review," which was the SDKPiL's principle theoretical publication.

THE PERIOD OF DECLINE AND DISINTEGRATION

Relations between the various socialist groups continued to be embittered by internal fights and frustration. In spite of extensive atomization, each fragment claimed to represent the majority of the proletariat of Poland.

The years 1908–1912 marked the lowest point in the history of the socialist movement in Russia. A similar decline could be observed in the ten Polish provinces of the empire, where both the repressions of Stolypin and the changing mood of the country did not favor the socialist cause. The internal weakness of the movement was reflected in bitter factional polemics and a slackening tempo of organizational life. The Central Committee of the RSDWP, elected in 1907, was supposed to meet every three months, but in reality it gathered but once in 1908 and then failed to meet again until 1910. Interferences in each other's affairs and ideological recriminations mixed with personal intrigues took up most of the time of the warring groups. Rosa Luxemburg, following the steps of Trotsky, made fruitless, repeated attempts to mediate between the quarrelling factions of the RSDWP.[21]

The close connection between the SDKPiL and the RSDWP resulted in recurring crises. Tensions within the RSDWP invariably were reflected in the life of the Polish group; even the split between Bolsheviks and Mensheviks was mirrored in the SDKPiL. One of the reasons for the Polish split was the tactlessness of Jogiches (Tyszko), who modelled his dictatorial ways on those of Lenin. His methods hampered free internal discussion and, at the end of 1911, produced a split which lasted several years and cost the party almost all the Warsaw section. For three years the Warsaw district had been in a rebellious mood, and decided to reject the authority of the Central Committee. It accused Jogiches and his followers of centralist tendencies, of refusal to submit their actions to the control of elected bodies, and of "trying to save the party against the party's membership." Finally, the Warsaw group objected to the Central Committee staying abroad permanently and opposing, from behind the scenes, a merger with the PPS-Left. The old leadership reciprocated with vitriolic attacks, accusing the rebels of being spies of the tsar's political police, the *Okhrana,* of having committed acts of banditry, and of preaching anti-Semitism. For more than four years after the resultant schism there were two hostile SDKPiL groups in Warsaw, Łódź, and other localities; one supported the émigré Central Committee, the other the Warsaw Committee. Generally speaking, the Warsaw group was much closer to Lenin. It accepted his point of view on organizational matters and all his general theories, with one traditional exception — there was no more willingness to accept Lenin's approach to national self-determination than that of Jogiches or Luxemburg. In spite of this, Lenin supported the secessionists and defended them on numerous occasions against the furious attacks and accusations of Jogiches and Luxemburg.[22]

The prosperity of the years 1907–1914 in Russia proved a satisfactory deterrent to revolution. Stolypin's agrarian reform in 1906, the enactment of the insurance law in 1912, and the slow but steady increase in wages, though far from satisfying more radical demands, helped to keep the revolutionary movement under control. Workers' associations were strictly supervised, but tolerated; peaceful strikes were permitted. The press enjoyed limited freedom. The insurance law covered the great majority of industrial workers, and provided for payment by the factory owner of from two thirds to three quarters of the normal wage in case of sickness or accident. Workers themselves elected the delegates to the insurance council. Even partial implementation of reform legislation appeased the more moderate labor groups, such as the PPS-Left. The PPS Revolutionary Faction, although regaining some influence, was split several ways and its extreme right wing was deviating from socialism. The SDKPiL remained separated in two warring factions.

At the beginning of 1914, any violent social revolution and any dictatorship of the proletariat seemed a distant proposition. The socialists of Poland were torn and dissident. But World War I and its aftermath gave the radical Marxist camp a new and unexpected chance.

Part II

The COMMUNIST PARTY of POLAND

4 WORLD WAR I and the FOUNDATION of the PARTY

The atomization of the Polish socialist movement was fully revealed at the outbreak of World War I. No single Marxist group could claim a really large following for itself; all of them realized this and looked for sympathetic support outside the movement. The PPS federated with nonsocialist parties which aimed to restore Polish statehood in alliance with the Central Powers. The Left Marxist groups of Russian Poland formed a loose coalition to pursue their common anti-war policy.

Thus the onset of the war consolidated the two rival camps within Polish socialism: pacifist and internationalist revolutionaries on the one hand, and the "social-patriots," on the other. The latter professed a pro-Austrian orientation, hoping to gain the favor of Austria-Hungary's Dual Monarchy. The PPS envisaged either a Triple Monarchy, with the Slavic segment (composed of Galicia and of Russian Poland) counterbalancing the Germans and Magyar parts, or restoration of some sort of separate Polish statehood. This school of thought, or "orientation," as it was then called, was headed by Piłsudski and supported by most of his friends from the former right wing of the PPS, the so-called Revolutionary Faction, as well as by Galician socialists; it proved to be the dominant view among socialists.

A majority of the SDKPiL and PPS-Left, however, remained as hostile as ever to any such "social-patriotic" solution, and advocated more or less active resistance to war, on an international scale and in cooperation with Russian comrades. Of the two factions of the SDKPiL, the oppositionist Warsaw Committee was closer to Lenin and the Bolsheviks.[1]

The bulk of the divided country continued to follow Dmowski and his National Democrats, with their platform of reconciliation and collaboration with Russia. The main purpose of this policy was to support all forces interested in checking German expansion, which Dmowski considered Poland's most dangerous enemy. Unification of all Polish lands by Russia, argued Dmowski, would lead toward full independence. The proclamation of the commander in chief of the Russian forces, addressed to the Poles, exhorting them to fight the German powers shoulder to shoulder with the Russians, was greeted almost with enthusiasm in Warsaw. Never had a policy of understanding with Russia been so widely accepted as in the years preceding the war and during its initial stages.

Immediately upon the outbreak of the war the Warsaw Committee of the SDKPiL took the initiative in coordinating the activities of all Marxist groups in the country. On August 1, 1914, it appealed to workers to demonstrate against the war by means of a general strike.[2] The next day, August 2, representatives of both factions of the SDKPiL, the PPS-Left, and the Jewish Bund met in Warsaw and issued a manifesto, taking a strong anti-war stand. Only socialism, said the pacifist manifesto, could end wars. "The proletariat declares war on its rulers and oppressors. In a struggle for national rights, the Polish proletariat will derive its demands from its class policy . . . In order to carry them through, the Polish proletariat must seize political power . . ."[3] This appeal had little effect on the masses who in most cases remained passive or followed either the pro-Russian or pro-Austrian orientation described previously.

The Warsaw conference of the SDKPiL and the PPS-Left also elected an interparty committee to coordinate the anti-war policies of the Left socialist parties of the Congress Kingdom. The common anti-war declaration did not involve any change in the program of the respective parties. The right of veto, which each party reserved for itself, indicated their mutual distrust.[4]

The Russian authorities promulgated a decree on March 30, 1915, which enlarged somewhat the local self-government of the Congress Kingdom and proved to be a fatal blow to the interparty committee. The decree provoked some mild criticism from the Menshevik-inclined PPS-Left, but only a sharp rebuke from the Social Democrats who branded it a "self-government of the money bag." In October 1915, the PPS-Left, joined by the Bund, made their more hopeful viewpoint prevail. This caused the Warsaw Committee of the SDKPiL to recall its representatives and thus ended, after fourteen months, the only attempt at collaboration on the part of Marxist parties in Russian Poland.

THE SOCIALISTS OF POLAND AND THE ZIMMERWALD
MOVEMENT

On the international scene there were three major socialist attitudes toward the war. On the right wing were various patriotic
socialists, pledged to what each of them styled the defense of their
fatherland. They refused to have anything to do with their comrades
on the other side of the front line, and each group claimed to be
fighting a defensive war only. Next to them stood the pacifists who
opposed any armed conflict and wanted to terminate hostilities by
all means short of civil war or complete defeat of their respective
governments. The pacifists preached the necessity of reconstituting
the Second Socialist International at the end of the conflict, and were
inclined toward mutual amnesty and forgiveness of past mistakes.
Their objective was a "white peace," a peace "without annexations
or indemnities." The third wing was made up of a small but determined leftist minority led by Lenin and his lieutenants. They claimed
to be the only really consistent revolutionary socialists, and insisted
on putting an end to the war by means of internal civil war which
would destroy capitalism and cause the inevitable triumph of socialism. They aimed to organize a new International which would exclude the hesitating, soft, "opportunistic" elements and unite the
socialist movement around the hard revolutionary nucleus.

Polish socialists split along these same lines. The PPS, the former
Revolutionary Faction, and the Polish Socialists of Galicia, belonged
to the first or patriotic group, with modifications deriving from the
particular position of their nation. The PPS-Left, represented by
Stanisław Lewinson (Łapiński), like the Left Mensheviks, belonged
to the "vacillating left fringe" of the pacifist trend, which was
slowly evolving towards Lenin's attitude. In the beginning the Main
Committee of the SDKPiL, represented chiefly by Adolf Warszawski
(Warski), also took a position not very distant from that of the
PPS-Left. Their evolution toward the Left, however, was somewhat
more rapid. From the beginning the Warsaw Committee threw its
lot with the Bolsheviks, and, with a few exceptions, remained faithful to this line.

The gradual assimilation of the Warsaw Committee by the
Leninist team could be observed both in domestic and in international
activities. As far back as February 1915, "The Workers' Journal"
contained an article entitled "The Downfall of the Second International," which took a viewpoint similar to that of the Bolsheviks.[5]
A proclamation to workers published by the Warsaw Committee on

May Day, 1915, appealed to them to turn the bourgeois war into a social-revolutionary struggle, to abolish tsardom, and to introduce an eight-hour work day. A parallel appeal by the SDKPiL Main Committee was much less revolutionary and stressed only economic demands.[6]

Meanwhile the war was dragging on. This played into the hands of Lenin and his associates by deepening the war-weariness and bringing about a progressive shift to the Left. On July 11, 1915, an information conference was summoned to Bern to discuss the possibility of a broad international socialist gathering. The conference was limited to those organizations which were represented at the International Socialist Bureau, the clearing house of the Second International. The Marxists of Poland were represented by the SDKPiL Main Committee's Warszawski (Warski) and the PPS-Left was represented by Maksymilian Horwitz (Walecki).[7] Both regularly voted against the motions of the extreme Left and opposed the invitation of Radek as a representative of the Warsaw Committee. These objections, however, had to be dropped under Moscow pressure.

In September 1915, at the Zimmerwald Conference, all three Marxist groups of Poland were represented. The left wing of the conference was led by Lenin. The manifesto of the conference condemned the war and the policy of the International, but did not include an appeal for civil war. Although the content of the manifesto made the Bolsheviks and the majority of the Left, including the Warsaw Committee of the SDKPiL, issue a separate statement, the left wing, nevertheless, subscribed to the manifesto so as not to break the conference unity.

The second conference of the Zimmerwald movement took place at Kienthal, at the end of April 1916. The growth of anti-war sentiment among the masses and the behind-the-scenes work of the Bolsheviks were reflected in the continuing shift to the Left, which almost doubled its strength at Kienthal. All three representatives of the Warsaw Committee systematically voted with the Bolsheviks.[8] On some matters the Left managed to poll as many as nineteen to twenty votes, almost half the total. The representative of the Main Committee, Warski, also shifted toward the Left in two essential matters: condemning the French socialists for voting in favor of war credits and supporting a Bolshevik amendment to summon the International Socialist Bureau.[9]

At the Kienthal Conference the main contest centered around the International Socialist Bureau. The left wing not only insisted upon condemning the line followed by the Bureau but also strongly opposed any idea of summoning it again. This implied a definite break with the Second International and both Warszawski and Lewinson opposed such a step. This time, however, the matter was not decided either way. A compromise resolution proposed by the Bolsheviks won the support of the SDKPiL Main Committee and finally prevailed. It made any convocation of the International Socialist Bureau dependent upon the convocation of another conference of the Zimmerwald movement. The Bolsheviks obviously played for time, which, as events proved, was working for them. Important also was the fact that the resolution marked another step in the evolution of the SDKPiL Main Committee toward the Bolshevik position.

With the spreading of the war and the inevitable discussions about future peace settlements, interest in the national problem and in its relation to a program of social revolution revived again. In autumn of 1915, the Warsaw Committee of the SDKPiL decided to publish a resolution passed by the editorial board of the committee's press organ, the "Workers' Journal." The declaration was mainly the work of Radek. The Journal stated:

The development of the war has proved that the epoch of national states is over . . . The bourgeoisie of Poland, has further renounced the battle-cry of independence. On the other hand, the Polish proletariat has never made national independence one of its aims. The proletariat has sought to destroy not the existing state boundaries but the *character* of the state as an organ of class and national oppression. In the face of the experience of the war, the advancement of the slogan of independence as a means of struggle against national oppression would not only be a harmful utopia, but would constitute also a repudiation of the basic principles of socialism. The right of self-determination is impracticable in capitalist society and unnecessary under socialism. Under socialism, cultural autonomy would be quite sufficient. The working class of Poland renounces all "defense of fatherland." The proletariat of Poland will fight neither for the unification of Poland [stressed by the pro-Russian orientation] nor for independence [emphasized by the pro-Austrian camp]. The Polish workers will struggle, in solidarity with the international proletariat, for a social revolution, which is the only possible solution of social and of national problems.[10]

Lenin replied to the statement of the *Journal* with a declaration entitled "The Socialist Revolution and the Right of Self-Determination (Theses of the Central Committee of the RSDLP)." [11] The SDKPiL, Lenin pointed out, rejected all war, which meant that it rejected even war against national oppression, war which was both necessary and progressive because of its revolutionary character. Lenin added that autonomy, meekly advocated by the Social Democrats of Poland, tended only to modify the existing state of things and hence it was merely a reformist measure, while self-determination spelled complete revolution. In another article, written in November 1915 although published later, Lenin pursued his criticism of Radek and his colleagues. He again insisted on his interpretation of self-determination as potentially including the right of complete separation. He said, among other things: ". . . we demand the freedom of self-determination, *i.e.*, independence, *i.e.*, the freedom of separation for the oppressed nations, not because we dream of an economically atomized world, not because we cherish the ideal of small states, but, on the contrary, because we are for large states and for a coming closer, even a fusion of nations . . ." [12]

In the autumn of 1916 Lenin wrote still another article in which he criticized the ideas of Radek and the "Journal" from the point of view of a realistic politician.[13] The SDKPiL, however, stuck to its guns as stubbornly as ever.

REVOLUTIONARY DISCONTENT IN POLAND

The continuation of hostilities worsened the economic crisis and caused a wave of popular discontent. This was reflected in several strikes occurring throughout Russian Poland, and evacuation of the country by Russian forces, in many instances similar to a scorched earth policy, still further increased misery, and, consequently, revolutionary ferment. On the other hand, forcible evacuation of entire factories and their personnel to Russia drained the proletarian reserves of the country. Consequently, the working masses were not only dissatisfied but also decimated.

The victorious German and Austrian summer offensive in 1915 resulted in the occupation of the rest of Poland by the Central Powers. On August 5, 1915, Russian forces abandoned Warsaw and the city was occupied by the Germans. A new era opened for the country. The Congress Kingdom was divided into two occupation zones, roughly corresponding to the former Prussian and Austrian shares in the partition of 1795. The northwestern part, with Warsaw as its capital, was taken over by Germany; the southeastern, with Lublin, was left to Austria. It was obvious from the beginning that the occupation regime was geared to economic exploitation of Poland for the immediate benefit of the Central Powers. It was also calculated to preserve the uncertain political status of the country in order to leave it as a bargaining stake in the event of peace negotiations.

The German economic policy was far more ruthless than that of

Austria. At the end of 1915, after consolidating their grip on the country, German authorities embarked upon systematic destruction of Polish industries or their removal to the Reich. This policy had a triple purpose: first, to remove a competitor; second, to turn the country into a purely agricultural *hinterland* of the German Empire; and third, to supply a vast reserve of manpower for the industries of the Reich. To achieve this last end, very low food rations were introduced and subsidies to charitable institutions were cut down. Simultaneously, a recruiting drive was opened, and higher rations, good wages, and better working conditions in Germany were propagandized. When these did not produce sufficient results, compulsory deportation was applied. In this way over six hundred thousand men and women were transferred to Germany.[14]

In contrast to this methodical economic exploitation, a certain degree of cultural and even political liberalism was exhibited by the German, and particularly the Austrian, occupation authorities. This gave a wider scope for action to the socialist groups who, under the Russians, had suffered more than other political parties. All groups took advantage of the opportunity offered by this development; most of all the so-called Activists, groups who favored collaboration with the Central Powers. To this latter camp belonged the PPS, supporting Piłsudski and his legions. The leftist Marxist groups were neither Activist nor Passivist. "We are," they repeatedly said, "neither for the Central Powers, nor for the coalition, but for *social revolution*." Nevertheless, they accepted with good grace all the marginal advantages of the new regime and tried to exploit both the legal possibilities and the loopholes in the occupation legislation.

The negative position of the SDKPiL on the national question was expressed by its attitude toward the Central Powers' proclamations of "an independent Poland," on November 5, 1916. The new state was to remain in permanent alliance with Germany and Austria-Hungary and was to have a monarch selected by the protecting powers. This proclamation was issued in order to extract a contingent of recruits from the country and to blackmail Russia into a separate peace. The Social Democrats criticized this act not so much for its provisions as for the fact that it was a revival of a hated idea. They also attacked the PPS for supporting the policy of the Central Powers.[15]

The Kienthal Conference marked a definite, although limited, success of the Zimmerwald Left, to which the Warsaw Committee belonged, and strengthened its position toward the less enterprising SDKPiL Main Committee. The growing confidence of the Warsaw Committee caused it to take the initiative in unifying the two factions of the party which had been at loggerheads since 1912. On November 4, 1916, these factions held a congress in Warsaw, and confirmed the editorial board of the paper "Our Tribune." The common resolution, mainly drawn by the Warsaw Committee, stated that the war was opening a new period of sharpened class conflicts and mass revolutionary movements. Only the complete destruction of capitalism and the establishment of socialism could prevent wars. The reunited party pledged its support to the Zimmerwald Left, elected a common Central Committee,[16] and expressed determination to fight the opportunists and pacifists, like the Bund and the PPS-Left, as long as the latter did not completely abandon its past mistakes and subscribe to the Social Democratic program.[17] This success of the Warsaw Committee was an indirect triumph for the Zimmerwald Left and for the Bolsheviks as well. Thus, after four years, the split ended which had sapped the scanty energies and resources of the party.

THE RUSSIAN REVOLUTION

The spring of 1917 brought the temporary triumph of liberal revolution in St. Petersburg and deeply affected both the internal political situation in Poland and the international position of the country. Generally speaking, the overthrow of the tsarist regime, which the Poles had considered a symbol of oppression, was joyously acclaimed by the majority of the Polish population. The radical groups, moreover, saw the establishment of the Russian Republic as an omen of growing democratization brought about by the war, a process which sooner or later was bound to extend to other belligerent countries. On March 29, 1917, the Russian Provisional Government issued a manifesto declaring its intention to restore the independence of Poland, which, however, was to remain in a free military alliance with Russia. The eastern frontiers of the country were to be defined by the Russian constituent assembly. This assembly was also to formulate the terms of the alliance. Its proletarian rival in the struggle for power, the Soviet of Petrograd Workers and Soldiers, had earlier issued a bolder "Proclamation of the Polish Nation." It pronounced itself for the unconditional right of Poland to self-determination and full independence.

The socialists of Poland greeted the revolution with enthusiasm. Initially even the PPS was not an exception. "Our Tribune" welcomed the event as the beginning of a broader and longer process, the dawn of a new era.[18] "The March upheaval," said the paper, "was a prologue to further revolutionary change." The SDKPiL press also paid tribute to the judgment of the Zimmerwald Left and the Bolsheviks, whose analysis of the situation had proved to be correct. The SDKPiL expressed its solidarity with the proletariat of Russia and repudiated any idea of a national bourgeois state.

The Russian revolution, by proclaiming Poland's right to separate national existence, hastened the polarization of the Marxist camp in Poland. One wing, headed by the PPS former Revolutionary Faction, accepted both the declaration of the Provisional Government and that of the Petrograd Soviet with satisfaction, but tended to regard them as mere confirmation of Poland's legitimate rights. To the SDKPiL and the PPS-Left both statements, but especially the declaration of the Petrograd Soviet, were a major set-back, a challenge to their whole program and their past as well as current activity. A new and desperate attempt was again made to obtain a repudiation of Polish self-determination from Lenin. Especially active in this respect was the group of Polish Social Democrats in Russia, headed by Dzierżyński and Julian Leszczyński (Leński). This group was very close to the Bolsheviks; from the beginning of the revolution it had managed to establish its own paper, and propagandized for the future incorporation of Poland into the Russian Republic. The members of the PPS-Left hesitated about whether or not to support the Bolsheviks.[19]

As far as the efforts of the SDKPiL in Russia are concerned, the minutes of the Seventh All-Russian Conference of the Bolshevik Party in Petrograd make a most interesting document.[20] At this conference Lenin, supported by Stalin, defended the right of self-determination against Dzierżyński, Pyatakov, and Makharadze. Lenin warned the Polish delegation not to overlook the aspirations of their native country and once more outlined the dangers of such a position. Lenin's speech of May 12, 1917, was especially strong. Replying to a statement of Dzierżyński, who presented the traditional point of view of the SDKPiL, Lenin gave an exposition of his doctrine. He praised the SDKPiL for its uncompromising internationalism, but he also spoke some harsh words on its failure to understand the Bolshevik tactical line. Lenin said:

The Polish comrades come and tell us that we must renounce the freedom of Poland, its right to separation . . . We make no pretense at seeking to liberate Poland, because the Polish people dwell between two states capable of fighting. But instead of teaching the Polish workers that chauvinists have no place in the Socialist Party and that only those Social Democrats are real democrats who maintain that the Polish people ought to be free, the

Polish Social Democrats argue that just because they find the union with the Russian workers advantageous, they are opposed to Poland's separation. They have a perfect right to do so. But these people fail to understand that to enhance internationalism it is not at all necessary to reiterate the same words. In Russia we must stress the right of separation for the subject nations, while in Poland we must stress the right of such nations to unite.[21]

But the SDKPiL, both in Russia and in Poland, was not convinced by these repeated arguments. Both branches failed to understand Lenin's intentions and tactics. Lenin, obsessed with the idea of seizing power, was willing to subordinate all other considerations and, for the time being, forget about this disagreement.

The March Revolution, in addition to stimulating the revolutionary forces of Poland, profoundly affected the international position of the Polish question, as well as the attitude of political parties in Poland toward the war. To understand the new situation fully, we have to return to the end of 1916. The camp led by Piłsudski had grasped that the act of November 5, 1916, did not foreclose the possibility of a separate peace between the Central Powers and Russia, which would probably result either in the return of the Congress Kingdom to Russia or simple incorporation into Germany. Hence they pressed the occupation authorities to take a first step and create concrete administrative and military institutions, which would later become obstacles to another straightforward annexation or partition. After some hesitation the Germans and Austrians, in the winter of 1916–17, decided to create a puppet government in the form of a Provisional State Council. It was composed of representatives of the groups favoring collaboration with Berlin and Vienna, the so-called Activists. Thus, reluctantly, the Central Powers laid the foundations of the future Polish state. The Social Democrats condemned this move violently in a sharply worded declaration which decried the Council as a Polish camouflage for the Austro-German occupation.[22]

These changes inside Poland were accompanied by several moves of a more important international character. The policy of the Russian Provisional Government gave the Western Powers, especially France, greater freedom to deal with the tricky question. Now they became free to take steps which had been impossible hitherto because of the fear of a hostile reaction on the part of their ally. In June 1917, the French government announced its decision to organize a Polish army in France. Thus, during the period between November 1916 and June 1917, the Polish question ceased to be an internal problem of the partitioning powers and re-emerged as one of wide international significance. This greatly bolstered the morale of the Poles and strengthened the National Democrats who staked their hopes on the Western Powers. On the other hand, it played against those groups which, like the Social Democrats, denied any possibility whatsoever of independent statehood for their native country. This statehood was slowly and painfully taking shape, developing like a slow-motion picture before their eyes, and they were powerless to stop the movement.

Such was the situation in the summer-autumn of 1917. The Bolshevik *coup d'état* produced an outburst of joy on the part of active SDKPiL members in Poland. "The working class of Poland," reads one of their proclamations, "greets with enthusiasm the victory of the Great Russian Revolution . . . The proletariat of Poland, which had endured common hardships in a unified struggle to defeat tsardom, now unites itself with the brotherly victorious proletariat of Russia." The Bolshevik revolution was an example to be followed by the toiling masses of Poland.[23]

No less enthusiastic were the SDKPiL groups active in Russia. As a result of the evacuation of the Congress Kingdom, carried out by the tsarist government in 1914–15, over two million Poles were in Russia, many of them skilled workers. Leszczyński (Leński), a leading representative of the SDKPiL in Moscow, was designated by the Council of People's Commissars to head the newly created Department for Polish Affairs. This was to be part of the Commissariat for Nationalities, under Stalin, and, at the beginning, all Polish socialist groups in Russia, including the PPS, accepted the new office and tried to cooperate with it.[24] Soon, however, the PPS was discouraged and slowly withdrew its support,[25] and other parties became more defiant. When, for example, in Moscow and Petrograd in 1918, delegates to the Council of Revolutionary Organizations were to be elected out of 60,000 resident Poles, some 3,000 voted for the Bolshevik list.[26] Only the SDKPiL and the extremist wing of the PPS-Left firmly supported the Bolsheviks. After the Bolshevik victory SDKPiL members were absorbed by the administrative apparatus, by the Red Army (including some ephemeral Polish units), and by the Commissariat for Polish Affairs.[27]

But even then the members of the SDKPiL, who had so wholeheartedly merged with the Bolsheviks, angrily objected to the repeated emphasis on self-determination, and reiterated instead their old battle cry of simple incorporation into Russia. This was, however, opposed by the Soviet government.

The demand for incorporation of Poland into the proletarian republic of Russia was put forward . . . by the representative of the Social Democracy. In spite of this demand, which is in accordance with the interests of the proletariat, the Bolshevik government decided for the principle of self-determination.[28]

At the beginning of 1918 another, but less important, difference threatened to alienate the former Polish Social Democrats from their new party. During the Brest negotiations and after the conclusion of the treaty, the SDKPiL, both in Russia and in Poland, supported the Left Communists, and, at the same time, protested half-heartedly against the injustices caused their native country by the treaty.[29] But in spite of such differences of approach to two vital questions, the former members of the SDKPiL continued to follow Lenin and his party.

THE SDKPiL AND THE PPS-LEFT AT THE CLOSE OF THE WAR

The Bolshevik revolution galvanized the forces of social upheaval throughout Europe; yet the Polish territories, in spite of the febrile agitation and the fiery exhortations of the Marxist groups, remained relatively quiet. Misery and starvation were widespread but the discontented were scattered and leaderless. Only strikes by municipal employees in Warsaw and demonstrations in Łódź and the Lublin area sporadically disturbed this strange silence.[30] In spite of some recent growth, neither the Social Democrats nor the PPS-Left had sufficient resources or followers to support their highly explosive words with deeds. The strikes called by them were, for the most part, unsuccessful.[31] By denying the only popular solution of the national problem they placed themselves largely outside the main stream of national life. Moreover, the failure to establish contact with the villages limited SDKPiL activity to urban labor.

The radical agrarian parties advocated outright expropriation of large estates for division among the peasants. By taking this stand they outbid the more moderate socialists, all of whose programs were limited to some sort of land nationalization. In August 1918 appeared the first issue of the SDKPiL newspaper for the villages, and it preached socialization of land and communist farming. The PPS at its Fourteenth Congress in September 1919 voted an agrarian program which compromised between orthodox Marxist doctrine on the subject and the realistic requirements of everyday struggle. While the program called for immediate and unconditional expropriation of large estates without compensation, it accepted individual ownership of small farms.[32]

Lack of leadership is also a factor in explaining the impotence of the revolutionary movement in Poland at the end of 1917 and the beginning of 1918. The leaders of both revolutionary groups were scattered all over Central and Eastern Europe. Those members of the SDKPiL and the PPS-Left who happened to be in Russia during the Revolution became more and more integrated with Lenin's team. Of their own accord these men renounced their party identity and united with the Bolsheviks. Dzierżyński, freed by the liberal Provisional Government, immediately became a close collaborator of Lenin, with Radek and Hanecki as his most trusted lieutenants. The latter were assigned to various important tasks abroad, mainly in Stockholm or Berlin. Another social-democratic group, which included Rosa Luxemburg, Jogiches (Tyszko), and Marchlewski (Karski), was then in Germany. Along with Liebknecht and Mehring they were editing the "Spartacus Letters" and laying a foundation for the future Communist Party of Germany.[33]

The SDKPiL in Poland watched the unfolding of events first in Russia, later in Austria-Hungary, and then in Germany with a mixture of anger, envy, and hope. They were angry because of the formation of new national states, which they had foredoomed to failure in their sweeping predictions. This meant a triumph for the hated principle of self-determination, which was proclaimed simultaneously from two corners of the world, Moscow and Washington. Moreover, the revolutionary ferment initiated and stimulated by the Bolshevik revolution actually helped Poland to regain her national independence by undermining the Central Powers. On the other hand, the Russians were envied for being the first to achieve what the SDKPiL themselves had only talked about: a proletarian revolution. But there was also hope that if the initial steps toward revolution were achieved in Poland by local forces, the more successful Russian comrades would rally with support from across the border.[34]

The German occupation and particularly the Austrian one were already tottering, undermined by revoluntionary ferment in both countries. At the beginning of November 1918, with the first signs of breakdown in Germany, the SDKPiL issued a proclamation appealing to the proletariat to assume all power.[35] It insisted both on the right and the duty of workers to form councils of workers' and peasants' and soldiers' deputies, as well as their armed fist, the Red Guard. "All power in the hands of the people," became the slogan of the day.

At the close of 1918, after the end of hostilities and disarmament of the German and Austrian troops, economic and social conditions in Poland were profoundly disturbed. In November of that year only the Dąbrowa coal basin employed more workers than before the war. The metal and textile industries had sunk to a very low level and were almost at a standstill because of lack of raw materials and removal of machinery to Germany. With the cessation of hostilities many industries were suddenly closed down, throwing large numbers of unemployed and discontented workers on the market. Agriculture, although it had suffered bitterly from lack of both machinery and fertilizers, was relatively better off, and agricultural production did not suffer as much as that of industry. Owing to favorable prices on the one hand and devaluation of the currency on the other, debts and mortgages were reduced and the high price of food products made agriculture a good business. Inflation sent all prices sky-high, but especially those of food; profiteering and black market operations were rampant. The prolonged industrial unemployment resulted in the pauperization of the working class. Moreover, workers had been dispersed throughout neighboring countries, mainly to Russia and Germany. The new bourgeois Polish state emerging from the chaos bit by bit was a far from impressive structure. At the war's end over three million Poles of all classes were outside the undefined frontiers of the Polish Republic. The new state had to face unprecedented difficulties, growing together as it did out of different administrative parts. There were no less than eight kinds of currency in use and nine separate military formations from which the new army was to be formed.

Immediately after the Brest Treaty, the Regency Council started a re-evacuation of Poles from Russia and Germany. Some of the returning workers not only swelled the ranks of the jobless but spread Communist agitation as well. On their way home millions of German, Austrian, Hungarian, and Russian soldiers passed through Polish territory. Some of them formed armed bands, usually called "green cadres," which pillaged the countryside and increased the general chaos.

COUNCILS OF WORKERS AND PEASANTS

The chaos which had preceded the disintegration of the Austro-German occupation in Poland, and the few weeks of turmoil which followed these events, merit closer examination. This was the only period when the forces of social upheaval had a chance of achieving some success in their struggle for power. The failure of those forces was to affect the subsequent history of the Communist movement in Poland for years to come. Under the circumstances in Poland at that time the formation of numerous local councils of workers and peasants was mostly a spontaneous process. To a large extent it was, of course, only a reflection of what was going on in neighboring countries. On the other hand, it was a not unnatural reaction to the state of chaos prevailing throughout the country. Not all the councils had a genuine revolutionary character, however, though all of them had pronounced radical social features. Not satisfied with their influence on the workers, the Polish Socialist Party, the radical peasant parties, and the National Labor Party tried to outdo the Communists in the work of organizing the workers' and peasants' councils. Several thousand of such local councils were organized by various political groups. The difference between the pro-Communist councils and those sponsored by other parties was that the latter regarded these new bodies as instruments for building a democratic Republic, while the Communists wanted them to be instruments of the dictatorship of the proletariat.[36]

The emergence of the councils could be observed first under the Austrian occupation where the military administration broke down as early as the end of October, immediately after the downfall of the Hapsburgs. The first workers' council was set up in Lublin, the capital of the Austrian occupation, on November 6, 1918. The following day, November 7, Lublin witnessed the unexpected appearance of an organized group which claimed to be the government of the whole country. This "people's government" was headed by Ignacy Daszyński, leader of the Galician socialists, and was composed of other prominent socialists and peasant politicians, as well as some representatives of the radical intelligentsia. A manifesto was issued declaring the new state to be a republic, with a one-chamber parliament. A minimum wage, protection of labor, and social security were provided for, and radical land reform was promised, to be achieved by wholesale expropriation of all large estates, without compensation to previous owners.

Most of the newly constituted Lublin Council pledged its support to the government of Daszyński, in spite of the protests of the council's Social Democratic minority. Since this government proved to be of short duration, the support was shifted, a few days later, to the Warsaw government of another socialist leader, Jędrzej Moraczewski.[37] It was formed as a more moderate coalition by the authority of the new head of the state, Piłsudski, to whom the Regency Council had transferred power.[38]

The formation of the council in Łódź developed along slightly different lines. Two hostile councils appeared almost simultaneously:

one formed by the PPS and another by the SDKPiL. Under pressure from workers the two councils soon merged into one; the majority proved to be non-Communist members, mostly PPS partisans. Thus support for the Warsaw government was assured in Łódź, the largest industrial center of the country, in spite of the protests of the pro-Communist elements.[39]

Some significant events also took place at the Dąbrowa industrial basin, the second largest center of heavy industry in Congress Poland. On November 8, 1918, in two neighboring towns of this district, Sosnowiec and Dąbrowa Górnicza, two councils of workers' deputies were established about the same time. They soon merged, but unlike the case in Łódź or Lublin, the Dąbrowa council had a majority of Social Democrats, supported by more radical members of the PPS-Left. This majority was already, at that time, drifting toward communism, and during one of its first meetings the council expressed its solidarity with Soviet Russia, condemned the government of Warsaw, appealed to workers to form their own detachments of Red Guard, and proclaimed an eight-hour working day. Several detachments of about 400 men were organized and mass street demonstrations were staged in support of their demands. On November 15, the council issued an appeal to workers to take over various factories and mines, and proclaimed a general strike. It also appealed to the armed forces not to execute the orders of the Warsaw government of Moraczewski and to refrain from taking part in reprisals.[40] Some enterprises followed the appeal of the council and chose their separate local councils. Some of them also appealed to peasants to elect village councils. Many groups of workers and even whole factories, however, remained indifferent.

Between November 8 and December 21, 1918, something like two independent and mutually hostile powers existed in the Dąbrowa region. On one side were the organs of the Warsaw coalition government, with their hastily assembled People's Militia under the Ministry of Interior, and some detachments of more or less regular soldiers taking orders directly from the Ministry of War. On the other side stood the councils of workers' delegates, with their small units of "Red Guards" armed with small weapons and some machine guns. In those days there was no shortage of secondhand weapons. As far as one can gather, these detachments never numbered more than 800 to 1,000 men, their strength lay in the support of an angry, starved mob of unemployed and a large section of discontented and excited workers. Both contestants were weak and the future of the duel depended on mass support. The situation was bound to end in a clash and, indeed, there were several bloody skirmishes between the Red Guards and the units of the Warsaw government. Criminal elements, *la grande canaille populaire,* to use Bakunin's phrase, took full advantage of the ensuing chaos. Several victims fell on both sides and numerous acts of robbery occurred. As the council was still unable to enlist the support of the broad masses of workers, its days were numbered. Finally, by the middle of December, the Moraczewski government managed to consolidate its power in the rest of the country. It then decided to reassert its authority in the Dąbrowa basin and on December 21, 1918, a detachment of the regular army disarmed the Red Guard, which put up little resistance. The rebellious councils were disbanded.

Events in Warsaw, if less violent and bloody than those of Dąbrowa, proved, however, of more significance for the whole country. The Warsaw council was formed on November 11 by the SDKPiL, the PPS-Left, and the council of the Trade Unions.[41] The PPS proper, whose rank and file were greatly affected by the example of Bolshevik theory and practice, joined the new council. The sentiments of the left wing of the PPS were strongly revolutionary and the idea of a united working-class movement was still alive. Many prominent members also supported the idea of a social revolution, provided it was strictly an internal affair of the proletariat of Poland, carried out according to its needs and wishes, without outside intervention from Russia or Germany. These PPS members were attracted to the principle of self-determination and deluded themselves that the Communists would respect a separate Polish Social Republic. The leaders of the PPS, however, more cool-headed than the membership, were soon convinced of the subversive character of the council, and they decided to secede. By November 21, 1918, the PPS had formed its own workers' councils.[42] After two days of separate, parallel existence, the two councils of Warsaw merged, again due to pressure from workers who were annoyed with factional bickering. The result was that the PPS obtained a slight majority and was able to outvote the Communists and their supporters on practically all major issues.[43] Many smaller councils followed the Warsaw example. The balance of strength varied in each of them but generally speaking, the PPS was in the majority.

There were belated Communist attempts to organize the peasant councils but, in most cases, these failed. The Social Democratic agrarian program, which advocated nationalization of land and large-scale communist farming, proved to have little appeal even to poorer peasants, and the half-hearted and sporadic support of agricultural workers was not strong enough to counterbalance the solid hostility of the farmers.[44]

The Moraczewski Cabinet, which took over from the Lublin government of Daszyński, had only a slightly milder social and economic platform than its predecessor. Its program was carried out in a series of decrees which continued to appear throughout November and December 1918, in spite of repeated accusations by the right-wing groups that the government was "Bolshevizing" the country. The government introduced an eight-hour working day in industry, without decrease of pay, and state inspection of factories. There were provisions for enforced protection of labor, organized obligatory insurance against accidents, illness, and unemployment; rent control, food rationing, labor exchanges, and the like.

The emergence of an independent Polish state proved a painful blow to both left-wing Marxist groups. It was a rude shock to the chiefs of the SDKPiL, who had ridiculed the idea of a possible rebirth of Poland at every step and branded it both utopian and undesirable. The reality of a separate Polish nation was like the sudden appearance of someone whose death and funeral had been announced several times with joy and relief. To the leaders of the PPS-Left who, after numerous hesitations and zigzags, had abandoned a program of political independence as no longer practicable, it was also an unpleasant surprise. The new circumstances afforded very little choice for the Bolshevik-oriented Marxist groups in Poland. In Russia the Bolshevik party became the most powerful single factor in the world socialist movement, and the ruler of a temporarily weakened but potentially mighty state. This state was already marshaling its forces in order to extend its doctrine throughout the exhausted and restless countries of Central and Eastern Europe. Across the border stood weak and shapeless Poland, besieged with overwhelming internal contradictions and headed by the despised "social-patriot," Piłsudski.

There was, then, a double challenge to action: to transplant Russia's achievement under Lenin to Poland, and to establish soviets of workers and soldiers who would then seize power. But to effect the overthrow of even a weak bourgeois government, like Poland's, would seem to require nothing less than a united front of the two main working-class parties.

THE FOUNDATION OF THE COMMUNIST WORKERS' PARTY
OF POLAND (CWPP)

In those days Communist parties mushroomed all over Europe. On November 4, 1918, the Austrian party was founded; the Hungarian followed on November 21, and the German on December 18. Poland, argued the SDKPiL leaders, should not stay behind her neighbors. Closing the ranks of Communist sympathizers became not only a matter of prestige but a necessity. Accordingly, on November 15 and 16, 1918, the SDKPiL, convened in Warsaw to prepare for merger. It deliberated in an atmosphere of confidence.[45] According to the resolution issued by the conference, the war had proved that the line which had been followed by the party was correct and, therefore, unification with the PPS-Left should be carried out on the basis of the SDKPiL program. The war, said the resolution, was the mortal crisis of capitalism which was unable to manage the forces it had unleashed. Social revolution and dictatorship of the proletariat were the only solution and it was the duty of the party to organize an immediate fight for power. This could be done by continuing to foster councils of workers' deputies as springboards for further struggle.

The resolution accepted the view that after a successful revolution the best conditions for development of native agriculture would be created by large-scale, centralized, communal farming. With the introduction of dictatorship of the proletariat, private ownership of land as well as private trade in agricultural products would be abolished, and land would become the exclusive property of the socialist community. During the transition period, however, small farms would be left in the hands of those who were willing to work them without hired labor. The final disposition of these small farms would be decided by the National Congress of Councils of Workers' and Peasants' Delegates. But, the resolution added confidently, the small owners would, with the lapse of time, be obliged to recognize the advantages of communal farming and they would, voluntarily and in their own interest, join the communal farms. All agricultural planning must be a monopoly of the state.

The date of December 16, 1918, was fixed for a unification congress to meet in Warsaw with the task of formulating a more definite program for a new united party. This party, to be called the Communist Workers' Party of Poland, should prepare to undertake an immediate armed struggle for power and should not refrain from any sacrifice to attain this objective. The instrumentalities of the struggle were to be the councils of workers' deputies and detachments of

the Red Guards. Increasing strikes throughout Poland and the outbreak of the German revolution were considered two favorable developments that ought to act as stimuli. Russian revolutionary groups
were consolidating their grip in Russia and marshaling forces; among
the units of the new Red Army a western rifle division was being
organized, to be composed of five regiments manned mainly by Poles.
Thus, brotherly Soviet aid seemed at hand and the conference closed
on a note of optimism and enthusiasm.

At the end of 1918 the PPS-Left was already under the spell of the
Social Democrats and merger was in the air. It had gradually swal-
lowed the Bolshevized platform of the SDKPiL, with emphasis on
dictatorship of the proletariat, and had forgotten its early humani-
tarian and democratic principles. The PPS-Left reconciled itself to
such methods as were deemed necessary to achieve a revolution in
the Soviet manner. In October it had condemned all "illusions connected with creating an independent Polish state," and decided to
end its traditional good relations with the Bund, described as a
"petty nationalist" and "reformist party," and to unite its forces
with the SDKPiL.[46] Subsequently the party's internal equilibrium
was thrown out of gear by the secession of the Łódź and Poznań
groups, both of which protested against Bolshevization of the party
and went over to the PPS.

A general statement of aims for the Unity Congress was prepared
beforehand. A draft was speedily dispatched to Rosa Luxemburg and
Jogiches (Tyszko) for their approval. Karl Liebknecht, informed
by them of the plan, also sent his greetings in the name of the Bolshevik inclined German *Spartacusbund,* which was to be transformed in a few days into the Communist Party of Germany.

The Unity Congress took place as scheduled in mid-December, in
Warsaw, and deliberated in an atmosphere of excitement and antici-
pation. On the night of December 15, after a debate lasting almost
twenty-four hours, the congress achieved its initial task. Both parties
decided to give up their separate identity and to merge into one.
The congress continued its work for two more days, December 16
and 17, in order to lay down the ideological and organizational foundation of the new party. The name, Communist Workers' Party of
Poland (CWPP) was chosen, in an attempt to combine elements of
the name recently acquired by the Russian party with traditional
Luxemburgist stress on the primary importance of the urban proletariat.[47] The congress issued a proclamation emphasizing that the
immediate aim of the new party was social revolution and dictator-

ship of the proletariat. It was to be achieved through the councils of workers' delegates in towns and villages.[48]

Ideologically the SDKPiL had triumphed: its program was accepted as the basis of the new party's ideology. Thus the SDKPiL attracted a group with considerable following and resources much superior to its own. To illustrate this, Marxist circles of Warsaw produced an epigram constructed in rather bourgeois terms: the merger of the SDKPiL and the PPS-Left was a *mariage de raison* between a poor young man of good family and a rich girl of doubtful reputation. The epigram alluded to the scanty following and the consistent Marxist internationalism of the Social Democrats, on the one hand, and to the "social patriotic" past of the PPS-Left and its sceptical attitude toward the possibility of radical revolution, on the other.[49]

The unconditional surrender of the PPS-Left to the program of the Bolshevized SDKPiL produced a new series of local revolts and secessions on the part of many of its rank and file members. The remaining moderate groups in the PPS-Left abandoned the party and joined the former Revolutionary Faction, now being reconstituted under the old name, the PPS.[50]

The new party's program was outlined in three main parts.[51] The first part described the factors of world revolution and their development, and the forms which the fight for dictatorship of the proletariat was taking. The second part analyzed the disintegration and downfall of the Second International. The third part defined the special tasks of the new party.

Long before 1914, read the first part of the program, the policy of imperialist expansion was resulting in an accumulation of contradictions. On the one hand were preparations for an inevitable armed conflict. On the other hand inner conflicts within capitalist countries were intensifying the class struggle. The war had bolstered those forces that had been working for a long time toward revolutionary liquidation of the capitalist system. After analyzing the role of the Bolshevik-controlled Russian state and the influence of the German and Austrian revolutions, the program concluded that, despite the reconstruction effort of capitalist economies, the revolutionary situation would inevitably result in a complete destruction of the capitalist system. "The World War leads to world revolution."

The second part of the program was a short restatement of the point of view held by the Zimmerwald Left. The Communist revolution in Russia brought victory to the forces that had fought treacherous and opportunistic majorities at the Zimmerwald and Kienthal conferences. These forces had shown how to accomplish social revolution and establish dictatorship of the proletariat. Thus The Communist International of Social Revolution had been created. This International rejected all attempts at half-hearted solutions, as advocated by moderate socialist groups, seeking instead to unify the great majority of the working class and achieve socialism through dictatorship of the proletariat.

The third part of the program defined the immediate tasks of the new party and expressed its attitude toward the perennial socialist controversy, that of Poland's political future: all power should go to the proletariat of towns and villages, organized in the councils of workers' delegates. The land problem — the rejection of land distribution among the peasants, the lack of mention of the worker-peasant alliance, the stress on land workers — this was the main point of variance with the Bolshevik position.[52] The platform was edited in distinctly Luxemburgist terms:

In the epoch of international social revolution which destroys the foundations of capitalism, the Polish proletariat rejects every political solution that is to be connected with the evolution of a capitalistic world, solutions like autonomy, independence, and self-determination. Since the proletariat is fighting against all its enemies and for the dictatorship of the proletariat, it will oppose all attempts at creating a bourgeois, counter-revolutionary Polish army and oppose every war for national frontiers. The proletariat will create its own revolutionary armed forces. For the international camp of social revolution there is no problem of national frontiers.[53]

As far as the agrarian problem was concerned, the differences were only tactical; Polish Communists refused to follow the Leninist line and thereby to sacrifice orthodox Marxist doctrine for the sake of expediency. In regard to the national problem the differences were deep-seated. Here the new party stuck stubbornly to its original Luxemburgist position which had been taken repeatedly in 1893, 1896, 1903, 1915, and restated again in May 1917: self-determination is impossible under capitalism, unnecessary under socialism, and would be applicable only during a period of transition. But, said the party, there will be no transition period because of the imminent disintegration of the capitalist system and the inevitable triumph of the Bolshevik revolution throughout East Central Europe. This revolution, in alliance with the German and Austrian revolutions, would soon extend the rule of socialism to Poland and thus end the provisional state of affairs. To be bothered about a transition period would be simply a waste of time.[54]

The leaders of the new party reasoned that since the Polish Republic was a semi-feudal, semi-bourgeois state, it should be fought against and its institutions sabotaged at every step. This should also be done because the new state was a potential partner of the *Entente* in international intervention against the Soviets. Poland, preached the party, was an ephemeral creature, a *Saisonstaat*. It was bound to be torn to pieces by its internal contradictions, and swept away by the mounting revolutionary wave. The downfall of the "bourgeois bastard," however, should be accelerated by an active and conscious contribution from the inmates of the new capitalist penitentiary. The task of the Communist Workers' Party of Poland was to organize and lead the impending revolt.

The YEARS
5 of HOPE

The period during which the Communist Workers' Party of Poland was being organized coincided with that stage of the Russian revolution when its fate seemed to depend on the dynamic power of other revolutionary movements in Europe. The Bolsheviks were convinced that the Soviet experiment could not survive unless it ignited a blaze of revolution, at least over East Central Europe and in Germany. It was partly as a result of this assumption that Lenin continued to overestimate the explosive potentialities of the social movements in Europe and even in America. The Bolsheviks feverishly attempted to create revolutions where they had failed to develop, and to bolster them up where they did not live up to expectations.

Industrial unemployment, exorbitant food prices, and the general weariness prevailing in postwar Poland all created conditions in which communism could find fertile ground. The war for Eastern Galicia against the Ukrainians was a further serious drain on the resources of the ruined and starved country. The newly organized Communist Workers' Party tried to exploit the sufferings and social grievances of the underprivileged for its own purposes. In numerous leaflets and proclamations the party summoned the masses to a direct fight for power; the Council of Workers' Deputies was to be the chief instrument in the struggle and the party its leader.

The internal struggle for power in Poland was observed closely in Moscow. To help the rather ineffective leadership of the new party the Office for Polish Affairs in the Soviet Commissariat for Nationalities put forward a plan of action. As early as April 1918, at a party conference in Moscow, it was resolved that agitation in Poland should be directed by experienced leaders and that these men should be sent to Warsaw under some pretext. As one speaker described it: "It is in the interest of the Soviet Union that we should go to Poland." [1] This idea was considered in the autumn of 1918 and a Soviet Red

Cross mission was planned for Warsaw. The mission's official task was to negotiate the evacuation of some Russian prisoners who had been captured by the Germans during the war and then left behind in a few camps located in Poland. After brief negotiations, the Warsaw government agreed in principle to admit the mission and to help in its work. Taking advantage of the general confusion, the mission entered the country secretly, without notifying Polish authorities on arrival.

There was considerable excitement among Communist followers when Marchlewski and Wesołowski, the mission's leaders, were interned. On December 29, 1918, spurred by rumors that the Communists had seized power in Berlin, the party organized a street demonstration, demanding the release of the Soviet delegates. The demonstration turned into a violent skirmish with police and troops; five people were killed and fourteen wounded. Warsaw and Moscow, meanwhile, had negotiated for the mission's return to Russia, and accordingly the delegation left the country a few days later, escorted by military police. However, before he could cross the border, Wesołowski was murdered by his escorts; the guards were brought to trial and later sentenced to imprisonment.[2] Thus ended one attempt to supply the Communist movement in Poland with more experienced leadership. This incident was one of the factors which contributed to the resignation of Poland's Moraczewski government, hard pressed by criticism both from the Right and the extreme Left. The new government was under the much more conservative leadership of Ignacy Paderewski. The downfall of the Socialist-dominated cabinet, which had been accused by the Right of Communist leanings, was greeted by the Communist press with unmitigated joy. In the face of revolution in Russia, Germany, and Austria, wrote a Communist weekly, the bourgeoisie of Poland entrusted power to the slaves of capitalism.[3]

In February 1919, the first parliamentary election to the Constituent Assembly took place in Poland. With little hesitation the Communist Party decided on a boycott. This attitude was the logical consequence of the party's contemptuous approach toward bourgeois parliamentary institutions, as well as its conviction that capitalism was about to collapse, and consequently the time for direct struggle for a dictatorship of the proletariat was at hand.[4] This over-optimism, largely an expression of what Lenin was soon to term "the infantile disease of leftism," was discarded by the party in Poland only very much later, and then rather half-heartedly.[5] The election proved successful for the Right and Center parties.

THE PARTY GOES UNDERGROUND

Revolution had failed in Germany by the end of January 1919. On the other hand, with the upheaval in Hungary in March, the hopes of the party revived again. Moreover, in February, without formal declaration, a small war had broken out between the Red Army and Polish forces. The former, in their westward expansion into the void created by the German capitulation, ran into Polish detachments which were endeavoring to occupy parts of the former Polish-Lithuanian Commonwealth. There were sections in this area which contained a Polish population and which preserved strong cultural and economic ties with ethnographic Poland. The hostilities with Russia were immediately condemned by the party as being provoked by Polish imperialism. The hearts of Polish Communists were now again rekindled with the hope for Soviet armed help.[6] A party council which gathered in February 1919, proclaimed with insistence:

The working class of each country has the right and the duty to render active assistance to the workers of other countries in their revolutionary struggle; in view of this, the armed help of the Russian proletariat, such help being needed by the Polish revolution, would be neither an invasion nor an expression of imperialist tendencies alien to the essence of socialism . . . such an intervention would simply be an embodiment of the principle of solidarity of the international proletariat . . . Revolution knows no boundaries . . .[7]

The party's situation within Poland continued to be unstable. After the failure of the Dąbrowa experiment, election to the workers' councils took place at the end of 1918 and the beginning of 1919. One delegate was to be elected for every fifty workers. In addition, each trade-union was to be represented by one delegate, while each socialist group was to have two representatives. Again two programs clashed: that of the PPS, supporting the principle of constituent assembly sovereignty, and that of the Communist Party claiming full power for the councils. The elections revealed the considerable influence of the Communists. In Warsaw, for instance, the new party polled 297 votes, against 303 for the PPS, while the two Jewish socialist parties, the Bund and the *Poalej Sion,* held the balance, often siding with the Communists. Similar results were achieved at Łódź and around Lublin. In some parts of the Dąbrowa industrial basin and in some villages around Lublin the party even managed to obtain an absolute majority of votes. The tug of war between the PPS and the Communists lasted until the middle of 1919. On June 15, 1919, the PPS finally seceded from the Warsaw Council of Workers' Delegates and set up its own councils. Beset by external troubles as well as administrative measures later undertaken by the government, the Communist-dominated councils gradually disintegrated; those sponsored by the PPS socialists disbanded spontaneously by the autumn of 1919.[8] Thus, by the end of that year, even the semblance of duality of power had disappeared completely. The government was firmly in control of the country, and liquidation of the councils deprived the party of its most powerful weapons. Emphasis was shifted to another instrument of class struggle — the renascent trade-union movement.

Other events occurred which determined the fate of the party for many years to come. On January 17, 1919, a new decree had been issued requiring all associations and organizations to register with the administrative authorities. Those already in existence were given one month to comply.[9] The party faced a fateful dilemma: to register or not to register? Registration, argued party leaders, would imply recognition of the existence of the Polish state, and hence, submission to its authority. Such a surrender would be contrary to the fundamental position of the party, a denial of its very reason for existence. The decree was not complied with, and thus, after February 7, 1919, a new era opened for the party. From that time it was treated by the authorities as a subversive organization, aiming not only at the overthrow of the existing social and political order, but also at the very state itself. Deprived of legality, the party went underground, where it remained for a quarter of a century.[10]

In March 1919, the Eighth Conference of the Bolshevik Party took place in Moscow in order to accept the program elaborated by the Seventh Conference in May 1917. At this time Lenin again warned the Polish comrades about their stubborn attitude on the national question and reiterated his defense of self-determination. In spite of the defiance of his Polish followers, the news of Communist successes in the recent elections of the Warsaw Council of Workers' Deputies, filled Lenin with optimism. "It proves," he said, "that over there [in Poland], according to our Communist calendar, the 'October' is not far away. What we see now may be something like our 'August' or 'September.' . . . ." Nevertheless, he admitted that the majority of Polish workers were "social-patriots." When Marchlewski objected to this, Lenin broke out: "You should achieve it [the revolution] in a different way than we did," to which Marchlewski retorted: "No, we will do what you did but will do it better." [11]

FOUNDERS OF THE THIRD INTERNATIONAL

Meanwhile, the problem of setting up a new International increasingly preoccupied the Bolshevik leaders. In 1903, in "What is to be Done?" Lenin had written: "Give me a body of revolutionaries and we will turn Russia upside down." After having achieved his preliminary objective in Russia, he decided to start a similar experiment on a world-wide scale. In this respect most of the Polish comrades went along with Lenin wholeheartedly. At this point, however, his old antagonist, Rosa Luxemburg, reopened her feud with the Bolshevik leader.

As Luxemburg's enthusiasm for the Bolshevik way of making revolution dwindled, another difference of opinion arose. Although she feared splitting off irrevocably from the world Marxist movement, Luxemburg opposed the immediate establishment of a new International; she felt that the world proletarian movement was not yet ripe for such a step. Luxemburg believed that, with other Marxist parties in chaos or in process of transition, a new International would be moulded in the image of the Bolshevik party and, consequently, would become a tool of Moscow, a *Russian* International. The Leninist concept of a monolithic party, led by a small group of professional revolutionaries, was alien to her, and Luxemburg was afraid that with the premature formation of a new International, its creator would breathe the same idea into this body. Her belief in a spontaneous evolution of the proletariat, driven by conscious opposition to the existing order and climaxing in an uprising, clashed with the idea that the main thing was to seize power first and thus get sufficient time to convince the people that the seizure was inevitable and would prove beneficial. Luxemburg formulated her ideas in her well-known "Theses for the Reconstruction of the International," which were published in 1918 as an appendix to her book "Crisis of German Social Democracy," usually known as the Junius Pamphlet. But, by this time, the revolutionary movement of Poland was firmly in the grip of Bolshevik-minded people. Rosa Luxemburg still wielded considerable intellectual authority, but, as far as purely tactical or organizational problems were concerned, she was absorbed by German issues and had little immediate power over the Communist groups of her native country. Consequently, the newly founded Communist Workers' Party of Poland joined the Communist International as one of its constituent members. The party was officially represented by Józef Unszlicht, a long-time member of the Russian Bolshevik Party and a resident of Moscow.[12]

A "Manifesto" was published on January 29, 1919, inviting representatives of the thirty-nine socialist and workers' organizations to Moscow and foreshadowing the creation of a "center of the Communist International, which would subordinate the interests of the movements in each country to the common interests of the revolution on a global scale." To hasten world revolution, the open conspiracy known since as the Comintern called for concerted mass action. The platform adopted by this First Congress urged "direct collision with the bourgeois state machine in open combat." Stressing the possibility of more overt techniques, the platform suggested "revolutionary utilization of the bourgeois parliamentary system."

The Polish party was far behind the tactical directives of the new International in respect to the platform outlines above, almost as far apart as it was on the national and agrarian questions. Nevertheless it had to be forgiven for the time being. Poland's key position in East Central Europe was of such importance that Moscow, although impatient with these deviations, could not afford to do anything which would upset the precarious structure of the party in Poland, for on its performance depended the possibilities of Poland's being either a wall or a bridge in the future march of communism toward Germany.[13]

PAINFUL RECOVERY

Spring and summer of 1919 brought some slight relief to the Polish population, which for several years had suffered from acute shortages and upheavals. The administrative and economic chaos was slowly overcome, textile and metal industries were begun again, and, compared with 1918, native production had increased 20 per cent by May 1919. The American mission, headed by Herbert Hoover, distributed welcome gifts. The effect of these supplies was not only economic, but also political and social.[14]

All these developments took some wind out of the sails of the Communists, who continued to prophesy an immediate economic collapse. The situation was indeed still difficult, but the violent strike of agricultural workers, which broke out in February 1919 in the Lublin area, although potentially dangerous, was never widespread enough to threaten the stability of the young Republic. The strike was soon settled by means of arbitration, performed by a government mediation commission, and resulted in some improvement in the miserable lot of agricultural workers, heretofore probably the most exploited social stratum of the country. Rural labor inspectors were introduced and collective bargaining, supervised by the state, was established. Although the Communists were unable to exploit the strike because of the rigidity of their agrarian doctrine, the strike impressed the Polish Diet, or the Sejm, with the need for urgency in dealing with the long overdue agrarian problem. From the very beginning of Poland's independence agrarian reform became one of the principal worries of a country suffering from a faulty land structure. More than half the rural population lived on dwarf holdings, and public debate centered not around the issue of whether reform was necessary but around the problem of its extent and its timetable. In July 1919, after a lengthy debate, the Diet laid down fundamental principles for reform which provided for the gradual distribution of large estates.[15]

At the same time that the Communist Party was waging its relentless struggle against the existence of the Polish Republic, its traditional rival, the PPS, in spite of vigorous opposition from its extreme left-wing group, accepted the Branting resolution of the International Socialist Conference in Bern, reaffirming adherence to democratic socialism. The PPS had been active primarily in what was formerly Russian Poland; now it merged, in 1919, with the Social Democratic Party of Galicia and Silesia, and the Socialists of Prussian Poland. Now the party undertook to unify the trade-union movement. In 1919 the movement was in a state of chaos, plagued by unemployment and split into numerous groups — Socialist, Communist, Christian Democratic, and nonpartisan trade-unions. Moreover, national subdivisions existed which cut across ideological orientation: Polish, German, and Jewish unions competed and fought with each other. In March 1919, the PPS summoned the first all-Polish Trade Union Conference, which laid down basic principles for unification. The Communists did not participate directly in the conference, merely sending observers. Again Communist and Socialist principles clashed, but finally the PPS won the day. The trade-union movement, the congress decided, should be nonpartisan, based on class principles and organized within various autonomous branches of industry and commerce. When actual unification was carried out, in July 1919, the Communist-sponsored Council of Trade-Unions saw no other course but to join the reorganized Central Commission of the Class Trade-Unions. By September 1, 1919, the movement numbered 566,000 members; by 1921 the membership passed the one million mark.[16]

In spite of the gradual normalization of internal conditions throughout most of Poland, the scars inflicted by the war were too deep to heal immediately. In addition, the small war that was going on along the eastern approaches of the Republic taxed its resources heavily. Inefficiency and lack of administrative experience in the young state aggravated the situation. Strikes of agricultural and industrial workers burst out sporadically throughout 1919. Members of the Communist Party infiltrated seemingly nonpolitical organizations and through them sabotaged both the war and the reconstruction efforts of the country. One of the organizations which absorbed a number of Communists and their fellow travelers was the Union of the Workers' Cooperatives, acting under the anarchistic and Bakuninist slogan "Let us destroy while creating." The creation of cooperatives was regarded as a stepping stone toward achieving full socialism.[17] Bolesław Bierut, the future leader of the Polish Workers' Party, started his activity in postwar Poland as a member of the Union of Workers' Cooperatives.

THE POLISH-RUSSIAN WAR OF 1920

The armed strife which broke out between Poland and Russia at the very beginning of 1919 was a result of the clash of two different concepts for organizing Eastern Europe. The first was represented by the Bolsheviks, who wanted to upset the traditional, bourgeois order, to split that order along horizontal lines by means of class struggle led by local communist parties, and, consequently, to establish a chain of friendly states. Communist buffer states created in this manner were to be linked with the Russian Soviet Republic by means of a special kind of federalism. When Lenin sent Stalin, then on the southern front, a draft of his "Thesis on the National and the Colonial Question," which had been prepared for the Second Congress of the Comintern, he emphasized that "Federation is a transition toward complete unity." Stalin did not agree completely. In his reply he pointed out that more advanced nations, such as Germany, Poland, Hungary, and Finland would not be suitable members of a Soviet federation immediately. He insisted that before merging into a federal Soviet Republic these nations should first pass through a period of looser confederation.[18]

Another concept for the organization of Eastern Europe was represented by Piłsudski. He, as well as most leaders of Polish political parties, including the PPS, realized that the national revival of Lithuanians, Byelorussians, and Ukrainians made impossible any reconstruction of the ancient Polish-Lithuanian Commonwealth in the form in which it had existed prior to 1772. On the other hand, in accordance with the main stream of the Polish democratic tradition, and in accordance with the program of his own party back in

1892, Piłsudski believed that unless a strong federal bloc was created between Germany and Russia, there would be little chance for the smaller nations to survive in Eastern Europe. Piłsudski thought the nucleus of such a bloc might be formed by the Baltic States, Byelorussia, and the Ukraine, federated with Poland. Accordingly, on April 21, 1920, Poland signed a political and military agreement with Simon Petlura, the leader of the anti-Bolshevik Ukrainian independence movement. Piłsudski was convinced that in order to help the German revolutionary movement Moscow would resume its westward push as soon as all the white Russian armies were defeated. The Poles, supported by Petlura and his small forces, launched an attack against Russia with the purpose of liberating the Ukraine from Soviet power. The ensuing war may be roughly divided into three phases: the first, from the end of April until the beginning of June, was characterized by rapid Polish-Ukrainian successes; the second, from the first days of June until the middle of August, brought the Russian counter-offensive to the very gates of Warsaw; the third and final phase was marked by an upsurge of Polish national spirit and by a lightning and decisive defeat of the Red Army at the battle of the Vistula. The war was ended by the treaty of Riga of March 1921.

THE COMMUNIST PARTY OF POLAND AT WORK

The changing fortunes of the war influenced the attitude of the Communist Workers' Party of Poland.[19] As the Polish-Ukrainian offensive toward Kiev got under way, the party protested by declaring a general strike. When this appeal found no response among the populace, a series of local strikes followed but they were also largely unsuccessful. Individual acts of sabotage, diversionary tactics, and intelligence work for the Red Army were all that party members could achieve.[20] On February 17, 1920, even before the Polish-Ukrainian attack, the International issued an appeal "To the workers of all lands." The proclamation presented Piłsudski as an agent of the *Entente,* determined to wage war against Communist Russia to "the last drop of blood of the last Polish soldier." Workers of all countries were implored to sabotage any attempt at war with Russia.[21] Polish Communists, who happened to be on the other side of the front, were supported by the resources of the Soviet state and made some efforts to follow the International's appeal. From the very beginning of the campaign The Polish Bureau of the Central Committee of the Communist Party of the Ukraine collaborated closely with Soviet military authorities in organizing indoctrination and propaganda courses on Poland for the Red soldiers. Great masses of material were printed,[22] but attempts to organize Polish military units failed completely.

With the westward advance of the Soviet forces, the weight of the political problems the Russians had to face increased. Consequently, in spite of a certain reluctance to put the federalist principles he preached into practice, Lenin was finally compelled to supplement his doctrines with some tangible acts. The original practice of incorporating conquered Byelorussian districts directly into the Russian Soviet Republic was abandoned. The Soviet Socialist Byelorussian Republic which was proclaimed on December 31, 1919, now, on the eve of the battle of Warsaw, was declared "independent" and endowed with trappings of sovereignty by the Soviet Revolutionary War Council. The Polish problem was both more difficult and more urgent for the local Red Army commanders and political commissars to deal with. As early as May 19, 1920, the commander of the western Soviet front had ordered his army commanders to set up provisional revolutionary councils in localities abandoned by the enemy. The order, however, entrusted the military authorities and not the councils with supreme power as long as hostilities lasted. In most cases the councils, formed in the wake of the Red Army's advance, represented merely a transformation of local Communist cells under a new name. On July 1, 1920, there were about thirty such councils,[23] and their number increased with the westward advance of the Red Army. Consequently, it seemed to Moscow that the time was ripe for setting up a provisional revolutionary committee for Poland.

In order to understand this Soviet policy in regard to Poland it is necessary to analyze two important conferences which were held in Moscow in May 1920, as well as the Second Congress of the Communist International, which coincided with the most successful phase of the Red Army's Polish offensive.

THE WAR COUNCIL

On May 5 a special council was created to deal with the problems of war against Poland. During a sitting of this war council Karol Radek made a programmatic speech which, at a later time, was to be reprinted in several languages and widely distributed all over Europe. In his speech Radek made an attempt to define the Soviet war aims and political tactics to be used.[24]

Piłsudski, according to Radek, was supported by France but not by England, and Poland thus became the chief French satellite in

Eastern Europe. Soviet Russia was fighting a defensive war against the unprovoked invasion of the Polish bourgeoisie. The Soviet government was determined not to negotiate for peace with the present rulers of Warsaw, but only with a workers' and peasants' government of a Soviet Poland. The Red Army, Radek said, was an instrument of the dictatorship of the proletariat. The Soviet government had two major war objectives: first, to liberate the nations of the Ukraine and of Byelorussia from the Polish yoke, while recognizing the right of the Polish nation to full independence; second, to liberate the Polish toiling masses from the social oppression of the native bourgeoisie. Soviet Russia could not exist without the Ukraine.

Toward the end of its meeting the council drew up an appeal addressed to "the Polish workers, peasants, and soldiers"; the appeal was signed by the All-Russian Central Executive Committee. This proclamation embodied the main points of Radek's speech and offered Soviet brotherhood and alliance to the Polish masses.[25] In an article written at approximately the same time, Radek, while conceding that a future proletarian Poland should freely determine her relation to Communist Russia, formulated a slogan which precisely described the role assigned to Poland by Moscow: "Poland" [wrote Radek] "must cease to be a wall protecting Europe from Russia and become a bridge between Russia and Germany." [26]

On the very same day, May 5, after the war council meeting had ended, a gathering of top ranking Polish Communists took place and a report on the situation in Poland was made by S. Budzyński (Tradycja). His speech emphasized the internal tensions within Poland and ended with the conclusion that the country was ripe for full-scale social upheaval.[27] Such optimistic views, expressed by Polish experts, were of considerable importance later when Moscow had to decide whether to stop its offensive at the ethnographic frontiers of Poland, at the Bug River, or to press on further into the heart of the country.

THE SECOND CONGRESS OF THE INTERNATIONAL

On July 19, at a time when Soviet military successes were reaching a peak, the Second Congress of the Comintern convened in Petrograd, only to be moved to Moscow a few days later. At that moment the Bolsheviks appeared to be at the height of their success, and their self-confidence rose tremendously. They had established themselves firmly as rulers of Russia and were igniting other mighty revolutionary movements. Throughout the globe the rift between the Left Socialists and the Social Democrats had deepened. The

Communists had managed to create their own International, now more than a year old. Practically all Left groups were ripe to enter this new organization. In addition, Soviet armed forces were marching victoriously westward. This unbounded optimism was reflected, among other ways in a comparison of the current situation with that of the previous year. Addressing the gathered delegates, Lenin said:

If the First Congress was only a Congress of Public Propaganda . . . now we have everywhere advanced detachments and proletarian armies, although poorly organized and requiring reorganization. We are able to organize these into a single force. If you will help us to accomplish this, then nothing . . . will prevent us from accomplishing our task . . .[28]

The Polish comrades, most of whom had been optimistic from the very beginning, were now completely carried away by the spirit of martial optimism pervading the congress:

Now our Red Army is rapidly marching forward [declared the rising strong man of the group, Marchlewski] and the proletarian revolution in Poland will go very promptly . . . It is the task of the Russian proletariat to assist the Polish workmen and peasants in their struggle against the bourgeoisie . . . Polish Communists swear that they will not retreat a step from their aims and they beg for assistance in their struggle . . .[29]

In answer to this appeal the congress issued a message to workers of all countries, and particularly to Polish proletarians, exhorting them to fight for the liberation of Poland.[30] A similar appeal was broadcast to transport workers of the world, urging them to sabotage all shipments of war materials destined for the armies of Piłsudski. The appeal had considerable effect on workers in Great Britain, Danzig, and Czechoslovakia causing them to refuse to handle war supplies for Poland.

In addition to fiery appeals, however, the Second Congress did extensive ideological work. It adopted the famous "Twenty-one Points" which was to be the credo of revolutionary discipline, the needle's eye through which no opportunistic or nationalistic camel could possibly pass. Sensing the close interrelation between national and peasant problems in the countries then at stake, the congress declared: "Communists should support the national liberation movements, but only when these movements are, in fact, revolutionary. The peasantry is usually the support of such national-revolutionary movements. In such countries, the Communist Party is not able to attain success unless it supports the peasants." [31]

On the other hand, a certain ambivalence in attitude was also reflected. While stating rather regretfully that "the prevailing prac-

tice in Russia . . . was that of partition of . . . landed property
for the benefit of the peasantry . . . ,"[32] the congress resolution
quickly added:

> The preservation of large landholdings best serves the interests of the
> revolutionary elements of the population, namely the landless agricultural
> workers and semi-proletarian small landholders, who get their livelihood
> mainly by working on the large estates. Besides, the nationalization of
> large landholdings makes the urban population, at least in part, less
> dependent on the peasantry and their food.

Under the circumstances it was not surprising that the Provisional
Revolutionary Committee of Poland had a certain amount of freedom
in deciding one of the essential questions left to its competence: the
solution of the agrarian problem. In a speech made by Marchlewski
at the Second Congress of the Communist International, a short time
before the establishment of the Provisional Revolutionary Committee, the choice was frankly made. In Poland, declared Marchlewski, as all over East Central Europe, predominantly a grain-produc-
ing area, large scale farming was a necessity. Consequently, squires'
estates should not be destroyed but taken over and run by the state
as grain producing factories.[33] These ideas were to remain the basis
for Marchlewski's actions during the fateful summer of 1920.

THE SOVIET PROVISIONAL REVOLUTIONARY COMMITTEE FOR POLAND

The Provisional Revolutionary Committee for Poland was established on August 2, 1920, soon after the occupation of Białystok,
the first large city which the Kremlin considered to be undisputably
Polish. Marchlewski acted as chairman, Feliks Dzierżyński, Feliks
Kon, and Józef Unszlicht as members of the committee, and Edward
Próchniak as secretary. The political supervisor of the whole western
front, J. T. Smilga, was appointed by the Revolutionary War Council
of the Soviet Republic as an advisory member of the committee,
which, in addition, employed about eighty officials.[34] The major
functions of this would-be government of Poland were: first, to
act as adviser to Soviet occupation authorities on Polish matters;
second, to coordinate, under the supervision of Red Army commanders, the activities of local revolutionary committees. The committee was given both legislative and executive power within the
limits allowed it by Soviet military authorities.[35]

The committee opened its activity by issuing numerous appeals
and pamphlets which were printed in millions of copies and dropped

all around the country by Soviet airmen.[36] The platform of the committee called for nationalization of factories and mines, as well as large estates and forests, while promising to leave peasant farms intact. Administrative power was to be taken over eventually by workers' councils in towns and peasants' councils in villages. After the expected occupation of Warsaw, the temporary revolutionary committee would "deposit its power in the hands of the Communist Workers' Party of Poland," and after liberation of the whole country a socialist government of the Polish Soviet Republic would be established.[37]

From the very start the committee realized that the land problem was of crucial importance. The attitude of the peasants, at that time about 70 per cent of the entire population, would be decisive for the success or failure of the whole experiment. Marchlewski was an expert on agrarian matters; this field was his major subject of study and preoccupation. Several years before the war he had written a series of articles for the chief theoretical organ of the SDKPiL, in which he suggested that large estates should be expropriated and handed over to farmers' cooperatives composed of agricultural labor and poor peasants.[38] The land itself would become the property of the nation and would be worked only by cooperatives. In the first stage of development more prosperous farmers would be left in possession of their property and only gradually won over to collective forms of production. In 1918 Marchlewski published a pamphlet on this subject which reiterated his former views.[39] He merely added a new conclusion: Poland should profit by the Russian example and avoid agrarian anarchy. This might be achieved by persuading peasants not to grab land and implements and not to destroy farm buildings. For this purpose peasants' cooperatives should be established. "Cooperative farming is the only possible stepping stone toward socialism." Marchlewski's avowed aim was to achieve as peaceful a transition as possible from individual to collective farming. It was this aim that he had in mind when he boasted in front of Lenin that he and his party, while following the Bolshevik example, would do a better job.

Now, Marchlewski wrote another pamphlet outlining his policies and addressed it to the peasant class. The pamphlet was widely circulated among Polish farmers,[40] distributed to them through the Red Army political apparatus and dropped by Soviet airmen. It was also given to Polish prisoners of war who had been taken by the Russians. Like the bulk of Communist propaganda in this period it produced little effect.[41] Only Dzierżyński argued with Marchlewski in favor of following the Leninist policy and letting the rural masses "expropriate the ex-proprietors."[42] The majority of the committee supported the chairman's policy. Thus, Marchlewski carried the day rather easily. This proves that the Soviet advisers attached to the provisional committee were sure of victory and therefore did not care about the obvious sentiments of the Polish peasantry.

After reading numerous Soviet reports which describe the attitude of the Polish masses toward the invaders, one wonders whether even the promise of immediate, direct, and unreserved distribution of land could have won them to the Russian side.[43] There were too many fresh and painful memories of national and religious oppression connected with the tsarist domination. Moreover, neither the efforts of the committee to restrain loot and rape by the Red Army, nor the various promises of civil liberties and religious tolerance attracted the masses.[44] Polish peasants, as well as most of the urban proletariat, remained mistrustful and unconvinced.[45] This hostility was reinforced by the fact that more than one million Poles had been deported to the interior of Russia during the early part of World War I. The deportees had been witnesses to Bolshevik ruthlessness and had seen much suffering and devastation caused by the revolution.[46]

To the above factors must also be added a basic suspicion of Soviet intentions. When the Red Army did not stop east of the Bug River but began to march on Warsaw, the last doubts that might have been entertained by the Poles vanished. The Russian Army, whatever the color of its banners, reappeared as an invader. The national instinct of the masses, so underestimated by the Social Democrats now turned Communists, revealed itself as an elemental force. Moreover, the Communist Workers' Party of Poland proved to be neither a very reliable nor a very powerful instrument. This was frankly admitted by the party later. On the tenth anniversary of the Russo-Polish campaign the theoretical organ of the party wrote: "Not . . . always and not everywhere were we sufficiently active in a revolutionary way . . . In various sectors the certainty of the Red Army's victory . . . created an atmosphere of passivity . . ."[47]

THE AFTERMATH

The war was finally decided on the battlefield, ending in a Polish victory. The conflict played a great role in the formulation of the Polish Communist Party's subsequent position on the national and agrarian questions. On the other hand, the invasion of Poland by the Red Army and the memories of violence and hardships inflicted on the population became powerful deterrents to the spread of

Communist propaganda in the years to come. The Communist Workers' Party of Poland was to pay a heavy price for encouraging the Red Army invasion.

For a considerable period of time after the battle of Warsaw, up to the very eve of the Riga Peace Treaty, the party still hoped that the tide would turn. The near-catastrophic economic situation in Poland at the end of the war and the growing unrest throughout Europe induced the party's Central Committee to submit a resolution to the Second Party Conference which included the following sentence: "The outbreak of revolution in Europe will be a signal for the red proletarian regiments of Russia to resume their westward march." [48] Acting in accordance with this hope, the party endeavored to organize strikes and acts of sabotage. These tactics were to win a laconic condemnation from an anonymous Communist writer who, with three years' perspective, later wrote:

In 1920 and partly in 1921, the party laboring under an illusion concerning the tempo of the development of the revolution, continued to apply tactics which were entirely calculated for an immediate conquest of power. As the new bourgeois state began to consolidate itself, the Party was threatened with the danger of losing contact with the masses.[49]

In Poland, meanwhile, three significant and almost simultaneous acts occurred which consolidated both the internal and external power of the country. On March 17, 1921, the Polish parliament voted a new constitution which laid the foundation for a democratic political system. On March 18 the Riga Treaty was signed, drawing the eastern frontiers of Poland and marking the end of Piłsudski's federalist plans to set up a confederation of Poland, the Ukraine, and possibly, the Baltic States. Poland was allotted the western fringes of territory inhabited largely by Ukrainians and Byelorussians, but also containing a strong Polish minority. In some urban centers in this area, such as Lwów and Wilno, the Poles actually formed a large majority of the population. To stress its support for the national aspirations of the Galician Ukrainians, the Comintern set up an autonomous Communist Party of West Ukraine with its own Central Committee at the end of July 1921.

Finally, on March 20, a plebiscite in Upper Silesia gave Poland a major share of that industrial and mining basin. It was under these circumstances that the Communist Workers' Party of Poland was to enter a new period of its existence.

In SEARCH of a NEW BEARING (1921-1926)

From the Communist viewpoint, the Polish Republic created after the World War was an "ugly bastard of the Versailles Treaty." It was a fragment of the *cordon sanitaire,* "the easternmost segment of Western imperialism," an enemy state whose foreign as well as domestic policies were influenced by Poland's chief sponsor and ally, France of Foch, Millerand, and Poincaré. As a pillar of the new *status quo* and of the "League of Robbers," this Poland was a major stumbling block for the revolution in Russia and for those forces of social upheaval which, according to Moscow, were about to triumph in Germany, the key country in the Comintern's European strategy.

As long as there was a possibility of revolution in the Weimar Republic, Moscow valued highly the party of Marchlewski, Dzierżyński, and Radek. It was considered an important section of the Comintern, and the party was to be an instrument by means of which Poland was to be undermined and either neutralized or paralyzed in order to make future Soviet intervention in Germany possible. On the other hand, Soviet diplomacy pursued the policy of alliance with Germany, initiated in 1922 by the Treaty of Rapallo, until well after Hitler's rise to power. In the eyes of the Polish government, and for the majority of ordinary citizens, the members of the Communist Party, with their insistence on joining the Soviet Republic outright and their willingness to give away Poland's western provinces to Germany, were considered simply as foreign agents who would once again turn their country into a Russian province. This widely held view was the main obstacle which prevented the party from becoming a spokesman for native Polish radicalism.

Conditions were generally favorable at that time for the development of radical ideas. Between the spring of 1921 and that of 1925 a bitter struggle for power took place between conservative and progressive forces in the country. Those parties which by and large represented the propertied classes — National Democrats, Christian Democrats, and other smaller groups often allied with well-to-do peasants — endeavored to maintain the existing system and to adapt it still further to their own social and economic interests. The Left, (the PPS, smaller socialist parties of the various national minorities, and the peasant group called Liberation), represented a large segment of workers and opposed attempts to preserve the *status quo,* endeavoring to consolidate and even expand social gains obtained during the 1918–19 period. The Left insisted on shifting the brunt of social and economic reforms to the shoulders of the propertied; they demanded that the promised agrarian reforms be carried out and a comprehensive social security system, initiated by the Moraczewski government, be established.[1]

Until well after the *coup d'état* some years later, in May 1926, the hopes of the Left were to remain fixed on the person of Piłsudski. Although he had left the PPS in 1916, he was still popular with many socialists and with most radical democratic groups. Until the end of 1922, Piłsudski was head of state, and the chief opponent of the National Democratic Party. The latter was now Poland's foremost conservative and nationalistic party and showed increasing authoritarian leanings. Piłsudski's popularity, or his "legend" as it was then commonly called, was an important political factor; against him and his supporters stood the extreme Right and the extreme Left, both opposed to the existing democratic form of government. The extreme Right included some conspiratorial Fascist groups of little importance, as well as a fanatic fringe of National Democrats. The extreme Left was composed mostly of Communists and their fellow travelers. Until the beginning of 1926 the bitter hostility of the extremists, against a background of economic crisis and monetary inflation, was kept essentially within the framework of the parliamentary system. In May 1926 the struggle for power was to move into the streets of Warsaw, where it was finally resolved.

THE CWPP EXPANDS

By the early part of 1921 the Communist Workers' Party of Poland (CWPP) had gained considerable reinforcement in the form of splinters from various other radical groups. One of the reasons for this realignment was a general mood of dissatisfaction prevalent at that time. The Polish people had expected a variety of immediate benefits from their reconstituted state. When these hopes failed to materialize, the Communists, offering lavish promises, proved attractive, and managed to offset some of the discredit earned during the war in 1920.

The harsh reality was that Poland faced great economic difficulties. Wartime ravages had rendered her industries incapable of competing in foreign markets, in spite of an export advantage caused by rapid currency depreciation. The loss of Russian markets was also painfully felt, especially by Poland's textile industry. As a result, the country suffered from chronic unemployment, a continuous rise in the cost of living, and a consequent struggle for higher wages as prices rose. The year 1921 witnessed a wave of strikes which shook the young state to its very foundation. Demobilization of the armed forces only increased the already widespread unemployment. Land-hungry peasants clamored for promised agrarian reform, and unrest among agricultural workers spread even to the more prosperous western provinces.[2] Moreover, more than 30 per cent of the Polish population consisted of national minorities; among them were, over five million Ukrainians, about three million Jews, over a million and a half Byelorussians, and some one million Germans. Some of the more radical minority members were naturally attracted to a doctrine which advocated full self-determination as well as social and economic equality. There were, in addition, many sincere Polish socialists who were deeply disappointed because the "bourgeois revolution" had stopped half way, far from what they had expected as a "minimum program."

In the second half of 1920 the Communists acquired members from the so-called Left Opposition of the PPS, including many able people such as Stanisław Łańcucki and Jerzy Czeszejko-Sochacki.[3] Łańcucki was a Sejm deputy and the party thereby gained its first parliamentary representative. Later some socialist youth groups joined the party, and in 1921 Communist ranks were somewhat further reinforced by the accession of small extreme left-wing splinter groups from the Jewish Bund, led by Aleksander Minc and Abe Flug, and from two other Jewish Marxist parties, *Poalej Sion* (Saul Amsterdam and Alfred Lampe) and *Vereinigte*.[4] These successes were later followed by the rapid spread of Communist influence among Ukrainian and Byelorussian social democratic groups.[5] In addition, a Sejm deputy of the Radical Peasant Party, Tomasz Dąbal, also joined the party.[6] Thus, the CWPP, which had boycotted the first parliamentary election in 1919 and had no representation in the Sejm, now acquired two deputies. This was of considerable importance to the movement, for although it had not been officially outlawed, it was being treated as a subversive group and deprived of normal facilities for propaganda.

During this time important changes were taking place in Germany and Russia. The failure of the German Communists to seize power in March 1921 had far-reaching consequences, not only for the German party but also for the Comintern leaders. Moscow now realized how far the Communists were from winning over a majority of European workers. A full-scale withdrawal was accordingly sounded. After proclaiming a New Economic Policy inside Russia, Lenin was now determined to retreat on an international scale and to enter into practical compromises even "with the devil and his grandmother." Overnight the political line of the Comintern was reversed, and the Third Congress of the Comintern, which met during the summer of 1921, shifted its tactics radically. The slogan "To the masses" meant, in practice, "To the Social Democrats," because they controlled the workers throughout Europe. The principle that no democratic government could possibly help the working classes was abandoned. The accusation that "the Social Democratic leaders do not want to fight, not even for a piece of bread," was temporarily forgotten; the offer to cooperate within the framework of a democracy was extended to hitherto despised social democratic "opportunists." Henceforth an immediate effort would be made to meet partial demands of the proletariat, postponing more long-range goals. For this purpose the petty bourgeoisie was to be attracted to the program and trade-unions were to be cultivated and held together. In exchange for their assistance in the struggle against the "offensive of capitalism," Lenin was determined to support his allies "as the rope supports the hanged man."

The united front tactics on the international level coincided with a further consolidation of dictatorship within Russia which took place after the bloody suppression of the Kronstadt uprising of Soviet sailors of March 1921. This also increased an already incipient trend toward stricter control over the national sections of the Comintern. A "front line" party like that of Poland was first to feel the new line.

THE UNITED FRONT TACTICS IMPOSED

The Third Party Conference opened in April 1922 and hotly debated the merits of a "united front" policy.[7] There were three main approaches to the problem. The left wing feared that united front tactics and the formulation of only partial demands would blur the goal of the movement and actually lead to abandonment of the social revolution's more far-reaching objectives. The center tended to accept the new policy as far as the International as a whole was concerned, but refused to apply it to Poland where, it was argued, the program would be unacceptable because of the extraordinary antagonism in inter-party relations. The Communist Party was hardly on speaking terms with the PPS, and any idea of negotiating with the "social-patriots" was most hateful to many left-wing leaders of the movement. After an intense debate the majority eventually accepted the Comintern viewpoint and reluctantly submitted to instructions from Moscow. One of the speakers expressed this capitulation quite openly: "having to chose between two evils: to talk with the Second or the Second and a Half International, or to harm the interests of Russia, we have chosen the former." [8]

The Third Conference also formulated basic party tactics for the internal problems of Poland in the period to come:

> The following three vital problems [said the final resolution of the conference] will be the point of departure for the revolution: first, the growing revolutionary ferment among the working masses following the increasing offensive of the capital and the government, who, together, are resolved to shift over all the cost of the capitalist reconstruction on the shoulder of the working masses; second, the revolutionary sentiments of the broad masses of landless and small peasantry, resulting from the failure of the agrarian reform . . . , third, the progress of the revolutionary tension in the eastern Territories, a consequence of the colonial policy of the Polish government . . .[9]

During the Third Conference the leadership of the Polish Communists was taken over by three right-wing, intelligent, and experienced politicians — Warski (Warszawski), Walecki (Horwitz), and Wera Kostrzewa (Koszutska), or the "Three W's," as they were commonly called. In spite of insistence by these three, neither the national nor the agrarian problem was settled fully in accordance with Moscow's wishes. The bulk of the party was still permeated with the traditions of the SDKPiL,[10] and it is significant that almost two years after the Second Congress of the Comintern, which had solemnly proclaimed the right of self-determination to all national groups and distribution of land to peasants, the CWPP, while hinting indirectly at these solutions, still hesitate to subscribe to them directly. The conference decided that the party should publish its theoretical paper called "New Review."

Before a party congress could cope with these two problems the first regular parliamentary election took place in Poland, in November 1922. By this time the CWPP was cured of the "infantile disease of leftism." Since the Communists remained an illegal body, and thus could not openly participate in the electoral campaign, "Red Factions" in the trade-unions formed a Central Electoral Committee and forty-five local committees. An electoral list called the "Union of Town and Country Proletariat" was presented. This was a grudging and indirect recognition of the Polish Republic. Despite vigorous electioneering, the list gathered only slightly more than 130,000 votes, mainly in Warsaw and in the Dąbrowa industrial basin, and two parliamentary seats were won.[11]

The new Diet was a more polarized body than its predecessor, the Constituent Assembly of 1919. The Right was now much more powerful than before, but did not manage to obtain an absolute majority, the Left was only slightly stronger than formerly, and the Center was considerably weaker. The Polish two-chamber Diet was rather like its French model: split into numerous rival factions, eloquent and unruly, emotional but slow in producing a clearcut majority. Despite these shortcomings the Diet acted as a useful safety valve for political tension in the freshly reunited and rather heterogeneous Republic, serving, as well, as a training ground in practical democracy. For the Communists the Diet represented the only important official propaganda medium; speeches of deputies could not be censored, were printed in the *Parliamentary Record,* and were distributed free of charge. The parliamentary rostrum became a major way of spreading Communist ideas throughout the country and both Communist deputies, Łańcucki and Dąbal, and later on also Stefan Królikowski, treated all parliamentary debates and disputes as "internal quarrels within the bourgeois family." Posing as "the only true representatives of the toiling masses," they fought with vitriolic vehemence against the capitalist system as such and opposed the existence of the Polish Republic, a "vassal of the imperialist France" and a reactionary state organically unable to cope with the problems of reconstruction.[12]

During the period 1924–1928 the Communist Parliamentary Faction, led by the able speaker and publicist, Warski (Warszawski), and supported by some radical Ukrainian and Byelorussian deputies, became a factor of some importance in the Diet.

ECONOMIC AND POLITICAL CRISIS

Since the election of November 1922 produced no clear-cut majority, a majority could be formed either by a coalition of the Right and *Piast,* the strongest peasant party, or by a coalition of the peasant and labor groups with support from the national minorities. Piłsudski, still a champion of the Left, and favored by it for presidency,

refused to run. He considered the Constitution of 1921 as an obstacle to effective government. It was his friend, Professor Gabriel
Narutowicz, who was elected. He had been a distinguished scientist,
a member of the Liberation Party, and a former foreign minister.
The new president of Poland owed his office in part to votes of the
bloc of National Minorities, which had been originated by Jewish
political parties. This in turn gave rise to increasing anti-Semitism
among nationalist groups, and a few days after his election the president was murdered by a fanatic.[13]

For some time after this murder Poland was on the verge of civil
war. A coalition government was formed by General Władysław
Sikorski and tried to steer a middle course. Soon afterward Wincenty
Witos, leader of the Piast and the most prominent peasant politician,
decided on a shift toward the Right. A pact signed in the spring of
1923 between Witos and representatives of the two main right-wing
parties provided, instead of compulsory agrarian reform, that the
state should parcel out up to one million acres of land yearly, paying
full compensation at market prices. The land was to come first from
state farms and only second from private estates which would volunteer to dispose of a part of their land; 60 per cent of the total area
to be distributed would be situated in the eastern part of the country
where the squires' estates were largest and were in the worst financial
shape. This shift in the policy of the Piast reflected the clash of interests between rich and poor peasants. The rich had enough money
to purchase land, and wanted only to bring pressure to bear upon
landowners so that they would dispose of part of their estates to
those who could afford to buy land.

In order to appease the restless urban masses, the new prime minister, Witos, declared that he did not intend to diminish the rights
of the working class, and even promised to introduce a bill improving
labor inspection in factories and establishing unemployment insurance. In practice, however, the Witos cabinet tended to shift a disproportionate share of the cost of reconstruction and currency reform
to the shoulders of workers.

The government, however, proved weak and incompetent. Inflation
became rampant; the note circulation, which in January 1922
amounted to 160 billion Polish marks, rose to 793 billion marks by
January 1923. The cost of living rose accordingly and at the beginning of 1923, after a year and a half of relative calm on the industrial
front, a number of strikes broke out. The summer and autumn of
1923 were filled with economic strife, equal in extent and intensity
to that of the first half of 1921. During 1923 the number of striking

workers amounted to almost one million, while the total number of industrial workers did not exceed a million and a half.[14] Although the struggle was headed by the trade-unions, the role of the Red Factions was also considerable. In spite of this Red Factions' activity, however, a Communist proposal to form a united front with the PPS and the Bund was turned down by these parties.[15] Numerous attempts to engineer united front tactics from below and to centralize the scattered efforts of various Red Factions failed also.[16] But the movement of protest against living conditions went on, to burst out later with considerable force.

THE SECOND PARTY CONGRESS

The Second Congress of the CWPP gathered in Moscow in August 1923. The congress was carefully prepared and skillfully run by the Warski-Walecki-Wera Kostrzewa team.[17] The decisions of the congress were shaped both by the critical situation within Poland and by Moscow's pressure to bolster the Polish party before unleashing a German revolt.

The policy of ignoring the aspirations of a large majority of the Polish population in regard to the national and peasant questions had been repeatedly criticized since 1920 by numerous party members. The mistake was frankly and officially admitted during this Second Congress by several speakers who gave some fine examples of self-criticism. Warski (Warszawski), then the actual leader of the party, pleaded eloquently for an immediate change in program, and quoted a passage from a letter of Dzierżyński written in November 1921:

Our mistake was in repudiating Poland's independence for which Lenin always rebuked us. We believed that there could be no transitional period between capitalism and socialism and consequently that there was no need of independent states, since there could be no state organization under socialism. We did not understand that there would be a rather long transition period between capitalism and socialism, during which, under the dictatorship of the proletariat, classes as well as a proletarian state supported by the peasantry will exist side by side . . . As a result of repudiating every independence, we lost our struggle for an independent Soviet Poland.[18]

Instead of denying the necessity for a Polish state, the party, despite the bitter opposition of its left wing, now assumed "the defense of the interest of the whole nation," menaced by the "offensive of international capitalism." The party recognized Polish rights to Upper Silesia and insisted on the necessity of preserving a national army, merely reformed and purged of its "undemocratic elements." The only way of saving the country's sovereignty would be to conclude a close alliance with the "brotherly Soviet Republics." A joint intervention on behalf of European revolution would be a just war. Poland should cease to be a pawn of France and become a bridge between the triumphant Russian and the nascent German revolutions. This policy could be carried out solely by a government of workers and peasants. To achieve such a government the party would be willing to collaborate with other progressive forces in the country. In the event of a clash between the National Democrats and the "camp of Piłsudski," the party would stand by the latter, alongside all the forces of the Left.[19]

Almost simultaneously, the main theoretical press organ of the Comintern issued a significant article on Poland, written by one of the leading members of the CWPP. The article ended with the following suggestions:

. . . a workers' and peasants' government, land for the peasants without compensation, the right of self-determination for national minorities, withdrawal from the military alliance with France and Rumania, and friendship with Soviet Russia. To the Piłsudski's parties (little as we believe in their willingness to fight, in consideration of the great masses who are still following them) we offer the united front; not for the sake of Piłsudski, but for the clear-cut class program which we have outlined. We need not fear that if our common fight will be victorious, we shall have thereby worked for Piłsudski. A new Moraczewski government, coming to power, as a result of a real fight of the workers' and peasants' masses against the bourgeoisie, would not be a second edition of the first. But it would be a step forward in the direction of the proletarian dictatorship.[20]

This amounted to an outright offer of support, but it was neither accepted nor specifically rejected, by those for whom it was intended, leaving the party full of hopes as to the role of Piłsudski as a possible Polish Kerensky.

As far as the peasant problem was concerned, the party launched the slogan of immediate expropriation of large landowners with no compensation. All large and medium-sized estates were to be confiscated outright and placed at the disposal of agrarian committees elected by landless and poor peasants, with prosperous farmers excluded. A new approach lay in the stress on two points of the agrarian program: first, that in parts of the country where there was no overpopulation and no land hunger the party proposed to keep some modern industrialized estates intact as collective farming models; second, all other land was to be divided among the rural proletariat.

The eight-hour working day should be put in practice in industry; factory committees composed of workers should control production. Worker-peasant alliance was proclaimed as a cornerstone of the party strategy.

While assuming a new role as the only champion of Poland's political and economic independence, the party put forward still another slogan which had been intimated during the Third Party Conference of April 1922, but never, hitherto, clearly formulated. This plan called for "the national unification of the Ukrainians and the Byelorussians with the Soviet Ukrainian and the Soviet Byelorussian Republics." The Luxemburgist view that self-determination was superfluous and even harmful under capitalism was rejected. Also rejected was an exclusive emphasis on class struggle as the remedy for all social evils. This was a momentous step, but, although it attracted a larger following for the party in the eastern border regions of the Republic, it tended to weaken Communist influence among the Poles.[21] Immediate arrangements were made to set up autonomous organizations, the Communist Party of Western Ukraine and the Communist Party of Western Byelorussia. Both of these were to be subordinate to general directives of the Central Committee of the CWPP and decisions of the party congress; the autonomous parties were each to have at least one representative on the Central Committee of the CPP. The affairs of the Jewish and German minorities were entrusted to the special departments of the Central Committee.

The importance of the Second Party Congress lies in the fact that it reversed the party's traditional, "un-Leninist," policy on the national and land questions, and accepted the Polish state as a fact to be reckoned with. The congress ended in a mood of extreme elation and expectation. The old rightist leadership, now safely entrenched in power, left Moscow taking with them the assurances of Zinoviev, head of the Comintern, that the triumph of revolution in Germany, and consequently in East Central Europe, was around the corner. And indeed, arriving home, they found a native revolution in the making.

NOVEMBER 1923 IN POLAND

Poland's worst inflation came in the second half of 1923. In October of that year most of the state employees, headed by railway and postal workers, went on strike for higher wages. Bent on checking the inflation, the government refused to accede to the demands and both railway and postal services were put under military control.

Court martials were introduced in some parts of the country, including Cracow and the Borysław oil district. To protest against these
steps the PPS, which was the main political force behind the trade-
union movement, declared a general strike to start on November 5
and to last indefinitely.[22] The strike, however, never became general;
it failed to spread throughout the whole country or to all the branches
of industry.[23]

Nevertheless, in Cracow, Borysław, and Tarnów, the strike order
was taken more seriously than elsewhere. Introduction of martial law
had increased the hostility of workers in these sections. On November 6, 1923, refusal to admit a group of Cracow workers to a meeting
place became a signal for stormy street demonstrations. Skirmishes
with military detachments which ensued proved disastrous for the
army; a battalion of infantry was disarmed and a cavalry charge also
failed pitifully. Within a few hours the whole center of Cracow fell
under the control of an angry mob. The military detachments withdrew, leaving 14 soldiers and 18 civilians dead, as well as numerous
wounded. The workers captured some 5,000 rifles, several machine
guns, and armored cars.

The situation was critical for both sides: The authorities were
bewildered and temporarily powerless; the rebels were leaderless
and unprepared to continue the struggle. To restore its shaken prestige the Witos government insisted on regaining control of the city,
but deliberated about the means of accomplishing this. The event
took the CWPP completely by surprise. The Cracow revolt was
spontaneous and neither started nor controlled by the Communists.
Here the party had a unique chance to spread civil war throughout
Poland, thus helping their Communist comrades in Germany, but
could do nothing. As one of the party leaders described the situation,
the party "got frightened by the very goal, the reaching of which it
had preached." [24]

Since the PPS leaders had never advocated civil war, they became
alarmed and decided to check the outbursts, which had flared up
principally in Cracow but also in various other places. After PPS
parliamentary pressure was applied, military detachments were withdrawn from Cracow altogether and the victorious workers' militia
took charge of the city. The government cancelled its order of martial law and promised to deal favorably with the striking workers
demands. The situation in Cracow returned to normal; other strikes
in Warsaw, Upper Silesia, and the Dąbrowa and Borysław basins
had been much less violent in character. Thus, in a few days' time
some pacification was achieved, but a great deal of bitterness per-

sisted among the working class. Relations between the Communists and the PPS, which had improved since 1922 despite the latter's refusal to join a united front, now became worse than ever. The slogan of "Social Democratic treason" was revived. All sorts of calumnies and libels were rehashed. Analyzing the recent failures, the theoretical organ of the CWPP concluded: "the road to the proletarian revolution leads over the corpse of the social-patriotic leadership . . ."[25] A trial was held in June 1924, for fifty-six ringleaders of the uprising; the non-Communist character of the riots was confirmed at that time, as well as was the limited influence of the party on the masses.

The party's weakness would have been more easily overlooked by Moscow had the Polish bosses remained in line with Comintern wishes. As long as Warski, Walecki, and Wera Kostrzewa faithfully supported Zinoviev and, consequently, also Stalin, the Left Opposition within the Polish party was kept under control through Comintern pressure. When the CWPP Central Committee began to differ with Zinoviev on the German question and, even more important, on the internal conflict in Russia between Stalin and Trotsky, the Comintern then withheld its support from the "Three W's" and new perspectives opened for the left wing of the Polish party.

THE POLISH QUESTION AT THE FIFTH CONGRESS OF THE COMINTERN

The Fifth Comintern Congress was forced to deal with the aftermath of the Communist defeat in Germany.[26] Moreover, the prophesied catastrophe of capitalism had not materialized. Increasingly the possibility of economic stabilization in Europe had to be taken into consideration. The idea of a "permanent revolution" was beginning to recede into the background, and the slogan "Socialism in one country" loomed on the horizon. This was coupled with the first phase of a feud within the Russian party: Stalin, supported by his allies, Zinoviev and Kamenev, or the so-called "Troika," was rapidly gaining an advantage over Trotsky. The orthodoxy of European Communists was immediately judged in the light of their attitude toward the rival Russian leaders.

Enraged by the alleged betrayal at the hands of the Social Democrats, the Comintern decided to turn left. The idea of a united front was not entirely abandoned, but it was reinterpreted in the light of recent experience. Only "united fronts from below" were to achieve "true workers' and peasants' governments," now to be understood as a synonym for the dictatorship of the proletariat. Social Democrats were denied the once honorable qualification of "right-wing working-class party," which had been accorded them since 1921, and were now branded as "the third party of the bourgeoisie."

Despite considerable success in local elections and some conquests among socialist youth, the Polish delegates went to the Fifth Congress of the Comintern in Moscow with a not very impressive record. Moreover, before dispatching its delegation to Moscow, the party committed the supreme imprudence of meddling in the internal affairs of the Russian party. What was far worse was that it backed the wrong horses. In December 1923 the Central Committee of the CWPP sent a letter to the Russian party which read in part:

> . . . for our party, nay for the whole Comintern, for the whole revolutionary world proletariat the name of Comrade Trotsky is insolubly connected with the victory of the Soviet Revolution, with the Red Army, with communism. . . . We refuse to admit any possibility of Comrade Trotsky being put outside the ranks of the leaders of the Russian Communist Party and those of the Communist International . . .[27]

In January 1924, the politbureau of the Polish party wrote another letter, which canonized Trotsky as the only man in Russia who could be "idolized" by the masses. "With Lenin's death there might be a need for such a man . . . Toward Trotsky will be directed the eyes of the masses." [28] It is no wonder that the CWPP was not very popular in Moscow at that time. At the Comintern Congress the barrage of criticism against the CWPP was opened by Zinoviev himself, who said in his programmatic speech:

> . . . for quite a long time, we regarded the Polish section as one of the Bolshevik sections of the Communist International. This is true with regard to the working-class revolutionary traditions, and the splendid proletarian elements in Poland, who are bearing all the burdens of illegal party work. I must openly state that things are not so well with the leadership. The leadership of the Polish party indulges in too much diplomacy on the most important question — determining the tactics of the Comintern, the German and Russian questions.[29]

To deal with this "over-diplomatic" party, the congress set up a special commission. The importance of the commission may be gauged from the fact that Stalin, busy at that time with elemental power problems, let himself be elected chairman. This was his first really significant step in the international field. The Polish commission included, among other people, Molotov (as vice-chairman), Dzierżyński, Unszlicht, Piatnitsky, Manuilsky, Skrypnik, Thaelmann, Ruth Fischer, and most of the members of the Polish Left

Opposition to the "Three W's" leadership. The role of accuser was left to Warski's chief antagonist, Leński (Leszczyński). Thus, Zinoviev arranged the whole affair as if one faction of the CWPP fought another, while the Comintern merely reserved the position of arbiter for itself. Leński, in addition to giving a detailed criticism of his native party's shortcomings, insisted that it "must cease to be an obstacle between Leninist Russia and the West." Bolshevization of the party, he went on, was a vital necessity. This should be done by removing the present "opportunistic" leadership and replacing it with a Bolshevik nucleus. The incumbent CWPP leaders endeavored to persist in defense of Trotsky and Brandler, but their efforts at opposition soon weakened. A climax was reached when the floor was taken by Stalin.[30]

The Russian question has the decisive importance for the whole revolutionary movement in the West as in the East. Why? Because the Soviet power in Russia is the foundation, the mainstay, the refuge for the revolutionary movement of the entire world. Thus, upsetting this power would mean upsetting the revolutionary movement throughout the world.

Exactly this sort of interference in the affairs of the Russian party, Stalin continued, was attempted by the Polish leaders because they tried to support Trotsky. Next to the Russian question in revolutionary importance stood the German problem, because no other country was so close to revolution and because triumph of revolution in Germany would mean Communist control over the whole of Europe. Here again, according to Stalin, the mischievous activity of the Polish comrades who had dared to back Trotsky's partisans with the Communist Party of Germany contributed to defeat of communism in that country. After having enumerated the sins of the "Three W's," Stalin, wanting to display his studied magnanimity and benevolence, declared himself opposed to an outright purge. "One had to bear in mind that, generally speaking, a surgical operation carried out without much need, leaves an unpleasant aftertaste in the ranks of the party . . ."

While preaching clemency, Stalin let others do the harsh part of the job. A large segment of the Central Committee of the CWPP was removed without consulting the Party Congress, and replaced by one composed of men who seemed to support the rising "Troika" during the first phase of the struggle for power in Russia. The new committee included Leński (Leszczyński), Leon Purman, and Henryk Stein (Kamiński), among others. Since most of these men had resided in Moscow for some time, they were ordered back to Poland.

The Polish commission issued a resolution condemning the defunct Central Committee as inept and opportunistic, incapable of leading the party toward revolution. This action of the Comintern set a precedent which has been followed consistently ever since. All subsequent central committees were to be imposed from outside, and then merely confirmed in power by an obedient party. The party was compelled to accept without any change the centralistic statute of the All-Soviet Communist Party. A principle was introduced that each party member must have a definite job to which the bulk of his time is to be devoted. In consequence of this arrangement, not only the leaders of the movement, but sometime even its rank and file partly depended on the financial assistance of the Comintern. Very few people had time to spare from their normal activities to devote to underground work. Thus, the CWPP started on the road to forced Bolshevization. Gradually, subordination to the Russian party became the touchstone of Communist orthodoxy.

CRISIS OF RECOVERY AND NATIONAL TENSIONS

By the end of 1923 Poland's inflation entered its last phase, superinflation, threatening the very fabric of the country's economy. Peasants were hard hit because they had accumulated large amounts of paper money, working-class people were unable to live on their wages, and their repeated strikes ruined industrial production. State employees and railway workers also demanded salary increases, but the government continued only half-hearted attempts at financial reform. Industrialists who had once benefited from the inflation also became its victims. The bloody events of October and November, 1923 had dramatized the necessity of coping with the catastrophic financial situation. The right-of-center cabinet of Witos fell soon after the Cracow uprising. A new cabinet, headed by a nonparty conservative, Władysław Grabski, assumed control, with a program of radical financial reform. After receiving extensive powers from the helpless Diet, Grabski proceeded with his task and showed a great deal of vigor.

Grabski's attempts at financial and monetary reform were based mainly on resumption of the people's self-confidence. He departed radically from a policy of inflation, and by drastic fiscal measures, including a capital levy, enlarged the Treasury's basis of revenue. Grabski founded a new central bank and this Bank of Poland assumed responsibility for exchange stabilization with a new currency, the *złoty*. Simultaneously with financial reform, Grabski proceeded to expand the already extensive social insurance system.[31]

After brilliant initial successes, the financial reform revealed its shortcomings. The program proved too ambitious; it tried to do too many things at once and too rapidly, and was not sufficiently integrated with the whole economy. Moreover, both weather and international events seemed to conspire against Grabski. Droughts in 1924 and 1925 were disastrous. The price of coal, timber, and sugar, three staple Polish export items, dropped on the world markets. Finally, at a crucial moment, in the middle of 1925, Germany declared a tariff war on Poland. The situation became critical and overnight Poland lost more than 40 per cent of her export markets. Unemployment figures jumped sky-high as did prices, which were calculated, mostly upward, to fit the new, relatively high exchange unit. Grabski, bent on the idea of financial reform, ruthlessly subordinated all sectors of the national economy to his purpose. He abolished the cost of living index as an automatic basis for wage adjustment. Consequently, the income of wage and salary earners deteriorated rapidly. The eight-hour working day was suspended in Upper Silesia and a ten-hour norm was temporarily introduced, following the German example, in order to enable industries in the Polish part of the basin to compete with German ones.[32] Agrarian reform was slowed again, provoking a great deal of bitterness among the rural proletariat. A new wave of unrest now swept the country.

In the eastern provinces social ferment was coupled with an upsurge of national grievance. This was caused by the establishment of standard primary schools which introduced Polish as a second language of instruction, parallel to the local tongue (German, Ukrainian, Byelorussian, or Lithuanian).[33] The whole struggle of these nationalist groups in the eastern provinces took place against a background of Soviet promises which seemed to offer both land and freedom from across the border to Ukrainian and Byelorussian peasants. The movements for Ukrainian and Byelorussian irredentism were conducted, on the one hand, by extreme nationalist groups and, on the other, by the respective branches of the CWPP, recently reorganized into two autonomous subparties. In addition there was a Soviet organized and supported guerilla movement. The tactical character of Soviet nationality policy was not, at first, discerned by many Ukrainian and Byelorussian leaders who, although not Marxists and mistrustful of Moscow, had been temporarily carried away by the amalgamation of national and social slogans which the CWPP had propagated since 1922. For several years this illusion was widespread and became a potent factor among national minorities in states bordering the Soviet Union. It was at this time that the Communist inclined Byelorussian peasant organization called *Hromada* began transforming the rather vague regional and ethnic aspirations of the peasants in Poland's northeastern provinces into something approaching a national movement. During the course of the same year the Ukrainian Alliance of Peasants and Workers (colloquially known as *Selrob*) was formed, later becoming the strongest Marxist organization in Galicia.

The Constitution of 1921 had guaranteed fully equal rights to all citizens of the Republic, regardless of their religion, race, language, or social class. That these guarantees sometimes proved insufficient to assure the enjoyment of these rights was largely due to the national passions aroused immediately after the end of the war, and to the irredentist tendencies of some extremist groups. These latter tendencies were quite openly encouraged by the Soviets. Moreover, Poland's nationality policy was far from consistent, and the early federalist tendencies of Piłsudski also helped to encourage false expectations among Ukrainians and Byelorussians.

The renewed economic crisis, the "crisis of recovery," and national tensions instilled hope in party ranks. Party membership swelled considerably despite severe police and administrative measures taken against the movement by Polish authorities. In February 1924, four deputies had seceded from the Ukrainian Parliamentary Faction and set up a new party, The Ukrainian Social Democratic Party; nine months later this group joined the Communist Parliamentary Faction. The Communist representation in the *Sejm* now jumped from two to six members. At the same time four radical peasant deputies left their original groups and, under the leadership of a former army officer, Sylwester Wojewódzki, set up a group called the Independent Peasant Party.[34] They were soon joined by two Byelorussian deputies who were disappointed with the national and social policies of the Liberation Party. The program of the Independent Peasant Party included: immediate expropriation of all landed property without compensation to owners, transfer of land to the peasants, national self-determination, and a fight against imperialistic war, with the slogan "All power to the peasants and workers." These were all familiar features of the program of the CWPP, with which the Independent Peasant Party closely collaborated.

"NATIONAL BOLSHEVISM"

A sense of frustration deepened as the apparent successes of the Soviet Federation were contrasted with the multiple shortcomings of the Polish Republic: the slow tempo of agrarian reform, the setbacks in financial reconstruction, and the zigzags of policy on nationality matters. This frustration, in turn, contributed to the spread of a peculiar form of social radicalism, similar to the so-called National Bolshevism in Germany. This new trend, which emphasized distinctness of Polish social and economic conditions and autonomy of the Polish revolutionary movement, found adherents among the intellectuals, particularly social workers and school teachers, and even penetrated the ranks of the CWPP. There were a few disciples among Piłsudski's followers and some hoped that the Marshal would head such a crusade.[35] This vague and rather amorphous undercurrent was brought to the surface by the publication by a literary monthly called *Skamander*, of a series of essays by Julian Brun (Bronowicz), from the end of 1923 member of the Party's CC, then in prison for his conspiratorial activities. The essays soon appeared in collected form and proved a literary success;[36] they analyzed a book by a leading novelist, Stefan Żeromski, in which the hero, a Polish youth returned from Russia, becomes disappointed with persistent political and social injustice and the clumsy tempo of Poland's reconstruction. Despairing of other remedies, the youth sides with the revolution.

Both the book and the essays caused a great uproar. The novel was regarded by most progressives as the warning of a great writer to a complacent society: the danger of communism was not to be underestimated but ought to be forestalled by means of timely reform. While many reviewers tended to condemn the book's author, Żeromski, as a Bolshevik, Brun criticized him as not Bolshevik enough, but merely a radical democrat preaching the idea of social justice in the wilderness. What was needed, according to Brun, was a native revolution similar to, but not identical with the Russian upheaval. The Bolshevik revolution, argued the author, despite its outwardly cosmopolitan character and its international slogans, had been essentially a "Russian, national revolution" directed against the colonial rule of financial feudal lords over the country. By expanding sovereignty over economic affairs the revolution had strengthened the political sovereignty of the Russian nation. Poland, argued Brun, should follow this example in essence though not in method. At the bottom of Brun's reasoning lay the vaguely formulated idea that there was a peculiarly Polish way of achieving the upheaval, and that an alliance of the two revolutions would be the proper way to fix relations between Poland and its neighbor, Soviet Russia. This was a continuation of a weak undercurrent in the Polish Marxist movement which had been evident since the beginning of the century. It presupposed if not ideological at least organizational and tactical independence for each Communist movement in a given country. Similar ideas were widespread among members of the Ukrainian and Byelorussian subparties, both crowded with individuals who tended to treat communism as an instrument of national liberation.

The ideas of Brun exerted some influence on the Polish Communist Party.[37] Instances multiplied in which prominent Communists took an apparently "nationalistic" stand and made pronouncements which would have been unthinkable prior to 1923 or 1924. The idea of "grafting the Bolshevik scion on the Polish body," while paying due respect to the needs and conditions of this body, took hold of a considerable section of the party. Speaking at the Diet, a Communist deputy gave expression to his party's anxiety for the country's economic independence. "We Communists," he said, "we have always been patriots; not bourgeois but proletarian patriots, because an independent Polish state, free from capitalist exploitation, is a guarantee of cultural and economic welfare of the toiling masses." [38]

It is against the background of this strange undercurrent of "national communism," as well as the ambivalent position of Piłsudski, still the idol of the Left, that one should view the struggle for power which took place in May 1926 and the stand taken by the CPP at that time.

THE THIRD PARTY CONGRESS

A Third Congress of the CWPP gathered in March 1925 near Brest Litovsk, summoned under the slogan "Bolshevization of the Party." To the honorary presidium of the Congress was invited "Comrade Stalin." The congress convened primarily to rubber-stamp the decision of the Comintern's Polish commission with regard to the party's leadership.[39]

The congress confirmed and expanded the stand taken by the Second Congress of the CWPP on the land and national problems, and on the question of workers' and peasants' government, emphasizing more vigorously, however, the need to prepare for an armed uprising. This was to be achieved by energizing the discontent of the workers, the peasants, and the national minorities. Their right to self-determination, including separation, was emphasized over again.

The congress issued a special resolution on "Bolshevization" which was a kind of provisional party statute. The resolution remained valid until the actual party statute was formally endorsed by the Sixth CPP Congress in 1932. Bolshevization consisted of four main points. First, the basic party unit was to be a cell, or a small group of people acting in a given enterprise; workers must not be grouped territorially, but rather according to the place of their work.[40] Second, only those who fulfilled certain concrete functions could be considered party members. Third, leadership of the party had to be in the hands of a group of professional revolutionaries entirely devoted to their task, and appointing people of their choosing to subordinate posts. Fourth, "all factional tendencies" had to be excluded from party life. This point amounted, in practice, to complete exclusion of any independent thinking, and required blind obedience toward party leaders who, in turn, had to be subservient to the Comintern. Thus, discipline was tightened, and the party became a more rigidly centralized structure, a party of a "new type."

The rightist Three W's, although formally still at the head of the party, were deprived of their right to vote. They meekly submitted and promptly confessed their "sins." The name of the party was changed: the adjective "Worker" was dropped. Henceforth the party was known as the Communist Party of Poland (Section of the Communist International).

The leftist leadership of the CPP, which for all practical purposes had taken control even before the congress, tended to transmit some of its intransigence and combative spirit to the rank and file. In consequence of this, propaganda for a boycott of taxes and administrative regulations followed and sabotage of military installations occurred in various parts of the country. Terrorist activities and assassinations of police agents multiplied. The death sentences which ensued (Botwin, Hibner, Kniewski, Rutkowski) provoked a wave of protest which the CPP and the International Organization of Assistance to Revolutionaries, known as the Red Aid, tried to make international.[41]

But the span of life of the leftist Central Committee was to be as short as that of its rightist predecessor. Despite the fact that the new group was hand-picked for its docility, it soon revealed a spark of independence: it took a stand on matters pertaining to Germany, France, and Bulgaria. The Polish Central Committee sharply disapproved of the German party putting forward its own presidential candidate, thus splitting the vote of the Left and permitting Marshal von Hindenburg to win the contest. The German comrades were censured for withdrawing from communal elections, while the Bulgarians were reprimanded for too frequent contacts with certain democratic groups. This represented neither a consistently left nor a right position. In all three cases, however, it happened to be contrary to the policy ordered by the Comintern. The CPP leaders were summoned to Moscow and tried by a second "Polish Commission," in a general atmosphere of heresy-hunting. Another group of Polish leaders was condemned wholesale and instantly dismissed.[42]

So ended the second attempt of the CPP to pursue a tactical course somewhat independent of Moscow. Gradually the Polish party was being shaped into a disciplined section of the *Russian* International.

TOWARD A COUP D'ÉTAT

In the absence of an alternative, party veteran Warski (Warszawski) was taken out of cold storage and put back in control of the Polish movement. From the beginning Warski tried to steer a moderate rightist course: in the Diet he championed the economic independence of Poland, "about to become a semi-colony of foreign capital," and put a new stress on fulfilling partial demands and everyday needs of workers, attempting to attract broad nonpartisan masses to the Communist movement. He recommended utilizing the services of various fellow travelers for the open work of the party. Following the slogan of the worker-peasant alliance or the *smychka* in Russia, Warski endeavored to establish a united front with the peasant parties of the Left, and boldly spoke of peasant grievances. He also supported the national minorities on a government bill regarding the fulfillment of agrarian reform.[43]

A Fourth Party Conference, summoned in December 1925, confirmed Warski's policies. It put forward a new, partly successful slogan which connected the interests of workers with those of peasants: "Workers have no employment because peasants have no land." The conference also concluded that Poland, threatened in her economic independence by Western capital, should seek protection in the East. Close alliance with the Soviets and the opening of Russian markets for Polish industries would be the only way out for the country. Bolshevization of the party, or "shifting the party to the Leninist position" was to go on.[44]

Meanwhile, the economic situation went from bad to worse. Disappointment in financial reform brought on a feeling of despair. The cost of living and the number of unemployed mounted constantly. In December 1925, the number of jobless reached 300,000, one fifth of the entire industrial labor force, and a new wave of social disturbances occurred. In November 1925, the Bank of Poland had refused to supply any more foreign exchange necessary to save the *złoty*. Then, after almost two years at the helm of state, Grabski resigned.

A new coalition cabinet decided to increase taxes and also prices of most monopoly products, and to introduce drastic cuts in expenditures, including salaries. This was opposed by the Socialists, who insisted on a public works program and reduction in the armed forces. In April 1926 the Socialists left the cabinet. The mutilated coalition was soon ousted by a new bloc of the Right and Center, similar to that of 1923 and again led by Witos.

Witos intended to amend the existing constitution and to strengthen the executive power. This was assumed by the Left to be a step toward rightist dictatorship, which might then eventually lead to an outright Fascist regime. The parties of the Left issued a statement warning the president of the Republic that "the government is a challenge to the whole Polish democratic camp," and, consequently, should resign. This statement, in conjunction with certain secret military preparations on the part of Piłsudski, clearly indicated that the struggle for power might at any moment transcend the constitutional framework. Piłsudski's retirement from the army had been caused by the Witos cabinet in 1923, a cabinet dominated by his National Democratic opponents. He now regarded the new government as a personal provocation. Both the acute economic crisis and the government's apparent inability to cope with it enhanced the prestige of the retired Marshal.

The country's economic situation was deteriorating. During March and April of 1926 there were various stormy demonstrations by the unemployed. By the beginning of May unemployment reached 345,-000. In Warsaw, during the workers' May Day parade, PPS squads clashed with those of the CPP and three workers were killed. The hopes of the Comintern ran high. "If there is one land," said Zinoviev, "in which an immediate revolutionary situation might crystallize in a comparatively short time, it is Poland." [45]

The CPP leadership watched the mounting crisis develop and tried to analyze it carefully. In April 1926 Warski set forth some political directives for future guidance of the party; the directives, unanimously confirmed by the Central Committee, were designed to support ". . . the struggle of the democratic elements, including the followers of Piłsudski, provided they fight actively in defense of the republican and democratic institutions and the demands of the workers and the peasants." Even Warski's leftist opponent, Domski, while warning at the Sixth Congress of the Comintern against the danger of Piłsudski's dictatorship, suggested remedies not very different from those of the Central Committee:

It is well known that there are many elements in Piłsudski's ranks who really believe that their leader is a revolutionary and that under certain circumstances, they must proceed together with the Communists. This situation must be exploited in order to expose Piłsudski by a correct application of the tactics of the united front.[46]

Nevertheless, Piłsudski's *coup d'état* surprised the Polish Communists no less than it did other groups by its rapidity. On May 13, both the CPP and the PPS proclaimed a general strike. It proved particularly useful to Piłsudski as far as the railways were concerned, because only trains transporting his troops were let through, and this factor was to contribute greatly to his swift victory. At the beginning of a street fight in Warsaw a small group of Communists took part in an offensive against loyalist troops. Then, on May 14, the CPP approached all leftist political groups in order to form a united front in the fight against "the Fascist government of Witos."

"Red Banner," published on May 14 by the CPP, demanded:

The arming of the workers and peasants and the liberation of political prisoners, that should be the first act which will kindle the enthusiasm of the masses . . . Bread and work for the workers! Land for the peasants without payment! Freedom for the suppressed nationalities! [47]

Before a few replies could even reach the party the struggle was already over.

Yet even before the end of the struggle most of Piłsudski's Communist allies were arrested, interned in a military fort, and released only when pacification of the country became complete. Meanwhile, in a press interview, the Marshal destroyed the lingering illusions of the Polish Left: he declared that he was in favor of neither Left nor Right, but of social equilibrium. His revolution, he emphasized, ought to have no revolutionary consequences.

It soon became obvious that the CPP had let itself be carried away by events. There were several reasons for this phenomenon. The party had become frightened by the idea that the rightist government, dubbed Fascist, might have come to stay, if only it could manage to amend the constitution and the electoral law. The party soon forgot its theory of "two Fascisms": that of the Right, represented chiefly by the anti-Semitic and authoritarian National Democrats, and that of the "petty bourgeois diversion" headed by Piłsudski. It also forgot the necessity of neutrality as long as possible in order to watch the two hostile forces destroy each other. Pressed by its rank and file, the CPP decided to choose what appeared to it as a lesser evil.

On the eve of the coup Stalin was busy with his own factional strife and left the CPP to itself. During the short struggle that followed he watched events more closely, hoping for civil war. The rapid solution of the possible "revolutionary situation" fell as a rude shock. The shock was all the heavier to bear because Piłsudski's success had been achieved with CPP assistance, minor though this was. Nevertheless, at first, no one dared to condemn the Polish comrades, whose intentions had been previously known in Moscow and not rebuked by the Comintern.[48] The signal for blame was given by Stalin himself. In a speech of June 8, 1926, at Tiflis, Stalin said:

How could it happen that the revolutionary discontent of a considerable portion of the workers and peasants in Poland brought grist to the mill of Piłsudski, and not to that of the Communist Party of Poland. It is because the party is weak, exceedingly weak, and that it has become still weaker in the past struggle through its incorrect attitude towards Piłsudski's troops; that in view of all this it could not take its place at the head of the revolutionary-minded masses . . . I must confess that our Polish comrades have, in this case, committed a very great error.[49]

The analysis of what was called "The May error" was to become one of the chief topics of self-criticism for years to come, a virtual time bomb.

7   Under PIŁSUDSKI

Communist theoreticians elaborated ingenious and often brilliant ex post facto theories explaining the causes and mechanism behind the coup of May 1926.[1] These many theories, however, overemphasized economic factors and neglected the personal element which was so important in Piłsudski's case. The coup was a revolt by a strong and ambitious man against the Constitution of 1921, which had been designed by the National Democrats to keep him out of power. In 1922 he refused to run for the presidency under that constitution and soon afterward resigned as commander in chief. When all other attempts to change the established system and to get back into political and military life on his own terms failed, Piłsudski decided to strike.[2] Economic conditions undoubtedly created a favorable atmosphere for his return to political life and the Marshal exploited them skillfully.

Immediately after seizing power Piłsudski advanced a nonrevolutionary program. It embodied three main points: first, a fight against the "overflow of party politics," second, a moral cleansing of public life, and third, an improvement of economic conditions, by which the Marshal meant primarily stabilization of the *złoty,* a balanced budget, and reduced unemployment. The economic part of the platform was firmly and consistently put into effect, the task being greatly facilitated by currency depreciation and a general strike in Great Britain. Poland was able to conquer the Scandinavian and Baltic coal markets, temporarily abandoned by the United Kingdom. During the summer of 1926 unemployment declined, exports increased rapidly, the budget was balanced, and the currency was stabilized. A considerable prosperity, which was to last about three years, enhanced the prestige of the new regime both at home and abroad.[3] The "moral cleansing of public life" was not practiced to the extent which might have been expected. The only major case to be brought for trial was that of a former deputy minister of national defense, General Michal Żymierski. He was duly convicted and sentenced to six years in prison.

Soon after his triumph Piłsudski made a bid to win over his old comrades of the Left. His offer was accepted by some who had remained under his spell, among them many of his former soldiers and associates from the period between 1903 and 1908. But the bulk of the Left, after several fruitless attempts to come to an agreement with its former champion and to influence the evolution of his regime in the direction of democratic reform, reluctantly went over to the opposition. Although only verbal at first, the opposition gradually became more active. As a result of Piłsudski's failure to gain support from the Left, his government disregarded parliamentary majorities and emphasized efficiency and quasi-military discipline. Several changes of cabinet were no more than a "changing of guards" and simply amounted to a shift of influence within the same ruling group. Piłsudski, however, was reluctant to apply dictatorial methods openly and to eliminate the party system altogether. The old parliamentary framework was outwardly preserved until 1935, but was manipulated to suit the purposes of a regime which refused to be called a "dictatorship," preferring "directed democracy."

During thirteen years of its existence the regime underwent a constant evolution toward the Right. Agrarian reform, although not abandoned altogether, lacked emphasis and social policy became progressively more conservative. While emphatically rejecting Fascist models, an effort was made nonetheless to strengthen executive power and to establish an authoritarian kind of regime. A new constitution was prepared, designed to reverse the trend toward democratization in social as well as political life. This deepened the chasm still further between the regime and the bulk of the people. In 1930 the government underwent further militarization and became known as the "regime of colonels," who threatened their political opponents with "breaking their bones." The country split between those who defended democratic institutions and those who opposed them. Almost at the same time the country entered another period of economic depression, which in Poland proved deeper and more protracted than in most European countries. This provided the CPP with great opportunities. However, the party encountered unexpected obstacles, and went through a series of crises which prevented it from exploiting the devastating effects of the depression. Among the main difficulties experienced by the party at that time were the "May error" debate, the shift in the nationality policy of the Soviet Union, and the Trotskyite heresy.

THE CPP AND THE COMINTERN

While Piłsudski was consolidating his power in Poland, Stalin was embarking upon his "Thermidor." With the support of Bukharin and Rykov he continued to crush the Left Opposition of Trotsky and Zinoviev. The latter, though still formally the head of the Comintern, was rapidly losing his influence and, in October 1926, was replaced by Bukharin. With the growing emphasis on "socialism in one country," the Comintern was becoming less an instrument of international revolution than one of national power.[4] Communist ideology became canonized in a rigid set of rules that had to be accepted by all sections of the Comintern. To be a Communist now one had to believe and not question. Naturally this reflected on the status of all non-Russian parties including, of course, the CPP, which was not renowned for its ideological orthodoxy. Moreover, with the deaths of Marchlewski in 1925 and of Dzierżyński in 1926, and with Józef Unszlicht's shift from the secret police to military affairs, the CPP influence in Moscow was on the decline. Lenin had been a close friend of the "Old Guard" in the Polish party; both his death and the aftermath of the "May error" speeded the downward process.

It seems beyond doubt that CPP tactics in support of Piłsudski's coup had been approved by Moscow. The pattern in Poland was the same as in China, where Communists were ordered to collaborate with the Kuomintang. Limited cooperation with Piłsudski was openly and repeatedly announced by Warski (Warszawski) and his associates; the collaboration was discussed and blessed by the main theoretical organ of the Comintern, the *Communist International*. Then, when the new disaster of Piłsudski's regime ensued, a scapegoat was sought. But now any change in CPP leadership was extremely difficult, because all factions of the party acted unanimously, after recently undergoing a series of Comintern-sponsored purges. Consequently, there was no serious "blood-letting" on this occasion. After severe admonitions and a meek submission by CPP leaders, the story was closed, with only a slight reshuffling on the Central Committee. Warski and his rightist group remained in control temporarily. By tacitly allowing the CPP to support Piłsudski, Moscow hoped to provoke civil war or to aid in establishing a "democratic dictatorship of workers and peasants."[5] When all these plans miscarried, the Soviets were unexpectedly confronted with their old enemy, now firmly entrenched in power in the key country of Russia's western approaches.

The CPP's theoretical organ, the "New Review" of August-September 1926 reprinted the article of the *Kommunisticheskii internatsional* that admonished the party for having "forgotten all about the danger to the Soviet Union" which was bound to result from the seizure of power by Piłsudski.[6]

Suddenly, memories of the 1919–20 *cordon sanitaire* revived in Russia. The Comintern gave currency to the version that Piłsudski's coup had been devised and supported by Great Britain and represented the triumph of English and American capital in Poland over the hitherto prevalent French influence. Although an American financial expert, Dr. E. W. Kemmerer, had been conducting a study of Poland's economic resources since the autumn of 1925, his presence was assumed to corroborate Soviet apprehensions in regard to Piłsudski. Then in 1927, when a so-called "stabilization loan" was finally granted by the United States, Moscow interpreted this whole development as a new victory for Anglo-American imperialism, a victory which endangered the Soviet position in Eastern Europe. This, coupled with a similar interpretation of Soviet difficulties in China, led the Kremlin to formulate a theory of a new "capitalist encirclement" being plotted in London, with Poland as the key country in the western arm of a gigantic pincers.[7]

Thus, in the eyes of the Kremlin, the Poland of 1921–1926, which had been merely a passive barrier between Communist Russia and the West, swiftly became a potential jumping-off place for military intervention against the USSR. The bogey of impending war was exploited by Stalin in order to facilitate his struggle against Trotsky and the Left Opposition. A "state of siege" mentality was artificially created and nurtured, with France and England pictured as the instigators of an imminent intervention, and Poland depicted as their main instrument in Eastern Europe. Even after Hitler's seizure of power, in 1934, the Treaty of Rapallo was renewed and Russo-German military collaboration was allowed to continue. The attacks against Poland abated somewhat after a Polish-Soviet nonaggression pact was signed in 1932, but were redoubled after the nonaggression pact between Poland and Germany in January 1934.[8]

THE "MAY ERROR" DEBATE

Meanwhile, the "May error" debate continued with increasing ferocity. The debate was initiated by the reprinting in the August-September 1926 issue of "New Review," of the already mentioned article of the *Kommunisticheskii internatsional*. The discussion was soon transferred to various other Communist papers and then became international in character. Two rival camps within the CPP, imitating the Russians, adopted the traditional terms "Minority" and "Majority" faction.

The Minority, led by Leński (Leszczyński), saw the source of the "May error" in the "opportunistic" attitude of the rightist leadership. The argument of the Majority was that the coup had many appearances of a revolt by radical intellectuals and petty bourgeoisie, with support from broad masses of workers and peasants, a sort of "petty bourgeois conspiracy" directed against the rule of the great capitalists and landlords. To this Leński and his faction replied that even if the upheaval had been truly radical and democratic, it should not have been assisted by a proletarian party, which should reject the antiquated concept of the two stages of the revolution, one bourgeois, another socialist. The Minority ascribed a Fascist character to the coup; according to the Majority it was merely a military dictatorship evolving toward fascism. Poland's imperialism was evaluated by the Majority as feudal and military in character, with only a few capitalist features. The Majority also regarded the rival "social fascists," who represented the petty bourgeoisie, as an independent third force between fascism and democracy but opposed to both systems of government. This view was bitterly contested by the Minority, who denied the independent role of the petty bourgeoisie.

In accordance with the contemporary views of their protector Bukharin, the Majority viewed rather optimistically the capitalist future of the Polish economy, then approaching a period of stability, prosperity, and expansion. The Minority took a contrary position and prophesied that internal contradictions would prevent any substantial stabilization in Poland. Low wages, high taxes, the turtle tempo of land reform — all of these factors were bound to render the growing internal market ineffective. In accordance with Stalin's view, this group saw the boom years 1926 to 1929 as a "rotten stabilization" which would end shortly in a slump. While the Majority was rather inclined toward limited cooperation with opposition parties holding democratic views, the Minority was intransigeant on this point and insisted on going it alone.[9] This internal conflict soon intertwined with the struggle for power within the Soviet Union. Roughly speaking, the viewpoint of the Majority coincided with that formulated by Trotsky, while the Minority followed Stalin.

The "May error" debate almost broke the party asunder during the Fourth Congress of the CPP, which took place in Moscow in September 1927.[10] After more than three months of deliberation, vitriolic recriminations, and even fist fights, the congress could hardly reach any conclusion. Endless debate, bickering, and intrigues were carried over to the Comintern's Sixth World Congress. During the congress Bukharin said:

At the last congress of the CPP, which lasted over three months . . . the representatives of the Comintern were unanimous in declaring that political differences within the Polish party had been practically reduced to nought. And yet, after this congress, the only thing that prevented the disruption of the party was extremely strong pressure brought to bear upon it by the executive and the whole Comintern. Had we not intervened there would now have been two parties . . .[11]

Finally, Warski was excluded from the party's Central Committee and two trusted outsiders, the Ukrainian Communist Dmitri Manuilsky and the Finnish leader, Otto Kuusinen, were added as supervisors. A resolution forced on the CPP congress by the Comintern admitted that the coup had been a severe setback for the proletariat of Poland and that the CPP was far from blameless. "Fascism" and not a "petty bourgeois conspiracy" had triumphed in a country reputed to be one of the weakest links in the capitalist system. Condemning the thesis of Ernest Brand, a prominent economist and a leader of the party's right wing, on the immediate peaceful intentions of Poland, the party congress resolved that "development of the internal market cannot be the basis for effective capitalist development" and that the objective conditions ". . . are gradually driving and will drive the Polish bourgeoisie to an accentuated expansion to the East." Piłsudski was to be denounced as an agent of British imperialism. The theory of the two-stage revolution was condemned as denying a possibility of an immediate triumph of socialism in Poland. The Fourth Congress launched a new slogan: "The peasants have no land because the workers have no power." [12]

The declining influence of the CPP in Moscow and the growing importance of Germany in Comintern strategy were both reflected in another point of the dictated resolution. The CPP now proclaimed "the right of national self-determination of Upper Silesia, including the right of secession," a measure not likely to increase the party's popularity in its native country.[13]

By 1928 Stalin had managed to extirpate all organized opposition within the Bolshevik party. Trotsky continued to maintain that it was impossible for a socialist revolution to succeed within the boundaries of a single country. According to him, the building of socialism in the Soviet Union could only succeed in connection with a general social revolution. Stalin, on the other hand, although he never aban-

doned the long term objective of world revolution, was determined
to apply different tactics. The Soviet Union was to be the focal point
for world communist movements, all of which were now pledged to
defend communism whatever its transformations or tactical moves
inside Russia.

The Sixth Congress of the Comintern opened a new era of Comintern policy which was to last from 1928 until Hitler's consolidation
of power in 1934. The congress also reflected a Left trend in Soviet
domestic policy. The Comintern decided to separaté Communist
movements still more sharply from moderate leftist and progressive
labor parties, all of which were denounced anew as "traitors" and
"sleeping partners of fascism." Once more, world revolution was
deemed so imminent that no collaboration with "social traitors" was
necessary.[14] Stalin's pre-eminent position within the Soviet Union
was reflected both in the program of the congress and in the internal
structure of the Communist International.[15]

Polish matters occupied a prominent place at the congress gathering. Using the congress forum, both factions of the CPP made numerous complaints. To cope with the aftermath of the "May error"
debate still another Polish commission was appointed. On the recommendation of this commission, the Executive Committee of the
Comintern issued a strongly worded letter to the CPP's Central Committee, in which the party was accused of not fulfilling its basic objective, defense of the Soviet Union.[16] The Polish delegation promised
to reform and rushed to sign a declaration against the Trotskyist
opposition.[17]

As previously stated, the CPP right wing, or Majority, had supported Bukharin's evaluation that Poland was now in a period of
stabilization and even capitalist expansion. Bukharin's replacement
by Molotov as head of the Comintern spelled the end for the faction
led by Warski, Kostrzewa, and Brand. In April 1929, the party was
purged in accordance with the Comintern's wishes. Leadership was
now captured by Warski's old rival, Leński, and his leftist followers,
who were always careful to consult the Kremlin before saying or
doing anything whatsoever, Alfred Lampe, Saul Amsterdam (Henrykowski), and Leon Purman.

EXPANSION OF THE CPP

Piłsudski's victory in May 1926 was not followed by a blood bath,
such as occurred in Bulgaria in 1923 and in China in 1927. Those
Communists arrested in Warsaw during the coup were promptly
released and, contrary to Soviet propaganda, there was no "white

terror." [18] At the beginning, the new regime was somewhat lenient toward the movement compared to the previous conservative government, thus earning accusations that it "appeased" or "wooed" the Communists. Really stern measures against the party came only during the decade of the thirties; [19] in 1934, a concentration camp was established at Bereza Kartuska, and Communists were interned together with members of various Fascist and semi-Fascist groups, and with common criminals.

The years 1926 to 1928 brought the CPP considerable expansion both in active membership and in the number of satellite and fellow-traveling organizations. [20] Popularization of the party's new agrarian program was influential among landless peasants in central Poland, particularly in the heavily overpopulated Lublin and Kielce provinces. This ascendancy was achieved for the most part indirectly, first through the Independent Peasant Party, and then through its ideological successor, the Peasant Self-Help. [21] During this decade favorable illusions about the Soviet Union were also a potent source of strength among national minorities in the states bordering Russia. Propaganda, skillfully combining social and national agitation, began bearing results and the mushroom growth of both the Byelorussian *Hromada* and the Ukrainian *Selrob* [22] raised great hopes within the CPP. Moreover, during the summer of 1926 some extreme elements broke away from the PPS and, under Andrzej Czuma, set up a separate party, which used the traditional name, the PPS-Left. [23]

The CPP also had several front organizations whose programs hardly differed from its own, yet these groups enjoyed all the privileges of legal bodies and rendered valuable service to the outlawed party. Despite the "May error" debate, the dissolution of the *Hromada*, and a split within the *Selrob,* the CPP was making some progress. During the election of March 1928, the last free election in prewar Poland, the party polled 829,416 votes out of a total of 11,-758,094. Including invalidated ballots, the party polled over 940,000 votes or 7.9 per cent of the total, more than double the results obtained in 1922. [24] The CPP won seven seats: two in Warsaw, two in Łódź, and three in the Dąbrowa basin. In Warsaw, the Communists this time proved stronger than their traditional rival, the PPS. Together with other Marxist parties the CPP now had at least nineteen deputies in the Sejm.

This expansion of the party's influence continued until the time bomb, the "May error" debate, began producing its paralyzing results. The consequences of that debate were aggravated by the leftist course inaugurated by the Sixth World Congress of the Comintern in 1928. At that meeting Communist parties had been ordered to close ranks in defense of the USSR, both the PPS and the Bund were dubbed "direct branches of fascism," and all cooperation with their leadership was forbidden. The establishment of separate trade-unions was condemned as "ultra-left deviation," but the formation of Red Factions within existing unions was made obligatory.[25]

This change of tactics, together with the "May error" crisis, retarded the growth of the party just on the eve of the economic depression which created a new potential "revolutionary situation."

"IMPERIALIST INTERVENTION" AND THE NATIONALITY PROBLEM

The nationality problems in Eastern Europe constituted a first-class offensive weapon for Moscow. It was a life-and-death struggle, *"Kto kago"* (who whom), eat or be eaten. Either the Soviet Union would paralyze its neighbors by a skillful use of the nationality question or its opponents would spilt the "Soviet nation" in the making.[26] The Byelorussian problem was a good case in point. Soon after its foundation in 1925, the leftist Byelorussian organization, known as the Hromada, passed from mere political activities to a boycott of administrative authority, and finally to terrorism. The dissolution of the Hromada by Polish authorities that followed in 1927 brought a storm of protest from the CPP and other minority groups, as well as from the Soviet Union.[27]

Older instruments of Soviet diversion in Poland were the Communist parties of Western Byelorussia and Western Ukraine. But soon after their formation these two groups became sources of constant trouble both for the Soviet Union and for the CPP. As a consequence of the more dynamic personalities of the Galician-Ukrainian leaders and a greater freedom of expression within these parties, they tended to draw the more enterprising and intelligent elements from the Soviet Ukraine in a westward direction, away from Moscow. A good example of such difficulties may be found in the spread of a "nationalist deviation" called "Shumskyism," from the name of the Ukrainian Communist leader. Although the "deviation" orginated in the Soviet Union, it spread to Eastern Galicia where it found a ready ear among some groups who either accepted Lenin's writings quite literally or embraced communism because it seemed to promise national liberation. The Communist Party of Western Ukraine soon became an active center of "Shumskyism," or "bourgeois nationalism." [28]

Relations with the CPP were no happier; constant bickering and factional feuds predominated. Survival of the Luxemburgist heritage, "national nihilism," and centralist tendencies within the CPP all formed rather frequent complaints on the part of Ukrainians and Byelorussians.[29] The CPP, on the other hand, could not bear criticism of the Soviet nationality policy which was repeatedly voiced by Ukrainian and Byelorussian leaders after 1930–31.[30]

Despite the difficulties which the CPP experienced with both autonomous subparties, the nationality problem remained one of the chief weapons of the party until 1932–33. This was facilitated by the numerous mistakes which Warsaw committed. The aging and ailing Piłsudski was increasingly unable to impose his federalist ideas on his following, among whom a strong undercurrent of nationalism was growing. The wavering nationality policy of Poland, alternating between promises and reprisals, created a state of confusion throughout the eastern provinces of the Republic. In the summer of 1930 numerous acts of terror and sabotage were perpetrated in Eastern Galicia, largely by members of the nationalist Ukrainian Military Organization. Warsaw lost its temper and applied martial law in Eastern Galicia. When acts of civil disobedience and guerilla warfare continued, the Poles applied punitive measures generally known as the "pacification of Eastern Galicia." By widening the breach between Poles and Ukrainians, these measures rendered any sensible modus vivendi in the Borderlands very difficult, at the very moment when a shift in Soviet policy toward the Ukraine and Byelorussia from encouragement of the local nationalism to Russification made such a compromise a real possibility.

The initially negative attitude of the CPP toward the Ukrainian nationalistic, "petty bourgeois" guerilla movement changed in the autumn of 1930.[31] "The mass setting on fire of the landlord and church manors," wrote the "New Review" of September-October 1930, ". . . the destruction of households of colonists and kulaks, the mass struggle against the Polish occupation administration . . . all these are the symptoms of the revolutionary right of the toiling peasants and the broad masses of the Ukrainian petty bourgeoisie against Polish imperialism." It was decided that the CPP now should lend a helping hand to such a movement. This was not the case, however. At that time, the party had hardly emerged from a period of internal paralysis and was not equipped to cooperate militarily with the Ukrainian rebels.

The CPP was further prevented from capitalizing on the Polish government's mistakes in the border areas by the increasing Russification being undertaken in the Soviet Ukraine. This was coupled with a great famine which had followed on the heels of collectivization. Next came the decapitation of the Ukrainian intelligentsia, followed by the dramatic suicides of Ukrainian leaders Skrypnik, Chvylovy, Shumsky, and Maxymovich, as well as liquidation by the Soviets of the Byelorussian Hromada leaders that had fled the Soviet Union. All of these events echoed loudly in the Polish borderlands, and deeply affected the morale of the Ukrainian and Byelorussian autonomous subparties.

THE FIFTH CONGRESS OF THE CPP

In 1930 the paralysis of the CPP leadership was still alarming. Consequently a Fifth Party Congress was summoned near Leningrad in August and September of 1930, with its chief objective to heal the wounds inflicted on the party by the "May error" debate.[32] Soviet leaders were now haunted by the nightmare that the West might attack the Soviet Union before its First Five Year Plan had been completed. A famine had followed collectivization and brought the country to the verge of civil war. The Soviet leaders believed that a new intervention was imminent. Hence, in addition to internal consolidation, the CPP Congress proclaimed defense of the Soviet state as the principal task of the party. This was to be achieved by integrating the struggle of workers, peasants, and national minorities into one action. Poland's economic crisis, accompanied by mass unemployment, a rising tide of revolution in towns and villages, and "the decay of the Fascist dictatorship" would facilitate achievement of the party's objective. The proletarian revolution would wrest Poland from the capitalist front and include her in the system of Soviet Republics. The congress insisted that the proletariat of the national minorities ought to fight not only the bourgeoisie of Poland but also their own bourgeoisie, because the latter was inclined to compromise with the government.

Armed party squads were made autonomous units, each containing a Communist cell. Workers and young party members were to be trained for these squads in order to perform acts of sabotage and wage guerilla warfare in the event of a Polish-Soviet conflict.[33] Propagation of the idea of armed insurrection was made obligatory, and the necessity of infiltrating the Polish armed forces was reemphasized. The slogan of self-determination for Upper Silesia was reaffirmed; to this was added another concerning "the nationally mixed regions of Pomerania." [34]

Opposition by other Left and Center parties against the Piłsudski regime was again declared an "internal affair of fascism." This was in accordance with the policy set forth by the Comintern in 1928 and followed by the leftist leadership under Leński, secretary-general of the CPP since 1929. Exploitation of Poland's growing unemployment was to be the party's paramount task. In spite of bitter attacks from the CPP right wing, an independent course within the trade-union movement was confirmed,[35] and the congress commissioned the party's Central Committee to develop a program as recommended by the Sixth Congress of the Comintern of 1928.

The CPP, according to the platform, should work directly for a socialist revolution, which, however, under Polish conditions, especially in the Eastern Marches, would have certain features of a bourgeois-democratic upheaval. As for the industries, "complete nationalization could not take place at once and should be brought about by means of several consecutive transition measures." Poor peasants with a strongly rooted property instinct being a dynamic force in the villages, the platform advocated winning them over by dropping the slogan of nationalization of land. "Land for the peasants without redemption payments," now became the battle cry of the party. Large estates were to be confiscated and rented out to poor peasants with some "model state farms" set up. The cooperative movement, both in the towns and the villages, should be regarded as a stepping stone toward socialism. "The proletarian revolution," emphasized the platform, "will remove the obstacles to the unification . . . of the Ukrainian and the Byelorussian nations," and assures to the German population of Western Poland "the right to reunification with the Reich." "The Polish Soviet Republic," stressed the program, "will conclude a fraternal alliance with the Soviet Union, and any country that will liberate itself from capitalism, on the basis of a voluntary unification and centralization of military forces and economic resources."

The program, an expression of the Left trend within the Comintern, foresaw a possibility for realizing the united front only from below. The platform was put into practice on the eve of another twist of the "general line," which followed the consolidation of power by Hitler. That twist made the program largely outdated, even an obstacle to the party's plans of forming a united, let alone a popular front.[36]

The congress put an end, at least formally, to the schism within the party. The Right Opposition capitulated, recanted, and was finally removed from power. Now Leński and his team felt they were firmly in the saddle.

The Fifth Congress speeded the evolution which the CPP had been undergoing since 1925. Reflecting similar changes in their

Russian counterpart, the Political Bureau of the party was strengthened at the expense of the Central Committee. Small individual cell
meetings were to replace the deliberations of the former broad party
conference, thereby atomizing party membership. Control from the
top down became still more rigid, and nomination of party officials
was made not on grounds of competence, but rather subservience to
the new Stalinized Comintern. Financial dependence on Moscow also
increased. Dictatorship of the party bureaucracy was rapidly being
consolidated.[37]

The congress concluded by framing a series of slogans for daily
use during the coming period of intensified revolutionary struggle
— "Let us face the big factories" and "Watch the toiling peasant
masses." Although party propaganda directed toward the countryside had been using the slogan "Land for the peasants" since 1923,
the leftist leadership modified this by adding the words "and for
land workers." The congress declared a tax boycott and launched the
slogan "Not a penny for the government of unemployment, hunger,
and war."

Several months before the Fifth CPP Congress convened, Poland,
together with the rest of the Western world, entered into a period
of severe depression which almost paralleled the span of the First
Five Year Plan. The economic crisis in Poland began in agriculture
and an unfavorable trade balance once more menaced the country's
economic stability. Moreover, even the limited domestic market was
shrinking rapidly as industrial unemployment mounted. The depression once more aggravated class antagonisms and renewed the
struggle for power between democratic and authoritarian elements
in the country. Although Piłsudski's coup had slowed the trend
toward political democracy and social levelling, it had not halted
these processes entirely. Now, the impoverished peasants and
workers again began to claim their share in shaping Poland's destiny.

A climax was reached in June 1930, at the Cracow Congress
called by labor and peasant parties. This gathering, which has
usually been referred to as the "Centroleft Congress," issued a
proclamation addressed to the Polish people as well as to the outside
world. The resolution stated that the parties assembled at Cracow
were determined to pursue their joint fight against the dictatorial
methods of Piłsudski and to restore democracy in Poland. A few
weeks after the Centroleft Congress its organizers were arrested
and imprisoned at the fortress of Brześć. This act of violence marked
a new epoch in the political history of Poland between the World
Wars and the regime became progressively more alienated from the

working masses. The newly affirmed "left" course of the CPP determined its negative attitude toward this latest display of democratic opposition to the regime.[38] The consolidation of the Left was regarded as a danger by the party that emphasized its monopoly for genuine leftism. In turn, the Centroleft parties showed no willingness to fraternize with the Communists whom they regarded as enemies of Poland's integrity and independence which they themselves were pledged to defend.

After 1930 the Piłsudski regime used openly dictatorial methods to consolidate its hold. The 1928 parliamentary election had still been a free contest between opposition forces and those of the government and rather faithfully reflected the actual state of public opinion. In this vote the Piłsudski bloc remained a minority. The government, however, dominated the election in 1930 which took place under the shadows of Brześć and the "pacification" of Eastern Galicia. Although the most blatant abuses were later corrected by the law courts, the election could not be called free. The CPP and its front organizations were among the first to suffer from this policy of tightened control; the number of CPP deputies dropped to four and representation of Communist-inclined groups also decreased. Restriction of overseas emigration hit the Polish countryside severely.

In December 1928, the general index of industrial production stood at 136.2 (1927 = 100); in February 1931, it was at 92.3 and continued to drop until it reached a level of slightly over 50 per cent in 1933–34. Prices of agrarian products dropped catastrophically; already, by 1931, the index of wholesale prices had dropped to 56.9 per cent of the 1927 level. The plight of the peasants was reflected in their increasing willingness to join CPP rural cells.[39]

The government's economic policy actually delayed the process of recovery. As Professor F. Zweig emphasized in his book *Poland Between Two Wars,* the Piłsudski regime came to power with a slogan of economic stabilization. It stuck desperately to the gold standard and fought a hopeless battle against the current world revolution in prices and money. A far-reaching economic and fiscal readjustment was then undertaken by the government. The closing of the so-called "price-scissors" was one of the most difficult problems; for both economic and political reasons the government adjusted nominal wages to changes in the price structure and thus weakened the bargaining power of trade-unions.

After 1930 the government, while still tolerating PPS-dominated unions, proceeded to establish its own unions in order to broaden the mass basis of the regime. After achieving limited results, the government then embarked upon an unsuccessful policy of unifying the whole labor movement. Furthermore, a 1919 law which had established a 46-hour working week in industry and trade was amended in 1933 to the disadvantage of workers, while payments for overtime were decreased. Both of these measures met with opposition.

During the period 1928–1936, the index of nominal wages declined by 21 per cent, while real wages rose 36.2 per cent. Real income of the working class as a whole, however, dropped during that period by 22 per cent as a result of widespread total or partial unemployment.[40] After 1931 a series of strikes by peasants occurred throughout the country, accompanied by violent demonstrations on the part of the urban unemployed. The peasant strikes took the form of stoppage of food deliveries to the cities. Profound discontent in the villages was followed by expansion of the CPP's peasant membership.[41]

The CPP's "left turn" also found a spontaneous though not very consistent response among the masses of unemployed. Being unable to pay their dues, the jobless were leaving their trade-unions *en masse*. Trusting Communist propaganda, they believed that the unions had betrayed them or at least were powerless to help them in their predicament. The party, competing with the PPS and the Bund, made a considerable effort to organize or encourage economic strikes and to turn them into political ones. Included were some "sit down" or "Polish" strikes, which became a characteristic feature of the industrial scene in Poland during the thirties. But generally speaking, the unemployed were not so much interested in the achievement of revolutionary objectives as in the immediate satisfaction of their elementary needs. And here the party showed little imagination. The suffering of the masses in the depression created widespread exasperation and a readiness to do violence. But the unemployed were ill-suited to a consistent struggle; their mood wavered between desperate outbursts and prolonged spells of apathy.[42]

Both the fifth and sixth CPP congresses devoted much attention to the problem of unemployment. However, full utilization of the latent revolutionary potentials in mounting unemployment was prevented by "the organizational weakness of the revolutionary trade-union movement" and the party's inability to further the concrete, daily demands of the jobless. CPP secretary-general Leński admitted that the party exhausted the unemployed masses by daily street demonstrations, hasty strikes, and riots.[43] These manifestations, which were supposed to prepare the workers for a general strike, soon came to be called "ineffective and pseudo-revolutionary gymnastics." They contributed greatly toward alienating even the more militant among the unemployed from the Communist movement.

CPP AND TROTSKYISM[44]

These years of economic crisis coincided with another internal crisis within the CPP, one which was a direct reflection of the feud raging in the Bolshevik party. The CPP had inherited its sympathy for Stalin's chief rival, Trotsky, from the teaching of Rosa Luxemburg and from the whole tradition of the SDKPiL. The latter, during the period 1906–1914, was often ideologically closer to Trotsky than to Lenin.[45] These proclivities revealed themselves strikingly in 1924, during the Fifth Congress of the Comintern, when the CPP lent its support to Trotsky. Later, with the growing ascendancy of Stalin and the Polish party's increasing financial and organizational dependence on the Comintern, the pro-Trotsky sentiment was suppressed. Outwardly, CPP leaders such as Warski and Kostrzewa pretended to submit and conform.[46] But the defeated leader's pronouncements had a certain grandeur and brilliance which made his teachings attractive to the intellectual strata of the movement. Criticism of Comintern strategy and daily practice also appealed to Polish members because Stalin's hand had weighed heavily on the CPP. Moreover, Stalin's theory of "socialism in one country" sounded like an expression of revolutionary pessimism, of profound disbelief in the potentialities of the movement outside the USSR. The theory implied that other Communist parties might, after all, be expendable, or at least condemned to remain in capitalist purgatory for an indefinite period. Consequently, among the party rank and file, the pro-Trotsky sympathies were still lingering by the late twenties. From time to time these sentiments would find some outlet in the party press and internal debates, but in each case the leadership managed to keep the statements within bounds. Speaking at the Ninth Plenum of the Comintern's Executive Committee, a CPP delegate, Leon Purman, declared: "Trotskyism was many times fought against in the Polish party, and hence [the party] has become immune to the Trotskyist danger . . . [N]ot a single party organization came out in favor of the Opposition."[47]

Indeed, until 1930, there was little of Trotsky's articulate influence on the surface, but a great deal of it underneath. Officially the party was thoroughly Stalinist, although rather reserved and reticent, refraining, as far as possible, from the outspoken denunciations of anti-Stalinist elements, which were already customary in other parties. Generally speaking, the CPP leadership submitted to Stalinist

rule, but in the inner recesses of leaders' minds were preserved
their own views on the rights and wrongs of the Stalin-Trotsky clash.
This attitude, however, began changing by 1930.

At that time, disappointed by the lack of internal party democracy
and by the CPP's tactics, a small group of party members in Warsaw
began to criticize their leaders, although not the Comintern itself.
The platform of the opposition was broadly formulated in order to
unite all its heterogeneous elements, which included some sympathizers of Trotsky, Brandler, and Bukharin. Isaac Deutscher, Paweł
Minc, and Abe Flug were among the most active leaders of this
revolt. In 1931 the rebels addressed an appeal to the Comintern,
insisting upon intervention in their behalf against the autocratic and
arbitrary rule of Leński. They particularly criticized Leński for
his indiscriminate denunciation of both the government and the
government's opposition as "fascist" or "social fascist." The conflict
within Poland, stressed the rebels, could not be treated as a "comedy"
or a "family quarrel," and the party ought to back all the democratic forces in their fight against the regime of colonels, as the
government had come to be called after 1930. While the CPP, for
tactical reasons, should fight the ideas represented by the PPS and
the Peasant Party, it should also defend bourgeois democracy
against authoritarian attack.[48]

The rebels accordingly advocated a united front with the PPS
and the Peasant Party against Piłsudski, and opposed the "sectarian"
tactics of the party with respect to trade-unions. The CPP had been
splitting the labor movement in an attempt to create is own groups;
the opposition favored a unified movement with clandestine Communist activity inside the unions.

Without answering their specific charges or satisfying their demands, the Comintern invited the opposition leaders to visit Moscow
and to explain the whole matter personally. This offer was prudently
refused. The opposition persisted in its demand that the Comintern
first admonish the Central Committee to stop its campaign of
vilification against the opposition faction.

Initially, the bulk of the opposition was strongly opposed to many
of Trotsky's ideas. This was due to the fact that most CPP members
judged them largely on the basis of Stalinist summaries which pur-
ported to reproduce the exiled leader's policy. Trotsky's own writings
and the documents of the Russian Left Opposition were available at
that time to the rank and file of the party only in official Comintern
version. But in 1931 Trotsky began to publish his articles and
pamphlets on the German problem in a variety of European lan-

guages. The "Bulletin of the Opposition" began reaching Poland regularly; immediately a large section of the opposition was convinced of the correctness of Trotsky's arguments[49] and Isaac Deutscher became a spokesman for this group. However, when Trotsky communicated his intention to establish a Fourth International, his Polish followers opposed the move. The Comintern was still a taboo to these supporters.

The rebels now recognized that those aspects of CPP policy which they criticized were common to all sections of the Comintern, especially to the German party, which in the conflict between nazism and bourgeois democracy took an attitude similar to that of the CPP in regard to the Centroleft. In the spring of 1932, Deutscher, then editor of several party papers, wrote an article in which he did not openly attack the party but did advocate a united front of all labor parties and trade-unions against fascism in general and against nazism in particular. In the article Deutscher also gave an analysis of fascism, from which it followed that Hitler, in the event of his victory, would crush the Social Democratic as well as the Communist parties. This reasoning was then in flagrant contradiction to the party's, and parallel to that of Trotsky. The author was asked to admit that he had committed a breach of discipline, but was not yet required to renounce his views. Deutscher, however, bluntly refused to comply. A group of other Polish party members declared their solidarity with Deutscher, and they were all expelled as agents of "social-fascism" at the Sixth Party Congress in 1932. By 1933 this opposition group had about three hundred members in Warsaw alone, while the total membership of the party in the capital then hardly exceeded one thousand.

Gradually the opposition, which was strongest in Warsaw and Łódź, took a more pronounced "Trotskyist" line and began to oppose the "Thermidorian reaction" and the Stalinist methods as a degeneration of communism, "the syphilis of the working-class movement." There was increasing solidarity with Trotsky's basic thesis that "the fundamental condition for the . . . reform of the Soviet state was a victorious spread of the world revolution," and that a thorough reform of the corrupted, diseased "Stalintern" was a pre-condition for such a policy.[50] However, the opposition split on both these issues; one section wanted to confine its criticism to the Polish party and to refrain from any censure of the Comintern and Stalin.

Ridden by internal tensions and lack of central leadership, the Trotskyist faction began to disintegrate. The party's financial dependence on the Comintern also played its role in this decline. In

1935 Deutscher and a group of his followers joined the PPS, while Minc and his partisans sided with the Bund. Trotsky officially founded his Fourth International in July 1936, but the Polish delegation was conspicuous by its absence. A pro-Trotsky undercurrent continued to remain a factor of some importance until the party's dissolution, particularly among the Jewish membership.[51]

Thus the CPP, although weakened during the crucial period of the depression, managed, nonetheless, to weather the Trotsky crisis successfully. Meanwhile, Hitler's seizure of power in Germany had focused attention on matters of far greater importance and brought about a reversal of the Comintern's most protracted left turn.

BACK to the UNITED FRONT – DISSOLUTION of the PARTY

8

The Polish Communist Party was seriously affected by Hitler's seizure of power in Germany and by the subsequent eradication of the German Communist Party (KPD). Some of these consequences were far-reaching and ideological; some immediate and practical. The German party had been the world's largest outside the Soviet Union. Germany, together with the Free City of Danzig, had constituted a main base of operations for the CPP. As a rule relations between the Polish party and the KPD were cordial and intimate. The Weimar Republic naturally tolerated and even encouraged the activities of a party which pressed for revisions in the Polish-German frontier; all the successive German administrations had considered the CPP to be an instrument of anti-Polish diversion and, therefore, gave shelter and protection to party members who needed it. Until 1933 the principal theoretical organ of the CPP, the "New Review," was printed at Gleiwitz (Gliwice) in the German-controlled part of Upper Silesia.

The Nazi upheaval in 1933 dramatically reversed this situation. Germany suddenly ceased to be a base of operations for the CPP; the editorial staff of the "New Review" and other personnel had to be hastily removed to Danzig and, in 1934, to Czechoslovakia. When Czechoslovakia fell to Hitler most CPP officials fled hurriedly to Denmark, Holland, Belgium, France, or Switzerland. The party's head, Leński (Leszczyński), happened to be in Germany and was arrested by the Gestapo. He was released only because of the intervention of the German General Staff, which was still faithful to the spirit of Rapallo.

Moscow took more than a year to realize that Hitler was no transient figure that will be swept away by an outburst of popular revolt. It was only in January 1934, at the Seventeenth Congress of the Bolshevik Party, that Stalin, having reluctantly declared his decision to abandon a leftist strategy, returned to the idea of a more conciliatory approach toward all forces threatened by fascism. This was dictated by the fear that, in spite of Moscow's efforts to preserve the old policy, Hitler would eventually fulfill the threats of *Mein Kampf* and attack the Soviet Union. There was no time to lose. The Social Democrats, until recently branded the "moderate wing of fascism," now suddenly became the most desired of allies. In addition, thinly disguised advances were made to the leftist bourgeois parties.

The new policy found full expression at the Seventh Congress of the Communist International, held in Moscow during July and August of 1935. Georgi Dimitrov, who had gained prestige by his daring rebuttal in the Reichstag fire trial of 1933, was now entrusted with leadership of the Comintern. World revolution was to be abandoned for the time being; henceforth, the interests of the world proletariat could best be served by making the security of the "first socialist state" the primary concern of Communist movements throughout the world. The new battle cry was for a united front of Communists and Social Democrats to defend international peace and democratic freedoms, and to protect the hitherto abused Versailles settlement against Fascist menace. Pacifism was discredited as cowardice. The framework of the popular front was soon broadened to include all anti-Fascist forces, without much discrimination. The foreign policy of the Soviet Union, under Litvinov's direction, was coordinated with the new pronouncement of the Comintern and geared to "collective security." The USSR joined that "robber's den," the League of Nations, in 1934 and concluded military alliances with France and Czechoslovakia in 1935.

The conciliation of the bourgeois world in foreign affairs was paralleled by a policy of extermination of Stalin's opponents in Russia and in the Communist movements outside the Soviet Union. This took the form of a series of unprecedented purges and trials within the Soviet Union, unleashed soon after its people had been granted "the most democratic constitution in the world." The purges, first overlooked by the CPP press, and then hailed as inevitable and even beneficial, were soon to strike at the very existence of the party.

UNITED FRONT TACTICS IN POLAND: THE OPENING PHASE

The Nazi threat was felt more acutely by countries directly bordering on Germany than by the Soviet Union itself, like Poland and Czechoslovakia. Moscow still hoped to continue the policy of Rapallo, but in March 1933, shortly after the burning of the Reichstag by the

Nazis, the Communist Party of Poland approached the PPS, the Bund, and other smaller socialist groups with a proposal "for setting up of the united front of struggle against the capitalist offensive and against fascism." The letter in this regard reads: "The C.C. [Central Committee] of the CPP points out that the proletarian united front is rendered necessary by the complicated international situation . . . the danger of new imperialist wars, the raging of Fascist reaction in Germany, and the prospect of big class struggle of the Polish proletariat." [1]

The letter suggested organizing a twenty-four hour general strike to protest against limitations in the scope of social insurance, then being discussed by the Polish parliament. During their common struggle the CPP promised to refrain from attacking Socialist organizations. This offer was then followed by a series of other proposals for collaboration, both general and specific.[2] The plans called for unification of parallel trade-unions "on the basis of class struggle," while retaining ideological independence and freedom of propaganda and agitation. Immediate leadership would remain in the hands of respective party committees.

The PPS and other social-democratic groups, however, rejected the Communist offers. Although they were insistent on direct negotiations between the Second and the Third International to achieve broader understanding, the Polish socialists were not inclined to accede to more than a temporary nonaggression pact.[3] Negotiations were resumed repeatedly, but quickly broken off each time, sometimes by the parties of the Second International, sometimes by the Communists. "There can be no talk of a united front," the Socialists insisted, "as long as the Communists regard the policy of the Second International as a betrayal of the interests of the working class."

Despite the rather cool reception from Social Democratic leaders, the rank and file of most socialist parties in Poland were soon affected by what was then termed by a PPS publicist as "united front fever." As a consequence, some local success was achieved by the CPP, acting secretly "from below," that is, behind the back of Social Democratic leaders. Several united front committees were established in factories and some temporary interparty agreements (in Łódź, Białystok, Grodno, and Stanisławów) were made concerning cooperation in strikes and demonstrations, and even in the municipal elections, like those of Łódź in 1936. This occurred spontaneously in spite of the fact that both the PPS and the Bund had forbidden any official contact with the Communists. It was feared that the CPP would infiltrate the labor movement solely for the purpose of Soviet propaganda and diversion.[4] But the severe depression and the concurrent growth of various Fascist and semi-Fascist organizations had the cumulative effect of making the working masses progressively more radical and impatient. Consequently, Social Democratic leaders were compelled to proceed with caution in their efforts to expose the CPP's bad faith.

Another problem was that even before the Communist overtures, some PPS politicians had begun to doubt whether the intransigent course that they had taken in 1918–19 toward the CPP was actually justified by events. "In 1918, the revolutionary process was interrupted too early . . . [wrote a PPS politician]. Everybody, everywhere, with the exception of Russia, considered the liquidation of the revolutionary process as a most pressing task . . . One should not have liquidated the vital forces of revolution in the name of theoretical programs . . ." [5]

"NO ENEMIES ON THE LEFT"

With the passage of a new semi-authoritarian constitution, a corresponding electoral law, in the spring of 1935, and the expansion of various rightist groups, a favorable atmosphere was created for renewed Communist attempts toward a united front. In May, after the PPS again rejected Communist overtures for joint participation in the forthcoming elections, the CPP issued an appeal to all opposition parties and trade-unions, urging them to organize a general strike in protest against the coming election.[6] This pronouncement was soon followed by a series of appeals for the "anti-fascist popular front." According to the CPP the struggle against fascism depended upon the speedy formation of a broad democratic people's front. This front must concentrate around the Socialist Party, the People's Party (*Stronnictwo ludowe*), and the United Trade Unions.[7] A resolution, issued on September 8, the eve of the polling day, declared:

> The overthrow of the government can be hastened by its electoral defeat providing that in the immediate future a joint fighting front of all non-Fascist elements is formed. Otherwise the clique of colonels and generals will be made still more insolent by the importance of the opposition and proceed with still greater energy to turn Poland into a "totalitarian state" along Hitler lines.[8]

The basis of the front was to be "a number of democratic demands . . . which correspond to the strivings of the masses . . ." The platform was to include a demand for a "Constituent Assembly but not the slogan of Soviet power . . ." The PPS, acting independently, decided to boycott the election, but once more vetoed any idea of a united front.[9] All opposition parties boycotted the election; only 46.4 per cent of the eligible voters participated in it.

The Seventh World Congress of the Comintern, meanwhile, had given its official blessing to the policy that the CPP had already been trying to follow for more than two years. Leński (Leszczyński), elected a member of the Presidium of the Comintern, admitted in his report that until recently the CPP had "not devoted enough attention to the defense of democratic rights." Henceforth the party would be ready to participate in a democratic government and would insist on the convocation of a Constituent Assembly to replace the puppet Sejm, which had been elected on the basis of the new electoral law. The year 1935, reported Leński, had brought a revival of peasant discontent. "The urban petty bourgeoisie represents a very weak point in our campaign for a people's front: in spite of its radicalization it remained nationalistic." The united front was, according to Leński, in the process of formation. For the time being, "unity of action" with the lower strata of working-class groups remained a substitute for a formal united front agreement. Leński pointed out that this maneuver "applied in a new way, enabled our party to appear at the surface of political life on a much wider scale than in the past." [10]

During 1934 and 1935 the CPP finally abandoned its support of German revisionist aspirations and tried to give its own propaganda an increasingly patriotic tinge. "The Resolution of the Sixth Plenum of the C.C." in 1935 used language which would have been condemned earlier as "social-patriotic" or at least "opportunistic." "We, the Communists, respect the independence of Poland . . . We, the Communists, are heirs of the best traditions of the Polish nation's struggle for independence and democracy . . . We, the Communists, are deeply attached to our homeland . . . We will not allow our homeland to become a bridgehead or the marching ground for the Hitlerite generals . . ." [11] This sort of appeal did not remain without some effect in a country which, notwithstanding its nonaggression pact with the Third Reich, remained acutely conscious of Germany's aggressive designs.

Despite the avalanche of united front proposals on the part of the CPP, both the PPS and the Bund repeatedly rejected innumerable Communist proposals to concert the policies of the leftist parties. The final rejection took place during the 1937 PPS congress at Radom. The congress declared that "the slogan of the united front everywhere except Russia, cooperation with the socialists everywhere, but persecution in Russia, prisons and collective murder perpetrated on socialists . . . must be treated as an empty phraseology behind which there is hidden the goal of . . . weakening the labor and the socialist movements . . ."[12]

The PPS congress decided in favor of "a workers' and peasants' front," aiming at the downfall of the dictatorship in Poland. In order to achieve this objective the Socialist Party should use "all available means." Subsequently, during the period of transition, "a temporary dictatorship" might be necessary to keep power in the hands of the toiling masses and to reform Poland's social and economic structure along democratic lines.[13] All members of the PPS who belonged to organizations or contributed to newspapers outside its direct control were required to obtain permission from central authorities for carrying on such work.[14] The atmosphere of the congress was so anti-Communist that resolutions against the united front were passed unanimously. The most open protagonists of the front — Barlicki, Dubois, and Próchnik — voted for the resolution, and even Communist-inclined delegates such as Wanda Wasilewska, did not dare to challenge the general mood of the congress. Thus, the attitude of the PPS and, for that matter, of other social-democratic parties in Poland did not undergo any substantial change, despite Communist assurances of support for the workers' and peasants' government envisaged by the PPS.[15]

THE LIMITED SUCCESS OF THE UNITED FRONT

The united front never did materialize; it was impossible to achieve in the face of the CPP efforts to upset the leadership in existing socialist parties and to subordinate their rank and file to Communist direction. "The Communist International," said a CPP writer, "poses the question of the political unity of the proletariat as a problem of setting up a single proletarian party . . . a party of a new type, modelled after the Bolshevik party . . ."[16] This approach was unacceptable to the overwhelming majority of Social Democrats in Poland. Although Hitler's rise and the growth of native authoritarian movements created a favorable climate for cooperation among all parties of the Left, misgivings as to the methods and ultimate objectives of the CPP were too strong and too deeply rooted among Socialists to be erased overnight. A Bund leader declared that conditions for more permanent cooperation between Social Democrats and Communists would have to include a break with the Comintern and rejection of Stalinist policies which curbed democratic freedom.[17] This counsel was equally unacceptable to the Communists.

In addition, the CPP had acquired a reputation as an instrument of Soviet diversion, a prolongation of the arm of the Soviet state. Although the party's propaganda since 1935 had been increasingly spiced with patriotism, it could not overcome the widespread distrust of other groups. As a prominent PPS leader, Mieczysław Niedziałkowski, put it: "With you Communists one never knows where the ideological comrade ends and where the Soviet agent begins . . ."[18]

The CPP still persisted in their attempts to achieve "a united front from below," largely by penetrating other groups and undermining the incumbent leadership. Not only socialist but also peasant and other parties, including some Catholic organizations, were infiltrated by the Communists after 1934. There were Communist revolts in the youth branch of the PPS and Communist conspiracies among the youth of the Peasant Party. These organizations were flooded with Communist publications, books, pamphlets, and leaflets, all of which propounded the idea of a united front. The most important carriers of Communist propaganda and agitation were illegal leaflets; some were printed secretly in Poland, others were smuggled from the Soviet Union. During the late thirties the CPP also issued a host of minor periodicals. These were, as a rule, suppressed by the police, only to reappear shortly thereafter under new names. Hence, a kaleidoscopic change in titles occurred, for example: "The Popular Daily," "Face of the Day," "From the World," "The Labor News," "The Lever," "The Village News," etc. The clearest case of Communist penetration occurred at Wilno University, where a group of able and dynamic people (Dębiński, Jędrychowski, and Putrament) formed an efficient and expanding cell that had considerable influence on the whole academic evironment.[19]

In spite of the intransigent attitude of all social-democratic parties, there were several instances when some kind of spontaneous "unity action" actually did take place on the national scale. Such was for instance, the Congress of the Workers of Culture, which met in Lwów in 1936. But the most striking example of spontaneous action along parallel lines was provided by the Spanish Civil War, which broke out in July 1936. The CPP, in accordance with Comintern instruction, supported the Loyalist side, and formulated a slogan which, for all practical purposes, was accepted by the whole Left: "The fight for Spain is a fight for Poland."[20] To this was added the traditional battlecry of Polish national insurrections: "For your freedom and for ours."

The Spanish cause won considerable support among leftist workers of Poland, irrespective of their formal party affiliation. Not only Communist but also socialist organizations and trade-unions recruited volunteers and collected both funds and food for Republican Spain. Several thousand volunteers from Poland, together with many Polish workers living in France, joined the International Brigade which André Marty had organized. Not all of these recruits were Communists or even fellow travelers, but the hard core consisted of Communists and Communist sympathizers. This was reflected in the many Brigade publications, which were replete with Communist phraseology and, as a rule, adhered to the Comintern line.[21] Later a separate Polish battalion was organized and, in 1937, expanded into a brigade named for Jarosław Dąbrowski, a hero of the Paris Commune. This Brigade had separate Jewish and Ukrainian companies.

An official delegation from the Polish trade-unions was sent to Spain in 1937. The delegation consisted of Antoni Zdanowski, who represented the PPS-controlled unions, and Wiktor Alter, who represented the Bund and its labor organizations. The delegates visited Polish detachments in Spain and spoke at several meetings where a CPP delegate, Gustaw Rwal, also made speeches. On May 1, 1937, Rwal presented the Polish battalion with a banner in the name of the CPP.[22] For some time the Polish Brigade was commanded by the Soviet General, Karol Walter-Świerczewski;[23] it fought courageously and suffered great losses. Its leadership harbored grand expectations for the future. In a letter addressed to the Polish unit, General Walter-Świerczewski declared: "Your Brigade is the nucleus of the future army of the people's Poland."

After World War II many former soldiers of the Brigade, the "Spaniards" as they came to be called did return to Poland and played a considerable role in the new regime. Ranks and decorations acquired during the Spanish Civil War were recognized by the government in 1945 and pensions were granted to Brigade veterans, but their hope of becoming the nucleus of a people's army did not come true, and many came to be regarded with suspicion as "too Westernized."

POINT OF NO RETURN

Following the "May error" debate the party became the scene of successive purges. First to be eliminated were the Trotskyites; a series of accusations then ensued against "provocateurs, spies, and diversionists" allegedly "plugged into" the party by the Polish police or intelligence service. By 1935 the assumption was that anyone who did not prove his innocence was a spy or a

Trotskyite. Even the Polish police were charged with propagating Trotskyism "among the arrested anti-Fascists by promising them freedom in exchange for a pledge of joining the Trotskyite groups," or by printing Trotsky's propaganda at government publishing establishments.[24]

There were numerous cases of Polish Communist leaders who were liquidated in Moscow for having worked to destroy the CPP from within. Three of them, however, deserve special attention: Jerzy Czeszejko-Sochacki, Sylwester Wojewódzki, and Tadeusz Żarski.[25] Their cases are worthy of close scrutiny because they reveal the nature of the relationship between the CPP and the Comintern, or, for that matter, between the Soviet Union and any other non-Russian Communist party during the Stalin period.

At the end of 1934 and at the beginning of 1935, the press organs of the Communist International and of the CPP published two illuminating articles which shed an interesting light on the whole program of party penetration by Polish security agents.[26] The articles discussed "the demasking by our party of the provocateurs" — former members of the Piłsudski Military Organization and of the PPS. The first of the accused, Czeszejko-Sochacki, was arrested in Moscow at the end of 1933. Sochacki was not charged with any specific crime, except indirectly. Żarski's testimony allegedly stated that Sochacki, already a member of the CPP, had urged him to join the party. Sochacki was charged with being a "spy, provocateur, and diversionist" in the service of the Polish Intelligence.[27]

Then came Sylwester Wojewódzki, former leader of the Independent Peasant Party who eventually turned Communist. Wojewódzki was allegedly "a special agent" and "a trusted man" of "the Piłsudski elite." The Polish security forces were endeavoring to spy on CPP operations through various contact men, such as Wojewódzki allegedly was. These contacts were to supply the party with information concerning minor police agents, while at the same time they were managing to gain the party's confidence and plant more important agents at higher levels.

In fact, Wojewódzki had been a former officer in Piłsudski's legions but had broken with the army and Piłsudski's group in 1924 and sided with the Communists. By 1925, as leader of the Independent Peasant Party, Wojewódzki seemed to act as a Communist functionary, and in this capacity he followed Comintern instructions as reflected in both the program and the tactics of his party. A police investigation of Wojewódzki resulted after a bomb was planted in his party's press offices. According to the deposition of Mr. Jerzy Luxemburg, the judge who investigated this case, Wojewódzki, far from having contacts with the police, was actually shadowed by them as a suspect and dangerous crypto-Communist agent. A Sejm committee which had been established to investigate Wojewódzki's activity as leader of the Independent Peasant Party also revealed no traces of his contact with police, while there were numerous indications of Wojewódzki's work for the benefit of the CPP.

Since, under Polish law, there was no ground for his detention in connection with the bombing, Wojewódzki was set free and soon afterward he left for Danzig; his party, meanwhile, was dissolved by Polish authorities. In Danzig Wojewódzki immediately got in touch with the permanent agency of the CPP, and from there, full of great expectations for a brilliant career, he went to the USSR and his doom.

The accusations against another "provacateur, spy, and diversionist," Tadeusz Żarski, contain three points. First, Żarski was allegedly entrusted by the already dissolved Polish Military Organization (arbitrarily identified with Counterintelligence) with forming a left wing within the PPS and provoking a split to set up a separate revolutionary, but still nationalistic, party. This new party would, on the one hand, attract those socialists for whom the PPS was not sufficiently leftist and, on the other hand, "intercept" all revolutionary elements which would have otherwise joined the CPP. Second, after having created such a group, Żarski was to engineer a fusion with the CPP, thus introducing the nationalist Trojan horse into the proletarian movement in order to destroy it. We know that there was a Left Opposition in the PPS and that the opposition, in the middle of 1920, joined the CPP, but it had been neither engineered nor led by Żarski. He was not instrumental in effecting the split and did not personally leave the PPS for the CPP until a year later. Thus, if Żarski ever had instructions from Counterintelligence, he did not carry them out. His step seemed to be rather an independent act of a man disenchanted with the "opportunistic" tactics of his mother party. Żarski had also been an officer of Piłsudski's legions, and a member of the secret Polish Military Organization.

The third accusation was that Żarski "gave the chief of the Political Department of the Ministry of the Interior the names of people who had to be arrested, in order to permit Żarski to reach the party's leadership." Strangely enough, Żarski's confession does not mention the names of men who were his police contacts and also carefully omits the names of those arrested at his instruction. Moreover, if such arrests had been carried out over a period of ten years, the matter would have attracted the party's attention much earlier, which was not the case.

Whether or not there were valid reasons for the liquidation of these three men remains unknown. If there were such reasons no sufficiently convincing proofs were ever offered by the CPP or the Comintern.

On the other hand, it is known that insufficient docility on the part of non-Soviet Communists inevitably led to conflict with the Comintern. It was the essence of their tragedy that in their own lands such leaders were considered to be slavish followers of a foreign power, while the Soviet government regarded them with suspicion either as potential rebels or as persons having dangerously deep roots in the old society and traditions. Wojewódzki, Żarski, and Sochacki may be striking examples and sad victims of this double rejection. After having quarrelled with their native society, they turned to the society of their dreams, only to find that their views and ways were equally unacceptable, although for different reasons. Even if it is supposed that there was no real ideological or tactical conflict between these men and Soviet authorities, they nonetheless had to be liquidated because, as former officers of the Polish Intelligence Service and followers of Piłsudski, they could never have been trusted completely to follow the twists and turns of Kremlin policy.[28]

A MYSTERY WRAPPED IN ENIGMA

By liquidating Sochacki, Żarski, and Wojewódzki, the Comintern apparently sought to emphasize the contrast between a group of traitors and the solid, monolithic, "healthy basic mass" of faithful party members. If such was the Comintern's purpose, a decisive blow to this myth was struck during the Great Purge of 1937–38.

The purge affected the CPP more than any other section of the Comintern. Although there is little direct evidence of the motives or methods applied, the results are known.[29] Practically all Polish Communists who were in Soviet territory at that period were either physically liquidated or sent to various concentration camps. Those who happened to be abroad were lured back under one pretext or another.[30] It is not actually known who was shot and who was spared, but during the purge all the CPP's leadership disappeared. According to available evidence the following important political leaders were liquidated: Bronkowski, Krajewski, Unszlicht, Warski, Kostrzewa, Walecki, Leński, Bobiński, Heryng, Ciszewski, and Henrykowski. The fate of the political leaders was also shared by the party intellectuals: Sztande, Jasieński and Wandurski. During 1937 and 1939, twelve members of the Central Committee of the CPP and numerous minor functionaries, altogether several hundred active members of the party, disappeared in one way or another. Leński and Bronkowski were members of the Executive Committee of the Comintern, Walecki and Krajewski of its Control Commission or the supreme tribunal of international communism. Yet the CPP could not claim that during the entire period between World Wars I and II more than two or three dozen members had been executed by Polish authorities for high treason.

By Comintern reckoning the Polish Intelligence had, by this time, managed to win over the entire top strata of the CPP, a success without precedent in the annals of the secret service. Paradoxically enough, most Polish survivors of the purge other than those who were either too insignificant to be purged or who served with the NKVD, owed their salvation to the fact that they were protected from Stalin by the walls of bourgeois prisons. One of the CPP members told a former comrade the following story about the fate of Polish Communists who in 1938 happened to be in their native country behind bars: "In 1938 we were repeatedly transferred from one prison to another. Out of seventeen prisoners, eleven escaped; others, among them myself, quietly remained . . . Where could we have gone to? In Czechoslovakia, we would have fallen into the hands of the Gestapo; in the Soviet Union — we knew all about it although we were in prison — we would have been arrested as 'Polish spies.' By remaining on the spot, we saved our lives." [31]

The Polish party was quietly dissolved sometime in 1938, at the end of the Great Purge. The question of who formally signed the decree dissolving it is, perhaps, not worth puzzling over. Under the conditions then prevailing in Russia such an important decision must certainly have been undertaken by Stalin himself. Moreover the rehabilitation of the CPP in February 1956 makes the matter a problem of purely theoretical significance. Nevertheless, the matter is historically fascinating. The present-day official historian of the Communist movement in Poland, Tadeusz Daniszewski, discussing the problem ten years after the fact, at the peak of the Stalinist period, most probably against his innermost conviction, made the following statement: "In 1938 the situation became still more complicated. The CPP, infiltrated by the provocateurs sent over by Piłsudski, was dissolved by the Executive Committee of the Comintern." Daniszewski continued: "The purpose of the dissolution was to eliminate the provocateurs; to separate them from the healthy basic mass of the party. On this foundation, a new party was to be created, Marxist-Leninist in outlook, purged of Piłsudski's agents, able to perform the enormous task created by the international situation of the moment." [32]

Significantly enough, Daniszewski gave neither the date nor the place where the Comintern decree was published. It is not available either in the *International Press Correspondence* or in the *Communist International*. Nor is it given in the selection of documents concerning the CPP, albeit the volume was published during the "thaw," after the end of the Twentieth Congress of the CPSU, after the rehabilitation of the CPP. Thus, while the fact of dissolution is beyond doubt, the timing and the circumstances still remain obscure. This is, however, one more reason why one should reconsider every bit of existing evidence, as flimsy as it may seem. For instance, at the Eighteenth Congress of the Bolshevik party, which took place in Moscow in March 1939, greetings were sent by the "fraternal comparties" of the following countries: Bulgaria, China, England, France, Spain, United States, Czechoslovakia, Germany, Sweden, Austria, Rumania, Denmark, and Norway. There was no word about the CPP. A "Report on the International Labor Movement" for 1938 devoted the following passage to Poland: "It is characteristic of the increased influence of the labor organizations in Poland that the class trade-unions and the legal political parties, like, for instance, the PPS, and the Bund, scored considerable successes in the local government elections." [33] Here again the conspiracy of silence continues. What can be observed is that in the second half of 1938 Comintern publications cease to mention the CPP, as though it had never existed. From about this time underground CPP publications became increasingly rare and Communist activity in ethnographic Poland more sporadic and chaotic. It seemed as if the dissolution of the Polish party did not affect its Ukrainian and Byelorussian branches, the CPWU and the CPWB.

Soviet documentation of the dissolution of the CPP is also scarce. The only official Soviet pronouncement on the subject of the CPP dissolution is a report by Manuilsky on the Eighteenth Congress of the Bolshevik party. There the following passage is found:

In order to split the Communist movement, the Fascist and the Trotskyite spies attempted to form artificial "factions" and "groups" in some of the Communist parties and stir up a factional struggle . . . [The party that was] most contaminated by hostile elements was the Communist Party of Poland where agents of Polish fascism managed to gain positions of leadership. These scoundrels tried to get the party to support Piłsudski's Fascist coup in May 1926. When this failed they feigned repentance for their "May error," made a show of self-criticism and deceived the Comintern just as Lovestone and the police "factionalists" of the Hungarian and Yugoslav parties had once done. And it was the fault of the Comintern workers that they allowed themselves to be deceived by the class enemy, failed to detect these maneuvers in time, and were late in taking measures against the contamination of the Communist parties by enemy elements . . . The Communist parties . . . have investigated their leading workers and removed those whose political honesty was questionable. They have dissolved illegal organizations which were particularly contaminated, and have begun to form new ones in their place . . .[34]

Thus, if Manuilsky is to be believed, the CPP was penetrated to the core by hostile, subversive elements. It then overcame its paralysis, dissolved itself, and began to form a new and sounder organization, thus putting to shame "the Comintern workers" who "failed to detect" the plague and "were late in taking measures against the contamination." This pronouncement, unique in the annals of the Comintern, is, moreover, full of contradictions. How could the very party which had been most infiltrated by hostile elements reach such a courageous and self-effacing decision? There is no scrap of evidence, direct or indirect, to support the allegation that the CPP dissolved itself. Such a step would have been impossible in view of the centralized structure of the Comintern, in which each national party was merely one section of the hierarchy.

The reasons for dissolution which were enumerated by Manuilsky and repeated uncritically during the Stalinist era by numerous other writers on the subject are threefold in nature: first, disintegration of the party; second, infiltration of the party by provocateurs and spies; third, contamination of the party by Trotskyite influences. The first reason — disintegration — is contradicted by all available data, which seem to indicate that on the eve of dissolution the party was expanding numerically and was less rent by factional dissension than at any time since 1924. In addition to expanded party membership there was Communist infiltration of non-Communist and "fellow-traveling" organizations, the exact extent of which would be difficult to gauge, but which was nonetheless considerable.

As for the second reason — penetration by "provocateurs and spies" — existing documentary evidence and testimony of those familiar with the matter all strongly indicate that the Polish police had not penetrated the inner core of CPP leadership and had no influence on its policy. According to the testimony of the already mentioned former prosecuting judge in important cases of this sort and one Jerzy Luxemburg, who obviously could have no reason to minimize the efficacy of his work, there were countless cases of minor agents having been planted, but only at lower levels. Such penetration as there was decreased after the early thirties; the party, on the one hand, went deeper underground, and at the same time managed to extend its influence not only in cities but also in the countryside, and was able to find shelter in numerous outwardly non-Communist bodies.

The validity of the third reason given by Manuilsky for the dissolution — contamination with "Trotskyism" — is more difficult to judge. For one thing, "Trotskyism" was made to cover a multitude of sins. However, the disintegration of the avowed Trotskyite opposition after 1935–36, the lack of trials for members of this faction, and the paucity of Trotskyite publications all seem to indicate that this form of heresy had ceased to be an actual danger to the party's unity or policy. How much latent sympathy for the exiled leaders still lingered among the rank and file is hard to ascertain. It would be reasonable to suppose that much sympathy did persist here and there and Stalin, bent as he was on destroying all men suspected of harboring dissident thoughts, could never pardon the CPP for having sided with Trotsky in 1924.

It is obvious, therefore, that all three reasons given by Manuilsky for the dissolution of the CPP largely contradict the available evidence and are not sufficient to justify so radical a step. Even now, after the rehabilitation of the CPP, after the official rejection of the charges against the party as forged, we are still puzzled by the sudden suppression of an entire section of the Comintern and the physical liquidation of its whole leadership. The statement that "The evidence for [the dissolution of the CPP] had been faked by a gang of saboteurs and provocateurs whose real role was only brought to light after Beria was unmasked . . . ," does not explain *why* the party was actually dissolved.[35] Neither were we told who were those "saboteurs and provocateurs."

What were then the real motives behind Stalin's move? Here again only speculation is possible. It appears that the possibility of revolution in Poland had become fainter than ever by 1937, when the country emerged from the depression. Piłsudski's successors had consolidated their hold on the country and a period of considerable economic progress had ensued. Moreover, it must be remembered that the CPP had never been a factor of great importance in Comintern calculations, except as a bridge, or a "transmission belt" to

Germany. With Hitler's triumph the Soviet hopes for a German upheaval had evaporated. Consequently, there was no longer any apparent reason for maintaining a shaky and costly bridge that, according to Stalin's estimate, now led nowhere. At the time of the CPP dissolution Stalin had apparently decided to reshape his strategy completely and to build his own diplomatic and military bridge to the Third Reich.

Stalin was probably convinced that in the event of another "revolutionary situation" arising in Poland, the Red Army would do a better job than the CPP. He realized that any deal with Hitler would probably provoke opposition within CPP ranks, since the party, with its large Jewish membership on the one hand, and with its growing undercurrent of Polish nationalism on the other, could hardly accept such a step without some sort of protest. Consequently, the purge of the CPP's entire top strata and, finally, the complete dissolution of the party amounted to two things: first, the discarding of what Stalin must have regarded as an ineffective and unreliable instrument of policy, and second, the waging of preventive war against a potential opposition. Thus, it may be said that the CPP, one of the last major victims of the great purges, became one of the first victims of the Stalin-Hitler pact.

Part III

The POLISH
WORKERS' PARTY

9

The UNION of POLISH PATRIOTS and the POLISH WORKERS' PARTY

The whirlwind tempo of events in August and September of 1939 surprised the scattered groups of former members of the CPP no less than other citizens of Poland. Some bewildered Polish Communists actually volunteered to defend their capitalistic motherland against Germany, then an ally of the Soviet Union. But these, however, were exceptional cases.

Soviet policy during this crucial period of 1939 to 1941 was to be of paramount importance later in shaping the attitude of the Polish people toward the Communist Party. As a result of the Soviet-German pact of August 23, 1939, and the accompanying secret protocols of September 28, 1939, Poland was divided into two parts. Originally, the secret protocols had provided that the Vistula river be the line dividing Poland into "zones of interest." Warsaw was to be on the German side of the river, with Warsaw's suburb, Praga, on the Soviet side. During the German invasion the protocols were redrawn and Poland was divided roughly along the lines of the Second Partition (1793). From the very beginning there was little doubt about the ultimate aims of both powers; this was to be partition, pure and simple. The western provinces of the Polish Republic were incorporated into Germany and many Poles were removed from this area to make room for Germans from the Reich and Baltic countries. Central Poland was organized into a so-called *General Gouvernement*, with Cracow as its capital. The eastern provinces were incorporated into the Soviet Union.

The anti-Fascist and "popular front" verbiage of Soviet propaganda was scrapped overnight, and the full solidarity of Moscow and Berlin was proclaimed. A Soviet note to the Polish ambassador in Moscow, dated September 17, 1939, declared that "the Polish state and its government have, in fact, ceased to exist." [1] Even before the actual capitulation of Poland's capital, V. M. Molotov, the Soviet

Commissar for Foreign Affairs and chairman of the Council of the
People's Commissars, sent a message to the German ambassador
in Moscow: "I have received your communication regarding the
entry of German troops into Warsaw. Please convey my congratulations and greetings to the German Reich government." [2] In a speech
delivered on October 31, 1939, at the Extraordinary Fifth Session of
the Supreme Soviet of the USSR, Molotov said: ". . . one swift blow
to Poland, first by the German and then by the Red Army, and
nothing was left of this ugly offspring of the Versailles Treaty . . ." [3]

It is no wonder, therefore, that the endemic mistrust of Russia was
bolstered by Soviet participation in 1939 in the destruction of the
Polish state. Whatever temporary popularity the CPP had managed
to gather during the period 1935–1938 now vanished overnight.
Moreover, the Soviet regime in Eastern Poland was a tragic experience for the Polish population there. "The misery and destruction caused by the Soviet invasion of 1939 made the word Communist loathed," an anonymous Polish woman noted in her memoirs. [4]

Immediately after the end of hostilities many surviving leaders of
the former Communist Party of Poland moved from the German-
occupied part of the country and settled in the "Soviet zone of
interest." In order to hold together and utilize the remnants of party
membership and fellow travelers, some minor Communist associations were organized at this time. A literary and political monthly,
"New Horizons," was started in Lwów. The first issue appeared in
January 1941, under the editorship of two women, Wanda Wasilewska and Helen Usiyevich. [5] The editors received support from other
Communist writers, such as Jerzy Putrament, Stefan Jędrychowski,
Roman Werfel, Feliks Kon, Jerzy Borejsza, and Alfred Lampe.
Several non-Communist writers who held radical views gave somewhat reluctant collaboration to the paper, being fearful of persecution by Soviet authorities. Another group of Polish Communists,
headed by Stefan Jędrychowski, was active in Wilno and in the region ceded by the USSR to Lithuania.

Such were the activities of those few members of the defunct CPP
who happened to be considered potentially useful to the Soviet
cause. Others were less fortunate. Communists of the C.P. of Western
Ukraine and the C.P. of Western Byelorussia, were so weak and so
tainted by Western orientation that the Bolsheviks had neither the
intention nor even the opportunity of utilizing them as instruments of
Soviet rule. Most of the real or alleged followers of Trotsky who
remained were shot. Large-scale deportations were carried out in
1940; these had a twofold purpose — to liquidate politically active

non-Communist elements, and to make a clean sweep of dissidents before the planned election.[6]

The Soviet commander of the occupation forces arranged for elections to be held on October 22, 1939, in order to select a Supreme Soviet and local soviet bodies. In accordance with the customary Soviet practice, the electorate had no voice in the nominations of the candidates, who came mostly from the Soviet Union and were complete strangers to the voters. A vote was permitted only for the one candidate whose name appeared on the ballot, with no chance of proposing other candidates.[7] Deputies elected to the Supreme Soviet were formed into two "National Assemblies": one "Western Ukrainian" and another "Western Byelorussian." Each of these, by a show of hands, passed resolutions providing for the "admission" of "Western Ukraine" and "Western Byelorussia" into the Soviet Union,[8] and for the confiscation of big estates and nationalization of banks and industries. Shortly after the election deportations started anew, affecting a still larger strata of the population, and an anti-religious campaign was unleashed. Religion was banned from the schools and numerous churches, convents, seminaries, both Catholic and Orthodox, as well as synagogues, were closed.

The overall Soviet policy in regard to Poland and the ill treatment of both Polish Communists and the rest of the population in Poland's eastern provinces would all seem to indicate that, at this period, Moscow had no plans for the creation of a satellite government in Poland. Instead, the Kremlin's program between September 1939 and June 1941 called for extermination of all politically conscious elements, whether Polish or Jewish, Ukrainian, or Byelorussian. In addition, the eastern Polish territory which Russia had already annexed was to be incorporated in the Soviet Union. As far as the rest of Poland was concerned, Moscow resolved to leave it to the tender mercies of Hitler. Such an attitude was, of course, bound to embitter the overwhelming majority of Poles, including many genuine Communists. Both the German policy of extermination, carried out in the *General Gouvernement,* and the large scale deportations by the Soviets, as well as the Katyń massacre perpetrated by the NKVD, would indeed seem to indicate that liquidation of the politically conscious in Poland was a target for both occupying powers.

THE GERMAN OCCUPATION AND THE RUSSO-GERMAN WAR

The German-occupied part of Poland had been torn into two parts: the western provinces and the so-called General Gouvernement. The western provinces were directly incorporated into the

Reich; all available resources in this area were to be expanded for the benefit of a greater Germany. The native population was to be either Germanized or deported; Jews and highly educated Poles were to be exterminated or transferred to the General Gouvernement. The provinces incorporated into Germany were well off economically, but the Gouvernement was to be exploited solely for the benefit of the master race. All raw materials and industrial equipment useful to the Germans were to be removed to the Reich. Only such enterprises were to be left as were "absolutely necessary for the mere maintenance of the naked existence of the population." This policy was never fully executed. In the later years of the war it was found convenient to use industrial plants inside the Gouvernement because this territory was more sheltered from Western bombers. But ultimately, Poland was to be treated as an agricultural colony, and the Poles as slaves of the Greater German Reich. Soon blind, indiscriminate terror became the chief instrument of German rule in the Gouvernement. The concentration camps of Oświęcim (Auschwitz), Treblinka, and Majdanek became centers for the murder of the Jewish population not only of Poland, but of the whole of Europe. The Polish intellectual elite was treated as cruelly as were the Jews. The senseless brutality of German occupation authorities in Poland could be compared only with the later horrors of Nazi rule in the Ukraine and Byelorussia. These were the policies of genocide.

This rule of terror was bound to produce an equally uncompromising resistance, and already, toward the end of September 1939, a clandestine resistance movement had been organized by the major Polish political parties. There was the Polish Socialist Party,[9] the Polish Peasant Party, the Christian Labor Party, and the National Party. There were also some smaller groups in opposition, but as long as Soviet-German collaboration lasted, there was no Communist underground party challenging the Germans.[10]

In 1941 the Union of Armed Resistance emerged as the strongest of all the secret military formations. The next year the Union was renamed *Armia Krajowa* (A.K.). This was awkwardly translated into English as the Home Army. The A.K. tried, on the whole rather successfully, to unify the clandestine military forces of the various political parties into one single organization. Both the extreme rightist National Armed Forces (N.S.Z.) and the Communist squads took exception to this action.[11] By the winter of 1940–41, when Nazi-Soviet relations had worsened somewhat, some military preparations were made on the part of small Communist groups which were active in the Gouvernement territory. These Communists, however, refrained from any guerilla or sabotage activity until well after the outbreak of the Soviet-German war.

The German attack on the Soviet Union caused a dramatic reversal in attitude. A "united war effort" was accepted by Polish Communists without much hesitation. Nevertheless, it was some time before they could adapt themselves to this about face. In many respects, the period from 1941 to 1945 marked a return to the old united front policy. There were, however, important variations now. The Comintern had suspended the class struggle; charges of imperialism, leveled against the Western Powers during all previous strategic phases, were dropped. The Communists and Soviet Russia now shared with the Allied nations a desire to defeat the Axis. Military effectiveness in the struggle against the Axis powers became paramount.

In order to appease the Western Allies and to utilize resources at the disposal of the Polish government in exile, the Soviet Union sought a *rapprochement* with the Poles. Diplomatic relations between the Soviet government and the Polish government were resumed, and on July 30, 1941, a Polish-Soviet agreement was concluded in London. In this agreement the Soviet government declared that the "Soviet-German treaties of 1939 concerning territorial changes in Poland have lost validity." Moreover, the Soviets consented to the formation, on Soviet soil, of a "Polish army under a commander appointed by the Polish government in accord with the Soviet government." The agreement also provided for the release of those Polish prisoners of war who had been taken by the Red Army in September 1939. All Polish citizens who had been deported to the USSR from Eastern Poland during the two-year period of Soviet occupation were now to be released, and the Polish army to be formed in Russia was to be composed of these ex-prisoners.

With the outbreak of the Russo-German war and the signature of the Polish-Russian pact, the Poles somewhat altered their attitude toward the Soviet Union. Until the signing of the pact, Russia had been regarded as an enemy whose policies could hardly be distinguished from those of Hitler. Henceforward, Russia would be considered an "ally of our allies."

FORMATION OF THE UNION OF POLISH PATRIOTS AND
THE POLISH WORKERS' PARTY

While pursuing a policy of appeasement toward the Western Allies and outwardly restoring good relations with non-Communist Poland, Stalin began to forge the instruments of his future Polish policy. Negotiations with General Sikorski were still in progress in Moscow at the end of 1941 when a conference of Polish pro-Soviet politicians, led by Wanda Wasilewska, was called in Saratov on December 1, 1941. The date of the conference was by no means an accident; it was specifically chosen so as to put pressure on General Sikorski and show him that his cooperation was not essential. Should he resist Russia's demands, Moscow could solve all difficulties by making a deal with its own men. There is reason to believe that the conference in Saratov later formed the nucleus of the so-called Union of Polish Patriots. Among the most influential members of this latter group were Wanda Wasilewska, Stanisław Skrzeszewski, Stanisław Radkiewicz, Jakub Berman, and Stefan Jędrychowski. In May 1942, the fortnightly "New Horizons" resumed publication in Kuybyshev, after a temporary suspension. A radio station was established in Soviet territory which broadcast news and comment in Polish. The station soon became the spokesman of the Union and was given the name "Kościuszko." [12] The broadcasts mixed extreme patriotism with social radicalism of a democratic cast.

Simultaneously, still another group was forming in the German-occupied part of Poland. In November 1941, five months after the outbreak of the Soviet-German war, an organization called the Union of Friends of the USSR was established in Warsaw. The Union soon initiated a publication, "Sickle and Hammer," and after merger with another group called Association of the Struggle for Liberation, the Polish Workers' Party (*Polska Partia Robotnicza*), or PPR was created in January 1942. The Polish Workers' Party quickly established its own armed detachments, the People's Guard. The moment chosen for this rebirth of a regular Communist Party in Poland co-incided with the Red Army's recovery from defeat. The PPR was founded on the initiative of the old members of the C.P. of Poland, like Marceli Nowotko and Paweł Finder. [13] Both were dropped by parachute by the Soviets to perform the task. The first of the PPR's proclamations was issued in January 1942, and the first fighting order for the People's Guard came on May 5, 1942. An announcement of the PPR's Central Committee, with the same date, stated: "The PPR is no section of the Communist International or any other international organization. Nevertheless, the PPR bases itself on the Marxist-Leninist doctrine which teaches that national liberation is possible only when it is timed with social liberation." [14]

The reason for omitting the name "Communist Party" was probably tactical: Russia's two-year occupation of Eastern Poland and reports on the Soviet regime from hundreds of thousands of deportees and prisoners had made communism less popular than ever. Consequently, the Polish Communists preferred to act under the name "Polish Workers' Party." Moreover, the new party deliberately avoided Communist phraseology and tended to blur its class character by a broad use of such terms as "national front" and "national unity." [15]

Two clandestine papers contained the bulk of PPR propaganda. "Tribune of Liberty" was destined mostly for urban dwellers; "Peasant Tribune" was circulated primarily among the peasants. Both of these, as well as numerous leaflets and proclamations, had a patriotic flavor. The PPR decried the alleged passivity of those forces which owed allegiance to the Polish government in London and made consistent efforts to persuade the Poles that the new party was the main center of anti-German resistance. During the first phase of its activity, and until the end of 1942, love for the Soviet Union and for its leaders was not particularly evident. However, the importance of developing "the Polish-Soviet brotherhood" was often emphasized; practically no PPR article or proclamation failed to stress the urgent necessity of waging an unrelenting struggle against Germany and of helping the Soviet Union in its life and death fight.[16]

Emphasis in the PPR program was on friendship with the Soviet Union, not as the fatherland of the world proletariat, but as the big Slav brother, the liberator and protector of small nations now struggling against the German yoke. The PPR acquiesced in the loss of prewar Poland's eastern provinces, and advocated instead the reconquest of the once Polish western lands, not included in the Polish Republic by the terms of the Versailles Treaty. Initially the PPR focused its attention on Warsaw and its working-class population, and gradually extended its party organization to the provinces.

SOVIET DIVERSION IN POLAND

The more deeply German troops penetrated eastward, the more violent grew Soviet propaganda exhorting the Poles to revolt against their Nazi oppressors. Leaders of the Polish underground movement tried to counteract these appeals, warning that any large-scale uprising ought to be prepared and ordered by the legitimate Polish government and closely coordinated with activities of the Allied armies.[17] Communist propaganda systematically condemned this uncooperative attitude, charging that it assumed the existence of two "mortal enemies" — Soviet Russia and Nazi Germany — who would eventually destroy each other.[18]

During the first phase of war with Germany, Soviet armies retreating from the east left behind many scattered units which formed numerous pockets. For the most part these survivors took refuge in the vast wooded areas of Polish territory. By the beginning of 1942, when the Soviet high command had recovered from the first shock of attack, the organization of Red partisan groups behind German lines began; even earlier both well-equipped paratroops and political agents were dropped in Eastern Poland.[19]

Thus, new reinforcements were added to the small armed PPR squads, although the People's Guard confined its operations to the solidly Polish area west of the Bug River and the Ribbentrop-Molotov line, and only infrequently dared to cross into territory east of this point, which was regarded as already belonging to the Soviet Union. Soviet parachutists, however, were active throughout Poland. Until 1943 the People's Guard also refrained from taking action against other Polish clandestine units. In fact, there were several attempts made to come to an understanding with the commander of the Polish Home Army, General Rowecki (Grot). The latter demanded, however, that the PPR publicly announce its independence from the Comintern, its recognition of the former Polish Soviet frontier of 1938, and its unreserved submission to the Polish government in London.[20]

General Rowecki attempted to clarify the status of Soviet partisans on Polish soil. A Polish army was then being formed in Russia under the command of General Anders. Politically this army was subordinate to the Polish government in London; operationally, however, it was under the Soviet high command. General Rowecki maintained that he had the right to demand the same sort of allegiance from Soviet partisan forces operating in Poland. The Polish Home Army considered itself host on its own soil; Soviet units were to be treated as guests and allies.[21] This was in accordance with a Polish-Soviet agreement signed by General Sikorski on December 1, 1941, during his visit to Moscow.[22]

Activities of the Home Army were in most cases carefully planned in order to sabotage German war efforts or to retaliate against the most offensive Nazi leaders. Communist methods were quite different. Typical incidents included the bombing of a German column as it marched across Warsaw, planting a bomb in a fashionable cafe patronized by German officers, or a hand grenade thrown through an open window into a German field hospital in Warsaw. When such incidents occurred the Germans arrested and shot more than a hundred Polish hostages, announcing their action over loudspeakers. Public opinion placed responsibility for these anonymous acts at the

door of the Home Army, thereby undermining the moral authority
of the Home Army's leadership, for it was obvious that the casual
death or injury of a handful of Germans did not compensate for the
execution of a hundred or more Poles.[23]

Annex No. VII to the report of the commander of the Home Army,
dated July 1, 1942, characterized Communist activities in Poland
during this period. The report emphasized the coordination between
PPR and Soviet partisan activities and stated that the partisans were
less preoccupied with fighting the Germans than with spreading Communist propaganda and preparing the way for the future assumption
of power by the PPR. The looting of prosperous farms by the partisans, as well as German reprisals for reckless acts of terror against
local administrations, only deepened the misery of the population
and spread anarchy.[24]

But the Communist underground movement, although incompara-
bly weaker than the Home Army, had two great advantages: first,
it enjoyed shorter lines of communications with its base of supply,
and second, it was consistently supported by the one nation vitally
interested in future control of Poland. The Western Allies tended to
regard the Home Army merely as a temporary instrument of anti-
German diversion.

DETERIORATING POLISH-SOVIET RELATIONS

The increasing military success of the Red Army and the mounting
German terror both contributed to a step-up in the hitherto meager
PPR activity throughout Poland. There was an accompanying shift
in propaganda, for with the worsening of relations between Moscow
and the Polish government in London, which accompanied the growing self-confidence of the Soviet government, relations between the
two resistance movements also grew more embittered.[25] Both groups
claimed credit for acts of sabotage and reprisal against the Germans.
The PPR armed squads, or People's Guard, had been organized by
a Soviet officer who was dropped by parachute near Warsaw at the
end of 1941, with orders to direct intelligence and diversionary activities behind German lines. PPR armed detachments were supplied
with weapons and equipment similarly dropped by parachute from
Soviet planes.[26]

By the winter of 1942–43, relations between the Polish government in London and the Soviet government had deteriorated further.
Russia insisted on the validity of a plebiscite held in November 1939,
in Poland's eastern provinces, and refused to recognize as Polish citizens those Ukrainians, Byelorussians, and Jews who had been de-

ported to the Soviet Union between 1939 and 1941. Moreover, the Soviet government accused Polish diplomatic and consular authorities in Russia of spying on behalf of the Western Powers. The Polish army of General Anders was evacuated from Russia to Persia and in May 1943, following that evacuation, Soviet authorities began the formation of the first Polish detachments within the framework of the Red Army itself. This new Polish army, although still overwhelmingly non-Communist as far as its rank and file was concerned, was very carefully officered. Many top command posts were given to Soviet officers, while most political jobs went to Polish Communits. On March 1, 1943, the Union of Polish Patriots was officially formed in Moscow, under the leadership of Wanda Wasilewska. On the same day as its founding the Union began publishing a weekly under the name of "Free Poland."

As these events were unfolding in Russia, in Poland the PPR increasingly stressed the necessity for forming a "broad national front" of all anti-Fascist parties. A makeshift program was formulated which did not differ radically from that of the non-Communist groups; the main variance was an emphasis on outright confiscation of nationalized industries and land.[27] The PPR now more frequently voiced sentiments hostile to the Polish underground movement, to the Polish government in London, and to the Peasants' and Christian Labor parties for their refusal to collaborate within the proposed "national front." The party press denied accusations that it was dependent upon Russia, and in turn violently attacked the Polish government in exile and the Home Army, accusing them of following a policy of "waiting with arms at ease." The Soviet wireless from the Kościuszko station and the Union of Polish Patriots began a campaign of slander in Polish against "the London Poles" and against the underground leaders, condemning them for their view that Germany and Russia were equally dangerous enemies of Poland.

In April 1943, the German revelation of the Katyń massacre, and Moscow's refusal to submit the matter to an impartial international body for investigation, caused the rupture of diplomatic relations between the Polish government in London and the USSR.[28] The Polish embassy, then in Kuybyshev, and all Polish consular and welfare agencies were asked to leave the Soviet Union within a short time. The Union of Polish Patriots, with Soviet backing, seized the stocks of food, clothing, and medical supplies belonging to the Polish embassy. These provisions were used by the Union to win favor among the starved Polish deportees who had been released from camps and prisons on the basis of an agreement made in July 1941. Simultaneously, a policy of friendship toward the Poles as a nation was stressed at every step by the organs of Soviet propaganda. In 1943, Stalin asserted that the USSR desired "to see a strong and independent Poland after the defeat of Hitler's Germany," a Poland committed to good neighborly relations and to a postwar alliance with the Soviet Union, should the Polish people so desire.[29] On May 8, 1943, Moscow announced that a Polish Kościuszko division, under General Zygmunt Berling, would join the Red Army.[30]

On June 9 and 10, 1943, the Patriots arranged a congress in Moscow in which, the Soviet radio stated, "the Polish workers, peasants, and guerillas were taking part"; the object of the congress, the broadcast stated further, "was to mark the unity of the Poles with the Soviet Union and to strengthen relations between the two nations." The congress acclaimed the program which had already been presented in "Free Poland," and demanded that after the war Poland should receive new territories in the west, as compensation for the eastern provinces to be ceded to the USSR.

In its platform, the congress reiterated that the major objective of the Union of Polish Patriots was "everlasting friendship between the Polish people and the USSR." The congress dispatched a thanksgiving telegram to Stalin who, "in spite of obstacles and the efforts of enemies, together with the Soviet government, was maintaining friendly relations with those fighting for the freedom of the Polish people . . ." The congress further expressed its gratitude to Marshal Stalin for permitting the formation of a Polish Kościuszko division, and gave its pledge that the "Poles in the Soviet Union would carry out their duty as soldiers, fighting alongside the heroic Red Army against the German invader." The congress also affirmed that it would not allow "any trouble to be created or any wedge to be driven between the Polish people and the Soviet Union." In his reply Stalin declared that "the Soviet Union would do everything . . . to strengthen the Polish-Soviet friendship, and to aid with all the means within its power the rebuilding of a strong and independent Poland." The program of the Patriots provided for a "Democratic People's Republic" having a unicameral parliament. Land was to be divided among peasants without compensation to former owners, and basic freedom was to be guaranteed to all citizens. "Our eastern frontier must be a bridge and not an obstacle between Poland and her eastern neighbors," declared the congress platform, which at the same time demanded the return of East Prussia, Silesia, and "the mouth of Vistula" to Poland. There was no mention of nationalization of industry or collectivization of agriculture.[31]

Thus, by the middle of 1943, the Soviet Union managed to forge two outwardly independent, but actually closely coordinated instruments of its policy toward Poland: the Union of Polish Patriots and the Polish Workers' Party.

Russia's refusal to submit to an investigation of the Katyń massacre by the International Red Cross caused consternation and embarrassment in Communist circles in Poland.[32] The evidence produced by the Germans from the very beginning of the investigation was so overwhelming that Poles could have no difficulty whatever in determining the perpetrator of the crime. The consternation of the PPR was, initially, so great that the party press took no official stand on the matter; the Central Committee also failed to publish any explanation. At secret PPR meetings and conferences, however, the Communists openly avowed that "Polish reactionaries" had been liquidated. They also initiated a "whispering campaign" in Warsaw to the effect that a dangerous mutiny had broken out in one of the war prisoners' camps and that its ringleaders had to be executed.[33] After several days of official silence an oral party instruction ordered local representatives to explain the massacre as a fully justified "liquidation of the Polish reactionaries." [34] Then, when an official Soviet communiqué charged the Germans with the crime, the party reversed itself and accepted the Soviet explanation.

The rupture of diplomatic relations between Moscow and the Polish government gave full scope to Communist propaganda both in Poland and in Russia: henceforth the legitimate character of the Polish government and its right to represent the Polish people were denied, for it had allegedly betrayed Poland by conspiring with Hitler and by helping the Western Allies to prolong the war, thus making Polish liberation impossible.[35]

Russia's strategic position had continued to improve after the spring of 1943 and Soviet plans for Poland entered a new phase. While General Berling's army was being created in Russia, Polish Communists in German-occupied Poland formed the nucleus of still another army, and renewed attempts were made to secure cooperation from non-Communist parties of the Left and Center.[36]

INTERNAL CRISIS WITHIN THE PPR

PPR efforts to be accepted as a legitimate Polish political party met with immense difficulties, both internal and external in nature. Moreover, during 1943 the PPR experienced a severe inner crisis because of a conflict which arose between the party leadership, composed almost exclusively of former Polish Communists, and the newly recruited members who apparently were insufficiently steeped in "proletarian internationalism," and inclined toward a national brand of Bolshevism. The former CPP members, survivors of the great purges, formed a conspiratorial hard core, imbued with the principle of blind obedience toward the Kremlin. They wanted to maintain their exclusive influence on the new party, and insisted on indoctrinating their younger comrades with Stalinist discipline. Reports from the Intelligence Service of the Polish underground movement indicate that considerable friction arose during party debates concerning the acceptability of the Ribbentrop-Molotov line as a future eastern boundary of Poland. A plan for an immediate revolt in Poland solely to relieve German pressure on the Soviet front was also criticized by the PPR rank and file as an inevitable failure which would be bound to bleed Poland white. The old Communist nucleus, however, finally won the struggle and the Soviet policy was officially accepted.[37]

By this time German terrorism was dealing heavy blows to all secret groups, including the Communists. The party was weakened considerably by the brutal liquidation of the German-established Jewish ghetto in Warsaw. The Gestapo seized the PPR's chief press organ, "Liberty Tribune," and arrested many leading party members. To some extent these arrests might have reflected the struggle for power which went on among the leadership of the PPR. The first secretary-general of the Workers' Party, Marceli Nowotko, was assassinated in Warsaw, in November 1942, under mysterious circumstances. In autumn of 1943 Pawel Finder, the second secretary-general of the PPR, and Małgorzata Fornalska, a member of the Central Committee, were captured by the Gestapo, also under circumstances which were never sufficiently clarified.

In order to bolster the shaken morale of the PPR, some additional members of the defunct Polish Communist Party, including Bolesław Bierut, were sent from Russia to reorganize the PPR as a more militant organization. Bierut acted with vigor and efficiency. On July 1, 1943, the armed detachments of the PPR, until now known as the People's Guard, were reorganized; from this point on each member of the PPR had to join the People's Guard and in one way or another participate in its activities. Military ranks and a strict discipline were enforced. At the same time the armed squads were instructed to expand their propaganda by distributing pamphlets and leaflets among the population, as well as by increasing their personal contacts.[38]

Moreover, a special organization, called the Association of the

Struggle of the Youth, was established in 1943 and soon issued its own publication. At approximately the same time the PPR organized its intelligence units, staffed largely by NKVD people who had been dropped by parachute. In addition to collecting military information for the benefit of Soviet forces, these intelligence teams also gathered data on the organization and leading personalities of the various political parties in Poland. PPR members were strictly supervised by this group, and those members who were considered unreliable were liquidated. The dangerous anti-Communist leaders were also closely watched.[39]

During this period the PPR made further concrete preparations for taking over Poland. These preparations went in three directions. First, they aimed at inculcating public opinion with the idea that the PPR was a legitimate, Polish, patriotic party, often extreme in its social radicalism, but independent of Moscow. Second, the PPR wanted to impress the populace with the idea that the party and the People's Guard were the most militant anti-German bodies. And finally, the PPR wished to establish the fact that it represented the broad mass of Polish people and was their sole protector against the terror and exploitation of the Germans, and the only guarantee of a better future for Poland.

CREATION OF THE NATIONAL COUNCIL OF POLAND (KRN)

Non-Communist parties were taking a parallel course of action; they tightened their ranks and formulated their plans more precisely. On August 15, 1943, a formal statement signed by the four major political parties emphasized that government authorities of the future "shall be free of those elements responsible for the mistakes of the former regime, and also free from any totalitarian leanings." The statement urged that immediate steps be taken after liberation to achieve land reform "in order to create such divisions of arable land as shall insure the largest possible number of efficient strong one-family farms, which would guarantee an adequate supply of food for the whole nation . . ." The future government should also direct those key industrial establishments which were administered by the Germans during the occupation, and labor must be recognized as "the greatest social value, and the foundation of the economic development and welfare of the country."

A number of smaller, leftist non-Communist groups were dissatisfied with this policy of the four large political parties and, in October 1943, established what they called "centralization of the Socialist,

Democratic, and Syndicalist parties," the Supreme People's Committee (NKL).[40] This was a coalition of non-Communist leftist forces opposed both to the PPR and to the Polish government in London. The strongest of the groups was the left wing of the PPS, known first as the Organization of the Polish Socialists, and then, after March 1943, as the Workers' Polish Socialist Party (RPPS).[41] Early in 1944 the NKL merged with still other leftist anti-Communist groups and then formed its own armed detachments.

All these developments took place in spite of the fact that the shadow of the Red Army already loomed on the eastern horizon. The specter of forthcoming Soviet occupation stimulated PPR activities. In reply to the moves of its opponents, the party, thus far a small group, conceived the idea of creating the semblance of a representative body. This was done secretly in Warsaw on the night of December 31, 1943, a few days before the Red Army crossed the prewar Polish-Soviet frontier at Volhynia, on January 4, 1944. The timing was not accidental. The Red Army's re-entry into Poland was bound to bring up the issue of political power; the PPR, therefore, providently decided to be ready with an "underground parliament" of its own in order to endorse its claim to control of Poland. Consequently, the National Council of Poland [42] emerged, known as KRN (*Krajowa Rada Narodowa*) in Poland. The new body was an obvious rival of the two representative bodies connected with the Polish government in London.

Establishment of the National Council had been preceded by prolonged negotiations with the Peasant Party[43] and the NKL. Even under the pressure of impending occupation by the Red Army, these two political groups refused to join the National Council.[44] The PPR's failure to attract any other group of importance confirmed the narrow popular base of the party. In fact, most signatories to the manifesto of the council were artificially created for this special purpose.[45] Various fictitious names were printed under the manifesto in order to enhance its prestige and to camouflage the fact that, in reality, only the PPR, its front organizations, and a few small splinter groups stood behind the proclamation. It seems that the establishment of the National Council of Poland was a retort to the pending creation of the Council of National Unity sponsored by the Polish government in London. All negotiations aiming at a "broad democratic front," conducted by Gomułka, who had many personal ties with the non-Communist groups, failed.[46]

In its manifesto the National Council declared itself to be "the only democratic representation of the Polish nation and its sole spokesman." The council pledged itself to extensive social reforms and favored replacement of the Constitution of 1935 with the Constitution of 1921.[47] Close collaboration with the USSR was pledged, and the council expressed its willingness to cede Poland's eastern provinces to the Soviet Ukrainian and Byelorussian Republics. In a communiqué of February 5, 1944, the council accepted a Soviet suggestion that the Polish-Soviet frontier should run along the so-called Curzon line, or the armistice line that had been suggested by Great Britain in 1920, with some slight modifications in Poland's favor.

The function of the National Council was primarily that of a legislative body, acting until such time as democratic parliamentary elections could be held. According to the organic statute of the council, political organizations could send delegates to the council only *after* an understanding had been reached between their supreme authorities and those of the council. In other words, it was essential for other parties who desired to nominate representatives to the council to obtain the consent of the Polish Workers' Party. The number of delegates which various organizations could nominate to the council was decided by the Presidium of the National Council, also controlled by the PPR. After liberation the council was to establish a provisional government of Poland. The National Council of Poland was supposed to be the assembly of a whole network of lesser groups, variously called the National Committees, the National Struggle Committees, the National Councils, and the Factory Councils. In reality it was the other way around: initiative advanced from the top to the bottom, and not from the bottom to the top. Soon after its formation, the National Council of Poland feverishly proceeded to organize the very bodies it was supposed to represent. The first local national councils were established by the PPR in Lublin (February 18, 1944) and in Warsaw (February 25, 1944), some six to seven weeks after the creation of the higher council.

According to communiqués published by the PPR, the local national councils were composed not only of delegates from the PPR and the People's Guard, but also of non-specified representatives of the Peasant Party and the Peasant Battalions, the Association of Polish Teachers, the trade-unions, and the Association of White Collar Workers. The PPR also tried to organize factory councils but since so many clandestine cells had already been established by two rival leftist groups, the PPR determined to infiltrate these organizations, with the intention of controlling them eventually.[48] Peasants' councils were organized in villages, and a letter, allegedly from the Archbishop of Cracow, Adam Sapieha, was distributed, appealing for a welcome to Soviet troops entering Poland.[49]

The manifesto of the National Council of Poland declared the council to be the supreme legislative body; its Presidium was to play an executive role. The first decree issued by the council pertained to the organization of the People's Army. The council declared itself the supreme authority over all Polish military units, whether in Poland, Russia, or the West. The second decree concerned the command of the People's Army; posts of commander in chief and chief of staff of the army were created, and the right to appoint generals was reserved for the KRN. The council's third decree appointed General Michał Żymierski (Rola) as commander in chief, and General Franciszek Jóźwiak (Witold) as his chief of staff.[50]

The manifesto of the National Council of Poland unleashed a storm of protest on the part of most non-Communist Polish secret organizations.[51] Nevertheless, the approach of the Red Army was a powerful incentive to all leftist groups to seek shelter in the PPR camp and to accept the inevitable. By May 1944, a large segment of the Workers' Polish Socialist Party and a minor left-wing peasant group decided to join the National Council. The armed detachments of these groups merged with the People's Army.[52]

Despite these successes, the National Council was still a precarious structure, with a narrow political basis. This was fully realized by some Communist leaders, among them the secretary-general of the PPR, Gomułka; hence his repeated attempts to persuade his comrades that some kind of understanding should be reached with the left wing of the coalition supporting the government in exile; hence his efforts to strike a temporary bargain between the PPR and other political groups.[53] Gomułka apparently believed that the Socialist splinter groups led by Edward Osóbka (Morawski), a leftist social worker, would constitute a kind of bridge between the National Council and the Council of National Unity. He felt that at least the extreme left-wing Polish Socialists and some elements of the Peasant Party could be won over to the National Council. It appears that Gomułka was even ready to make far reaching concessions so the Communists might broaden their political basis, that they might not remain isolated. In this undertaking he was supported by a group of his friends, including Zenon Kliszko and Ignacy Loga-Sowiński. The Moscow trained leader, Bierut, however, opposed this "opportunistic" attitude of Gomułka.

Thus, already at this time, latent differences between the "native group" and the "Muscovites" were taking shape. The former, realizing the party's inherent weakness, remained cautious and willing to compromise. The latter, trusting in the all-powerful Soviet help, urged the party to take a bolder line. The two groups, while pursuing the same ultimate goal — seizure of power by the Communists — differed fundamentally on a tactical plane. The "Muscovites" emphasized the military force of their protector, which would place them in power in any event; the "natives" wanted to form a more representative instrument, including all groups of the Left and Center. The "Muscovites" accused the "natives" of being "radishes," that is, red outside but white inside, whereas they themselves were "beetroots" — red all the way through. Negotiations were conducted intermittently throughout 1943 and early 1944 between Gomułka on behalf of the PPR and the non-Communist groups, but no results were produced.[54]

When the Red Army finally entered Poland, the PPR stood condemned by all major political parties as the tool of a foreign power, and hence it was isolated except for a few satellite groups.

THE SOVIET ARMIES ENTER POLAND

When the first Soviet detachments crossed the Riga Treaty frontier between Poland and the USSR, on January 4, 1944, the Polish government in London not only called on its Home Army to collaborate with the Red Army, but made a new proposal for the restoration of diplomatic relations with the Soviet Union. The offer was rejected; the Kremlin pointed out that the Red Army was not yet actually on Polish soil, "as the Soviet constitution had established a Soviet-Polish frontier corresponding with the desires of the population of Western Ukraine and Western Byelorussia." The Soviet government continued to ignore the Polish government and dealt instead with the Union of Polish Patriots and with the newly formed National Council of Poland.

The London government now instructed the Home Army to take an active part in the fight against retreating German troops, to destroy communications, and to seize strategic points. Local Polish commanders were to establish contact with Soviet commanders and place themselves under Soviet orders, stating that they were doing so on instructions from the Polish government. A similar message was issued to civil servants.

Numerous units of the Home Army fought behind German lines

and achieved notable success in helping the Red Army to capture
Wilno, Lublin, Lwów, and a score of other small localities. But once
their role as the vanguard of the Red Army's advance was over, detachments of the Home Army were surrounded by the Russians, disarmed, and the officers arrested, along with some of their men. The
rest were usually forcibly enrolled in the Soviet-Polish army. This
pattern was invariable throughout Polish territory.[55] Naturally
enough, in many instances this procedure aroused opposition. Soldiers who had struggled for five or even six years against the Germans refused to be disarmed by the "Allies of our Allies." [56] This
spontaneous resistance was to be used later by Soviet prosecutors as
a major argument during the trial of sixteen Polish underground
leaders in Moscow in June 1945; it was also to be used in numerous
political trials held in Poland during the Stalinist period.

THE POLISH COMMITTEE OF NATIONAL LIBERATION

While the Polish government and its armed forces, now just emerging from underground, were being liquidated, a new administration
for Poland was being prepared.[57] In March 1944, a delegation from
the National Council of Poland, composed of Osóbka (Morawski),
General Żymierski (Rola), and Marian Spychalski, went to Russia
where Stalin received them on May 22. Once more a policy of wooing
other parties left of Center was approved and even encouraged. Once
more the National Council of Poland appealed to its countrymen to
increase their resistance to the Germans, to help the Red Army, and
to join the Polish forces fighting shoulder to shoulder with their
Soviet comrades.[58]

Another step toward the assumption of political power in Poland
was initiated on June 23, 1944: the Union of Polish Patriots formally
repudiated the Polish government in London, stating that "The Union of Polish Patriots recognizes the National Council of Poland as
the representative of the nation." The council based its claim to legitimate authority on the existence of a net of local national councils,
which it claimed to have nurtured during the German occupation,
and which the National Council of Poland now supposedly represented.

Meanwhile, Soviet forces were now approaching what Moscow
regarded as "an undisputable Polish territory." On July 20, 1944,
Bolesław Bierut, chairman of the National Council of Poland, left
Warsaw and, with the aid of Communist partisans and the Red
Army, was transported to Moscow and from there to Chełm and

Lublin. In a similar way, the major part of the PPR's Central Committee was secretly transplanted from the German to the Russian side of the front, in order to meet the Red Army as it advanced across the Vistula. Thus, the Communist leaders had assembled in Lublin before the Warsaw uprising was to begin, on August 1, 1944. On July 21, 1944, members of the PPR, together with those leaders of the Union of Polish Patriots who arrived in the wake of the Red Army (Wanda Wasilewska, Jakub Berman, and Stanisław Radkiewicz, among others), established the Polish Committee of National Liberation, or PKWN. Osóbka (Morawski) assumed the chairmanship of the committee while Wasilewska and Andrzej Witos (nephew of the great peasant leader), became vice-chairmen.

Seven of the fifteen members of the committee were pro-Communist: Wasilewska, Żymierski, Berling, Kotek (Arguszewski), Radkiewicz, Skrzeszewski, and Jędrychowski; some, like Osóbka and Drobner, were members of various radical groups dependent upon Communist favor. Andrzej Witos, Grubecki, Sommerstein, and Rzymowski, although non-Communists, were also following the line of the PPR. The committee was formerly created by a decree of the National Council of Poland, the decree having been marked as if it issued from Warsaw rather than Moscow. The committee was to act as a "provisional executive authority to lead the nation's struggle for liberation, to secure its independence and the re-establishment of the Polish state." In another decree the National Council declared itself to be the sole Polish representative entitled to lead and coordinate all activities directed toward Poland's liberation; the council also assumed supreme authority over the Union of Polish Patriots and the contingent of the Polish army created in the USSR.

The next day, July 22, the Committee of National Liberation issued the so-called July Manifesto.[59] This manifesto was a sketchily outlined program, containing outwardly democratic reforms, as well as an appeal to the Polish Nation to rise against the Germans, to submit to the committee's power "as the sole legal source of authority in Poland," and to collaborate closely with the Red Army liberator of the country. The committee promised a "broad agrarian reform" without compensation to former owners, but failed to mention any nationalization of key industry, commerce, or banking. Private initiative was, on the contrary, to be encouraged. The manifesto stated that Poland's eastern frontiers "should be settled by mutual agreement" with her neighbors: the Ukraine, Byelorussia and Lithuania. As for the western boundaries, the committee re-emphasized that it stood firmly for the return to Poland of East Prussia, of the "ancient Polish territory of Pomerania and Silesia," for "a broad access to the sea, and for Polish boundary marks on the Oder." The "broad principles" of the liberal and democratic Constitution of 1921 were declared binding. The manifesto stressed, however, that "enemies of democracy cannot be allowed to enjoy democratic freedoms." The words "socialism" and "communism" were not even mentioned. This crucial document, in accordance with the prevailing Soviet strategy, was designed to attract as many non-Communists as possible.

On July 26, 1944, the Polish Committee of National Liberation signed an agreement with the Soviet government which defined the relationship between the commander in chief of the Soviet armies and the new skeleton administration organized by the committee. This agreement left wide power in Soviet hands as long as Polish territories remained zones of military operations, and full cooperation was pledged between the new regime and Russian authorities.[60] The recently established administration was, on the one hand, based on the network of local national councils already described, which had allegedly formed spontaneously within Poland's democratic resistance elements;[61] on the other hand, the new government shaped its administration on traditional prewar patterns, but tended to put its own trusted men in key positions.

THE WARSAW UPRISING

At the moment of publication of the July Manifesto, the strength of Communist forces in Poland was still relatively small. The Warsaw uprising was to alter this balance considerably, to the advantage of the Lublin Committee. It is, therefore, necessary to discuss the uprising in some detail.[62]

From the outset of the Russo-German war, both Soviet and PPR propaganda endeavored to incite the Poles to a nation-wide uprising. There was hardly any Communist newspaper, pamphlet, or periodical which did not contain some exhortation of this kind. These efforts grew to hysterical intensity during the battle of Stalingrad; they did not cease when Red troops started driving Hitler's armies beyond the frontiers of the USSR. The July Manifesto was, among other things, also a fiery appeal to arms. The Polish government in London and leaders of the resistance movement in Poland were primarily oriented toward cooperation with the Western Allies; hence they distrusted such appeals and considered that only under their authority could

Poland's struggle be directed. Both the Polish government and the Home Army opposed the idea of a premature revolt and were determined to preserve the strength of the country for the decisive moment when it could be used to the utmost benefit of Poland and her allies. "Tempest," a carefully calculated plan to this effect, had been prepared as early as 1943; it provided for an increase in sabotage and diversionary activity and for a series of insurrections timed to assist Soviet troops as the front moved westward. The plan was put into operation from the moment Soviet troops entered Poland's prewar territory, in January 1944. Although the Polish underground opposed the Kremlin's political plans for Poland, it stood ready to cooperate militarily with the Red Army in order to defeat Germany.

Originally, according to General Bór-Komorowski, commander of the Home Army, "Tempest" was designed to avoid fighting in major towns, in order to spare the defenseless population and safeguard historical buildings. With this object in mind, the Home Army did not, at first, plan any action inside Warsaw; Home Army units from Warsaw were to be concentrated outside the city where they could attack the rear guard of German forces withdrawing from the capital. However, in mid-July, the Home Army command decided upon a modification of "Tempest" with regard to Warsaw, and prepared to capture the capital "just before the Russians would enter it." [63] Such a step, it was felt, would demonstrate the will of the Polish people to remain independent.

There were many reasons which made Polish leaders decide to order this insurrection. What interests us now are not the Polish-German aspects of this question but rather the Communist ones. The latter were enumerated by Bór-Komorowski in his Memoirs:

> Inaction on the part of the Home Army at the moment of the Soviet entry is likely to mean general passivity on the home front. The initiative for fighting the Germans is liable then to be taken by the PPR and a considerable fraction of the less-informed citizens might join them. In that case the country is liable to move in the direction of collaboration with the Soviets and no one will be able to stop it. Also, in that case the Soviet Army would not be received by the Home Army, loyal to the government and the commander in chief, but by their own adherents — with open arms . . . Finally, the participation of the Home Army in the battle for Warsaw would definitely silence the lies of Soviet propaganda about the passivity of our country and our sympathies towards the Germans, and the liberation of the capital by our own soldiers should testify with unquestionable strength to the nation's will to safeguard the sovereignty of the Polish state.[64]

As the front approached Warsaw it grew increasingly surer that the time was at hand for "Tempest." The Red Army's offensive seemed irresistible. The Germans were showing signs of exhaustion and demoralization as their disordered retreat continued. It appeared that they would be unable to offer resistance along the Vistula line. On July 28, 1944, an official communiqué from Moscow announced that Marshal Rokossovsky's troops, were "advancing on Warsaw from the south and east on a front nearly fifty miles wide," and were at points within forty miles of the capital. The following day, July 29, Mikołajczyk, prime minister of the Polish government in London, had flown to Moscow to see Stalin in order to attempt a restoration of Polish-Soviet relations, when the Russians formally announced: "In Central Poland, Marshal Rokossovsky's tanks, motorized infantry, and Cossack cavalry, powerfully supported by the Red Air Force, pressed on towards Warsaw . . ." [65]

On July 30 the Home Army's monitoring service picked up a call from Moscow, addressed in Polish to the people of Warsaw. This broadcast had first been transmitted on July 29 and was later repeated by the wireless station of the Union of the Polish Patriots: "Poles! The time of liberation is at hand! Poles, to arms! . . . Every Polish homestead must become a stronghold in the struggle against the invader . . . There is not a moment to lose." The appeal was worded in a very explicit and emphatic way and continued to be repeated; it seemed to indicate that the Russians judged the situation ripe for the uprising to begin. This was of special significance in view of the Home Army's subsequent inability to coordinate its actions with those of the Russians.

Inasmuch as a big Soviet attack toward Warsaw was expected at any moment,[66] the Polish government in London gave the commander of the Home Army discretion to fix the precise moment for fighting to begin in Warsaw. Accordingly, the uprising broke out as planned on August 1, 1944, at 5 P.M. From that day on Soviet broadcasts changed entirely. For several days no mention of the struggle was made; instead, the Kościuszko station in Soviet territory resumed its attacks on non-Communist political groups. In Warsaw, on the other hand, the Communists and their fellow travelers behaved quite differently. The PPR branches in Warsaw had been left without precise instructions from their leaders, who had hastily departed from Lublin ten days previously. On the fourth day of the fighting, the PPR posted a declaration calling on all its members to join in the struggle and to accept tactical orders from Home Army sector commanders. This act of cooperation, however, revealed the numerical weakness of the PPR, for the Communists mobilized some 500 men. The so-called Security Corps of the People's Guard formed one battalion which took part in the defense of a central sector. At the time the Home Army numbered about 46,000 men.[67]

Polish Communists took an active part throughout most of the uprising, as if, cut off from their Moscow-inspired leadership, they followed their own patriotic impulses. PPR propaganda was currently placing more emphasis on the necessity of rebuilding a strong and democratic Poland than on propagating Communist doctrine.[68] As time went on, Polish Communists tended to become angry and disillusioned with Soviet tactics: "The People's Army has staked its young life, its souls, and its hearts [said a PPR proclamation pasted on the walls of Warsaw at the beginning of the revolt], to show the world that it can afford a heroic deed of such magnitude, to which other nations can only listen!"[69]

While this handful of Communists was giving a good account of itself at the barricades of Warsaw, Soviet-controlled broadcasts continued to be silent on the subject of the uprising. Moreover, the Soviet troops which, according to Moscow's own communiqué had been about to capture Poland's capital, stopped their advance while a Russian offensive on the Balkan sector of the front was stepped up. Numerous dispatches of General Bór-Komorowski were addressed to the Soviet command, asking for help and coordination of military operations, but all were ignored.[70]

On August 13, 1944, Moscow broke its two weeks' official silence. The Moscow radio, as well as the B.B.C. from London, broadcast a statement from the official Soviet Press Agency, Tass. This statement, while acknowledging the uprising, accused its leaders of having failed to coordinate their move with the Soviet high command. General Bór-Komorowski's numerous appeals directed to Marshal Rokossovsky continued to be unanswered until the latter half of September, when some scanty supplies of arms and food were dropped by Soviet planes. By that time, however, it was too late.

The insurgents, on September 13, finally managed to establish liaison with the Polish division of General Berling, which then occupied the eastern bank of the Vistula. In response to a request, Berling sent an infantry battalion across the river; further help was expected any day, but did not materialize. Even supplies for the lonely battalion were not dispatched. On September 14, when it had become obvious that Warsaw must surrender any day for lack of food and ammunition, a new, dramatic Soviet appeal to continue fighting and a promise of help was made by the Lublin station.

To fighting Warsaw: The hour of liberation for heroic Warsaw is near. Your sufferings and martyrdom will soon be over. The Germans will pay dearly for the ruins and blood of Warsaw. The first Polish Division Kościuszko has entered Praga. It is fighting side by side with the heroic Red Army. Relief is coming. Keep fighting! . . . The whole Polish nation is with you in your self-sacrificing struggle against the German invaders. A decisive fight is now taking place on the banks of the Vistula. Help is coming. Victory is near. Keep fighting!

Although all proposals made by the commander in chief of the Home Army concerning practical cooperation were ignored by him, General Berling was soon dismissed from the command of the Kościuszko division.[71]

On October 3, 1944, the surviving insurgents capitulated, after sixty-four days of fighting. For six weeks the Soviet army had held a bridgehead on the western bank of the Vistula. The Warsaw uprising provided them with diversion in the very midst of the German lines; consequently, the Russians had extremely favorable conditions for the capture of Warsaw. They stubbornly refused to use this chance, vetoed any idea of Western planes using the Soviet bases, and passively watched the Poles being destroyed by their common German foe. An early capture of Warsaw would have been a military success of the first magnitude, but Moscow deemed it to be politically inadvisable and this consideration proved to be decisive. The Soviet tactics during the Warsaw struggle may be largely explained as a determined effort to destroy the most active elements among the non-Communist groups.

When, soon after the end of the war, General Eisenhower made a short visit to Poland, the United States ambassador accompanied him on his sight-seeing tour.

I showed General Eisenhower through an arch which was still standing, a magnificent view of the Vistula River below and Praga beyond, with the dome of the Russian Orthodox Church glittering in the sunlight. I explained to him that during the insurrection of 1944 this part of town had been initially held by the Polish Home Army, which was daily expecting the Soviets to join forces with them from the other side. Emphasizing that he was speaking purely as a soldier, the general observed, "What a perfect bridgehead!" [72]

The failure of the uprising in Warsaw cost Poland at least 200,000

victims from among its most politically active non-Communist element, and destroyed the organizing center of the most numerous and
powerful resistance movement in Europe. Thus the catastrophe considerably facilitated the subsequent Communist assumption of power.
This was underscored by a Communist member of the new Polish
government, who in 1946 said to a prominent American visitor in
Warsaw:

"Had General Bór-Komorowski and his underground army succeeded in liberating Warsaw, they would have been the heroes of
Poland and would have formed the nucleus of the government within
Poland. It would have been most difficult under such circumstances
for the Soviet government to maintain in power the Lublin Committee of National Liberation." [73]

The prestige and influence of the Polish government in London
were now lowered, and new vistas opened to the Lublin Committee.

10   SEIZURE and CONSOLIDATION of POWER

The first few months of the existence of the Polish Committee of National Liberation (PKWN) were of crucial importance for its future. The committee had been placed in power by the Red Army, but its leaders realized that they could not depend solely on Soviet bayonets. Accordingly, the Lublin Committee, as it had come to be called, took appropriate steps to expand its political base and consolidate its position. The Constitution of 1921 had provided that the Speaker of the Sejm act as president of the Republic whenever the latter was unable to discharge his duties. On September 11, 1944, a new law was passed which interpreted this provision conveniently for the Lublin Committee. The post of president of the Republic of Poland was declared vacant, its functions were transferred to the chairman of the National Council of Poland,[1] the veteran party member Bolesław Bierut. Thus, the three highest state posts were merged in the person of Bierut. First, he was chairman of the Home National Council, hence the presiding officer of an assembly to which was ascribed the role of a parliament and the source of sovereignty. Second, Bierut was chairman of the Presidium of the National Council, which wielded full authority in the name of the council. Third, Bierut now possessed the prerogatives attached to the post of head of state.

In October 1944, Mikołajczyk again went to Moscow. This time Stalin shifted the burden of negotiations to members of the Lublin Committee, who simply repeated Soviet demands concerning the acceptance of certain territorial changes and the composition of Poland's government.[2] In this manner Stalin attempted to represent the whole problem of Poland as an internal quarrel between rival Polish factions. Mikołajczyk, pressed by his British friends, was increasingly inclined to accept the terms offered, at the same time trying to save at least the Galician oilfields for his country. Upon

Mikołajczyk's return to London, his colleagues rejected his suggestion that already accomplished facts be accepted, namely, Russia's
annexation of Poland's eastern provinces, a general westward shifting
of Poland's boundaries, and the sharing of governmental administration with the Communists. Mikołajczyk resigned at the end of
November 1944 as prime minister of the Polish government in
exile and the Socialists formed a new government without the
participation of the Peasant Party. Soon, Mikołajczyk and a group
of his followers decided to seek reconciliation with the new master
of their native country.

By the close of the year it had become obvious that the Soviet
Union intended to make the Lublin Committee the nucleus of Poland's future government. The Western Powers made some feeble
attempts to prevent this; on December 16, 1944, President Roosevelt
pleaded with Stalin not to recognize the Lublin administration as
Poland's provisional government. The Soviet leader replied on
December 27 by paying tribute to the reconstruction work already
accomplished by the Lublin Committee; he skillfully emphasized the
security requirements of the Soviet Union, and declared that, if
the committee were to become the government of Poland, he would
have no serious ground for postponing recognition. And, indeed, on
December 31, 1944, anticipating the capture of Warsaw by Soviet
troops, the Lublin Committee declared itself to be the provisional
government of Poland. This act was preceded by a vigorous propaganda campaign designed to prove that the masses of the people were
demanding the immediate establishment of a regular administration.[3]

The provisional government was composed of seven PPR leaders
(Gomułka, Zawadzki, Korczyc, Radkiewicz, Skrzeszewski, Raban-
owski and Minc), three Socialists, three Peasant Party members, and
three politicians of the Democratic Party. Only five members of the
old Committee of National Liberation entered the new provisional
government: Osóbka (Morawski), premiership and foreign affairs,
Żymierski (Rola), national defense, Radkiewicz, security, Skrzeszewski, education, and Rzymowski, culture and arts. Only one member of the provisional government, Marshal Żymierski (Rola), could,
with some effort, be considered an independent member. Nonetheless,
because of the prevalent feeling of suspicion both at home and abroad,
the PPR took great care to stress that several parties were represented
in the government, encompassing a group broader than the Polish
Committee of National Liberation. On January 5, 1945, Moscow extended prompt recognition to the new government, but Washington
and London continued to recognize the Polish government in exile.

Less than two weeks later, on January 17, 1945, Warsaw was captured by the Russians. The courageous decision to retain Warsaw, then a heap of snow-covered ruins, as the capital of the country was of considerable psychological importance, and the provisional government stubbornly clung to this traditional seat of power.

At the Yalta Conference, in February 1945, the Big Three leaders of the anti-German coalition, acting without Poland's participation, reached an agreement in principle regarding Poland's future. While the government in exile was completely disregarded, the PPR-dominated provisional government was to be "reorganized on a broader democratic basis" so as to include a more representative group from Poland itself and from among Poles abroad.[4] The new government was made to promise that free and unfettered elections would be held as soon as possible on the basis of "universal suffrage and secret ballot." In these elections all democratic parties were to participate. The Yalta Conference proved to be a great success for Moscow because it confirmed the provisional government's sovereignty and, consequently, strengthened both the internal and external position of the new government.

Yet, despite the Yalta Conference, despite the successes of the Polish units fighting alongside the Soviet army, then approaching Berlin, and despite the distribution of land, the new government remained insecure. A large portion of the country's population was suspicious of the government's real intentions, and resistance by the so-called "forest detachments," which continued to pay allegiance to the Polish government in London, was vigorous. Consequently, it became an important task of the new regime to liquidate the representatives of the London government in Poland. On March 28, when negotiations were in progress for the formation of a unified government for Poland that would be recognized by all the Allied Powers, leaders of the former Home Army were approached by Red Army members in order to negotiate a modus vivendi between these two groups. The avowed purpose of these negotiations was to "ensure law and order at the rear of the Red Army as it entered the last phase of its offensive against the Germans," a task which apparently exceeded the powers of the provisional government. Trusting the Soviet offer, the chief delegate of the London government in Poland, the commander of the Home Army, and fourteen other leaders revealed themselves to the NKVD. Instead of negotiating, the Russians arrested these men and, during the San Francisco Conference of the United Nations, Moscow announced that the Poles had been accused of crimes against the Red Army and would be tried by a Soviet court.⁵ The show trial was soon after staged in Moscow.

The imprisonment of the sixteen Poles thereby eliminated the most promising non-Communist leaders from the political scene during the crucial period of negotiations on the creation of a government of national unity in Soviet-occupied Poland. The trial took place in Moscow from June 18 to 21, 1945, at the very time that Mikoła-jczyk in his capacity as leader of the Peasant Party was also there discussing the formation of Poland's new government, to be established with the blessing of the Big Three.⁶

Simultaneous with the trial of the sixteen Polish resistance leaders, a conference was held in Moscow, presided over by Molotov and by the American and British ambassadors to the Soviet Union.⁷ Representatives of the Lublin Committee and a few other political figures selected at random were brought from Poland. This gathering was joined by Mikołajczyk, who arrived from London with two former members of his cabinet. As a result of this conference a new provisional government of national unity was established on June 28, 1945.

This government was nominally a coalition of five parties: Polish Workers' Party (PPR), Polish Socialist Party (PPS), Peasant Party, Democratic Party, and Labor Party. Of the twenty-one government posts, seven were given to Peasant Party members. Mikołajczyk himself held two posts, deputy prime minister and minister of agriculture; one of his followers, Kiernik, was given the ministry of public administration from which, however, control of the police was withdrawn in favor of an experienced NKVD-trained man, Radkiewicz. Sixteen posts were given to representatives of the old provisional government, while only five ministries were relinquished to Poles living abroad. The government thus formed was promptly recognized by Great Britain and the United States on July 6, 1945.

The Potsdam Conference (July 17-August 2, 1945) provisionally fixed the western frontiers of the new Poland, "pending final delimitation at the future peace conference." The Three Great Powers awarded most of East Prussia to Poland (except for the Koenigsberg region), and also Danzig (which now became Gdańsk), and the territory east of the Oder and Neisse rivers, including Breslau (Wrocław) and Stettin (Szczecin). German residents in these areas were to be transferred to the Reich, with the assistance of the United States and Great Britain. A treaty signed on August 16, 1945, confirmed the previous territorial settlement between the Soviet Union and Poland. The Polish population in territories east of the

"Curzon Line" was to be transferred to the western provinces newly acquired by Poland.

HOW TO MAKE FRIENDS AND INFLUENCE PEOPLE

While establishing itself in power, the Polish Workers' Party (PPR) faced a harder task during 1944 and 1945 than did other Communist parties in East Central Europe. Out of the ordeal of the war the Polish nation, although bled white, emerged more homogeneous than ever, both socially and politically: class distinctions were largely obliterated and party differences blurred, thus blunting the slogan of class struggle; religious sentiments both broadened and deepened. This also tended to increase resistance toward the new regime. The great majority of Poles were traditionally both anti-Russian and anti-Communist. Experience under the first Soviet occupation from 1939 to 1941, the Katyń massacre, the Warsaw uprising, and the behavior of Soviet troops in the recent fighting all strengthened these feelings of hostility. Despite the party's denials, the people of Poland regarded the PPR as a tool of Moscow, a direct heir of the Communist Party of Poland.

The extent of the hatred encountered by the new regime at every step may be gathered from the following reminiscences of a leftist Socialist, Bolesław Drobner. Referring to his experience in the summer of 1944, he wrote: "I found myself before the Polish teachers of Przemyśl. Their eyes burned with hate for us. We answered: 'You can hate us . . .' In August 1944, I found myself before the doctors of Lublin where the same scene took place as at Przemyśl. Again we answered: 'You can hate us . . .' " [8]

The small size of the party, from twenty to thirty thousand members,[9] and its unpopularity made the use of fellow travelers and opportunists a necessity. The Germans had smashed the prewar Polish state structure; they had been especially ruthless with the educated classes. Consequently, lack of trained personnel was a major difficulty facing the new administration. There were very few native Communists on which to draw, and those who were available were ill-equipped to assume public office. Therefore, in the initial stages of organization offices were filled with random people who often lacked the confidence of the authorities but who were deemed indispensable for the job. The new regime had little choice in the matter, nor did the remnants of the prewar intellectual group; the starved urban population necessarily depended on those who controlled the country's meagre resources: "Food, not money [noted an American observer], was the basis of life in Poland. Six free dining

rooms for upper civil servants were the cornerstones of the state . . .
The wages and salaries paid in paper zlotys counted for little. Permits
to eat three times a day in some dining rooms were more valuable
then any amount of printed cash." [10]

Yet material comforts were not the only means of attracting and
managing adherents. The vivid memory of Nazi atrocities gave any
anti-German regime a certain degree of popularity. Moreover, a
widespread desire to play an active role in the open after five years
of clandestine activity also played a part.

Generally speaking, five distinct groups assisted the party in its
seizure of power. The first group was composed of those army
officers and professional people who had compromised themselves
in some way and could thus be easily blackmailed into subservience
by the Communists who knew their record. To this category belonged
such people as General Michał Żymierski (Rola) and Wincenty
Rzymowski. Their former anti-Communist activities, coupled with a
questionable past, now served to guarantee their obedience to Communist dictates. Żymierski was appointed commander in chief of
the People's Army and minister of national defense; Rzymowski
became a member of the Polish Committee of National Liberation
and was in the Polish provisional government of Lublin as minister of
culture and arts, representing the satellite Democratic Party. With
the formation of the Polish provisional government of national unity,
Rzymowski became minister of foreign affairs.

The second very large category assisting the party consisted of
prewar civil servants and intellectuals. This group and the Communists were mutually useful, for membership in the PPR or one
of the government-sponsored political parties was a form of temporary personal reinsurance. The returning émigré politicians formed a
third group, which quickly polarized into two camps: those who, like
Mikołajczyk and his friends, began to oppose the establishment of
a totalitarian regime, and others, like the two PPS politicians, Stań-
czyk or Grosfeld, who proved docile instruments of the PPR. Some
of the latter were simply opportunists; others sincerely believed
that the inevitable had to be accepted, that Poland, now destined to
live in the Soviet sphere of influence, must have good relations with
her powerful neighbor, and that the rule of the PPR would be the
best guarantee of such relations.

The fourth assisting group was made up of politicians with totalitarian proclivities, like Bolesław Piasecki, prewar leader of the
Fascist group called Falanga. Piasecki soon formed a Social Catholic

movement which ardently preached a synthesis of Catholicism and Marxism.

To the fifth and final category belonged those leftist politicians actually won over by the PPR. Examples were Edward Osóbka (Morawski), Józef Cyrankiewicz, and Kazimierz Rusinek. Morawski and his group in the Workers' Party of Polish Socialists had signed the first Manifesto of the National Council of Poland. In Lublin, during the summer of 1944, Osóbka recruited an executive committee from the PPS, which he was bent on re-creating as his own party. In September 1944, while most of Poland was still under German occupation, the new PPS arranged an All-Poland Party Congress in Lublin, and after the formation of the Lublin Committee, Osóbka was proclaimed chairman of the Central Executive Committee of the Polish Socialist Party, while Stefan Matuszewski, a defrocked Roman Catholic priest and a member of the Union of Polish Patriots, was assigned to the post of secretary-general of the new party. Later, Matuszewski and Osóbka were joined by two genuine PPS leaders of some prewar standing: Cyrankiewicz and Rusinek. Between 1935 and 1939 Józef Cyrankiewicz had been secretary of the Cracow District Committee of the PPS. In 1939 he joined the PPS resistance groups; arrested by the Germans in 1941, Cyrankiewicz was sent to a concentration camp where he was converted by his Communist fellow prisoners to the idea of close collaboration between socialism and communism in the name of "unity of the working class." Kazimierz Rusinek had also been active in the PPS. Before the war he led the Seamen's and Dockers' Union of Gdynia. During 1939 Rusinek too was taken prisoner by the Germans and sent to various concentration camps where he came under the influence of the Communists. After the war Rusinek returned to Warsaw and placed himself at the disposal of the provisional government. Soon afterward he was appointed secretary-general of the Polish Trade Unions.

At first the bulk of the old PPS protested these highhanded tactics. Gradually, however, seeing no chance of rebuilding their old movement, many former members of the PPS joined the new party. This development had a twofold result. First, to a certain extent the party lost its puppet character. Second, Osóbka, Cyrankiewicz, and Rusinek, emboldened by the discovery that the PPR had finally gained the backing of a genuine mass movement, began to act more and more independently. This marked the beginning of a revival of the Socialist movement which soon became a powerful force.

Similar tactics were applied to the peasant movement. As far back as 1943 the Communists had set up a bogus Peasant Party. With the return of Mikołajczyk, however, leaders of the genuine Peasant Party gradually rallied around him. In the course of the summer of 1945, Mikołajczyk concluded that collaboration with the Communist elements within the Peasant Party was impossible. Backed by the Peasant Party's general secretary, Stanisław Bańczyk, and supported by the rank and file, Mikołajczyk decided to sever his ties with a group which he believed was bent on destroying the genuine peasant movement. Accordingly, on September 22, 1945, a new party was established under a new name, Polish Peasant Party (PSL).

As a consequence of this bold move, the Communist-sponsored Peasant Party lost a great deal of its membership and became an obviously bogus organization. However, the provisional character of the government at that time forced the regime to consider the possible reaction of the Western Powers if every form of independent political activity in Poland were suppressed. Moreover, the overwhelming support given to Mikołajczyk forced the PPR to tolerate his defection for the time being. Around Mikołajczyk soon gathered most non-Communist forces in Poland, and this was a challenge to the PPR.

THE PPR 1945–1947

Thus, by the end of 1945 the PPR, while struggling against a general opposition, had to face one open rival for power, the reborn peasant movement, and another potential competitor — the slowly reviving Socialist movement. Moreover, the party itself was far from united. The chief internal weakness of the PPR was its division into two groups, almost equally strong: the "Muscovites" and the "native" factions.[11] The differences between the two were three-fold: psychological, organizational, and tactical.

Psychological conflicts arose from the different background and experiences of the two groups. These differences became magnified by the conviction of each faction that its own contribution was of decisive importance for the triumph of the *cause*. Differences in organization and tactical approach resulted from the fact that the homegrown Communists were closer to the party rank and file and, consequently, better known. This caused an undue reliance upon a misleading feeling of popularity. The Muscovites, on the other hand, being closer to the Kremlin, relied on the real masters of the situation; they distrusted any sort of "spontaneity" or "elemental trends" as "un-Bolshevik" and "dangerous." Most leaders of the Muscovite faction were products of the Stalinist school; by that time the type of professional revolutionary so characteristic in the early history of the CPP was gone. Having faithfully followed all the turns and twists of the party line, having witnessed the massacre of their comrades (and in some cases probably contributing to it), these people were by now sufficiently "Bolshevised," that is, thoroughly acclimated to the Communist Party of the Soviet Union. They had become accustomed to the changing infallibility of their master. As far as tactical matters were concerned, the native Communists realized better than the Muscovites the inherent weaknesses and limitations of the party. Hence, they tended to compromise with other radical groups, mainly with the Left Socialists and more extreme peasant elements. The Muscovites, on the other hand, while paying lip service to the idea of a "broad democratic front," tended to rely mainly on the armed might and police skill of their Soviet protector. In view of the strength of the anti-Communist forces this could provoke an open civil war.

The first clash between the factions took place in the spring of 1944, soon after the establishment of the People's Council of Poland; another was to occur in the summer of 1948. The first conflict gave the upper hand to the natives, probably because the Kremlin supported them in their cautious tactics. An open civil war was obviously against the best interest of the Soviet Union. The Home Army had already been ravaged by the Warsaw uprising and by "Tempest" in general, so with Soviet support it was possible to achieve the first phase of Communist take-over without a major upset.

After the seizure of power, native Communists continued to compete with their rivals for control of the state and party apparatus. Gomułka, while remaining secretary-general of the party, also later became vice-prime minister and minister of the recovered territories. Spychalski was placed in the ministry of national defense as vice-minister in charge of political matters and deputy commander in chief. Kowalski was appointed head of the association, Struggle of the Young, or youth branch of the PPR. Władysław Bieńkowski, as head of the educational section of the party, became a powerful figure in the cultural life of the country.

On the other hand, the Muscovites also managed to gain control of some of the highest posts in the state administration. Bierut, as chairman of both the National Council of Poland and its Presidium, became head of state. His close friend, Jakub Berman, an old Communist hand, established himself firmly at the Presidium of the Council of Ministers, as vice-minister, in order to keep an eye on every successive premier. In this position he became the "gray eminence" of the regime. Berman's and Bierut's friend, Radkiewicz, a man with thorough NKVD training, was assigned to the key post of minister of security. In Jóźwiak (Witold), commander of the Militia and the Voluntary Reserves of Citizen's Militia (ORMO), he found a faithful assistant. Another Muscovite, Hilary Minc, was entrusted with industry and commerce, and soon became the economic overseer of the country.

To this group should be added Roman Zambrowski, Edward Ochab, and Aleksander Zawadzki. Zambrowski, an old party member, originally chief of the political administration of General Berling's Polish army in Russia, became a member of the Presidium of the National Council of Poland. Ochab, who was originally deputy commander for political education of the Third Infantry Division, became vice-minister of public administration in the provisional government of national unity, with the task of watching the nominal head of the ministry, Władysław Kiernik, a partisan of Mikołajczyk. Zawadzki was also a political officer in Berling's army in Russia. Soon after the formation of the provisional government of national unity, he was transferred to a new position as governor of Silesia.

At the beginning, one of the party's major objectives was to expand numerically. This was an understandable ambition on the part of a small group of some 20,000 members who were bent on demonstrating to a hostile country that they could, after all, attract and lead the masses.[12] Hence, the first four years in power was a period of "spontaneous," "elemental" expansion of the party's membership. At the First Party Congress, which took place in December 1945, the membership rose to 235,000, about 62 per cent of which were workers. During its very first year in power, a vigorous recruitment drive was undertaken and numerous privileges were granted to those in possession of a party card: jobs, food, clothing, housing, and so forth. During this initial period, which lasted between two and three years, almost anyone was accepted as a party member, including people with a doubtful past, political or otherwise. This became an established policy of the party, which viewed an expanding membership as a token of confidence on the part of the masses.

Despite these successes the country's resistance to the new regime continued to be widespread.[13] In order to enhance the chances of recruitment, a member of the politbureau, Roman Zambrowski, emphatically stated that the PPR was not a "Communist party," but a "new party." [14] He called for building this new party's membership to one million.[15] With this objective in sight, the PPR continued to expand its ranks until a second internal crisis upset the party's development temporarily.

FROM THE POTSDAM CONFERENCE TO THE REFERENDUM

Following the Potsdam Conference, the PPR made capital of Poland's Oder-Neisse frontier and used the new territories to consolidate its power.[16] At the end of 1945, a separate ministry of regained territories was created, with the party's secretary-general Gomułka, at its head. These areas had previously been under the direction of the ministry of public administration, headed by Kiernik. The new territories now became a special domain of the PPR, a state within the state, an experimental ground for the first "producers' cooperatives" or collective farms. Integration and resettlement of these newly acquired western and northwestern territories became the most successful battle-cry of the regime, supplementing that of reconstruction.

But, although there was response to the party's nationalistic slogans, the country at large remained hostile to the new regime. In November 1945, on the eve of the first PPR Congress, Edward Ochab defined the needed strategy for the party. According to Ochab, the PPR faced a threefold task. First, it had to "crush the reaction," that is, to liquidate remnants of the resistance movement that still gave allegiance to the government in exile in London. Second, it had to "tighten the alliance with the peasants" while "protecting the unity of the working class." Third, it had "to have a political platform that does not terrify the peasants." [17] In plain language this meant that the peasant masses had to be neutralized for the time being, and to accomplish this the government had to refrain for the time being, from collectivizing the country's agriculture too forcibly. The party also had to prevent Mikołajczyk from forming an opposition movement around the Polish Peasant Party, and it had to bar any *rapprochement* between the peasant group and the PPS, which would have been disastrous for the Communist regime. "The unity of the working class" meant absorption of the PPS, which then controlled by far the largest segment of the urban proletariat and dominated two important mass organizations: trade-unions and cooperatives. Then an alliance between Communist-controlled peasant and socialist movements would complete this subtle game of division, absorption, and control.

To accomplish these objectives, after the Potsdam Conference had ended, the PPR embarked upon a broad program to discredit, disrupt,

and destroy the remaining remnants of the underground movement. A violent propaganda campaign was launched against the
Polish government in exile and its supporters, the chief targets being
the Polish armed forces in the West and the Home Army traditions.
In both cases the regime concentrated its barrage against leaders
rather than against rank and file members. Since Mikołajczyk, as
Prime Minister of the government in exile, had planned and directed
the anti-German resistance movement, he was held responsible for
all alleged mistakes and crimes. The PPR campaign aimed, among
other things, to discredit Mikołajczyk generally and thus prepare
the ground for a showdown with his Polish Peasant Party.[18]

In October 1945, as these attacks were occurring, the government
granted amnesty to rank and file members of underground organizations still existing, provided that these members would make known
their identity and surrender their weapons. The amnesty, however,
did not include the underground leaders. Notwithstanding this, most
officers of the Home Army ordered their men to come out in the open.
The order was obeyed by some two hundred thousand people but
the amnesty was not fully observed by the government. Some right-
wing underground groups refused altogether to accept the amnesty
and remained in hiding. Reprisals were taken against these so-called
"forest detachments" during the end of 1945 and most of 1946. These
mopping-up operations sometimes involved skirmishes on a considerable scale and gave the regime a pretext to expand its "security
apparatus" by creating new detachments of militia to cooperate with
the ministry of public security. Consequently, several concentration
camps, which had been erected for soldiers of the Home Army
as far back as 1944, began expanding again. The new regime claimed
to have lost 14,876 men in the struggle against the remnants of the
anti-Communist underground. Many of them were party members.[19]

Meanwhile, the Western Powers were pressing the provisional
government to fulfill its obligations regarding parliamentary elections. The Potsdam communiqué had included the following paragraph:

The three Powers note that the Polish Provisional Government . . . has
agreed to the holding of free and unfettered elections as soon as possible
on the basis of universal suffrage and secret ballot in which all democratic
and anti-Nazi parties shall have the right to take part and to put forward
candidates, and that representatives of the Allied press shall enjoy full
freedom to report to the world upon developments in Poland before and
during the elections.

The pledge to hold elections at the earliest possible date could only be interpreted as meaning that they should be held without unnecessary delay. After World War I, under similar conditions, elections for the Polish Constituent Sejm were held barely two months after the armistice, on January 27, 1919. But the provisional government of national unity was reluctant to keep its word on elections. A delay was apparently necessary to further soften the opposition and to carry out changes in the social and economic structure, such as nationalization of industry, banking, and commerce, which would consolidate the party's grip on the country.

In April 1946 the PPR decided on a move designed to postpone the elections. The Communist-controlled National Council of Poland, acting as a temporary parliament, voted a referendum on reforms introduced by the provisional government. Besides being a pretext for putting off the election, the referendum was to serve an additional double purpose. First, it was to test the actual strength of the regime's opponents, now gathering in increasing numbers around Mikołajczyk. Second, it was to check the efficiency of the government's electoral machine.

The referendum asked the voters three questions:

1. Are you in favor of abolishing the Senate?
2. Are you in favor of the economic reforms instituted by the new regime, the nationalization of industry, and the land reform?
3. Do you want the western frontier with Germany as fixed on the Baltic, the Oder, and the Neisse to be made permanent?[20]

Voters were asked to answer each question "yes" or "no." Mikołajczyk, despite his party's traditional policy of opposition to a two-chamber legislature, appealed to his supporters to answer the first question "no" and the remaining two "yes." The purpose of this step was to demonstrate to the regime, and indeed, to the Kremlin, the growing strength of the PSL and its following. In reply to this move, the PPR opened a fierce campaign of terror against the PSL. The secret police and the militia were active against Mikołajczyk's followers throughout the spring of 1946.

There is no doubt that the referendum was conducted in an atmosphere of moral pressure and even physical terror, with several hundred PSL agitators arbitrarily imprisoned and, in some cases, tortured. Polling took place on June 20, 1946. According to the official figures, the results of the referendum were as follows:

Question number one: Are you in favor of the abolition of the Senate?

Yes   No
7,844,522   3,686,029

Question number two: Are you in favor of the economic reforms?

Yes   No
8,896,105   2,634,446

Question number three: Are you for the Polish western frontiers as fixed on the Baltic, the Oder, and the Neisse?

Yes   No
10,534,697   995,854

The PSL challenged these figures and claimed that there had been systematic falsification of the ballots on the crucial first question. In 2,805 polling areas in fourteen provinces, where voting commissions had managed to save the poll-boxes from the hands of the police, the results were 83 per cent against abolition of the Senate, indicating a vote of no-confidence in the government.[21] Almost no impartial observer questioned the genuineness of the answer to the third point of the referendum.

"As to the third point, the people, who had already lost that portion of their country east of the Molotov-Ribbentrop Line to the Soviet Union, naturally desired the compensation in the north and in the west which had been promised in the Yalta and Potsdam decisions." [22]

SOCIAL AND ECONOMIC REFORMS, 1944–1947

The new Poland was a different country from the pre-1939 Polish Republic. As a result of the ravages of war and the decisions of the Big Three during the Teheran and Yalta conferences, the country lost over ten million inhabitants and 198,000 square miles of territory. At the Potsdam Conference the country was moved one hundred and fifty miles to the west. The allotment to Poland of East Prussia and the regions east of the Oder-Neisse rivers made the country less land locked and agricultural, more maritime and industrial. The nation's social structure was also considerably altered as a result of the war, the German policy of genocide, and the Soviet deportations.

When the new regime assumed power, it proceeded to carry out two sets of economic reforms: agrarian reform and nationalization of industry, banking, and commerce. These measures were to give the party the "commanding heights" of Poland's economy.

Radical land reform without compensation to former owners was a major point in the platforms of both the Union of Polish Patriots and the Polish Workers' Party.[23] Both groups bitterly criticized the sluggish and conservative land reform with compensation, which had been voted by parliaments in 1920 and 1925.[24] The objective of prewar reforms had been to create "a healthy peasant class" of well-to-do medium-size farmers, owning from 25 to 50 acres of land. The Communists regarded this as an attempt to strengthen the "kulak" strata in the villages, a thoroughly reactionary step in Communist eyes. Nonetheless, for tactical reasons, the PPR advocated land reform measures differing little from those proclaimed by the bulk of the non-Communist resistance movement and by the government in exile. Although the government in London and the non-Communist resistance parties had criticized both the slow tempo of reform and the high maximum which landowners had been permitted to retain, and urged a wider and more even distribution of soil, they also insisted on compensation to former owners. To the PPR land reform was merely a stepping stone toward more far-reaching objectives; to the rest of the resistance movement, individual farming combined with voluntary cooperation, remained an axiom.[25]

The principle of "broad land reform" was again proclaimed in the Lublin Manifesto of July 22, 1944, and implemented immediately. On September 6, 1944, well ahead of Soviet occupation of all of Poland, the Polish Committee of National Liberation issued a law expropriating all landed property exceeding 250 acres, if more than half the acreage was arable land.[26] Even before publication of the law, in fact as soon as a given region was occupied by the Red Army, teams organized by the Department of Agriculture and Agrarian Reforms and led by local PPR men were sent to the villages. These visitors encouraged the peasants to seize and distribute medium estates among themselves. The PPR's zeal for reform led the distribution of land to become largely an absurdity, since the parcels were divided into ridiculously small bits.

The confiscation of forests was ordered by a separate decree on December 12, 1944. Altogether, the new regime seized approximately fifteen million acres of land from the larger landowners: slightly less than five million acres in prewar territories, and about ten million acres in the western provinces allotted to Poland by Potsdam. Over five million acres were retained by the state and "public bodies."[27] Consequently, less than ten million acres remained to be parcelled among the peasants. Out of this land, 981 thousand holdings were created: 498 thousand in the old Poland and 483 thousand in the new territories. Moreover a part of the land was distributed among the so-called dwarf peasants having plots of land not much larger than an ordinary garden. The average new farm amounted to about seven acres. According to the expression of some farmers, it was "too small to live on but too large to permit us to die immediately." [28]

When Mikołajczyk joined the government in June 1945, as minister of agriculture and vice-premier, he made a considerable, though not a very successful, effort to remedy the shortcomings of the reform by supplementing the small farms with additional parcels, by encouraging the pooling of dwarf holdings, and by supplying, as far as possible, both cattle and implements. He endeavored also to grant legal deeds of ownership to peasants settled in the newly acquired western provinces.[29] Mikołajczyk's efforts ended when he left the government in January 1947.

As the result of land reform, the prewar agricultural structure of Poland was replaced by a new one, in some ways basically similar to the old. While the number of small farms increased slightly, the state now emerged as a single huge landowner, retaining almost as much land as the squires of old. Both before and after the war some 60 per cent of Polish farms were smaller than twelve and one half acres. On the other hand, liquidation of prewar bank debts and mortgages, an increase in the amount of usable land per capita of the agricultural population, as well as electrification of the countryside helped the rural masses, especially the poorest group of them. In addition, the first phases of a "cultural revolution," initiated by the new regime soon after land reform, benefited the rural areas by diminishing illiteracy and spreading technical skills throughout the villages. Until the middle of 1948 rumors of impending collectivization were branded as "malicious gossip," "reactionary gossip," or at least an "oversimplification of the tempo of historical process." [30]

Although the reform failed to produce all the results hoped for by the peasants, it fulfilled the expectations of the party. The distribution of land appeased and consequently neutralized the peasantry during a crucial period in the struggle for power.

The first eighteen months of the new regime saw a slow process of reconstruction, coupled with a hasty confiscation by the state of all large and medium-size industries, banking, and foreign trade. Foreign commerce was, from the beginning, a state monopoly, although until mid-1947 considerable latitude was given to domestic trade. All banks, with two exceptions, were taken over by the state, which refused to grant them banking licenses.[31]

Generally speaking, there was less opposition in Poland to the nationalization of industry and banking than in other countries of East Central Europe. Even before the war a considerable number of the country's large industries and most of the banks were either state owned or dependent on, if not owned by, foreign capital. As far back as 1943, all political parties except some of the most extreme conservative groups had agreed that key branches of the national economy should be directed by the state. Moreover, in 1945 and 1946, opposition to a nationalization law was reduced in the hope that this measure would put an end to the hasty and often violent methods applied by the provisional government during the immediate postwar months. To understand the mood of the country at the end of 1946, on the eve of the law's promulgation, one must bear in mind the clever and misleading assurances of the country's economic boss, Hilary Minc, minister of industry and commerce. At that time Minc, together with Gomułka, insisted that the new regime would follow the "specific Polish way to socialism," and that the country's economy would be organized into three separate autonomous and balanced branches: state, cooperative, and private sectors. Consequently, the only controversial point between the PPR and non-Communist parties was the scope of nationalization, and the question of compensation. Mikołajczyk and his PSL, who in this respect represented the bulk of public opinion, insisted on dropping the principle of compensation in favor of raising the ceiling on employment in privately owned enterprises to 100 workers per shift. By this means, small and medium-size entrepreneurs, mostly natives of Poland, would be compensated, while large capitalists, to a considerable extent foreigners, would be deprived of any compensation whatever. The PSL also wanted to exclude from nationalization all printing presses and food processing industries. On all these points the PPR supported by the government-controlled PPS, won the day, and the National Council of Poland (KRN) voted the Nationalization Law by a large majority.

The Nationalization Law of January 3, 1946, nationalized all industrial establishments "capable of employing more than 50 workers per shift." The principle of compensation was written into the law. But, with the exception of some foreign owned enterprises which were backed by diplomatic intervention, no compensation was actually paid. The law was promulgated simultaneously with another, "encouraging private initiative." This law was described as a "safe conduct letter" for all those industries working in conformity with existing law. Article 3 of the Nationalization Law stipulated that a decree of the Council of Ministers would be sufficient to nationalize any category of enterprises not specifically exempted.[32] This soon became an instrument for the confiscation of all sorts of industrial enterprises employing more than 50 workers per shift, as well as smaller concerns spared by the limited scope of the Nationalization Law.

The Nationalization Law of January 3, 1946, was the most important single step legalizing dictatorship of the state in economic matters. The old assurances concerning private initiative and a balance between the state sector on one hand, and private and cooperative sectors on the other, were now irrelevant in view of the dynamics of nationalization. More than 70 per cent of the workers employed in industry and crafts and more than 80 per cent in industry proper now worked for the state. By the end of 1946, the production of the "socialist sector" of industry, that is, state and cooperative industries, was 91.2 per cent of total industrial production, while that of the private sector was 8.8 per cent; in 1948, this ratio amounted to 94 per cent and 6 per cent respectively.[33]

Consequently, by 1946, before the Three Year Plan of Reconstruction was launched, the "commanding heights" of Poland's economy were safely in the hands of the new regime.[34] The period of the Three Year Plan, 1947–1949, saw a great increase in industrialization and a marked rise in the standard of living as compared with the immediate postwar period. The ravages of war were largely healed and the new territories were successfully resettled with 6,000,000 Poles, refugees from the eastern provinces and colonists from central Poland. Warsaw's reconstruction proceeded rapidly. The foundations of the industrial giant Nowa Huta, near Cracow, were laid.

The increasing emphasis on industrial rather than agricultural production is illustrated by the following figures. Considering combined output in industry and agriculture to equal 100, industry's share in 1937 was 45.5, while agriculture's was 54.5. By 1948 the corresponding figures were 64 for industry and 36 for agriculture. The growing industrialization was indicated not only by a rapid expansion in overall industrial output, but also by a swift increase in production of capital goods as opposed to consumer goods. In 1937, 47 per cent of the total industrial output represented capital goods and 53 per cent consumer goods; in 1948, the production of capital goods rose to 54 per cent and that of consumer goods dropped to 46 per cent.

The achievement of this industrial progress depended on great sacrifices courageously borne by the Polish people and on the bold and ruthless drive of the party. There was no corresponding increase in the supply of consumer goods, especially agricultural products,[35] and despite repeated announcements that real wages of manual workers in June 1948 surpassed prewar levels, the general standard of living remained behind the level of 1937. In addition, the achievement of full employment and the expansion of social and educational services were counterbalanced by a growing trend toward a rigid "socialist labor discipline" and "socialist competition," modelled after the Soviet Stakhanovite system. The trade-union movement became subordinate to the aims of the Communist Party.

Rapid industrialization caused a marked increase in the number of wage earners. In 1938 there were 2,733,000 people employed outside agriculture; by 1948 that figure reached the 3,500,000 mark. Wage earners formed 8 per cent of the population in 1938; in 1948 they totalled 14.6 per cent.[36] This development, stressed Hilary Minc, "brings an absolute and relative growth of the proletariat and strengthens the position of the working class — the leading and most progressive part of the nation." The social basis of the party was thus potentially strengthened in turn.

THE SEJM ELECTIONS

After the referendum the struggle between the PPR and Mikoła-jczyk, still a vice-premier and minister of agriculture, continued unabated. With United States and British support, Mikołajczyk persisted in his demands to hold "free and unfettered elections" which he hoped to win decisively. Mikołajczyk had inherited a substantial following from many prewar parties which were now eliminated from the political scene, and consequently, he counted on winning most of the non-Communist electorate. Although stressing Poland's ties with the West, Mikołajczyk emphasized that it was his intention to establish a government "friendly to the Soviet Union" and to maintain the Soviet-Polish alliance. Thus he hoped to convince Moscow that it would be better in the long run to have as an ally a more stable and popular government than one led by a party compelled to depend on Soviet bayonets.[37] Like Benes and Jan Masaryk, Mikołajczyk still harbored the illusion that countries of East Central Europe could be a kind of bridge between the Soviet Union and the West, while Moscow regarded them merely as a bridgehead.

Probably because of the results of the referendum, the PPR was still reluctant to implement its pledges concerning parliamentary elections. Afraid to reveal its weakness, the PPR opened negotiations with Mikołajczyk concerning a joint list of candidates. The number of seats allotted to each party was to be settled in advance. One of the arguments presented by Communist negotiators was that unless a single list were agreed upon and an electoral bloc with the PPR established, Poland might fall prey to anarchy. Another standard argument of the PPR's intense whispering campaign was that only a pro-Russian, Communist-controlled government could guarantee Poland's independence; an electoral victory by Mikołajczyk would be an open challenge to Moscow, which would, in such a case, incorporate Poland outright into the Soviet Union.[38]

Protracted negotiations continued between Mikołajczyk and PPR leaders but no positive results were reached. Mikołajczyk intimated that he might join the bloc provided his party received 75 per cent of the seats in the Sejm and additional governmental posts. This was refused and a fierce electoral campaign began. The PPR press charged Mikołajczyk with provoking an electoral conflict at a time when reconstruction of the country and Poland's international prestige demanded complete unity at home.[39] In order to discredit Mikołajczyk and his alleged "Fascist" supporters and to distract the world's attention from the referendum, an attack on a Jewish settlement near Kielce was provoked, and probably even organized, by the ministry of public security for the purpose of throwing the blame on the PSL opposition.[40]

On November 28, 1946, during a visit to Moscow, Cyrankiewicz, on behalf of the PPS, signed a "unity of action" pact with the PPR.[41] The Democratic Bloc now included the PPR, the PPS, and two Communist-controlled satellite groups, the Peasant Party and the Democratic Party. Members of the bloc decided in advance how to divide the spoils of the election among themselves. In order to confuse the voters, the PPR left two small groups outside the bloc: the Labor Party, and the new "Liberation."

According to obligations assumed during the Potsdam Conference by the Polish government of national unity, "all democratic and anti-Nazi parties" were to be permitted to participate in free and unfettered elections. This formula was an unfortunate one because it implied that there were pro-Nazi parties in Poland, which was incorrect. It was left to the government to decide which parties were to be considered "democratic and anti-Nazi." The government took advantage of this opportunity, and on November 4, 1946, passed a resolution which announced that ". . . the structure of the community . . . has been already fully reflected in the differentiation of the socio-political platform" of the existing political parties. Six parties were mentioned in the resolution: the Polish Workers' Party, the Polish Socialist Party, the Democratic Party, the Peasant Party, the Polish Peasant Party, and the Labor Party. Thus, except for the Polish Peasant Party, only one other opposition group, the Labor Party, was allowed to participate in the election.

The Electoral Law had been issued on September 22, 1946 and, rather than applying principles of full adult suffrage, introduced a franchise arbitrarily restricting the right to vote by introducing various political qualifications.[42] According to the law, "persons who, during the German occupation, extracted benefits from economic collaboration with the occupation authorities to the evident prejudice of the Polish nation were to be disenfranchised." Another excluded group was "persons collaborating with underground Fascist organizations or bands striving to overturn the democratic structure of the state." In neither case, however, was a judicial verdict necessary for disenfranchisement. The final decision rested with PPR-dominated presidia of the provincial national councils. More than one million persons were deprived of their vote in this way.[43] In addition, the Electoral Law provided for representation in the Sejm on the basis of the number of inhabitants in a given polling district, rather than on the number of voters.[44]

As the polling day approached, the intensity of the terror increased and both the militia and the secret police became major electoral agents of the bloc. Simultaneously, the PPR press denounced "reactionary rumors" about impending Sovietization of the country, collectivization of agriculture, and establishment of a one-party totalitarian dictatorship. Free reign was given to Gomułka's pet idea of a "Polish way to socialism." Speaking on the eve of the election, Gomułka emphatically declared:

We have chosen our own Polish road of development which we have named that of People's Democracy. Along this road and under such conditions, the dictatorship of a single party is neither essential nor purposeful . . . Our Democracy and the social order built up and consolidated by us are unprecedented in history. Our experience so far demonstrates that they will successfully pass the test of life. Poland can proceed and is proceeding along her own road . . . along which our party desires to lead her.[45]

Wide appeal was made to the religious feelings of the population, and some PPR pamphlets were printed, as Mikołajczyk maintains, with the picture of the Blessed Virgin.[46]

After disenfranchising many voters, the regime then proceeded to deprive as many as possible of those entitled to vote of any choice among candidates. One week before the balloting, Polish Peasant Party candidates were stricken from the ballot in ten out of fifty-two election districts.[47] These ten districts constituted only 12 per cent of the country's territory but contained virtually a quarter of the total population (5,342,000 out of about 24,000,000). The ban was accompanied by mass arrests of candidates in the other forty-two districts where the lists were still admitted. Altogether, 135 candidates were arrested. The already limited freedom of the press was further restricted during the last phase of the election period. Circulation of the only daily PSL paper was arbitrarily limited to some 75,000 copies; five of its editors were arrested and similar methods were applied to the few weeklies which the PSL was allowed to publish in the provinces. Practically no broadcasting facilities were given to the opposition.

Having disenfranchised a considerable percentage of the electorate and having jailed a large number of PSL candidates, the PPR also decided to deprive remaining voters of their right to vote secretly. A vigorous propaganda campaign was initiated in favor of open voting two weeks before the election. This was a very potent weapon in view of the limited propaganda facilities left to the opposition and in view of the hold the state and the party apparatus already had over the Polish populace.

Voting took place on January 17, 1947, during the coldest winter month, when heavy snow made traveling difficult if not impossible. In most cases the PSL was prevented from sending its observers to check on the fairness of the voting.[48]

The official results of the election, published on February 22, 1947, were as follows:[49]

	Number	Percentage of Valid Votes
Registered electors	12,701,056	
Ballots deposited	11,413,618	
Valid votes	11,244,873	
Democratic Bloc (controlled by the PPR)	9,003,682	80.1
The Labor Party	530,979	4.1
The Peasant Party "New Liberation"	397,754	3.5
The Polish Peasant Party of Mikołajczyk	1,154,847	10.3
Other parties	157,611	1.4

Former United States Secretary of State, James F. Byrnes, reported in his memoirs that during the Yalta Conference President

Roosevelt said to Stalin: "I want the election in Poland to be beyond question, like Caesar's wife. I did not know Caesar's wife, but she was believed to have been pure." To this Stalin retorted: "It was said so about Caesar's wife, but in fact, she had certain sins." [50]

As a prominent member of the PPR Władysław Wolski (Piwowarczyk) said to a Polish-American writer, Alexander Janta: "Was anyone so naive as to expect that a revolution carried into this land on bayonets' points would yield before a ballot box . . . ?"

AFTERMATH OF THE ELECTION: THE SMALL CONSTITUTION

The next step of the triumphant government bloc was to present Poland with what was later labelled the Small Constitution. The disregarded "broad principles" of the Constitution of 1921 were now officially replaced, although the Lublin Manifesto had declared the 1921 document to be the fundamental law of the country in place of the semi-authoritarian Constitution of 1935. The provisional charter, often called the Small Constitution, was to be an interim law which would stand until a final fundamental law of the country had been prepared and promulgated.

The new charter was prepared in a hurry. All three readings of it were rushed through the Sejm with great rapidity. The parliament was convoked on February 4, 1947; by February 19 the constitution was approved and Bierut was re-elected as head of state, with the title of president.[51] The next day Bierut appointed Cyrankiewicz as prime minister, to succeed Osóbka (Morawski), who had lost favor by his surprising resistance to PPS-PPR merger. The new government finally dropped the "provisional" qualification from its title.

Perhaps the most significant feature of the Small Constitution was the establishment of a Council of State. According to Article 15 of the constitution, the Council of State was to be composed of the president of the Republic, as chairman, the marshal and vice-marshal of the Sejm, and the chairman of the Supreme Control Council, corresponding to the Office of the Controller General in the United States. Of the seven Council of State members, three belonged to the PPR and four others more or less willingly did the party's bidding. The Council of State was entrusted with "supervision over local national councils," which, in turn, would check on local administrations.[52] Furthermore, while the Sejm was to be convoked for only two ordinary sessions each year, the Council of State would rule throughout the rest of the year by means of its decrees.

Five avowed PPR cabinet members held the reins of government.

Gomułka, the vice-prime minister, was also the all-powerful minister for regained territories. Radkiewicz, as minister of public security, directed the police and the citizens' militia, "Ormo." Hilary Minc, as minister of industry and trade, was in charge of most economic affairs. The remaining two Communists, Skrzeszewski and Modzelewski, administered the ministries of education and foreign affairs respectively.

Immediately after the elections there followed mass arrests of PSL members and a wholesale closing of its local branches. It became obvious that the PSL's back was broken, and the only open political force opposing the regime now ceased to exist. In November 1947, Mikołajczyk and a handful of his friends, fearing for their lives, escaped from Poland. With the defeat of the PSL, the political weight of the already subservient PPS declined rapidly. By the close of 1947 it was clear that the days of the PPS were numbered also.

Thus, a crucial phase in the Communist assumption of political power in Poland, or as some like to call it, "the first revolution," [53] ended late in 1947. Political power was firmly in PPR hands; the property-owning class and its last liberal spokesmen had been eliminated as political and economic factors of importance. The country's economic life was now, at least outwardly, a mixed affair composed of three unevenly balanced sectors: private, cooperative, and socialist. In this respect there is a certain similarity between the years 1945 to 1947 and the period of the New Economic Policy in Russia. In reality, also in Poland the state dominated the whole economy because it controlled the "commanding heights."

The consolidation of power, which combined methods of friendly persuasion, nationalistic propaganda, terror, and ideological penetration, lasted three years: from the beginning of 1945 until the end of 1947. These years were marked by transformations that had certain genuine democratic and socialistic features, such as agrarian reform and the nationalization of large and medium-size industries. These reforms, generally speaking, found a broad measure of popular support. The loss of the eastern provinces, especially the cities of Wilno and Lwów, were deplored, it is true, and the subservience of the regime to Moscow was ridiculed, but the slogan of "reconstruction" and establishment of Poland on the Oder-Neisse rivers as well as on the Baltic Sea were received with a considerable amount of favor by the Poles.

During this period certain gestures of appeasement were performed, both for the benefit of the outside world and for the overwhelming majority of non-Communist citizens. The Catholic Church, for example, was interfered with less than in other people's democracies. Peasants were repeatedly reassured that they would be allowed to continue private ownership of their land. Petty tradesmen and small craftsmen were told to continue their occupations and were left relatively undisturbed. During the immediate postwar period, a certain latitude was allowed to non-Communist political and religious forces, provided they did not openly challenge the new order, the leadership of the PPR, and the fundamental principle of Polish-Soviet friendship. The degree of freedom, although insignificant in comparison with that prevailing in most Western countries and, indeed, in prewar Poland, was not negligible when compared with the Soviet Union or other people's democracies, among them Yugoslavia and Bulgaria. In 1947 four freedoms still existed in Poland: freedom of worship, freedom of movement and of choosing one's work, freedom to listen to the radio, even to foreign broadcasts and, finally, freedom of *private* criticism.

Poland, according to Communist theoreticians, was simply a "People's Democracy." As an American scholar writes:

Unlike the orthodox view of the dictatorship of the proletariat, in which its vanguard wields the effective power, the political power of the People's Democracy was to be shared in a formal sense by national coalitions and in the real sense (if we may use these distinctions of Marx) by an alliance of the working and peasant classes, but with neither exercising a hegemony . . . One must note, however, that a clear-cut, theoretical, and well-reasoned analysis of the People's Democracy, made within the context of Marxian ideology, was not elucidated systematically by the East European Communist leaders. It may well have been that most of them were not, trained as they were in the Stalinist Comintern or in local undergrounds, theoretically equipped or so inclined. In addition to this, they were faced with the many daily tasks inherent in the unfolding struggle for power and could hardly be expected to devote themselves to a serious formulation of an admittedly ticklish subject. Finally, they probably preferred to leave the field of theory, with all its dangerous quicksands, to their Soviet senior colleagues and limit themselves to mere elaboration of formulas shaped in Moscow.[54]

Although no longer part of the capitalist world, Poland was not yet a fully "socialist" state.

PURGES and
MERGERS

After the flight of Mikołajczyk, the PPR threw away any pretence of being merely the leading member of a governmental coalition and openly assumed a dominant role. After a brief period of relaxation following the elections Poland began to evolve toward a totalitarian form of government of the Soviet type, with emphasis not on democratic process but on the dictatorship of the proletariat. Gradually, however, the term "dictatorship of the proletariat" has been replaced by that of "dictatorship of the working class," since a people's democracy cannot have a proletariat. Both the Czechoslovak *coup d'état* and the Yugoslav crisis quickened this evolution. Major changes in Poland's development after the 1947–48 period were accomplished in the Soviet-like atmosphere which prevailed since that time, with the application of Stalinist police methods of indoctrination, intimidation, and coercion. Among other things, purges and show trials now became characteristic features of political life.

The PPR underwent its first major purge in two installments, the first milder phase occurring in September 1948, when Gomułka was removed as secretary-general of the party and a group of his followers were deprived of their posts. The second much harsher installment took place at the end of 1949. The purges were closely connected with broad policies of Moscow in respect to the captive East Central Europe.

THE GOMUŁKA AFFAIR

Earlier, in the summer of 1947, a Communist information bureau (Cominform) had been established, with the seat in Bucharest, as another Soviet instrument of control over the adolescent people's democracies. Gomułka indicated that he was rather frightened by this move,[1] and while acting as host at an inauguration conference of the nine Communist parties, which took place in Poland, he expressed

his misgivings about it. Some of Gomułka's utterances revealed overtones that were bound to alarm the Kremlin. When referring to work
the PPR was doing in eradicating anti-Soviet feelings in Poland,
Gomułka said: "The principal lever is the question of the western
territories and the knowledge that the Soviet Union helped Poland
to settle its frontiers on the Oder and the Neisse . . ." [2] This
sentence suggested the fear which certain PPR quarters shared with
a majority of Poles, namely, that Moscow might, at some future
date, once more strike a bargain with Germany at the expense of
Poland. These doubts, implicit in Gomułka's words, when coupled
with his constant emphasis on a "Polish way to socialism," must
have created the opinion in Moscow that the secretary-general of the
PPR was not so reliable a man as was expected.[3]

Further confirmation for the Kremlin was forthcoming. On June
3, 1948, just as the Russo-Yugoslav dispute was reaching its climax,
but three weeks before the Cominform meeting which condemned
Tito, a plenary session of the PPR's Central Committee took place.
In reporting this meeting, the Communist theoretical organ, "New
Roads," printed some extracts from Gomułka's speech in which he
attacked the party's Luxemburgist traditions and praised the PPS
for its stand on independence. On another occasion Gomułka affirmed
that the PPR and PPS were in agreement regarding Poland's independence: "Both for the Polish Socialist Party and for the Polish
Workers' Party, the independence of Poland is a supreme consideration to which all others are subordinated." [4] Once more Moscow
must have viewed this repeated stress on independence with suspicion.

The Central Committee meeting of the PPR, which lasted from
August 31 to September 3, 1948, took Gomułka to task. His past
attempts to compromise with other parties and his emphasis on the
difference between Poland's "way to socialism" and Russia's were
scornfully denounced. Gomułka was accused of favoring a conciliatory attitude toward Yugoslavia and of adopting a defiant
attitude toward the Soviet Union. He was denounced as a "nationalist
deviationist" who allegedly wanted to make the PPR a national
Communist party and, still worse, negotiate with the Bolshevik party
as an equal partner. Gomułka was accused also of attempting to
sabotage the collectivization of Polish agriculture, and branded,
moreover, as being thirsty for absolute power in the party.

After prolonged and bitter debate the Politbureau had already
suspended Gomułka as secretary-general and designated Bierut to
be chairman of the PPR's Central Committee. At the Central Com-

mittee session described previously, Gomułka's resignation was formally accepted, after the Central Committee heard his not too articulate recantation.[5] Four of Gomułka's followers were demoted from full to alternate members of the Central Committee; Włady-sław Bieńkowski, until now in charge of the party's educational department, was expelled from the Central Committee altogether.

At the end of 1949 the fall of Gomułka and Bieńkowski was fol-lowed by that of their friends, Spychalski and Kliszko, thus provid-ing the second installment in this major PPR purge. For a long time Spychalski, as head of the Chief Office of Political Administration, had been a key figure in the armed forces. He was an old CPP mem-ber, a founder of the PPR, a resourceful underground leader, and chief of the Intelligence Service of the clandestine People's Army. Because of his lack of Moscow training, his considerable popularity among the party rank and file, and his association with Gomułka during the underground period, Spychalski was now regarded as a potentially dangerous figure.

From the point of view of Moscow Spychalski's past was far from blameless. First of all, he had been so horrified by "the first Soviet occupation" of Poland (1939–1941) that, in spite of Moscow's in-structions, he refused to join the Wasilewska group and left Lwów for Warsaw.[6] There Spychalski eventually became a founder of the PPR, which he hoped would be allied to the Soviet party, on the basis of equality but not slavishly subordinate to it. Secondly, he had a brother, a regular army colonel, who succeeded General Bór-Komorowski in 1943 as Home Army commander of the Cracow dis-trict. Spychalski apparently refused to break his family ties, and when his brother was murdered by the Gestapo in 1944, he repeat-edly tried to help his widowed sister-in-law.[7]

In Spychalski's case the charges were similar to those made against his friend, Gomułka, and had little to do with the real reasons for the purge. As Intelligence chief of the People's Army, Spychalski had allegedly permitted enemies of the party and of the Soviet Union to occupy responsible positions in the party apparatus and in the armed forces. Numerous instances of his sheltering "spies" and "sab-oteurs" were cited. Moreover, he was charged with allowing "valu-able Soviet specialists to depart prematurely." There had, indeed, been a reduction in the number of Soviet specialists utilized in Po-land after 1946, due to the return of Polish officers from the West. This reduction must have been decided at the highest level and ap-proved by the appropriate Soviet advisers, but this fact was now used against Spychalski. In spite of his attempt to defend his viewpoint and to disassociate himself from Gomułka, Spychalski was discharged from his post of vice-minister of national defense and replaced by Ochab.[8]

Gomułka, whose case was reopened in November 1949, was further charged with such misdemeanors as "lack of vigilance," "tolerating spies in his ministry," allowing party ranks to be penetrated by former Trotskyites, and using Polish patriotism as a touchstone for his appointments. In the new atmosphere of rigid Stalinism created since the previous year, each of these alleged actions bordered on treason. Finally, Gomułka was accused of responsibility for the deaths of Nowotko and Finder, his predecessors in the office of secretary-general. All these charges were invented or, at least, twisted in order to compromise Gomułka. Gomułka defended himself in a courageous and dignified way. He refused to admit, as charged, that he had removed his predecessors, then he attempted a vigorous counterattack. His ideological mistakes, he said, had been shared by practically all his colleagues and by most builders of other people's democracies. Why was he chosen to be the scapegoat? The condemnation of Gomułka and his associates, however, had obviously been decided upon beforehand. What the Central Committee witnessed was a morality play staged for the benefit of the rest of the party. Gomułka and Spychalski were expelled from the Central Committee and forbidden to participate in any party work. This was, in reality, a thinly disguised expulsion from the party.[9]

The aftermath of the "Gomułka affair" lasted for more than a year. Three major purges (September-December 1948, January-March 1949, and November-December 1949) were successively conducted under the slogan of eradicating nationalist deviation; one fourth of the party membership was affected. Many leading native party members were deprived of their key posts and scattered, or in some cases, as with Spychalski, imprisoned. Gomułka was still present at the Unification Congress of December 1948, and was even allowed to speak, but his statement was not published. In November 1949 he was removed from the party altogether. In July 1951 he was placed under house arrest and began his "long retreat" in a suburban villa near Warsaw. For a couple of years his trial was awaited in vain, despite intermittent Soviet pressure. The second conflict between the "Muscovites" and the native faction ended in a complete victory for the former.

The scope and intensity of the purges revealed the strength of "national communism," as it was then branded in the PPR. The reaction of the broad masses of the party in the crisis of October 1956 showed that even the purging of a quarter of its membership had not innoculated the party against nationalistic tendencies. It had merely driven them underground to take still deeper roots. Thus ended the "nationalist crisis" within the Polish party. "[T]he crisis of 1948–49 brought out the true nature of Titoism as an organic disease of Communist parties when in power. Titoism in Poland was not successful. But it was merely . . . one outbreak of the disease and not its sources that were destroyed." [10]

PPR, THE BOLSHEVIK PARTY, AND THE SOVIET UNION

It would be erroneous, however, to interpret Gomułka's downfall only in terms of a struggle for power between two rival factions of the PPR. Certain fundamental misconceptions of the native Polish Communists concerning the nature and dynamics of the Soviet state and the Bolshevik party played a decisive role at this time. The personality of Gomułka was an important factor also.

By now it seems beyond question that the early attempts of Polish Communist leaders to find a specifically "Polish way to socialism" were guided by a Kremlin decision made during the war in order to intercept the nationalistic forces unleashed in the struggle. This approach had naturally been welcomed by many resistance leaders who were in close touch with the masses. Although determined to entrench his party in power, Gomułka, a man endowed with a great deal of common sense, believed the PPR ought to proceed toward communism in a way that would not necessarily imitate Soviet methods and would take into account the patriotic sentiments of the Polish masses, as well as peculiarities of the country's social and economic structure. He was convinced that Poland could evolve into a socialist state without applying wasteful terror on a large scale. His idea was that of a "mild" revolution, supported by the masses as far as possible, that is, spontaneous to some extent and not entirely engineered from above. Gomułka was not trying to sabotage collectivization, but he believed that collectivization should be preceded by cooperative use of machinery on private fields, the later stages coming gradually and voluntarily after a considerable period of training and careful preparation. His familiarity with the Soviet experiment led him to believe that the Bolshevik tempo of socialization would produce disastrous results in Poland and consequently would undermine the position of his party.

Gomułka's policies, which had been "correct" (that is, considered helpful to the Soviet Union) from 1944 to 1947, during the takeover period, became "deviationist" in 1948–49, during the period of consolidation. Gomułka, relying unduly on his personal popularity and the popularity of his slogans seemed to forget it was Moscow that called the tune. When the tune changed, Gomułka still insisted on dancing the old dance. The "Polish way to socialism," so popular with many native Communists during the period of underground struggle against the Nazis, now became a fatal "nationalist deviation," "denying the universal significance of the Soviet experience."

There was also a personal factor. It seems quite probable, as has been emphasized by Ulam in his *Titoism and the Cominform,* that Gomułka's spectacular rise to power turned his head. He became jealous of Soviet interference and arrogance and resentful of the colonial methods of exploitation applied in Poland by the Kremlin. He had to share control over the party with Bierut and Berman, but still he was the party's secretary-general and a vice-prime minister of Poland. Gomułka had an apparent temperamental inclination toward socialism of the PPS brand — militant and spontaneous, romantic and emotionally patriotic. When comparing the PPS record with that of the Communist Party of Poland, he often found warmer, kinder words for the former; he repeatedly disparaged the Communist Party for its "Luxemburgist heritage," its "nationalist nihilism," and its doctrinaire disregard of the peasant problem. A genuine synthesis of both movements, a synthesis which would balance his party in a manner more to his liking, was probably what Gomułka intended. There are some indications that he was pressing for a quick merger and searching for support among PPS members against his opponents within the PPR, who were distrustful of his insistence on the "Polish way to socialism." [11] This insistence must have been annoying to the Soviet leadership. Gomułka, steering the Polish party toward a more independent course, might indeed be following in Tito's footsteps. After the defection of Yugoslavia, Moscow decided to take no chances with local Communist leaders and to remove this man who showed an unmistakable reluctance to do the Soviet bidding.

In confessing his cardinal sin — his attitude toward Moscow and the Soviet Communist Party — Gomułka said:

[T]he core of my rightist, nationalist complex must have been my attitude to the Soviet Union — to the CPSU(B). . . . [M]y attitude could be reduced not so much to . . . the relationship between the CPSU(B) and the Polish Workers' Party as to the relationship between Poland and the USSR as states . . . It never entered my head that Poland could progress along the way to socialism without being supported by the

Soviet Union . . . These things I understood, but, . . . it was . . . difficult for me to shift my attitude as regards the Soviet Union to the ideological party plane.[12]

This, it seems, was the heart of the matter. It was correctly formulated by a French student of communism, who, analyzing the position of the Communist leaders in various Soviet-controlled countries during the Stalinist period concluded: "The important chiefs of the Soviet system and the party in various Soviet republics are primarily representatives of the party: they stand to their own nationals as representatives of the party rather than to the party as representatives of their nationals." [13]

The Stalinist ideological platform of the United Polish Workers' Party, of December 1948, emphasized that "every tendency aimed at loosening collaboration with the Soviet Union endangers the very foundation of the people's democracy in Poland and, at the same time, the independence of the country," since the alliance with the USSR is the best guarantee of Poland's territorial integrity and her very existence. The Polish Workers' Party "indissolubly links the cause of consolidating Poland's independence and her march towards socialism with the struggle for peace conducted under the leadership of the Soviet Union." [14]

By recognizing the leadership of the Bolshevik party, the Polish party became a junior party, subordinated to the Soviet one. Poland, as a people's democracy, and as a member of the socialist camp, led by the USSR, needed to remain "indissolubly linked" with the Soviet Union, with whose assistance its own government was established and maintained itself in power. The first dependence, however, the ideological one, was by far the most important, the political dependence following the partisan one. The satellite character of the Communist regime in Poland, lasting until October 1956, was but a reflection of its ideological partisan subordination to "The Rome of the Proletariat," to use André Gide's expression. And in the partisan relationship iron discipline is a must.

Here, it seems, lay the main cause of Gomułka's downfall: he was not Bolshevized, or Stalinized, enough, not indoctrinated deeply enough to accept the leadership of the Soviet Union, that is, complete and automatic subservience of his party and his country to the Bolshevik party and the Soviet state. For this Gomułka had to suffer the inevitable penalty. Only a combination of favorable circumstances saved his life, and allowed him to re-emerge as the leader of a Communist reformation in Poland.

LIQUIDATION OF THE PPS — THE SOFTENING PROCESS[15]

After crushing the Polish Peasant Party, absorption of the still semi-independent PPS became the next objective of the PPR. The ground for merger was prepared by the skillful use of the slogan, "unity of action," which was to be a step toward "organic unity" of the entire working class of Poland.

The new leaders of the PPS, who replaced the old Social Democratic team, had to pay constant lip service to the idea of merger with the PPR. But, after the new leadership had consolidated its position and some of the rank and file had reasserted their influence over PPS affairs, the idea of self-effacement began to appear less and less attractive to all concerned. The Communists quickly noticed this change of mood, which was bound to be reflected in a change of mind toward any merger.

The PPR used various devices to weaken the new Socialist leaders. The first, related previously, consisted of preventing a coalition between the PSL and the PPS and fostering a belief among Socialists that the only alternative to dictatorship of the proletariat was the "return of reaction." "Thanks to this concentration of the democratic forces [that is, of the PPR and the PPS]," said Bierut in 1948, "it was possible to unmask and finally destroy . . . the Polish Peasant Party." [16]

A second device was to capture two important mass organizations which had been traditional bulwarks of Social Democratic influence — cooperatives and trade-unions. Both groups were undermined by the transfer of some of their functions to state-controlled organizations. The ultimate tactic of the Communists was the use of force. At the height of Socialist resistance to the Workers' Party, during the summer of 1947, the Communists staged a series of trials of rightist Socialists.[17] The charges, usually of espionage and subversive activities, served to warn post-1944 leaders of the PPS that their failure to cooperate with the Communists would be tantamount to treason. The fate of the liquidated Social Democratic group (Żuławski, Pużak, and their followers), intimidated many of those members who, up to now, had opposed any outright association with the Communists.

During this period the problems of cooperation and eventual merger were sharply debated in the press of both parties. Some friction arose between the two, the Socialists being accused of cultivating petty bourgeois ideas on civil liberties and "harboring elements hostile to democracy." As the Sejm election approached, representatives of the two rival parties were summond to Moscow, in November 1946, and made to sign a united front agreement. This agreement, published simultaneously in the Communist and Socialist presses on November 29, 1946, stated that the parties were "separate, independent and equal political groups," which would "mutually respect each other's organizational structure."

The agreement embraced the following points: (1) The two parties were to endow their members with a spirit of working-class unity and forge a conviction in them of the importance of a united front. They were to combat all tendencies to return to policies contrary to the principle of working-class unity. (2) Leaders of both parties were also to combat anti-Soviet tendencies and the reactionary activities of right-wing Socialists. (3) Both parties were to support the agencies of public security charged with reestablishment of "peace and justice." (4) Both parties were to fight the Polish Peasant Party of Mikołajczyk, because his party "became a legal superstructure of reactionary resistance." They were to encourage the conversion of "true democrats from the Polish Peasant Party." [18]

At the same time it was announced that the secretary-general of the PPS, Cyrankiewicz, was to be appointed minister without portfolio, and Dr. Stanisław Leczycki, also a Socialist leader, was to receive the post of vice-minister of foreign affairs. Further concessions were made to the PPS after the Sejm election of January 19, 1947. Mikołajczyk's party was already weakened, but he was still potentially dangerous, so as a precautionary measure the PPR determined to appease the PPS. Consequently, the Socialist Party was given six cabinet posts and retained the premiership which Osóbka-Morawski yielded to Cyrankiewicz. The PPR received only five ministries, but succeeded in placing strong personalities as vice-ministers in most other ministries.

The pro-Communist faction among PPS leaders continued to press and plot for a merger. On May Day of 1947, taking advantage of the Marxist holiday, Gomułka issued a clear call for the amalgamation of the two parties. Common meetings were to be held throughout the country to discuss the fusion. Speaking for the Socialist rank and file, which was disturbed by Gomułka's declaration, the PPS press asked if the Workers' Party contemplated turning Poland into a one-party state. Organic unity of the two parties, the PPS added, could not be achieved during the period of people's democracy, but only when Poland was ready for socialism.[19] The Communists retorted that the PPR had no desire to create a *monoparty* state; that as long as different social classes existed in Poland, they must be represented by separate political parties. A PPR spokesman asked, however, what class interests the Socialists represented in contradiction to the Workers' Party, and vice versa. The task of the day, said the Communists, was to achieve complete ideological unity. Organic unity would be the logical consequence of an ideological agreement.[20]

Relations between the two parties were strained to the breaking point. Only skillful pressure exercised by Cyrankiewicz and Rusinek prevented further recriminations; they persuaded their comrades not to upset the united front in the face of the danger of "fascism" and "reaction" represented by the PSL. On July 26, 1947, at a conference in Warsaw, PPS and PPR leaders decided upon joint meetings throughout the country to organize mutual assistance in uncovering "reactionary and hostile elements" in both parties, and also to establish mixed mediation boards in order to eliminate mutual differences. The slogan was, "the enemy is only on the right; the ally is on the left." At this stage PPS leaders reversed themselves and, accepting the inevitable, favored a quick merger which would give the Socialists numerical superiority within the new organization. It is quite possible that Gomułka encouraged this new PPS policy. Meanwhile many Socialist leaders toured the country exhorting joint PPS-PPR meetings to maintain a united front. Some meetings were rather stormy; many local Socialists objected to the fact that the front was a one-way affair. The major protagonists of merger, Cyrankiewicz and Rusinek, were taken aback by the amount of local opposition to the fusion which they encountered during a speaking tour and at the annual PPS Congress in December 1947. Consequently, they proceeded to purge those whom they considered guilty of "rightist deviations." According to a socialist writer:

On January 15, 1948, a government delegation, headed by Cyrankiewicz, and including Gomułka and Minc, went to Moscow to negotiate a trade agreement with the Soviet government. What Cyrankiewicz was told there is not known, but his action was decisive. At a meeting of the Warsaw Committee of the Socialist Party on March 17 he declared, in effect, that the party was ready to merge with the Workers' Party.[21] Both parties started purges, however, and combined to give "joint schooling courses" to their members. As a result, it was believed in June that the merger would take place at the end of September. But just at this point the blast of the Cominform resolution against the Yugoslav Communist Party, and the implications it carried for Communists in Poland blew this hope out the window . . .

Apparently Moscow feared that unless both movements were purged before the merger, the Gomułka faction of the PPR might combine with like-minded PPS elements and, consequently, create a bloc difficult to manage.

Between September 18 and 23, 1948, following the crucial Gomułka purge session of the PPR's Central Committee, the Supreme Council of the PPS held its own "purge session." Disciplinary measures were taken against those members of the small group opposing fusion who still held leading posts in the PPS. Mass purges then followed.[22] The history of the PPS was hastily revised, rewritten, and ridiculed. On the eve of the amalgamation, the PPS was already a paralyzed rump.

LIQUIDATION OF THE PPS — THE MERGER

Formal fusion of the two Marxist parties took place in December 1948, at a Unification Congress held in Warsaw on the thirteenth anniversary of the founding of the Communist Party of Poland.

The congress, which lasted over a week, was attended by 1539 delegates; 1013 came from the Workers' Party and 526 from the Socialist Party.[23] Two guests of honor were Zofia Dzierżyńska, the widow of Feliks Dzierżyński, organizer and first head of the Cheka, and Wanda Wasilewska, the founding mother of the Union of Polish Patriots. Alexander Zawadzki read a telegram on December 20 to "the leader of genius," congratulating him on his sixty-ninth birthday; members of the gathering burst into shouts: "Sta-lin, Sta-lin, Sta-lin."

The new United Workers' Party elected a Central Committee of 65 members who, in turn, elected a Politbureau of eleven members. There were eight members from the PPR, including Bierut, Berman, Zawadzki, Zambrowski, Jóźwiak, Minc, and Radkiewicz, and only three from the PPS (Cyrankiewicz, Rapacki, and Świątkowski). Besides the three PPR deputy members of the Politbureau (Chełchowski, Mazur, and Ochab), there was one Socialist (Matuszewski). Bierut became chairman of the Central Committee, while the nominal mantle of Gomułka, the post of secretary-general, went to Cyrankiewicz, the man who was largely instrumental in bringing about the merger. But even Cyrankiewicz was not to be trusted fully. His power was limited by the appointment of two reliable, Moscow-trained secretaries, Zawadzki and Zambrowski. A governmental reorganization followed the merger, and the most important posts, with the notable exception of the premiership, were taken over by Communists. Previously, thirty-three out of sixty governmental posts of the rank of vice-minister or higher were occupied by party men; after the merger they held fifty-three out of seventy-four.

Thus the United Polish Workers' Party was established. The struggle against the "social-patriotic" PPS which had lasted for over half a century came to a close: the merger was a resounding triumph for the PPR over its traditional antagonist. From the start of the alliance the PPS, the junior partner of the team, was first pushed into a position of subordination and then finally absorbed. The merger, to use the expression of Lenin's Social Democratic rival, Martov, was reminiscent of a hungry man merging with a piece of bread.

The preamble to the United Party's Rules reaffirmed the Leninist concept of the party's role: "The United Polish Workers' Party is the vanguard of the Polish working class — the leading force of the Polish nation, the UPWP is the highest form of working-class organization and the exponent of the interests of the town and country working masses." According to the new ideological platform, "the United Polish Workers' Party is the wisdom, honor, and conscience of the working class," [24] it means its elite organization.

The platform stated that, although Poland had followed the example of the Soviet Union, she had not yet achieved the final goal:

The People's Democracy in Poland is accomplishing the collaboration of democratic groupings under the leadership of the united working-class movement . . . The setting up of a People's Democracy in Poland fully confirms Leninist-Stalinist teachings on the state . . . People's Democracy is the way to socialism; it is a new form of controlling power by the working masses, led by the working class, and brought into being thanks to the new historical situation and thanks to the assistance of the USSR. The system of People's Democracy can and should . . . effectively realize the basic functions of the dictatorship of the proletariat.[25] Thus the party is to be the instrument of the dictatorship of the working class.

Intensification of the class struggle and further expansion of nationalization were forecast by Bierut who, in his speech entitled "Ideological Foundations of the United Polish Workers' Party," forecast intensification of the class struggle:

[T]here cannot be any question of a freezing of the existing economic relations, no questions of the inviolability of the parallel positions of the various economic sectors . . . The working class must carry on a ruthless struggle against capitalist elements, must aim at the complete elimination of all forms and sources of economic exploitations. . . .[26]

Following on the heels of the Three Year Plan of Reconstruction and Development was a Six Year Plan to lay the "foundations of socialism" and to turn Poland into an industrial-agricultural country. Minc declared that the Three Year Plan would be completed ahead of time early in 1949. The Six Year Plan would be put into practice in 1950. By the close of 1955, at the end of the plan, Poland was to produce 4,000,000 tons of steel, 4,000,000 tons of cement, 95,000,000 tons of coal, and 18,000,000,000 kilowatt hours of electric power. The plan called for an expansion in the chemical industry of more than 350 per cent as compared with the prewar level. Industry was to become second in importance to coal production. The plan would give Poland 350 new large industrial plants and 65,000 new tractors which were indispensable for further collectivization of agriculture. "Voluntary transformation of small and medium peasant holdings into cooperative farms" was the official term for this latter process.[27]

This second industrial revolution was to be accompanied by a cultural revolution which would eventually abolish illiteracy and create a new intelligentsia of worker and peasant origin, fully dedicated to the task of "building the foundations of socialism in Poland."

THE UNITED PARTY IN ACTION: ORGANIZATION

In addition to presenting an ideological platform, the congress defined the rules of the UPWP which, in fifty-nine articles, set forth the organizational structure of the new party.[28]

The rules at least nominally adhered to the traditional principle of "democratic centralism" as the basis of the party's internal structure. The lowest level of party organization consisted of "primary cells," each based, as a rule, on "production links"; primary cells were to be supervised by district committees which, in turn, received their instructions from a provincial committee elected by the party congress, supposedly the highest party authority. Lower party executives, including party secretaries up to the provincial level, were to be elected annually. Usually, however, even these officials continued to be appointed from above. The Central Committee did not even try to conceal its authority in respect to provincial committees, and freely appointed, transferred, and relieved the secretaries of these bodies.

In accordance with the rules, a party congress was to convene every three years, but following the Soviet practice of taking liberties with such provisions there was actually only one congress after December 1948, that of March 1954. Plenary sessions of the Central Committee were to take place every three months. In reality, between the first and second congresses of the United Party, the so-called

Plenum convened less than twice a year. The Central Committee was supposed to direct all party work in accordance with instructions laid down by the Politbureau, but because it was an unwieldy body of some sixty-five to eighty people, it relied on its various bureaus such as the Orgbureau, the Party Secretariat, the Central Editorial Bureau, etc., in order to supervise party activity.

The party rules emphasized that "resolutions of the lower bodies may not be contrary to the resolutions of the upper bodies" and that "internal democracy may not be misused for purposes contrary to the interest of the party and the working class." The fact that upper bodies and, ultimately, the "Central Committee of the Central Committee" — the Politbureau — determined what these interests were gave the Politbureau a far-reaching control over the ideological orthodoxy of the whole party. For example, members of the Politbureau had to secure its permission in order to speak during its sessions. Even members of the Politbureau who wished to address a plenary session of the Central Committee were obliged to present the text of their speeches to the omnipotent bureau for approval beforehand. Resolutions which the Politbureau presented to the Central Committee were invariably passed unanimously. Consequently, the Politbureau really determined the party's policy and was its most important organ.

The Central Committee, supreme organ of the party between congresses, was to be elected by the congress itself, but individual deputy members of the committee could be selected or expelled by the committee's own decision. Going beyond the limitations of this rule, the Third Plenary Session of the Central Committee co-opted Marshal Rokossovsky on November 6, 1949, as a full-fledged member of the committee.[29]

Another means of control was party discipline. Absolute obedience and "guarding the purity of the party ranks and the ideological attitude of the party members" were successfully enforced, this task being entrusted to a Central Commission for Party Control which was elected by the congress.[30] Penalties consisted of warnings, reprimands, temporary removal from the party's social and professional work, and, finally, expulsion. Expulsion or purge had been increasingly applied since the end of 1948. Punishment was often preceded by public self-criticism which, in some cases, was a severe penalty in itself. After his confession had been torn to pieces by his comrades Gomułka said: "You've made a rag out of me . . . you've maltreated me!"

Although collective resolutions from lower party cells had to be directed to the next higher level of the hierarchy, individual members could communicate directly with the Central Committee, reporting, if they wished, on activities of lesser authorities in the party. Thus, although individual members were assured free access to the very apex of the party, the way was blocked for collective statements. The Communists argued that by this means factionalism was prevented and the "elemental pressure" of the party rank and file minimized. It was, of course, also an effective way for the Central Committee to keep a close watch on the lower strata of the party. Both the rules and the ideological platform of 1948 reaffirmed the "Leninist Character" of the party, which became "Polish in form but Bolshevik in content." Like all other Communist parties, the UPWP remained a hierarchical, military-type structure whose business proceeded along vertical lines from top to bottom. Both the rules and the ideological platform placed more stress on Marxist-Leninist-Stalinist tenets than did corresponding documents dating from the PPR's First Congress in December 1945. Traditions of "proletarian internationalism" and the heritage of Poland's Communist Party were re-emphasized, as opposed to the "social patriotism" of the PPS, the party's defeated rival. Soviet leadership became ever more exalted and any idea of a "Polish way to socialism" was discarded once again. This was authoritatively stated at the congress:

There can be no question of any particular, specific type of People's Democracy opposed to the party of the dictatorship of the Proletariat — the Communist Party of the Soviet Union (Bolshevik). Quite to the contrary, with due regard for the particularity of our development, the model for a party of the new type is and will continue to be for us the Communist Party of the Soviet Union . . .[31]

Soon after the absorption of the PPS the Communist-sponsored Peasant Party merged with the remnants of the Polish Peasant Party which had been meanwhile, after the flight of Mikołajczyk, increasingly infiltrated by the PPR. Thus was created the United Peasant Party, a "transmission belt" of the UPWP to the peasant masses. Its ideological platform was made to correspond with that of the UPWP, including the recognition of "the dominant role of the working class and its party."[32] Another tolerated political group, the Democratic Party was to play the role of transmitting the directives of the UPWP to the vestigial classes of craftsmen, petty shopkeepers, and members of liberal profession.

Part IV

The UNITED POLISH
WORKERS' PARTY

The PARTY,
the PLANS, and
12   the PEASANTS

The congress which incorporated the PPS into the PPR also opened a new era in Poland's history. Soon after the congress the united party embarked upon several ventures of great scope and intensity, among them a revised six-year plan calling for more rapid collectivization, and a struggle with the Roman Catholic Church.

The process of interpenetration between the state and the party apparatus accelerated since 1948 and the party consequently tightened its supervision over the state administration. Some party bureaus and departments are chiefly concerned with internal problems, but the majority correspond to various ministries in the government. In fact, no minister can make a major decision without securing the prior approval of a corresponding section in the Politbureau. The Six Year Plan, for example, was first approved by the Politbureau and only then voted by the Sejm. The new constitution was published only after the Politbureau approved it as being "in accordance with the party policy."

After 1949 the party assumed direction of most of the outwardly nonpolitical mass organizations, such as trade-unions, the Peasant Self-Help Association, the Women's League, the Union of Fighters for Freedom and Democracy, the Polish-Soviet Society, and various professional associations. All of these groups were utilized in an effort to fulfill the Six Year Plan. Most methods for influencing such bodies had been formulated in the party rules, which provided for the establishment of party cells inside various mass organizations in order to "carry out the policy of the party, enhance its influence and authority, and expand the activities of the masses for the implementation of aims set by the party."

The truly mystical aura enveloping the Six Year Plan affected all party activities, including its personnel policy, in which training of new cadres had to be increasingly stressed. The plan provided for an average yearly increase in the nation's output from 11 to 12 per cent and an annual growth in socialist industrial production of about 20 per cent, confronting the party with an almost superhuman task. In attempting to complete this second social and economic revolution, the party had to mobilize ruthlessly every ounce of the country's energy and tighten the already stringent controls to which the nation had been subjected ever since 1948. In the summer of 1950, after the outbreak of the Korean War, the ambitious original targets of the plan were markedly increased, apparently under Soviet pressure. The final plan, adopted at the Fifth Plenum of the Party's Central Committee (July 1950), contained substantially higher objectives to be attained by the end of 1955: 4,600,000 tons of steel; 100,000,000 tons of coal, and 19,300,000,000 kwh of electric power.[1] These revisions followed a prolonged visit to Moscow by the plan's chief architect and Poland's economic boss, Hilary Minc. There he was instructed to expand heavy industry and was promised more "fraternal aid"; an intricate commercial agreement, to last eight years, was signed at that time.

Minc, addressing the Fifth Plenum, proposed to reach the revised goal by discarding "cautious methods of planning" and introducing "the Bolshevik approach" to planning, management, and production, as well as Stakhanovite working methods and principles of socialist competition. "Utilization of hidden reserves," both in manpower and raw materials, became a new slogan; fulfillment of the revised industrial objectives became the main preoccupation of the party and the government.

While launching the Six Year Plan the party attempted to create an almost mystical atmosphere, resembling to some extent that which prevailed in the Soviet Union during the first two five-year plans. Although popular enthusiasm for the plan has been largely dampened by suspicion that the Soviet Union probably benefits as much from Poland's progress as does Poland herself, and that the plan is chiefly determined by the Soviet Union's military requirements, still the industrial achievements of the regime have been considerable. An *émigré* economist rightly pointed out that feelings of revulsion for Soviet economic exploitation and for the harsh methods of enforcing the will of the party have existed alongside an awareness that Poland's growing industrialization is a valuable by-product of the plan. Most of the peasants recruited from the villages for factory work are inclined to feel that they are gaining socially by joining the privileged urban proletariat, and an improvement in their economic status opens new prospects to them. The urban working class, now more than half the population, despite injustices and even horrors often accompanying the process of industrialization, is proud of the new mines and factories. Many young people believe that, at the cost of immense privation, they are laying the foundation for the future prosperity of their country.[2] The progress, impressive as it is, has sadly neglected the standard of living of the population, which has been gradually depressed to the Soviet level. From the beginning of the country's reconstruction the agricultural output has been lagging behind the industrial production.

Six months after the Moscow-imposed revisions in the plan, the party realized that it could not carry on its gigantic task without asking for new sacrifices and the substantial support of the entire nation. Only $120 million of an expected $600 million loan from the International Bank materialized. In order to get machinery from abroad, more food had to be exported and this depressed the already inadequate standard of living. On the occasion of a plebiscite of peace, a new call for a national front was made by Bierut, then president of the Republic and party boss. Problems of the Six Year Plan, Poland's western frontiers, and the United States-sponsored remilitarization of Germany were intertwined in the proposal for a national front. In February 1951, Bierut declared:

We realize more and more clearly that every single man, each and every one of us must continue the struggle for peace and that it should become part of the everyday toil of the entire nation, the very essence of its labor. It is obvious that the fight for peace must be carried on a wide front with the entire nation participating in it. We vividly recall the horrors of the last war. We remember only too well the inhuman faces of Hitlerites who are at present the *protégés* of the U.S.A. They are reaching with their greedy claws not only for our western territories, but for the entire country, which they would like to trample with their boots . . . Is there one honest Pole who would hesitate to take a courageous and unequivocal stand with regard to those criminal plans? Is there any other answer than a further tightening of our ranks on our national front in the struggle for peace and for the Six Year Plan? [3]

Thus, even those who opposed communism as a doctrine were asked to cooperate with the party for reasons of patriotism and national solidarity. The concept of a national front became a device to attract nonparty people toward collaboration with the Communists. At the same time the party pressed its argument that the Soviet Union was the sole power both ready and able to protect Poland's possession of the newly acquired western provinces. Exploiting the attachment which the overwhelming majority of Poles had for the western territories, and stressing the United States policy of bolstering the German Federal Republic, the regime stepped up its anti-American propaganda and its attack on the Vatican.

TOWARD A PARTY STATE

Parallel to the launching of the Six Year Plan came a reform in the top echelons of public administration. An endeavor was made to reject all Western patterns as unsuitable to the needs of a socialist country, and to introduce Soviet institutions and administrative practices. Existing agencies were expanded, various new offices were created, and remnants of the non-Communist element were gradually replaced by younger and more reliable people. Creation of numerous new ministries necessitated the formation of an inner cabinet, called the Presidium of the government, which, alongside the State Council, made decisions on matters of policy. The Presidium of the government was composed of the following persons: the president of the Republic, the prime minister, the vice-premiers, and the secretary of state for the Presidium of the Council of Ministers; all incumbents of these offices have been members of the party since 1949.

Along with these top-strata changes occurred a less spectacular but perhaps more essential process which transformed the whole internal administrative system of the country. On March 20, 1950, a "Bill Concerning Regional Organs of Unified State Authority" was obediently voted by the Sejm.[4] Democratically elected provincial and local legislative bodies (such as village, county, and provincial councils) had already been replaced in 1944 by a system of national councils. The most important aspect of the new bill lay in the greatly increased powers it granted to the councils, which now became the sole organs of local administration. By eliminating provincial and local executive officials and corresponding legislative bodies, and by transferring their functions to national councils, the regime abolished the last vestiges of prewar Polish local government and established a system which closely resembled that of the Soviet Union. As in the USSR, the councils (soviets) of smaller areas were made responsible to their counterparts in larger areas. At all levels the councils were permeated by party activists and ultimately controlled from above by the State Council.

After the reform of local administration, the time came to replace the out-dated provisional or "Small" Constitution of 1947 since it failed to reflect the tremendous changes which had taken place in

Poland since 1944. The constitution had been left intact largely as a decorative fig-leaf on Poland's developing totalitarian structure. With the consolidation of party rule, the need for a constitutional expression of the revolution became more imperative. After a prolonged "general national debate," a new constitution was unanimously approved by the Sejm on July 22, 1952, the eight anniversary of the July Manifesto of 1944, and became effective immediately.[5]

The preamble referred to "the experience of the Soviet Union," and rejected the hitherto accepted principle of dividing authority among the legislature, the executive branch, and "independent courts of law." The office of president of the Republic was now abolished. The Council of Ministers became an administrative body deprived of most of its political significance. Although the legislature was declared to be the highest organ of state authority, it was overshadowed by the State Council, composed of fifteen members acting collectively. Article 25 of the constitution specifically made the Sejm superior to the Council, but there was no provision for the revocation of the Council or of its individual members. Thus, the Council, once elected by the Sejm, became independent of it.

The Council was moreover given very extensive powers. It nominated the highest officers of the state, including ambassadors, and could ratify or denounce international agreements. The Council possessed the right of clemency and could award state decorations. Elections to the Sejm could be ordered and its sessions convened by the Council, which also was endowed with legislative initiative similar to that granted to the government and Sejm deputies. The chairman of the council and its secretaries were to sign all laws passed by the Diet; the Council could issue decrees having the force of law when the legislature was not in session. The Council could decree martial law, order mobilization in case of war emergency and, when the Diet was not in session (such sessions were to take place at least twice a year but no minimum duration was mentioned), the Council could declare war as well. Another major function of the Council was to interpret the laws of the country. In addition, it was to supervise the network of national councils which, according to the law of March 20, 1950, were the only state authorities in villages, towns, districts, and provinces. Consequently, the State Council formed the apex of the hierarchy of national councils and, according to the mandate of the constitution, was the most powerful body of the People's Republic.

The executive branch of the government became purely administrative, its functions being defined in a chapter entitled "The Leading Organs of State Administration," while the prerogatives of the State Council were significantly enumerated under the heading "The Leading Organs of the State Power." The administration was to carry out decisions of the policy-making Council and the laws passed by the Council and the Diet.

The legislature was to be elected by all citizens 18 years of age and over, for a term of four years, the right to nominate candidates being reserved to political and social organizations of citizens. Another article of the constitution stipulated, however, that: "Setting up associations, and participating in associations, whose aims or activities are directed against the political or social system or the legal order of the Polish People's Republic is forbidden." Article 70 separated church and state. "Freedom of conscience and religion" was guaranteed, but abuse of these freedoms could be punished.

The new Polish charter of July 22, 1952, is largely an adaptation of the basic features of the Soviet constitution of December 5, 1936: of 91 articles in the Polish Fundamental Law, 50 contain clauses similar, if not identical, to those of the Stalinist constitution. The second paragraph of Article 12 of the Stalinist charter says: "The principle applied in the USSR is that of socialism: from each according to his ability, to each according to his work." The third paragraph of Article 14 of the new Polish law declares: "Polish People's Republic puts into even fuller effect the principle: from each according to his abilities, to each according to his work." The great idea of socialism is to be "the final aim of the Polish People's Republic," while in the USSR it is allegedly an accomplished fact. There are differences between the two charters. The Polish constitution provides for two "supreme organs of state authority," the Diet and the State Council; these bodies are similar to the Supreme Soviet and the Presidium of the Supreme Soviet, respectively, but while the Soviet legislative body has two chambers, the Sejm consists of only one, as is the case with the Soviet National Republics. The Polish constitution, moreover, does not incorporate that provision of Article 126 in the Soviet charter which gives a position of monopoly to the Communist Party; Article 72 of the Polish charter enumerates citizen's associations permitted by law, and also mentions political organizations.

On the other hand, there is no difference between the Soviet constitution and the Polish one in defining fundamental rights and duties of citizens, such as "watchfulness against the nation's enemies and the close guarding of state's secrets," or "the observance of the socialist discipline of labor." A significant difference between the Polish and Soviet charters is that the former does not provide for nationalization of all means of production. Article 10 recognizes individual ownership of small farms, although "producers' cooperatives receive special assistance and protection of the state." The right of inheritance is limited to "personal property." The charter distinguishes three kinds of property: national and cooperative property, individual holdings of land, buildings, and other means of production owned by working peasants and artisans, and personal property of citizens.

The new constitution was followed by an election. Unlike the 1947 campaign, however, that of 1952, conducted during the darkest days of the Stalinist period, was rather apathetic and uneventful. The Electoral Law gave "mass social organizations of the working people" the right to nominate candidates. In each district one list, that of the "national front," was put forward. The election took place on October 26, 1952, and brought the anticipated results.

The opening of a new Diet coincided with still another reconstruction of the government. Cyrankiewicz was demoted to the position of vice-premier and replaced by Bierut, who retained chairmanship of the Central Committee of the Workers' party. Bierut, in addition to his key party posts, now became head of the government; he was also an ex officio member of the State Council, thus achieving a near-dictorial position.

Bierut's cabinet consisted of forty-two ministers, including eight deputy prime ministers. Five deputy premiers were members of the United Polish Workers' Party, while three came from the United Peasant Party. Aleksander Zawadzki, formerly one of six deputy prime ministers, became chairman of the State Council and, at least formally, head of state. As a result of the new constitution and new elections, party dictatorship was now complete, and at the same time Bierut became the unquestionably dominant figure within the party. An intensive propaganda campaign was put in motion to glorify "the first builder of socialism in Poland," a little local Stalin, surrounded by an appropriate personality cult.

Hardly had this new pattern solidified in Poland when the Soviet dictator passed away. That event and the ensuing jockeying for power caused a great deal of confusion among Polish party leaders. At the Eighth Plenum of the Central Committee the Polish party promptly accepted "the collective leadership" of the Communist Party of the Soviet Union and, fearing to back a wrong horse, refrained from more outspoken political pronouncements.[6] The May Day speech of Bierut mentioned no living Soviet statesman. The prevailing uncertainty was deepened after the fall of Beria. On the other hand, Stalin's death provided an opportunity for the party to turn the screw of "socialist competition" still more tightly. A new drive for greater output started, with reports from all over the country of individual production pledges to be fulfilled in honor of "the leader of the working class." But neither these pledges nor the propaganda of the national front could camouflage the fact of a deepening agricultural crisis, which became one of the most serious problems facing the regime after 1952.

THE AGRARIAN CRISIS

During the Three Year Plan (1947–1949), there was no significant attempt to quicken the tempo of collectivization, and Polish agriculture achieved an impressive recovery. By the end of 1949 fewer than 250 "producers' cooperatives" existed in the whole of Poland.[7] During this initial planning period the food situation in Polish cities was improving slowly but steadily. Food prices on the free market were consistently high and the economic position of farmers was rather favorable. Meanwhile, however, detailed preparations for a collectivization drive were in process: machine tractor stations were established, production of tractors and other machinery was bolstered, and a considerable amount of propaganda exalting Soviet achievements in the sphere of collective farming was forced on the reluctant peasantry, including numerous trips by selected delegates to Soviet collective and state farms.

At the same time a kind of "softening process" was applied to the peasantry. After 1949 the life of wealthy and middle-income farmers became increasingly difficult. In order to drive them into collective farms, the regime restricted proper supplies of fertilizers, forbade the hiring of outside help, set high delivery quotas, made contributions of thirty days a year of free labor to the community compulsory, and paid ridiculously low prices for compulsory deliveries of farm products. In addition, there were state-owned machine tractor stations, with highly differentiated fees for use of tractors, direct state subsidies to the collective farms, state control over the flow of goods to be delivered to village stores, plus a differentiated taxation policy administered on a "class basis."[8] All these measures were designed to undermine the independent farmer eventually and to "demonstrate to him the superiority of socialist farming."

Numerous statements made by Bierut, Minc, and others left no doubt as to the methods which would be used to demonstrate the advantages of joining collectives. At a meeting of the party's Central

Committee, Minc revealed that "the criteria of class division in the rural areas are not based solely on the number of hectares which are owned." [9] Roman Zambrowski, another member of the Politbureau, who had been in charge of the agricultural program for some time, stated that "the land tax paid by the poor peasants in our country accounts for 3.5 per cent of their cash income, while 378,000 kulaks and the most wealthy middle-peasant household pay taxes amounting to 27.6 per cent of their cash income." [10] Zambrowski's statement indicated that the regime regarded any farmer as a kulak who owned more than 10 hectares (about 25 acres) of land. Minc's pronouncement left little doubt that any farmer who showed too much independence toward the authorities could be branded a "kulak," regardless of the size of his farm. In this way the political rather than economic objectives of collectivization were stressed, as in the Soviet Union.

The decision to press forward on rapid "socialization" was officially announced by Minc at the Fifth Plenum of the Central Committee, which occurred in July 1950, and was devoted to a discussion of the revised Six Year Plan. Investment in machine tractor stations was to be increased tenfold. At the end of the plan, "producers' cooperatives" were to comprise from 20 to 25 per cent of the total cultivated area; together with state farms, the "socialist sector" would then cover about one third of all agricultural land in Poland.

The first vigorous collectivization drive began late in 1950 and lasted until the spring of 1951. On paper the results were impressive: more than 3000 "producers' cooperatives" were founded, mostly in the western territories. "Dizzy with success," the party applied pressure on an increasing scale, but soon strong opposition ensued. The peasants embarked upon a form of slowdown strike, consuming whatever they could themselves and delivering little to the government. The number of livestock declined. Alarmingly diminished food supplies reached the free market, where little was to be had in exchange. Although the regime's standard explanation was to blame the current drought, it was apparent that the pace of collectivization had to be slowed. Nevertheless, the drive was resumed more cautiously early in 1952, with similar results. Food shortages became acute and could no longer be explained away by bad weather or the potato bug.

During the Seventh Plenary Session of the Central Committee (June 14–15, 1952), Bierut, although promising to complete the Six Year Plan in five years, officially revealed that there were symptoms of an agrarian crisis. He accused the peasants of willfully upsetting the balance of the whole economic program by their failure to fulfill their share of the Six Year Plan. Bierut reported that agricultural production had fallen short of targets set in the plan, resulting in insufficient reserves of food for the urban population. This in turn forced the government to introduce rationing of food in the towns and compulsory deliveries from the villages. The party boss also revealed that a considerable amount of grain had to be imported from abroad. Moreover, he admitted that the management of state and collective farms had been inefficient. During the debate on the matter it was disclosed by another member of the Central Committee that during the past year state farms had incurred heavy losses and were unable to deliver their quotas. The full scope of the failure was revealed later when a government periodical stated that not only did agricultural production fail to increase since 1950, as had been calculated in the Six Year Plan, but even dropped by 0.9 per cent.[11] The population, however, rose by about 1,500,000 during this period and the export of food increased in order to purchase necessary machines and raw materials abroad. Therefore, Poland's standard of living, very inadequate even in 1950, dropped still further. An agricultural expert of the party, J. Tepicht, admitted that the socialized sector of agriculture produced less grain than did the despised and persecuted kulaks. As far as cattle breeding was concerned, small and medium farmers led the way.[12]

The Plenum disclosed the regime's oscillation between a desire to accelerate collectivization, and thus strengthen its political control over rural areas, and the fear of aggravating the critical problem of food supplies, consequently undermining its hold on the towns. The growing food crisis imposed a middle way. Kulaks were to be restricted but still tolerated; collectivization was to be continued, but more cautiously. It was clear that a slump in agricultural production was bound to slow progress in the industrial sector, thus undermining the success of the Six Year Plan and making the prospect of fulfilling it in five years illusory.

The agrarian crisis has become a standing feature of the country's life since the launching of the Six Year Plan, particularly in respect to shortages of food in the cities. Since 1952 the situation has assumed serious proportions. The party realized full well that a solution was of the utmost importance for the regime. The agrarian crisis in Poland coincided with Stalin's death and with the initiation of a so-called "new course" toward farmers and consumers in the Soviet Union and, ultimately, throughout Soviet-controlled East Central Europe.

The "new course" became effective in Poland in October 1953, much later than in other captive countries, and at the beginning it followed a much milder line. The policy was announced officially on October 29, 1953, at the Ninth Plenum of the Central Committee. At the Plenum Bierut proclaimed the necessity of raising the "material and cultural level of the living standard of the masses," and reiterated the regime's desire for "persistent realization of the socialist industrialization of the country." Admitting that the then current standard of living was unsatisfactory, Bierut explained that this was caused by a disproportionate expansion of industry coupled with neglect of consumer goods and food production. Industrial output of the new Poland had more than trebled since 1938, and had increased 150 per cent over 1949 figures; agricultural production, however, rose only 9 per cent since 1949. The Six Year Plan, slightly overfulfilled in industry, was 12 per cent below the target for agriculture. To remedy this, investments in heavy industry were to be decreased about 6 per cent, while investments in other fields were to be increased approximately 12 per cent. Nevertheless, said Bierut, "The goal of the new policy [improving the living standard of the masses] can be achieved only by continuing our general line of industrialization which is directed toward strengthening our defense, increasing the basis of our industrial production, and further expanding our industrial base . . ."

Neither Bierut nor another principal speaker at the Plenum, Berman, gave any indication that policies formerly pursued in the countryside would be radically altered. "All the measures we are taking," said Berman, "are a bridge to socialism, a bridge toward the collective economy."

Bierut submitted to the Central Committee a lengthy ten-point program of measures which were intended to induce peasants to increase their production. Bierut's plan, unlike those applied in Hungary, Rumania, and Czechoslovakia, included no far-reaching concessions to farmers, but he promised that obligatory deliveries would not be increased despite a planned increase in the production of individual peasants. This meant that if the farmer produced more he would be permitted to keep a larger share of his output and sell it on the free market. Bierut's second pledge was to increase the supply of consumer goods in the villages and thus create the only incentive the peasants really understood.

The Ninth Plenum launched a new slogan, "rapid raising of the living standard of the masses," and announced that a Second Party Congress had been summoned. The congress was to meet early in 1954.

THE SECOND PARTY CONGRESS

The Second Party Congress, which lasted eight days (March 10–
18, 1954), opened on the sixtieth anniversary of the First Congress
of the SDKPiL. The congress gathered over 1200 delegates, each
representing 1000 members. The Soviet Union dispatched no less a
personage than N. S. Khrushchev, First Secretary of the Communist
Party of the Soviet Union. There were also delegations representing
twenty-one Communist parties from all over the world. "The immor-
tal memory of Stalin" was honored by the congress, which stood for
a minute in silence to commemorate his work.

The congress, summoned under the slogans: "Let's face the
countryside" and "We must raise our standard of living," focused
around three major speeches, delivered by Bierut, Minc, and Zenon
Nowak. Bierut submitted a report of the party's Central Committee
covering the period since the Unification Congress of December
1948. Minc outlined the chief economic tasks to be faced in the last
two years of the Six Year Plan, while Nowak surveyed the state
of Poland's agriculture. Both Bierut and Minc placed considerable
emphasis on agriculture in their own reports,[13] and indeed, agriculture was the general focus of the entire congress.

After proudly reviewing the regime's industrial and political
accomplishments, Bierut turned his attention to less successful
matters. In 1953, he said, state farms and producers' cooperatives
included less than 9 per cent of the cultivated land, and their
production per acre was lower than the corresponding average output
of individual farms. Bierut admitted that "during the last years
Poland was obliged to import a considerable and constantly increasing amount of grain." The number of cattle, on the other
hand, rose by 23 per cent since 1949, but cattle breeding was the
domain of individual farmers. Bierut reiterated the party's determination to press collectivization: "In the next two years . . .
special attention will be given to a more regular development of
producers' cooperatives; greater distribution of them to central and
eastern provinces so that newly-formed cooperatives will embrace a
greater proportion of the inhabitants of the villages and the old
cooperatives shall increase the number of their members."

In his speech Minc discussed the Six Year Plan at length, and the
tenor of his speech was rather pessimistic. Annual production growth
of socialist industry for the last two years of the plan was to be
decreased from roughly 20 per cent to somewhere between 10 and
11 per cent.[14] Minc once more admitted that agriculture was lagging

behind industry and was repeatedly failing to fulfill its share of the plan. Grain, one of the very few products which collective farms could produce more or less efficiently, and previously one of the chief items of export, was now the major headache. "One should realize [said Minc] that without a solution of the grain problem . . . there can be no talk of an appropriate expansion of agriculture nor of the appropriate development of the entire national economy for the purpose of a speedier raising of the living standards of the people."

Minc added that agricultural machinery and fertilizer industries were still inadequate, and that output of consumer goods "does not catch up with the demand"; moreover, the goods were often of inferior quality. According to the plan, 25.5 per cent of all industrial investment was to go to light industry, but again the plan was not fulfilled. In 1953, for example, only half the scheduled amount was spent on consumer goods investment.[15] Minc declared that 1954–55 investments should increase 35.40 per cent over actual investment in 1953, but even so, consumer goods investment in 1955 would still be less than two thirds of what should have occurred in 1953. Minc was less than hopeful about the chances of fulfilling the plan as a whole. "An analysis of the present situation shows that full achievement of the Six Year Plan will not be an easy task; this very goal is even threatened, and the threat should be removed as far as possible." This amounted to official abandonment of the idea of fulfilling the plan in five years. Minc twice pointed out that "the plan is not a dogma." [16]

Both Minc and the principal speaker on agriculture, Nowak, advocated a middle line between Gomułka's position and "leftist sectarianism." Both short and long term credit were promised to all farmers, but especially to "working peasants," while containment and gradual elimination, not instant liquidation, remained the key note of the party's policy toward prosperous farmers. The principle of voluntary membership in cooperatives was at least nominally endorsed, and compulsion condemned. Nowak pointed out that "[some] comrades do not understand that today without the output of individual peasants we will not be able to feed the country." Our task, he quickly added, "will be to build new producers' cooperatives and to gain new members for the already existing ones." It was imperative that the party conduct a "relentless struggle against the kulaks" and "oppose the kulak's robbery."

Collectivization was also strongly reaffirmed by Berman. He stressed, however, that fulfillment of the party congress goal in respect to a 15 or 20 per cent rise in living standards over the next two years would require more energy than the party alone could hope to muster. For this task the whole nation must be mobilized, implying continuation of the national front policy initiated in 1951. Detailed measures to adapt the Six Year Plan to the new situation were formulated in a lengthy final resolution of the congress.[17]

External affairs occupied relatively little time. While furiously decrying "American imperialism," Bierut emphasized that "the German problem is the central question of European security" and that Poland, not unlike France, was vitally interested in its solution. Bierut even went so far as to suggest that the traditional French-Polish alliance be renewed. Poland's growing military potential was outlined by Marshal Rokossovsky.

Sixteen points in the party rules of 1948 were amended by the congress.[18] One of the amendments officially introduced the principle of collective leadership ("collegiality" as it is called in Russia and her orbit). Article 20 of the revised rules stated that collective leadership afforded a maximum guarantee for a balanced party program and also gave scope to party activists for the exercise of "broad initiative." Commenting on this change, Bierut made the discovery that "the principle of collegiality is an inseparable part of inner party democracy." Since the principle of collegial leadership clashed with the practice of accumulation of posts, Bierut gave up one of his main offices. The post of chairman of the party Central Committee having already been abolished, Bierut now resigned from the premiership and became the party's First Secretary. This was in accord with Soviet practice, Bierut remaining the keyman of the regime; he was still listed first, out of alphabetic order, among members of the Politbureau. Cyrankiewicz, the only former Socialist to survive politically, again became prime minister, a post of relatively lesser importance since the Constitution of 1952 made the cabinet a rather technical, administrative body. The division of power between Bierut and Cyrankiewicz was similar to that which occurred in the Soviet Union after Stalin's death.

The new Central Committee was expanded from seventy-five to seventy-seven full members, of whom twenty-two were newcomers. The number of deputy members of the committee was cut from sixty-one to fifty. The Politbureau elected by the Central Committee was largely composed of old-timers: B. Bierut, A. Zawadzki, J. Cyrankiewicz, H. Minc, Z. Nowak, K. Rokossovsky, E. Ochab, J. Berman, F. Mazur, F. Jóźwiak, S. Radkiewicz, W. Dworakowski, and R. Zambrowski. A. Rapacki (a Socialist prior to December 1948), had formerly been a full member but now became a deputy, while Dworakowski was promoted from deputy to full membership of the ruling oligarchy.

The growing emphasis on agriculture was reflected in a decision to overhaul local administration in rural regions. The administrative system had been based on a pyramidal structure of national councils since March 1950. As far as the villages were concerned, the system consisted of two levels. Slightly more than 40,000 village communes were contained within some 3000 rural municipalities. This dualism was to be discarded and a unified network of some 10,000 medium-sized village communes introduced. This reform provided for closer party control over passive peasant masses. Bierut left no doubt about the matter when he commented on the impending reform:

> The new village commune [consisting of from three to five villages] with a comparatively small area numbering from 1000 to 3000 inhabitants, will be an administrative unit linked far more closely than the present rural municipality [consisting of up to twenty villages] with the village population and problems of agricultural production. Rural communal national councils will have their own executive organ — a presidium — and standing committees which will make possible the attraction of the widest peasant masses to direct participation in exercising authority and in social supervision of all economic, social, educational and cultural activities in the area.

Administrative reform was indirectly linked to rejection of Gomułka's rather Bukharinist agrarian policy, and to the planned collectivization drive. Greater control over local party cadres was to be provided, and village communes, lowest rung in the administrative ladder, were to be under direct supervision of state organs.[19]

So-called "blind spots" on the map, those villages without party cells (more than 40 per cent were in this category) were to be eliminated by trebling the number of officials and communes in the planned expansion of the party's rural organization. Taxes and compulsory delivery quotas remained unchanged.

The congress, although held over one year after the death of the Soviet dictator was still an affair staged to some extent in the old Stalinist tradition. On the one hand, following the example of Moscow, "collective leadership" was established and some rather nominal concessions were made toward increasing production of consumer goods and improving the sorry state of agriculture by means of a series of half-hearted and mostly contradictory measures. On the other hand, however, renewed emphasis on collectivization and greater political control of the countryside seemed to indicate that the party was considering another offensive against the peasants, the main opposition force next to the Catholic Church.

The policy laid down at the congress contained at least three inherent contradictions. First, how was the low living standard to be raised some 15 or 20 per cent within the next two years while the overambitious industrial program continued with only slight alterations? Second, could agricultural production increase when a quarter of a million of the most industrious and efficient farmers, the kulaks, were being "contained" and "eliminated"? The kulaks held only about 14 per cent of the cultivated land but supplied up to 28 per cent of all marketable food products. The third dilemma inherent in the congress program was how to raise the standard of living without weakening the party's control over the masses?

Realization of these contradictions was already developing among some of the younger and more open-minded members of the party. Opposition to the official line was not yet voiced because the leadership of the party, in spite of its new label, was still successful in preventing any outspoken criticism. But the growing pressure of the masses, the fluctuation of Soviet policy, and the domestic economic difficulties — all these factors were already working for far-reaching changes.

13 The PARTY and the CHURCH

The Second Party Congress concentrated chiefly on the tremendous economic difficulties facing the regime and devoted little time to another problem which transcended even the serious agrarian crisis in importance. This was the religious question which, in Poland, meant the problem of the Roman Catholic Church. Because of changes in Poland's population caused by the war and its aftermath, Roman Catholicism had become the religion of nearly 98 per cent of the Polish people. Corresponding figures were 74 per cent in Hungary and 69 per cent in Czechoslovakia. Of some 50 million Catholics behind the Iron Curtain, 23 million or almost half the total were in Poland. As in Ireland and Spain, Roman Catholicism had a history of intimate association with nationalist sentiments. Moreover, the Catholic Church in Poland also had an excellent anti-German resistance record.[1] Consequently, after the war, when the church was very active in charity and reconstruction work, its prestige was probably higher than ever.

The party had never been very outspoken in its antireligious propaganda, being aware of the church's popularity among the broad masses, and initially took great care not to alienate either the hierarchy or the faithful. From 1945 to 1949 the party focused its attention on exploiting latent anticlerical feelings and conducted a small war against weak spots in the church's position, but the party refrained from open interference with freedom of worship. Land belonging to the church (about 450,000 acres) was excluded from agrarian reform; on the other hand, in September 1945, "the eternal concordat" of 1925 was unilaterally denounced by Warsaw. The Catholic hierarchy, while consistently and patiently trying to avoid an open clash with the government, repeatedly saw itself compelled to denounce "the atheistic and materialistic philosophy of communism." Pastoral letters were the only remaining public form of criticism to be heard in Poland after 1944.

A critical attitude toward the party in its capacity as carrier of an atheistic doctrine implied neither a negation of the existing regime nor wholesale condemnation of all changes which had taken place since the end of the war. The Catholic hierarchy, led by the courageous and progressive Cardinal August Hlond, Primate of Poland, shared the view of a great majority of Poles that initial actions (such as the first phase of agrarian reform and the nationalization of large industry), were simply the long overdue fulfillment of generally accepted programs common to all democratic forces in Poland, both before World War II and during the period of anti-German resistance. Such reforms had been advocated for years before the war by numerous Polish Catholic writers and politicians, with the official blessing of the Episcopate. Therefore, despite doctrinal clashes and polemics, the Episcopate accepted the new regime as the legitimate government of Poland and awaited further developments.

Until the end of 1948 the party's official position in regard to the Catholic Church was that the coexistence of Catholicism and Marxism in Poland was not only feasible but even highly desirable, provided Catholicism adapted its ways to the requirements of modern times and supported the Communists in their endeavors to build a new Poland. Both sides, it was argued, could profit from each other's experience. Numerous public debates were staged, with representatives of both groups participating.[2] In addition to this way of meeting controversial problems, the party made numerous gestures designed to appease the church temporarily: freedom of worship was free from interference, high Communist dignitaries (including party leader Bolesław Bierut) attended public religious ceremonies, the army was ordered to assist Corpus Christi processions, a certain number of Catholic publications were permitted to appear, and numerous church buildings were reconstructed with state assistance. When the party treated General Karol Świerczewski (Walter), a former commander of the International Brigade in Spain, to a state funeral on April 1, 1947, Roman Catholic rites were performed and a chorus was asked to sing religious chants, including the *De Profundis.*[3]

However, the party is itself a kind of secular sect with totalitarian proclivities, and no rival church could be tolerated indefinitely. "If, as the Gospel teaches, we must not do harm unto others, then perhaps we must not harm kulaks? If the highest glory does not belong to man, then perhaps worship of Lenin and Stalin is idolatry?" [4]

The ensuing campaign against the church was planned with obvious care and proceeded with caution. Negotiations had been in progress between the regime and the Vatican in order to secure recognition of the new government by the Holy See, and to reorganize the Catholic hierarchy in the recovered territories in conformance with the new German-Polish boundaries. When these efforts failed, Warsaw began to assail the position of Rome in the matter of the western provinces. The Vatican's alleged dependence on American imperialism and sponsorship of German revisionism became a favorite theme of Communist propaganda after 1946.

Religious instruction was increasingly subjected to interference after 1948. Employees of various state enterprises were compelled to work on Sundays and on church holidays young people were required to participate in official demonstrations, with the purpose of preventing them from attending religious services. The teaching of religion was allowed in schools, but priests were often accused of exceeding their duties and were closely supervised. A number of priests were arrested for engaging in "political activities."

In December 1948, at the Unification Congress of the Polish Workers' Party and Polish Socialist Party, prominent Communists fiercely attacked the Vatican and decried the negative attitude of the Catholic hierarchy toward the new regime and its reforms. By this time it had become clear that a more violent struggle, similar to that in Hungary, was approaching. Both sides, however, were interested in postponing a clash: the party, because it was afraid of provoking a civil war which would upset its economic plans; the church, because it counted on either internal changes in the Soviet world or some evolution of the international scene. There was no chance of a new concordat being concluded because of the lack of diplomatic relations between the Vatican and the new regime, but numerous outstanding problems of daily church and state relations urgently required some form of modus vivendi.

On July 13, 1949, came a Vatican decree excommunicating those Catholics who belonged to the party or who were its willing adherents. The Warsaw government denounced the decree, calling it an "act of aggression against the Polish state." The regime declared that the Vatican's edict could not be carried out in Poland and warned that it would prosecute all activities which threatened public

order or "weakened the peoples' democracy." At the same time, the
government announced that it was ready to negotiate with the Polish
Episcopate in an effort to reach an understanding.[5]

Simultaneously with the proposal to negotiate, the regime took
retaliatory measures against the Vatican. On August 5, 1949, the
government passed a law providing prison sentences of up to five
years for anyone refusing church sacraments to citizens because of
political or scientific opinions or activities. Moreover, all religious
orders and associations were to register within three months, and
religious processions were made dependent on a government permit.[6]
The Episcopate instructed the heads of religious orders not to comply
with the law and tried in vain to settle the matter with the government. The three-month deadline passed, with the orders failing to
register.

With a barrage of antichurch propaganda, the government now
attacked the hierarchy at a time when it was sure to have the
support of the entire nation, including the most pious Catholics. A
great deal of newspaper space was devoted to appeals from the
faithful in various sections of the recovered territories requesting the
permanent appointment of Polish priests and bishops in that area.
This had long been a sore point with the government, which had
sought to have the Vatican reorganize the five residential bishoprics
set up by Cardinal Hlond in the new western provinces and make
them permanent dioceses. Had it compiled, the Vatican would have
accepted the Oder-Neisse line as Poland's western frontier.

In this matter the attitude of the Episcopate (and of the entire
clergy) was not much different from that of the rest of the nation,
but the attitude of the Holy See made the position of the Polish
hierarchy rather embarrassing. Cardinal Hlond had repeatedly conferred with the Vatican on this matter, advocating early appointment of a permanent ecclesiastic administration in the Polish western
provinces, and warning that a refusal to do so might gravely en-
danger the unity of Roman Catholicism in Poland. The same attitude
was taken by his young and enterprising successor, Archbishop
Stefan Wyszyński.

To test the unity of the church, the regime began sponsoring
groups of so-called "patriotic priests" who, while not rejecting the
dogmatic side of Catholicism, might, on social and political issues
(especially in the matter of the regained territories), back the regime
against the Vatican. Increasing support was also given to a lay
group of "Social Catholics" who were working to bring about a *rapprochement* between Catholicism and Marxism. On October 10, 1949,

a strongly worded pastoral letter appeared from the new Primate of Poland, Archbishop Wyszyński. The letter was the first recognition of a schism existing in Poland. Without referring directly to the group that sought agreement with the government on the latter's terms, the Primate indicated there were "many who have strayed." We are deeply grieved by so many tragedies of priests' souls that do not withstand the pressure of perplexing circumstances." The letter added that Polish youth "is tired of the ideological vacuum and spiritual poverty of materialism" and, consequently is "falling into an abyss of apathy and inertia." [7]

The party replied to the pronouncement by breaking off negotiations which had finally begun with the Episcopate, and by organizing a series of strikes among workers on church estates. The latter were encouraged to refuse any work unless they received higher wages retroactive for two years. Moreover, the party undertook a series of drastic measures to blackmail the Episcopate into accepting its conditions. On January 23, 1950, the church's largest welfare institution, *Caritas,* was placed under state control, the government asserting that Caritas' funds had been used for political purposes hostile to the state. This action of the regime was followed by a wave of radio and press attacks against the Polish Catholic hierarchy; bishops were variously accused of graft, embezzlement, hostility to the "People's Poland," reactionary tendencies and close ties with foreign imperialists, warmongering, spying, and acts of sabotage. By the end of January 1950, more than 500 priests, nuns, and monks had been placed under arrest.[8]

Pressing its offensive still further, the government presented a draft bill to the Sejm on March 6, 1950, calling for seizure of all church estates in excess of 250 acres. The proposed decree affected approximately 450,000 acres of church property.[9]

THE MODUS VIVENDI OF 1950

By early spring of 1950, after one year of bargaining, it seemed that church-state negotiations could not possibly succeed. Suddenly, on April 16 of that year, an official communiqué issued by the government announced that an agreement had been signed two days earlier. The accord which was reached is an extremely interesting document, worthy of close scrutiny because its importance transcends the boundaries of Poland: it is the first and only agreement between a people's democracy and a Catholic hierarchy.[10]

Both sides made far-reaching concessions. It was stipulated that the Episcopate would oppose revisionist activity by the German clergy and would seek the Holy See's recognition of the Oder-Neisse line as Poland's permanent boundary. Basing its position on the assumption that the recovered territories constituted an inseparable part of the Polish Republic, the Episcopate was to ask the Vatican to establish permanent episcopal seats in place of the resident bishoprics established in the territories by the late Cardinal Hlond. Moreover: "Accepting the concept that the church's mission can be implemented within various socio-economic structures established by secular authority, the Episcopate will explain to the clergy that it should not oppose the development of cooperatives in rural areas because all cooperatives are essentially based on the ethical concept of human nature." The hierarchy was to "oppose the misuse of religious feelings for antistate activity" and combat the operations of antigovernment resistance groups, punishing all clergy guilty of such affiliation. Other duties of the church were formulated as follows: the Episcopate was to teach the faithful respect for state authority and state law and was to exhort the faithful to intensify their efforts toward Poland's reconstruction and increased prosperity. The Pope was to remain the supreme authority of the Roman Catholic Church "in matters of faith and ecclesiastic jurisdiction," but the Episcopate "would be guided in other matters by the Polish *raison d'état*."

These were the chief gains scored by the regime. On the other hand, the government agreed that the Lublin Catholic University could continue to function. Catholic associations were to enjoy the same rights they had held before the accord and the Catholic press and publications were to have the same privileges as others. Public worship was to be free of interference. Military authorities, after consultation with the Episcopate, were to draw up regulations governing the work of chaplains, and religious care in penal institutions and hospitals would be given to those desiring it. The government also promised not to restrict the existing program of religious instruction in the schools. In carrying out its decree of March 1950, whereby church estates were confiscated, the government pledged that it would take into consideration the needs of both the clergy and ecclesiastic institutions. Finally, the Catholic welfare organization, Caritas, was to be re-established and reorganized as the "Association of Catholics."

The agreement was not a concordat but rather a modus vivendi, a technical instrument and not an ideological compromise. The communiqué issued by the Episcopate underlined this point by saying that the work of the mixed church-state commission conducting the negotiations was not easy, because it was "carried on amidst mounting difficulties caused by insurmountable ideological differences." Neither the party nor the church gave up any ideological tenets, and both stuck to their respective ideological positions.

Although it had compromised on certain important but not essential points, the church preserved its doctrinal independence. Moreover, in the key article in the agreement which called on the church to teach respect for law and authority, to condemn underground activities, and to support all efforts to consolidate the peace, the Episcopate managed to insert the qualifying clause: "in accordance with the teaching of the church."

The most important concession on the part of the Communist government was recognition of the Pope's authority over the Polish church. On its part, the Episcopate explicitly recognized the new political and socio-economic pattern created by the party since July 1944. The alleged concession concerning the western territories was, in reality, no concession at all, since the Episcopate spoke for all the clergy when it declared the hierarchy's support for the Oder-Neisse line as Poland's permanent boundary and her just compensation for the tremendous territorial and human losses she suffered in the war. The only genuine compromise was the Episcopate's public promise to intervene with the Holy See on the matter of establishing ordinary bishoprics in the recovered territories.

Concessions granted by the government with regard to freedom of religious teaching, religious schools and associations, press, and charitable institutions, show that the party was forced to retreat from its previous position in the face of the hierarchy's determined resistance and its support by the masses of the faithful. An open struggle might have led to civil war. The party decided not to risk such a danger, which would of a certainty have upset the Six Year Plan and might have led also to international complications.

FAILURE OF THE EXPERIMENT

The agreement of April 14, 1950, opened a period of nearly three years during which the Episcopate made a patient effort to compromise and patch up, as far as possible, innumerable everyday conflicts arising between the two ideologically opposed groups. Since the hierarchy now officially recognized the new regime and its reforms, Catholics were encouraged to participate actively in the political life of the country. To emphasize the church's new attitude, Primate Wyszyński paid a visit to the president of the Republic, Bierut. The Episcopate, after some hesitation, finally signed the Stockholm Peace Appeal and supported the Second Congress of

Defenders of Peace. Bishops urged the faithful to participate in the
1952 elections, and although suggesting numerous amendments, took
a positive attitude toward the preparation of a new constitution.
Polish Catholic intellectuals and writers, backed by the hierarchy,
issued a vigorous appeal to their French colleagues, urging them to
oppose the remilitarization of Germany. In May 1951, after Primate
Wyszyński's visit to Rome, an episcopal letter was issued expressing
admiration for the economic effort of the nation and urging the
clergy and the faithful to respect the existing laws of the country.
The clergy was warned not to meddle in politics and to refrain from
evaluating people on the basis "of their political orientation." The
clergy was reminded that ". . . no one appointed us the distributors
of temporal goods . . . Priests serve the Motherland best not when
they fight with arms, but when they unite in Christ." [11]

Nonetheless, these endeavors did not end attacks on the church,
which resumed only a few weeks after the accord when the Episcopate displayed some initial hesitation in signing the Stockholm
Peace Appeal. On October 23, 1950, soon after an agreement between
Poland and the East German Republic in which the latter recognized
the Oder-Neisse line as "the inviolable and permanent borderline
between two countries" and "the frontier of peace," the government
sent an ultimatum to the hierarchy demanding abolition of the
provisional ecclesiastical administration in the regained territories.
A governmental decree followed on January 26, 1951; it provided
for the liquidation of the provisory status of church administration
in the western territories, along with the apostolic administrations,
and for the removal of priests who were acting as apostolic admin-
istrators. The government also ordered "the election of Capitular
Vicars and the acknowledgement of all present parish priests as
permanent managers of their parishes . . ." The specified election
ensued, and on February 18, 1951, the "Catholic Weekly" printed
the Primate's communiqué granting "Canonical jurisdiction to the
elected Capitular Vicars."

Despite the Episcopate's compliance in this matter, the regime
continued its attempts to drive a wedge between the lower clergy
and the hierarchy. An effort was made to persuade some priests that
they could rely on the support of the government, if only they would
dissociate themselves from "the reactionary politics of the bishops."
Attention was focused primarily on military chaplains and those of
the clergy who had been inmates of German concentration camps.
Out of these clerical elements "commissions of priests" were formed,
attached to the Union of Fighters and Defenders of Freedom and

Democracy. The union, while not rejecting Catholic dogma, attempted to reconcile religion with Marxism.

Throughout 1951 the problem of German revisionism became one of the most hotly debated topics in Poland. On December 12, 1951, a meeting of Polish clergy and secular Catholic leaders gathered in Wrocław in order to take a stand "against anti-Polish revisionist pronouncements of Bonn's political leaders and against the remilitarization of Western Germany, which constitutes a threat to peace." [12] Some 1700 persons, including several hundred priests and the apostolic administrator of Wrocław, participated; yet during this same time the regime was conducting a virulent propaganda campaign against the Vatican.

A significant example of the policies of the Vatican are demonstrated in the numerous demands for the rebuilding of the Hitlerite Wehrmacht which, according to the program of American warmongers, should become the main support of the aggressive Atlantic forces in the remilitarization of Western Germany, and the encouragement of revenge feelings of the German Episcopate and that of the Christian Democratic Party, which is closely connected with the Vatican.[13]

In spite of the Episcopate's conciliatory efforts, a violent offensive against the church was launched at the end of 1952, soon merging with a "hate-American" campaign. Numerous priests and some bishops were arrested, most of them being accused of using "their position for espionage activities and political subversion against the Polish People's Republic." To substantiate some of these allegations, the Polish press quoted from a book by Stanton Griffis, former United States ambassador in Poland, who described giving money to the Bishop of Cracow for an orphanage. At the beginning of November 1952, there was an indignant outcry in the press against the Bishop of Katowice because he had asked the faithful to sign a petition requesting the government to provide religious instruction in schools, in accordance with the agreement of April 1950.

On February 9, 1953, the State Council issued a decree giving the government control of all appointments to church posts, thus limiting the authority of the Pope in matters of church jurisdiction. The decree made it obligatory to "swear allegiance to People's Poland" and gave the regime the right to remove clergymen from their posts should they "support antistate activity" or "act contrary to law and public order." [14] This proved to be a useful pretext for the state to remove bishops and have them replaced by "patriotic priests" as Capitular Vicars, possibly with the intent of establishing a national church independent of Rome. The principle of separation between state and church, proclaimed in the April 1950 agreement and in the Constitution of 1952, was now supplanted by state intervention in ecclesiastic affairs. A party press organ stated: "The decree insures that only patriots will be appointed, that only persons who support the Polish state's interests will hold ecclesiastic posts." [15]

The church protested against the decree and accused the state of violating its 1950 agreement and of conducting an antireligious campaign. A detailed memorandum was sent by the Polish Episcopate to Prime Minister Bierut on May 8, 1953, in protest against the growing persecution of the Catholic Church. The memorandum cited numerous examples of violations by the regime of both the letter and the spirit of the church-state agreement and the new constitution. The history of church-state relations was summarized from the time the Communist regime in Poland was established until May 1953, with special emphasis on the period after the April 1950 agreement. The memorandum was also, in a way, a balance sheet of the Episcopate's relentless efforts to establish a modus vivendi with the regime. According to the church, the decree of February 9, 1953, definitely closed the experimental period which had opened on April 14, 1950: The regime's "mad desire to annihilate the church" was now apparent. It was expressed in its restrictions against the Catholic press and publications, elimination of religious instruction from educational establishments, attempts at diversion among the clergy, application of political pressure on the clergy and faithful, and constant intervention of the regime in internal affairs of the church. This intervention finally became institutionalized by the February decree on church appointments, stated the memorandum. As for the reasons for the failure of the experiment in coexistence, the memorandum pointed out, "The hostility toward the church was not so much the matter of the people involved but of the system; with the people we negotiated, as a rule, in a friendly atmosphere." [16] This passage seems to imply that the Polish party, in its relations with the church, behaved not as an independent agent, but as an instrument of Moscow. To illustrate an action of the party which was against its own better judgment and against Poland's obvious state interests, the memorandum referred to the fact that the Vatican, at the suggestion of the Polish Episcopate, had finally agreed to replace the apostolic administration in Poland's regained territories and only the government's veto prevented establishment of permanent church representatives.

The tense atmosphere created by the antichurch campaign was

manifest in various events which followed. On May 8, 1953, in spite of a governmental ban, huge crowds joined a religious procession through the streets of Cracow and security forces had to be withdrawn. In Warsaw, on the feast of Corpus Christi, Cardinal Wyszyński denounced "the intolerable attempt" of the Communists to suppress religion in individual and social life. The Polish hierarchy, said the Cardinal, would defend religion "even to the point of shedding blood." As in Cracow, the security forces had to withdraw in the face of a defiant mass of the faithful. In September 1953, Bishop Czesław Kaczmarek of Kielce was placed on trial for alleged spying on behalf of "the American ambassador, Bliss Lane, the Vatican, and the National Committee for a Free Europe." He was also accused of having helped Ukrainian anti-Soviet insurgents, and having provided British agents with secret information.[17] The bishop was sentenced to twelve years in prison. On September 28, 1953, a few days after this trial ended, the government issued a communiqué suspending Cardinal Wyszyński from his functions,[18] in reprisal for his failure to issue a public condemnation of the accused bishop and for his outspoken censure of the regime in a Corpus Christi speech. This action was taken on the basis of the February 9, 1953 decree permitting removal of clergymen who "act against state interests." According to the communiqué, the government would permit the Cardinal to "retire into a monastery." [19] The Cardinal was officially accused of failing to fulfill the 1950 church-state agreement, and in October 1953, two of the Primate's auxiliaries in Gniezno were also imprisoned. The charge against one was that he had smuggled abroad the text of an Episcopate resolution which protested against a government decree.

At the beginning of 1954 nine bishops and several hundred priests were held in prison.

14   The THAW

The last days of Stalin were the bleakest and most dreadful of the postwar decade in Poland. Arbitrary arrests and show trials became increasingly·frequent. Largely under the pressure of Moscow, over half of the country's investments had been pumped into heavy industry, while consumer goods, housing, and community services were grossly neglected. The standard of living gradually sank to the Soviet level.

The stern, stifling atmosphere of Marxist dogmatism descended also upon the intellectual life of Poland. Until 1948 a certain latitude had been left to writers, intellectuals, and scholars provided they did not openly attack the Soviet Union and the basic tenets of the Communist doctrine; now active participation in the process of "building socialism" was insisted upon. "Socialist realism" was sternly recommended as the only approved method of artistic creation. Literature was muzzled and emasculated; all other arts were subjected to party supervision; Polish scholarship consisted largely in quoting Lenin and Stalin, preferably the latter, all over again. At least lip service had to be paid to Russian art, science, and learning, and glorification and imitation of everything Soviet became the shortest and surest way to success. Culturally, the period 1952–1954 was one of abject sycophancy and incredible dullness. Polish books and periodicals written in the so-called "numb language," the Orwellian "double speak," became unreadable.

The death of the tyrant was bound to have a considerable effect on the whole Soviet Empire, yet all the consequences of his demise did not come at once. For a year or so everything appeared unchanged: for the time being the rigid concept of *sui generis* Communist feudalism linking the Soviet Union and its satellites remained unaltered; the Second Congress of the UPWP in March 1954, proclaimed policies only slightly milder than those pursued under Stalin; the collectivization drive was to continue. Nearly 75 per cent of all industrial investment was to go into heavy industry. The climax of the struggle with the church, the arrest of Cardinal Wyszyński, came after Stalin's death in September 1953. "Socialist realism" still remained a rigid rule of artistic creation; adulation of "the Center" (to use the terminology of *The Captive Mind*) was still imperative in all spheres of activity.

Nevertheless, powerful forces inside Poland and in the Soviet Union were already at work, undermining the unbearable Stalinist system. Its destruction was a gradual process brought about by a conglomeration of intertwined phenomena, which for better understanding have to be studied separately. The deep crisis within the ruling party and its youth organization was a critical factor, especially among the young Marxist intellectuals. One must add to this the breakdown of the economic and especially the agrarian policies of the regime, and the repercussions of the struggle for power within the Soviet Union. This struggle revealed a temporary disorganization of the Soviet leadership. The liquidation of Beria brought about first the discrediting and then the disorganization of the Soviet secret police, with which the Polish police apparatus was closely linked. Consequently, during 1954–55 the all-pervading fear of the midnight knock on the door and arbitrary arrest diminished considerably. The abating of the terror brought to the surface hitherto suppressed political ideas and basic human passions, revealing the smouldering crisis within the party.

"THE NEW CLASS"

Since 1945 the party had been the driving force which ruthlessly imparted direction and purpose to the "socialist revolution" in Poland. Under Soviet supervision, the party enjoyed a near monopoly of power: political control, ownership of the means of production, and all but exclusive control of communication and education. While imposing profound political, economic, and cultural changes the party itself had undergone a deep transformation.

At first the party expanded rapidly: from a small group of less than 20,000 in 1944–45 it became a mass party numbering over a million people at the end of 1948. In the spring of 1950, with the start of the Six Year Plan, a new principle of recruitment was announced: "The struggle for new cadres." A few thousand "activists" were to constitute the cadre: local party secretaries, members of executive committees, etc., were to form the backbone, the apparatus of the party. From now on the United Polish Workers' Party was to be not only a mass movement but also an elite organization and to achieve this end the party had to be constantly purified, tightened, and kept in a state of alertness by means of frequent and thorough purges of party personnel.[1]

All these purges and the "controlled recruitment" did not prevent the development of three dangerous trends: first, a decrease in the number of workers within the working-class party; second, a drop in peasant membership; and third, a marked growth of the bureaucratic element within the party. The first trend is significant in view of the rapidly expanding industrial labor force, which increased from 3,300,000 in 1948 to about 6,000,000 in 1954.[2]

The second phenomenon, the constantly decreasing number of peasant members, can be explained both by the disappointment with land reform measures and by resistance to the mounting collectivization drive. As for the third trend, the party tried in vain to limit the admission of officials and to increase the number of workers and peasants. All in vain; the bureaucratic sclerosis continued, as shown by the occupational composition of the delegation to the Second Party Congress held in March 1954. Out of 1228 delegates, there were only 272 workers and 108 peasants, while a variety of white collar workers, intellectuals, and party functionaries formed almost exactly half of the congress — 620 delegates.[3]

Parallel to the numerical expansion, and to the bureaucratization of the party, the enjoyment of total power with all its privileges affected the morale of the Communist movement. The almost religious fervor of 1944–1947 faded away amidst the comfort and even the luxury which the omnipotent bureaucracy displayed amidst general pauperization, and the enjoyment of hitherto undreamed of pleasures by a party elite alienated from the rest of the nation, a small group of political bureaucrats and party bosses having many features of an exploiting group characterized by "pharaseical morals of a privileged class."[4] The "new class" became isolated from the rest of the nation by a wall of special institutions, shops with "yellow curtains," luxurious summer resorts, special medical care, etc.

On the other hand, the very size of the party made it absorb from the bottom numerous elements having little to do with Communist ideology. After a decade of rule, the Communist regime in Poland, like any living political system, had succumbed to the inevitable environmental pressure and gradually adapted itself to the local conditions. Consequently, despite the lip service constantly paid to Marxism, "proletarian internationalism," and the "Polish-Soviet brotherhood" by the party rank and file, the party at the bottom became more and more permeated with "petty bourgeois, nationalistic," and even religious sentiments common to broad masses of the Polish people. Most party members had vivid memories of the Stalinist purges, the liquidation of the CPP, and the deportations of the years 1939–1941. They had witnessed the behavior of the "liberating" Soviet troops in Poland, their looting and raping; they knew about the deportations, the Katyń massacre, the role played by the Soviet army during the Warsaw uprising, etc. But among the older generation the memory of the wholesale purge and the dissolution of the CPP was especially vivid. A popular saying freely circulating among the party activists in 1955 was:

It is not fair that the French Communists call themselves the Party of the Murdered. It is we who deserve that name. And no Okhrana or Gestapo killed as many of our comrades as the Soviet NKVD.[5]

The Soviet colonial exploitation of the country, camouflaged by the slogans of the "fraternal aid," was a factor which even the skillful party propagandists were at a loss to explain away to the lower echelon of the movement. Thus, while the swelling party rank and file, especially the youth, preserved its ties with the broad masses of the people, frequently sharing their complaints and anti-Soviet sentiments, the leadership, even after Stalin's death still stuck to his rigid, dogmatic line of policy and his tyrannical methods.

The gap separating "the new class" and the masses of the Polish people was deepened by the disclosures made by a high official of the Polish ministry of public security, Józef Światło, who had fled to the West in December 1953. His revelations of the corruption of the "new class" and the bestiality of its secret police, broadcast by Western radio stations in 1954–55, increased the already spreading uneasiness and even disturbed many sincere Communists. Denied at first by the regime, the revelations eventually compelled the party to launch an extensive shake-up of the secret police in order to remove its most discredited and unpopular figures. On December 7, 1954, the ministry of public security was abolished, and the dreaded Radkiewicz dismissed; the functions of the *Bezpieka* were divided between the ministry of the interior and a newly established committee of public security responsible directly to the Council of of Ministers.

At the end of 1954, Gomułka was quietly released from detention, although this was not announced until much later. At the beginning of 1955, the fall of the "Polish Beria" was followed by the purge of many of his most vicious henchmen, like Roman Romkowski, Anatol Fajgin, and Jacek Rożański, who were also purged from the party ranks. Rożański was soon tried and sentenced to five years in prison for having systematically used sadistic methods to extract evidence from political prisoners. The *Nowe drogi* condemned the past role of the secret police, declaring that administration of justice should be entrusted to independent law courts. The changing attitude of the party toward its security apparatus was formulated by Bierut who, in his speech at the Third Plenum, admitted failure in curbing the *Bezpieka,* a virtual "state within the state," and promised to punish those guilty of violating "socialist legality." Thus without dissolving its secret police the regime destroyed its prestige and limited its role.[6]

The crisis within the party and its security organs was accompanied by a growing unrest among the youth and the intellectuals, eager for more freedom of expression. The leadership of the party, while initially acquiescing in the "thaw" as a means of appeasing the people's wrath, now began to put a break on the decompression as assuming dangerous proportions; but the pressure of the rank and file of the movement, supported and encouraged on by the broad masses of the people, was irresistible. Demands for relaxing the "iron corset" of the police system, and for more consumer goods were so elemental that the party leadership did not dare to resist them. After all, were not similar demands being gratified in the Soviet Union?[7] The party attempts to limit the "thaw" widened the chasm separating the Polish people from the "new class." It was in this post-Stalinist period in 1954–55 that the popular saying originated: "What is the best way of committing suicide? The surest way would be to jump into the abyss separating the party and the Polish people." And here the leadership of the party was meant first of all.

Yet the gap separating the party from the rest of the nation, as the events of the autumn of 1956 were to prove, was never as deep as that in Hungary. Despite its subservience toward the Kremlin, the Polish party managed to preserve a spark of independence, sometimes carefully camouflaged by outward servility. Polish agriculture was less collectivized than any other in the area. In 1955 the state farms covered only 14 per cent of the land, and all types of rural cooperatives only 9 per cent. Moreover, Poland was the only satellite country that erected no monument to Stalin. Numerous competitions were arranged, and many prizes awarded; but each time some pretext would be found not to proceed with the actual construction. Eight years passed and Stalin got no monument in Poland. Moreover, unlike Hungary, Communist Poland never staged a show trial of the leader of the Roman Catholic Church.

What was more important, however, from the party's point of view, Poland, unlike Czechoslovakia, Hungary or Bulgaria, did not bodily liquidate the chief opponents to the Stalinist line. No mock trial of Gomułka or Spychalski was ever staged despite repeated reminders from Moscow. In most cases, the Polish party bosses answered obediently that evidence is still being collected and that the trial will come in due time.[8]

Thus, the UPWP, had managed to save from destruction an alternate team of courageous, former underground leaders who automatically gained certain popularity in the eyes of the public because of their opposition to Stalin and his Polish stooges. This team was invaluable when the party eventually maneuvered itself into a truly "revolutionary situation."

THE MOSCOW CONGRESS AND ITS CONSEQUENCES

In February of 1956, came the Twentieth Congress of the Communist Party of the Soviet Union. At the beginning of the congress a special committee was set up composed of delegates of the parties of the Soviet Union, Italy, Bulgaria, Finland, and Poland. The committee examined the problem of the dissolution of the Communist Party of Poland and, on February 18, issued a communiqué which stated:

In 1938 the Executive Committee of the Communist International adopted a resolution of dissolving the Communist Party of Poland in view of an accusation made at the time concerning wide-scale penetration by enemy agents into the ranks of its leading Party *aktiv*. It has now been established that this accusation was based on materials which were falsified by subsequently exposed provocateurs.

The five parties concluded their communiqué by stating that "the dissolution of the Communist Party of Poland was an unfortunate act" and that the party should be rehabilitated. On February 19, *Trybuna ludu* published the communiqué followed by its own editorial entitled "The Historical Document," which states:

The evidence for [the dissolution] has been faked by a gang of saboteurs and provocateurs whose real role was only brough to light after Beria was unmasked. . . . The party honor of these [liquidated] comrades has been re-established and these were fully rehabilitated.[9]

Neither the article nor the communiqué stated, however, who those provocateurs were, and upon what evidence their decision was based.

Then came Khrushchev's speech attacking Stalin and the "personality cult." The speech put the little Stalin of Poland — Bolesław Bierut, on the spot: he was as guilty of arbitrary rule as Stalin had been. He duly attended the congress as head of the Polish delegation, addressed its opening session and praised the new "collective leadership" without mentioning Stalin. Less than a month after the rehabilitation of the Communist Party of Poland, Bierut died in Moscow on March 12. Bierut's place as First Secretary of the Central Committee was taken by an old party hand, Edward Ochab.[10]

Meanwhile, under the influence of the spirit generated by the Moscow congress, the atmosphere in Poland began changing rapidly, affecting even the party. The congress was both more meaningful and more dangerous to the UPWP than to any other Communist Party outside the Soviet Union. On one hand the congress spelled not only the debunking of Stalin but also rehabilitation of the CPP, the organizational and spiritual parent of the UPWP; on the other the discrediting of Stalinism was a risky operation, because for most Poles Stalinism and communism were one and the same thing.

On April 6, a conference of party activists took place in Warsaw, to discuss the resolutions of the Moscow congress. In a major programatic speech Ochab frankly admitted many past mistakes, officially announced the release and rehabilitation of Gomułka (without mentioning when it had taken place) and the restoration of party rights to twenty-six of his political friends, including General Wacław Komar. While condemning "hysterical criticism" of the past party line Ochab promised that "democratization" will go on, and that the Five Year Plan would remove the existing "disproportions," and restore the balance between agriculture and industry; the wages of the lowest paid workers were to be increased; defense spending to be curtailed.[11]

In the spring of 1956 events in Poland began snowballing. On April 20, a sweeping amnesty for 28,000 people, including well over a thousand political prisoners, was announced; so was the rehabilitation of several high ranking army officers condemned in 1951 for allegedly plotting against the regime. The purging and arresting of former high officials of the dissolved ministry of public security went on. The released prisoners and the Polish deportees, many of them Home Army heroes, returning from the USSR, began to tell their stories to friends and neighbors, thus further increasing the existing tension, restlessness, and bitterness against the regime. This deepened the ugly mood prevailing throughout the country. Under the pressure of public opinion, on May 6, Jakub Berman, responsible for security and ideological matters, was made to resign from the Politbureau as well as from his post as deputy prime minister. The puppet front organizations suddenly awakened from their slumber and began to stress their independence toward the party. The trade unions destroyed secret files on their workers and elected their officials by secret ballot. The Sejm ceased to vote unanimously and started to act as a genuine legislative body — it began to summon civil servants, and even ministers, and question them on their activities. The institutions of higher learning formulated new curricula and began to clamor for restoration of their ancient academic freedoms. The Polish press, even party organs, started to criticize not only minor shortcomings, as had been the case hitherto, but also to question some fundamental assumptions of the Communist doctrine. Within the ranks of the party the slogan of return to "pure Leninism" was advocated. In some cases Leninism was stretched conveniently to cover a simple rejection of Russian influence in Poland.

Now, the "thaw" became really dangerous for the party because the people began openly asking whether Stalinism alone was responsible for the soulless society created in Poland during the last decade. The party leadership was simply carried away by a trend which it considered dangerous, yet unable to stop.

THE CRISIS OF CONSCIENCE: THE REVOLT OF THE INTELLECTUALS

With the changes going on both in Poland and in the Soviet Union since 1954, the straightjacket of Stalinism became unbearable even for more sensitive spirits among the party members. The first signs of reawakening had already come in the spring of 1954, when the party itself, taking its cue from the relaxation of the Soviet cultural policy marked by the publication of Ilya Ehrenburg's novel *The Thaw,* acquiesced by somewhat loosening the hitherto rigid standards of "socialist realism." From the spring of 1954 to the summer of 1955, a vigorous controversy was going on in the literary press about the real meaning of "socialist realism" as an artistic method and an instrument of social engineering. Soon even some basic tenets of the Marxist ideology were tackled, at first cautiously. A Marxist scholar, Józef Chałasiński, attacked Marxist monopoly of scholarship, and the dogmatic party interpretation of doctrine, which practically destroyed Polish sociology, and stifled creative impulses of Polish men of learning.[12]

Symptomatic of the crisis of conscience experienced by the party intellectuals was the challenge of the official varnished reality by a leading Communist poet and writer, Adam Ważyk. Ważyk himself was an important person: at the end of the war he had been assigned a responsible job as an ideological watchdog of the Marxist weekly, *Kuźnica* (The Smithy). In this capacity he proved himself to be a leading exponent of "socialist realism" and an implacable foe of liberalism and all other "decadent and rotten" Western tendencies, which he ruthlessly crushed on behalf of the party. But by the middle of 1955, talented and imaginative men like Ważyk could no longer stand the atmosphere of boredom and sycophancy. On August 21, 1955, *Nowa kultura* (New Culture), the party literary magazine, published his "Poem for Adults." The "Poem" was a bitter criticism of communism in Poland, a merciless flogging of the ruling group, and a revelation of the atmosphere of frustration and despair prevailing in the country after eleven years of Communist rule. Ważyk attacked the atmosphere of gloom and apathy, hooliganism, and banditry, alcoholism and sexual depravity of the youth. He ridiculed the Communist brainwashing and regimentation of education, the dogmatism of official Stalinist orthodoxy, the attempts to exorcise social and economic evils with quasi-religious slogans:

> They ran to us, shouting:
> A Communist does not die.
>
> . . . .
>
> They ran to us shouting:
> Under Socialism
> A cut finger does not hurt.
> They felt pain.
> They lost faith.[13]

Ważyk decried the hypocrisy of party dogma, the discrepancy between word and reality. He lampooned the party purges with their witch hunting, and their obsession about "deviations." Despite the nightmare Ważyk still concluded his "Poem" with an appeal to the party demanding a new policy:

For a clear truth,
For the bread of freedom,
For burning reason
We demand these every day
We demand through the Party.

Immediately the "Poem" reverberated throughout the country, becoming a most popular topic of discussion and gossip, dramatizing the deep crisis within the ruling group. Hundreds of articles were written on the subject, mostly supporting the views of the author. *Trybuna ludu* of September 21, 1955, published an article which, while condemning the author, had to admit that at least in the cultural field, there was a great deal to be corrected; that there was an inflation of "vain declamation"; that "cold dogmas go together with actual emptiness of hearts and minds." Despite these admissions the party tried to reassert its authority; Ważyk was sharply reprimanded, and the editor and entire editorial board of the *Nowa kultura* were dismissed. For several months nothing from Ważyk's pen appeared in print.

The publication of the "Poem" opened a period of agonizing reappraisal by the press of many vital issues until that time camouflaged by fear, hypocrisy, and the varnish of official propaganda. Soon Ważyk's example was followed by other intellectuals who began insisting on priority of artistic criteria over political dictates. On March 24–25, in Warsaw, the Nineteenth Session of the Council of Culture and Art brought to the surface the ferment seething for a long time. The meeting witnessed a passionate attack on the part of some of the writers against the regimentation of literature.[14]

Parallel to the political "thaw" following the Moscow congress, liberalization of intellectual life continued, and on April 21, 1956, Włodzimierz Sokorski, the discredited minister of art, was removed from his post. Within a few weeks a new moral and intellectual climate was created. In the spring of 1956, Polish press, periodicals, and literature, till then as dull and monotonous as anywhere within the Soviet orbit, became witty, vivacious and often brilliant. Topics that had been forbidden for over a decade were now debated with amazing freedom. The mask of hypocrisy was suddenly torn down, and neither Soviet-Polish relations nor cultural developments in the West were taboo. Great interest in Western literature, especially American, manifested itself with great vigor; even the works of some prewar non-Marxist writers were now republished.[15]

Even the Soviet Union and its sacrosanct policies toward Poland became subjects of critical discussion. Purges, concentration camps, the treatment of the Polish Home Army — all these hitherto strictly forbidden themes were loudly debated. For the first time in ten years people began talking openly and frankly about questions which no one had dared to debate even at home. The "thaw" turned into a flood.

THE POLISH YOUTH IN REVOLT

The revolt of the intellectuals was paralleled by the revolt of the youth. From 1948 the political life of the young generation had been dominated by the Union of Polish Youth, numbering up to two million members. The Union had been created by compulsorily merging four already existing youth movements: the Communist Organization of Fighting Youth, set up in 1944 during the underground period by PPR; the old youth branch of the PPS; the Association of Workers' Universities, the Association of Polish Democratic Youth; and finally, the peasant youth movement, known in Poland as the *Wici*. The consolidation was preceded by infiltration and "democratization." When the forcible fusion took place in 1948, the Union of Polish Youth became a monopolistic youth organization, possessed of all the instruments of compulsion and allurement at the disposal of a totalitarian creature of this kind. The Union was a branch of the UPWP and all persons up to the age of twenty had, in principle, to pass through this organization before being admitted into the party. In the ranks of the Union, Polish boys and girls had to undergo a period of Communist indoctrination; "bourgeois nationalism" and religion or "metaphysical fideism," were elminated, and atheism, adulation of the Soviet Union and the cult of Stalin, were forced down their throat.

Soon, however, the mood of the "thaw" and of the Moscow congress penetrated into the ranks of the Union. Among the most vocal critics of the Stalinist systems was the Warsaw Communist weekly, *Po prostu*, the literary organ of "students and young intellectuals." The editorial team of the paper was mostly of proletarian origin, educated in the Stalinist school of "The Smithy," but by now thoroughly disgusted with the corruption, dullness, and hypocrisy of the "new class," and with the rigidity of the dogmatic interpretation of Marxism. Around the paper in Warsaw, there formed a debating circle, the model for a number of similar clubs throughout the country. Both the paper and the clubs confronted the Marxist dogma with concrete historical experience, and by their passionate, outspoken, witty, and often sarcastic ventilation of the vital problems of contemporary Poland, helped to tear down the superficial, stultifying veneer of Stalinism that had stifled the country for a decade. Soon *Po prostu* became the liveliest and most outspoken paper of Poland, and its circulation at one time reached 200,000 copies. Its editor, Eligiusz Lasota, became a well-known and a popular personality throughout the country.[16]

In March 1956, soon after the Moscow congress, the *Po prostu* published a bold letter from a member of the Union of Polish Youth, reflecting the soul-searching through the young Communist generation was passing as a result of the ideological earthquake produced by the Moscow congress:

I want to ask what the comrades in the highest positions did to prevent the development of the cult of the individual? And what about the Central Committee: To whom is it responsible? . . . And as far as Stalin was concerned, even if I had known the true state of affairs, I would not have been able to say anything. I would like to know why? [17]

The letter was followed by a series of similar eruptions of anger and bitterness on the part of the young people, most of them confessing disappointment with communism and rejection of the party's authority. The party authorities tried to curb the unbridled vivacity of the *Po prostu,* as well as the rapid expansion of the clubs, but this proved impossible because their activity was an elemental expression of the hitherto suppressed sentiments permeating a great majority of the Polish youth — a revolt against the monopolistic position of the bureaucratic and corrupted Union of Polish Youth "paralyzing the young intelligentsia," training people "with a religious and not a rational mentality," and preparing them not "for a struggle with evil but for uncritical submission." The criticism of the Union reached its climax when it was proposed that the Union be dissolved, and "a new revolutionary organization" be set up.[18]

The disillusion of the young generation with the official interpretation of the Word was reflected in the publication by the *Po prostu* of an essay entitled "Is this the twilight of Marxism?" [19]

THE ECONOMIC CRISIS AND THE POZNAŃ UPRISING

The crisis within the party, its youth, and its intellectual elite must be viewed against the background of the deepening economic crisis. Confusion and haste in preparing the Six Year Plan, with its emphasis on speed and heavy industry, resulted in chaos and waste of precious raw materials, many of which had to be imported from abroad. Foreign commerce was increasingly and often artificially directed toward the countries of the "socialist camp." Agriculture was neglected and brought to the verge of ruin. All this depressed the standard of living of Poland to the subsistence level, and by 1952–53 Poland began to feel the adverse consequences of hasty overindustrialization: the inadequate investment in housing, agriculture and consumer industries. Despite various artificial devices aimed at camouflaging the depreciation of real wages, they more than doubled between 1949 and 1955.

The Six Year Plan was a grandiose undertaking by Polish standards; its various aspects are difficult to evaluate from a perspective of a few years, but some of its negative aspects are obvious even now: "At the cost of enormous investments, officially estimated at around 25 per cent of national income, but more probably over 30 per cent, the plan was successful in its main goal: the output of producer goods, according to the official index, nearly tripled between 1950 and 1955. During this period nonagricultural employment increased by more than 60 per cent. Forty-five per cent of all investment went into industry (and most of this to metallurgy, machine building, and armaments), only 9 per cent to agriculture (mainly to the collectives and state farms) and 10 per cent to housing (primarily in the large industrial centers)." [20]

The year 1955 was the last year of the Six Year Plan, which officially was considerably overfulfilled. The new Five Year Plan, which began in January 1956, was to strike a better balance between the production of capital goods and consumer goods than was the case with its predecessor, and especially put more emphasis on the neglected agriculture. While the Six Year Plan, in its final year, devoted 63.5 per cent to production of capital goods, the Five Year Plan lowered this rate to less than 50 per cent. Nevertheless the industrialization of Poland was to go on; the production of steel was to be increased from about 4.5 million tons to 7 million tons. By the end of 1960 as much as 30 per cent of the land was to be collectivized. At the same time, however, the government promised that the inquisition methods applied toward individual farmers were to be relaxed; that raising of livestock was to be encouraged, and the supply of consumer goods in the countryside increased. These concessions, however, proved inadequate and the pressure of public opinion for further liberalization of economic policies was continued through the spring of 1956. Then came the Poznań uprising.

The uprising was precipitated by the strike of the Stalin Locomotive Works, locally known as the ZIPSO factory. The strike was a protest against exploitation, waste, bureaucracy, shortage of consumer goods, and appalling housing conditions. The immediate issues were irregularity of supplies of raw materials, which, by keeping the workers idle, cut down their wages, and the misapplication of wage regulations, including the excessive payroll tax reductions. When repeated protests and even the sending of a workers' delegation to Warsaw proved to be of no avail, on Thursday morning, June 28, the workers marched into the streets with "We want bread and freedom" banners. The general public so sympathized with the workers, that the peaceful demonstration of the ZIPSO workers snowballed as it marched toward the center of the city. Thousands of passers-by, especially young people, spontaneously joined the demonstration. Many shops were closed; communication in the center of the city was interrupted. Now "Russians go home" slogans appeared. All this time the militia remained passive. Thus the old working-class weapon, the general strike, was turned against the party.

When the demonstration reached the center of the city, however, shots were exchanged between the crowd and the secret police. Who fired first is difficult to ascertain. In any event, by 11:30 A.M. fighting had commenced between the crowd and the secret police. The demonstrators invaded several public buildings, including that of the party provincial committee, the headquarters of the secret police, and the arsenal and the army barracks. The soldiers of the Poznań garrison remained passive and in some cases willingly handed over their weapons to the crowd. Thus, the original peaceful demonstration was turned into a bloody struggle against the regime. By late afternoon the city was surrounded by crack troops stationed nearby and a curfew was imposed. The intermittent struggle went on until Friday, June 29. According to official data, 53 persons were killed and about 300 wounded.[21]

During the fighting Premier Cyrankiewicz and several party bosses flew to Poznań. There, by alternating promises and threats they tried to cope with the situation; a rebate of taxes was ordered to the ZIPSO workers, obnoxious officials were removed. After having repressed the revolt, the regime had to explain how it had happened that the workers had risen against the People's Republic run by the Workers' Party. Initially the alleged role of "imperialistic agents" and "provocateurs" sent from abroad was emphasized.[22] Even at this stage, however, the government did not dare to deny the fact that the workers had had legitimate grievances against the regime. Gradually, under the pressure of public opinion and the press, led by the *Po prostu*, the stress was shifted from the "agents" and the "provocateurs" to the wrongs and abuses of which the workers were victims.

Thus, after twelve years in power, the party realized that as far as the youth and the workers were concerned it was in a weaker position than it had been ten years ago. Formally, on paper, the number of Communists had been truly impressive. But while in 1944–45 the party had been able to count on a hard core of idealists and of fanatics, now even the young elite was undermined by doubt and despair about the validity of the Communist dogma:

At Poznań [wrote a party activist] within two to three hours this power-ful [party] organization was swept away from behind its desks . . . and played no role whatsoever.[23]

The destruction of the Stalinist myth was probably the last straw needed to complete the process of disillusionment of the generation brought up in the aura of the personality cult. As a keen observer of the satellite scene put it: "The collapse of the infallibility of the individual led to a collapse of the infallibility of dogma. . . ."[24]

The Poznań explosion, or the "Black Thursday," posed the problems: How far can decompression go without destroying the party control? Would the "thaw" survive the revolt?

Such was the moral and intellectual climate in Poland preceding the meeting of the Seventh Plenum of the Central Committee of July 1956.

The RETURN
of GOMUŁKA

The Poznań uprising, together with the series of lesser provincial strikes, riots, and demonstrations which preceded and followed it, dramatized the critical situation into which the party had maneuvered itself. The seriousness of the situation was obvious to the party bureaucrats, but they could not unite on a common solution. The partisans of the old Stalinist methods interpreted the uprising as a direct and disastrous result of the "thaw," and felt that further relaxation could mean the final collapse of the regime. The more liberal faction urged further decompression of the regime, and its further modification in ways which would make it more acceptable to the masses' of the Polish people, who keenly desired a higher standard of living, end of forcible collectivization, more religious freedom, especially freedom of religious instruction, and a greater independence from the Soviet Union.

To cope with the situation the Seventh Plenum of the Central Committee was convened on July 18, to sit for an unprecedented period of ten days. The Plenum deliberated in the shadow of the Poznań events, and under the wrathful eyes of Soviet Premier Marshal Bulganin and Soviet Defense Minister Marshal Zhukov who came ostensibly to celebrate the tenth anniversary of the establishment of the Communist regime in Poland. Bulganin's speech dwelt on machinations of foreign "provocateurs" as responsible for the Poznań events. In their statements delivered at the Plenum, both Ochab and Cyrankiewicz ignored the Soviet analysis of the recent developments in Poland; Ochab spoke of the moral shock produced by the Poznań events and of the "immense wrongs" suffered by the working class. He admitted that the official statistics were inaccurate, that their claims of increased standard of living over the prewar period were exaggerated. He blamed the heavy armaments imposed on Poland as a result of the Korean War as the main reason for the neglect of consumer goods and of agriculture, and even tried to defend the "Polish economic model," including collectivization. He placed, on the other hand, heavy responsibilities for the Poznań revolt on "bureaucracy and the soullessness of the authorities both central and local," and chartered a new role for the party:

Our party [he said] is the ruling party. Does this mean that its organs should exercise power directly? No, not at all. We should set the general direction [for the administrative authorities] . . . but must not replace them, we must not duplicate their work and hamper them in their functions. . . .

The policy of continued limited decompression was opposed by the Stalinist faction whose spokesman, Zenon Nowak, launched a frontal attack on the democratization as a camouflage of anti-Soviet agitation, and a gradual drift from socialist construction. While favoring economic concessions he was for muzzling the press, and tried to shift the blame for the failure of the past policies onto the intellectuals and the Jews who occupied high party and governmental positions. The stormy debate that followed witnessed the clash of these two concepts.

The resolution of the Seventh Plenum, apparently voted against the bitter opposition of the Stalinists, overlooked Bulganin's interpretation of the Poznań revolt; it conceded that the uprising had "caused a profound shock throughout Poland," and that "the link with the masses was broken" as a result of "economic neglect," the degeneration of the party work permeated with the "personality cult, bureaucratization," and "abandonment of the inner party democracy." "There can be no democratization of the country [we read in the resolution] without democratization of the party which leads the country." It was vital that the party tame the activity of the security apparatus, "observe socialist legality," expand "the workers' democracy . . . , transfer the center of gravity of their work" to the masses, and pay more attention to their sentiments and daily needs; economic planning should be reshaped to better suit those needs, and "all possible injustices done to the working people" were to be corrected. The resolution promised a better deal for workers in industry and agriculture: wages of the lowest paid employees were to be boosted and private initiative in handicraft encouraged; there was to be a revision of delivery quotas detrimental to the peasants. Cooperation with other political groups, the United Polish Peasant Party, and the Democratic Party was to be restored. The Diet was to become the main organ of legislation. Finally, the resolution of the Seventh Plenum proclaimed the end of discrimination against former members of the Home Army and other non-Communist underground groups.

The elections to the Politbureau showed that the faction favoring reform was in the ascendancy. The Seventh Plenum officially rehabilitated Gomułka, Spychalski, and Kliszko. Gomułka's "party rights were restored," but no responsible job was entrusted to him. Three new Politbureau members were elected: Edward Gierek, Roman Nowak, and Adam Rapacki; Stefan Jędrychowski and Eugeniusz Stawiński were made alternate members; none of them had any lengthy Moscow training, while all had a considerable Western background.[1]

The resolutions of the Seventh Plenum, while going in the right direction, did not go far enough. Even the speeches of the partisans of reform were halfhearted in their evaluation of party mistakes. It was obvious that party leadership was divided, and although the reforming wing was in the majority, even they were far behind the masses. There was, moreover, a marked discrepancy between words and deeds; despite its resolution about the scrutability of public life, the Plenum never published the full minutes of its deliberations. The compromised leaders were not completely removed and replaced by a new team. The all powerful Rokossovski was still in charge of the armed forces and Minc was at least nominally the boss of the Polish economy. With Zenon Nowak, Jóźwiak and Mazur, both hard-boiled Stalinists still in the Politbureau, and with Zawadzki and Zambrowski hesitating, the balance of power within the key body of the party was rather shaky. While the two shaping factions jockeyed for positions and worked at cross purposes, the masses were relentlessly pressing forward for more dramatic and essential changes.[2]

From the time of the Poznań uprising, negotiations had gone on between the Politbureau, represented mainly by Ochab, and Gomułka in order to enlist the support of the latter for the party; but he was apparently unwilling to accept a minor post, would come only to resume his old place, and insisted on removal of his main opponents: Minc and Jóźwiak, and especially Marshal Rokossovsky, the symbol of the Russian domination of Poland.

Meanwhile, throughout the summer of 1956, the ferment among the youth continued. In August, the Union of Polish Youth drafted a resolution "outlining the task of the Union as a revolutionary and independent leader of young people in the struggle for democratization and improved standard of living." [3] But the Union was to remain a branch of the UPWP. At the same time Jerzy Morawski, a secretary of the Central Committee assured the members that the party wanted the Union to "grow into an important political force," and to participate in the process of democratization.[4]

Simultaneously with the spreading riots and street demonstrations, a broad movement snowballed in the factories for relaxation of the draconic labor discipline and the fantastic norms. During the summer and early autumn, disregarding the trade-union officials and the local-primary party cells, both largely manned by the Stalinists, the workers took matters into their own hands and spontaneously elected genuinely representative workers' councils independent of both of these bureaucratic and largely parasitic instruments of governmental control. This trend was encouraged by the faction of the party supporting the idea of a thorough reform, because it undermined the position of their rivals throughout the country. The mood of dissatisfaction with the existing conditions prevailing among the workers found its expression in the words of a Silesian miner who declared to an American newspaperman: "We are getting tired of working for the next generation." [5]

On August 20–22, a three-day meeting of the Central Council of the Trade Unions was held. Chairman of the Council, Wiktor Kłosiewicz, while trying to defend the thesis that the trade-unions should be responsible for the implementation of production plans, admitted that the unions had failed in their primary task of defending the interests of the workers who had elected them. The resolution passed by the Council demanded the independence of trade-unions and insisted that the Council must review and abolish:

all decisions which stifle the independence of trade unions. . . . The plenum thinks it necessary to stress the need for strict observance . . . of democracy within the trade unions in the election of new officers and for fully respecting the will of the broad union masses.[6]

On September 5, the ninth session of the Sejm opened in a rebellious mood. The conciliatory speech made by Cyrankiewicz admitted the existence of mistrust "between the party and a certain segment of the people"; despite the Poznań uprising the government and the party were determined to go on with democratization, to turn the Sejm into the "main workshop" of legislative activity, and to remedy promptly the most immediate economic and social ills. The prime minister promised that the new Five Year Plan would raise the living standard of the population by at least 30 per cent. He announced that the Poznań trials would be public and conducted in accordance with "the strictest requirements of the rule of law and legality." [7] His speech was followed by an exceptionally lively parliamentary debate in which two former Socialists, Bolesław Drobner and Julian Hochfeld, took a leading part. Both these speakers and many other deputies insisted that the Chamber should perform its constitutional role. For the first time in the history of the postwar Sejm a governmental proposal, concerning legalization of abortion, was rejected by the deputies.

Parallel with the parliamentary debate, a penetrating analysis of the economic ills pestering the country went on in the press. It was revealed that six important crops had given a lower yield per hectar in 1954 than in 1934–1938, and that Polish agriculture was using less fertilizers than before the war.[8] Edward Lipiński, professor of economics at the Main School of Planning and Statistics, challenged a basic tenet of the Communist doctrine — the superiority of collective farming over individual farming. The assumption was based, according to Lipiński, on an "incorrect economic theory," the application of which in Poland had considerably damaged the country's agriculture. Socialism does not necessarily imply nationalization of agriculture "where previous capitalist development has not already organized agriculture in the forms of great farm factories based on hired labor." The chief objective of agrarian policy ought to be higher productivity, and not the forcing on peasants of a particular form of land ownership. Higher productivity cannot be obtained without supplying agriculture with machinery and fertilizers.[9]

On September 11, the government announced the closing of the communal machine stations and the sale of machinery to the peasants.[10] Hardly two weeks later, Zambrowski revealed that some collective farms were being dissolved because they had not been run efficiently and democratically. He declared that the government was to concentrate on strengthening the viable ones and supplying them with tractors directly rather than through the machine tractor stations. A group of prominent economists came to the conclusion that the decline of Polish agriculture had begun with the introduction of the Stalinist methods of collectivization, which one of them characterized as "legalized robbery." [11]

The failure of the past economic policy of the regime was dramatized by the resignation of the chief of the State Economic Planning Commission, Hilary Minc, on October 9. Minc had been the chief exponent of the rejection of the cautious "bourgeois planning" and following the "bold, Bolshevik planning," of attacking economic problems by means of all-out assaults or "Shturmovshchina." His resignation both from the Commission and from the Politbureau further weakened the Stalinist faction.

During the summer and early autumn of 1956 Poland lived in a state of upheaval. There were numerous meetings and demonstrations by students and workers, by youth and trade-union organizations; innumerable resolutions were passed urging the party to "deepen democratization of social life." "This program can be implemented," stated an appeal by the National Front, "only through the joint efforts of the whole nation and not the party alone." [12]

On August 4, the Politbureau officially invited Gomułka, Spychalski, and Kliszko to rejoin the party, and negotiations for Gomułka's resumption of power were begun.[13] Kliszko accepted the post of vice minister of justice, but Spychalski received no definite assignment at the time. At the end of August, the Council of Ministers appointed another friend of Gomułka, General Wacław Komar, to the command of the Internal Security Corps, in place of General Julian Hibner, who was named deputy minister of the interior.[14] Komar, a former soldier of the Dąbrowski Brigade in Spain, had been dismissed from the post of chief of military intelligence in 1953, and arrested for "treason." In his new office, he was not subject to the orders of Marshal Rokossovsky, since the internal security corps was not under his command.

From the time of the Seventh Plenum, the attention of a growing segment of the party, and of the nation, had been focusing on Gomułka. To the party rank and file, he was still a militant Communist, a hero of the underground; to many non-Communists, this man, who had been the personification of Soviet occupation between 1945 and 1948, became the epic warrior who had challenged Stalin and his stooges, who had fought for some independence from Moscow, and who had suffered imprisonment because of his courageous stand. In short, in the eyes of some people, he had been a martyr for the cause of Polish independence from Moscow, because of which they were willing to forgive many of his past excesses.

The summer of 1956, with its passionate self-criticism, soul-searching and breast-beating, brought about a far-reaching polarization of the party, and the crystallization of two rival factions. They became known as Liberals and Conservatives, or "Natolin faction," after the eighteenth century palace near Warsaw where the caucus of the faction usually met. The Liberals, or the moderate wing of the party, led by the former Socialists, Cyrankiewicz, Lange, and Rapacki, favored further democratization of the regime, and advocated entrusting Gomułka with a post worthy of his abilities and prestige. The Conservative group or "Stalinist faction," was led by Zenon Nowak, Rokossovsky, Mazur, and Jóźwiak, and favored stern reprisals against the discontent, and continuation of the policies of the previous period with only minor adjustments. While many of the intellectuals and almost the entire press and the radio was on the side of the Liberals, the "Natolin faction," ashamed and unable to openly defend their Stalinist past, used mostly whispering propaganda, including anti-Semitism, and conspiratorial methods to paralyze the action of their rivals. Initially both factions courted Gomułka. It soon became obvious that he was on the side of the reformation.

Much depended in this crisis on the position of the new First Secretary, a man with a strong Stalinist background. During his visit to Peking, Ochab had been impressed by the Chinese interpretation of the principle of "proletarian internationalism," with its emphasis on respect for national sovereignty and the necessity of respecting local differences and traditions. Under the pressure of the rank and file of the party, Ochab, a practical and coolheaded man, who already during the Seventh Plenum had emerged as a spokesman of moderate reform, now definitely shifted his allegiance toward the cause of the Liberals. He obviously sensed the mood of the country; he believed that continuation of Stalinist methods would spell a nationwide outburst and that Gomułka represented the only possible salvation for the tottering regime. Moreover, he was apparently disgusted with the slavish subservience in which the Polish party had hitherto been held by Moscow, and his Peking visit strengthened this sentiment. Ochab's attitude was supported by many party bureaucrats who were threatened with loss of their jobs, and so they were bent on perpetuating the regime regardless of its ideological platform.

Thus, the late summer of 1956 witnessed a considerable shift of the center of gravity within the party, each faction trying to win over as many members of the Central Committee as possible before the coming Eighth Plenum, but with the Liberals definitely in the ascendant, and public opinion bolstered by the press overwhelmingly behind them. As the time for the all-important Eighth Plenum drew near, debates became even more heated. The behind-the-scenes maneuvering in preparation for some sort of *coup d'état* continued on both sides with mounting passions, until the Eighth Plenum of the Central Committee was convened in mid-October.

Charged with tension, the members of the Central Committee met on Friday, October 19, excitedly debating rumors about the suspicious moves of the Soviet troops. Immediately the Committee co-opted Gomułka, Spychalski, Kliszko, and Loga-Sowiński. The entire Politbureau (twelve full members and three alternate ones) then submitted their resignation and asked the enlarged Central Committee to elect a new and smaller one composed not of thirteen but of only nine members.[15] The sentiments prevailing within the Central Committee at the time left no doubt that Gomułka would be elected its First Secretary and that his main opponent, Rokossovsky, the symbol of the Soviet domination of Poland, would be eliminated. This was anticipated by the Muscovite faction who had prepared its *coup d'état,* and compiled a proscription list of their enemies as well as their shadow cabinet. On Thursday night, on the eve of the meeting, the pro-Gomułka workers managed to get hold of a list of the leading Liberals, numbering about seven hundred persons, who were to be arrested by the Stalinists. The workers managed to forewarn the prospective victims, and sent messages about what was in store for them to the new commander of the Internal Security Corps, General Komar, to the key provincial centers, to the students of various academic schools of the capital, and to numerous units of the Polish armed forces, which were mostly on the Liberal side. The workers of the Zeran automobile factory, the largest in the Warsaw district, were especially active in this respect. Many units of the armed forces declared themselves for Gomułka.

The order of business was interrupted by the news that a formidable Soviet delegation led by N. S. Khrushchev, and including V. N. Molotov, A. I. Mikoyan, and L. M. Kaganovich, accompanied by some high ranking military leaders, had suddenly descended upon Warsaw by air. The Muscovite leaders were apparently "deeply apprehensive" about the development of the situation in Poland, especially by "the spread of all forms of anti-Soviet propaganda." They made a vigorous attempt to prevent the ousting of the Natolin faction from the Politbureau and the election of Gomułka. In the course of a highly explosive conversation with the delegation of the Polish Central Committee (which was headed by Gomułka and Ochab), the "Russian friends" threatened armed intervention. The Soviet troops stationed in Poland were alerted and began moving toward Warsaw, while the Soviet army in East

Germany and on the eastern border of Poland assumed a menacing attitude.[16] The Poles tried to argue that the party's most important task was to re-establish its shattered leadership, and then to regain the confidence of the masses by following their basic demands for more independence, democracy, and for a better life. When the Soviet leaders brutally brushed these agruments aside, as mere moves for popularity, and a thin veil for anti-Soviet activity, Ochab spoke boldly for the majority of the Central Committee. He rejected the threats and demanded that the military blackmail be stopped. All the time the Poles tried to alleviate Soviet fears and assure the Moscow leaders that the democratization meant merely a Communist reformation, establishment of a regime more palatable to the Polish people, and not a break from the Warsaw Pact, emphasizing that the Polish-Soviet friendship was the cornerstone of Poland's policy.

Meanwhile, news of the unwelcome appearance of the Soviet delegation and the purpose of the visit had been conveyed by special messengers, and by the overwhelmingly "liberal" press and the radio, to the pro-Gomułka Warsaw party organization, and to the workers and the students; they both staged calm but forceful street demonstrations supporting Gomułka. Meanwhile, the Internal Security Corps of General Komar had been summoned to defend the stand taken by the party leadership. At the critical moment the detachments of the corps, in full fighting gear, straddled the approaches to the capital and occupied its key buildings. Most of the regular armed forces were also ready to defend the attitude of the Plenum and ignored the suspected orders of Marshal Rokossovsky.

The atmosphere of the Polish capital during those critical days was charged with tension and patriotic excitement; it was reminiscent of the eve of the first days of September 1939, or the Warsaw uprising of 1944. Faced with the prospect of nation-wide armed resistance, backed by most of the armed forces of the country who had refused to obey Marshal Rokossovsky's orders, the Soviet leaders hesitated. Finally, convinced that, after all, their main objective, a Communist Poland within the Warsaw Pact, was not necessarily at stake, they decided to back down. The negotiations were resumed later Friday night, October 19, and completed by Saturday morning, October 20, at which time most of the Moscow delegation departed for home, leaving only a few military men, apparently to keep an eye on the situation. But by that time Gomułka already won the first round of the battle. The calm and

composure of the Polish masses combined with the determination
to resist force with force was a powerful factor in preventing Soviet
intervention. There were a few anti-Soviet manifestations, but the
country as a whole remained calm. On Sunday, October 21, the
rest of the Moscow delegation left Warsaw; but there was still a
lingering danger of an internal Stalinist coup supported by the
Soviet forces, both stationed in Poland and massing on the frontiers
of the country. To prevent a domestic revolt the Żerań workers
went to their factory, despite the holiday, and watchfully remained
there on guard until the danger passed.

Throughout those tense days the Central Committee continued
its deliberations. On Saturday, October 20, with the Soviet warships
still demonstrating in the Bay of Gdańsk, and the Red troops still
concentrating along Poland's borders, Gomułka addressed the
Central Committee, for the first time in seven years. Speaking with
remarkable self-control and without any personal vindictiveness,
he dispassionately analyzed the Stalinist system in its application
to Polish conditions as well as on the international scale. While
stressing the necessity of Polish-Soviet friendship, he submitted the
mutual relations between the parties and states of the "socialist
camp" to a critical analysis, and found them overshadowed by "the
cult of personality," in this case a euphemistic term for Soviet
dictation of both domestic and international policies of the lesser
members of the Eastern bloc. In the future, he insisted:

these relations should be shaped on the principles of international working-class solidarity, should be based on mutual confidence and equality
of rights; on granting assistance to each other; on mutual criticism, if
such should be necessary; and on a rational solution, arising from the
spirit of friendship and from the spirit of Socialism, of all controversial
matters. Within the framework of such relations each country should
have full independence, and the right of each nation to a sovereign
government in an independent country should be fully and mutually
respected. This is how it should be and . . . this is how it is beginning
to be.

Continuing to dissect the Stalinist system in Poland, Gomułka
pointed out that many "innocent people were sent to their death.
Many others, including Communists, were imprisoned, often for
many years, although innocent. Many people were submitted to
bestial tortures." He promised return to legality, and a thorough
democratization of the ruling party, which "must not govern but
merely guide" the state apparatus. He insisted on restoration of
the "democratic centralism" in inner party life, and pledged "to

insure adequate control by party bodies over the party apparatus, beginning first of all with the central apparatus."

Gomułka praised some of the basic achievements of the Six Year Plan, as far as industrialization of the country was concerned, but decried its distortions and exaggerations, especially the neglect of the consumer goods industries and agriculture, especially its private sector. He pointed to the progressing inflation, carefully camouflaged by manipulated statistical data to show fictitious advantages brought to the working class by the system. He condemned the Seventh Plenum for failing to exact the necessary consequences with regard to the people responsible for the disastrous economic and social policies which brought Poland on the brink of economic ruin, and the working class to the state of misery.

Gomułka's bold and well-documented speech revealed the bankruptcy of the past economic system in Poland, especially the follies of its agricultural policy, which consisted in subsidizing inefficiency and waste. Incompetence, corruption, neglect of human needs and aspirations, as well as the obsession with industrialization at all costs were mercilessly exposed. Gomułka promised to establish factory self-government, and provide more material incentive to the workers, the peasants, and the surviving artisans. The basic tenet of the Communist policy: the principle of economic compulsion, especially as far as agriculture was concerned, was rejected. "Abolition of the exploitation of man by man" was, according to Gomułka, the essence of socialism. "The ways of achieving this objective can be different. They are determined by various circumstances of time and place." [17] Gomułka implicitly rejected the Soviet type of economy planned in all respects by the state, and seemed to accept an economy coordinated by the market forces of supply and demand; the state would retain merely the commanding heights and general direction of the control. This was still communism but of a variety closer to social democracy of the Western type than to Soviet communism. During his "long retreat" Gomułka, a practical man, and a realistic politician, sensitive to the mood of the country, had obviously submitted the beliefs of his youth to a critical scrutiny; but basically his speech was a return to his ideas of eight or even ten years before: a mild, gradual transformation of the country's social and economic structure, whenever possible achieved with support of the governed, an autonomous Poland as a member of the "socialist camp."

The lengthy statement of Gomułka was followed by a most vivid and enlightening debate in which both his opponents and supporters freely participated. Perhaps the most revealing speech was that of General Spychalski, who compared the Stalinist party apparatus to "a mixture of a caste and a maffia." The Natolin faction tried to present the ousting of Marshal Rokossovsky as a provocative, anti-Soviet gesture bound to upset relations with the powerful eastern neighbor. Generally speaking the faction refrained from criticizing Gomułka's diagnosis of the past ills. Jóźwiak, however, launched a sharp attack on the planned abandonment of the forced collectivization — which he condemned as "an unhealthy development." Both Berman and Minc attempted to justify their past errors by various extenuating circumstances, mainly by the overwhelming Soviet pressure. Berman claimed that only his and Bierut's evasion and procrastination prevented physical liquidation of Gomułka. Zenon Nowak made an attempt to shift the brunt of the responsibility on the Jewish members of the party leadership. Despite the sporadic bickering of the Natolin faction Gomułka scored a resounding victory.

On Sunday, October 21, the Central Committee, still acting in the shadow of possible Soviet intervention approved his line of the "Polish road to socialism," and by secret ballot elected a new Politbureau. Ochab, Gomułka, Loga-Sowiński, Cyrankiewicz, Rapacki, Zawadzki, Zambrowski, and Jerzy Morawski were returned, while Rokossovsky, Roman and Zenon Nowak, Gierek, Mazur, Jóźwiak, and Dworakowski were dropped. Only Ochab received all the seventy-five votes of the Central Committee; Gomułka and Loga-Sowiński received seventy-four each. Stefan Jędrychowski, a former alternate member, was promoted to full membership. Rokossovsky received only twenty-three out of seventy-five votes from the Natolin faction. Six party secretaries were elected: Jerzy Albrecht, Edward Gierek, Witold Jarosiński, Władysław Matwin, Edward Ochab, and Roman Zambrowski. Then followed the unanimous election of Gomułka to the post of First Secretary of the Central Committee.[18]

The Central Committee approved the new political line chartered by Gomułka, but the resolution of the Eighth Plenum left no doubt that "the decisive task for further progress of Poland toward socialism is the strengthening of the leading role of our party as the guiding political and ideological force," and that "the false liberal bourgeois tendencies among the hesitant elements, particularly in certain circles of the intelligentsia," were to be overcome; so were the "conservative forces" within the party, the forces "hampering the development of intra-party democracy," "stifling criticism," "abusing legality," and "defending bureaucratism." Thus the party was to wage a struggle on two fronts, both rated as equally important. Democratization was to go on but the process was to be directed and controlled by the party, and channeled not toward democracy of the Western type but toward "socialism," which was, however, to be purified of its worst abuses, humanized and made more palatable to the Polish people. Poland, stressed the resolution, was to be closely linked with the "camp of the socialist states," and in an "unshakable alliance with the Soviet Union," although this alliance must be based "on principles of equality and independence."

The outcome of the Eighth Plenum, the defeat of the hated Stalinists, and the triumph of Gomułka were greeted with genuine enthusiasm by the masses of the Polish people. The Plenum was followed by further far-reaching changes in various fields of national life. On October 28, Cardinal Wyszyński was freed from house arrest, after nearly three years of detention; this was followed by the release of most ecclesiastics still remaining under arrest. Soon negotiations between the party and the Catholic hierarchy were opened, with the purpose of regulating the state-church relations. Meanwhile, Catholic organizations and publications were allowed a larger margin of freedom. At the beginning of November, a joint commission to mend church-state relations was set up. On December 10, the commission issued a joint statement outlining the main points of the new modus vivendi.[19] The statement stressed that the "representatives of the Episcopate expressed full support for the work of the Government aiming at the strengthening and development of People's Poland." Religious teaching was to be permitted in schools for children whose parents desired it. The decree of February 9, 1953, giving the control of church appointments to the government was abolished.

The revolution made it clear that the majority of Poles did not necessarily oppose all the changes which had taken place since 1944; they rather favored the first phase of the agrarian reforms and the nationalization of large industry or banking, and hated only the ultimate totalitarian objectives of the party as well as its brutal methods. The overwhelming majority of the Poles hoped to stop the revolution at a definite point beyond which there could be no more political and economic pluralism, and hence no basic freedom and respect for human dignity.

During the critical October days the Poles amazed the world by abandoning their attitude of insisting on everything or nothing, and showed a surprising spirit of compromise, in this part of Europe usually attributed only to the Czechs. After ten years or so of wait-ing for some sort of "liberation" most Poles gradually became con-vinced that as long as Poland was an abandoned island surrounded by the Soviet-controlled territories they must assume a sort of protecting coloring, and accept a regime friendly to Russia, a regime that Moscow would tolerate. Many politically-thinking non-Communists, professing the so-called "neo-positivistic" school of thought, agreed that within the existing international framework any change must be merely a Communist reformation, and not an anti-Communist revolution, and that under the circumstances Go-mułka was the best man available.[20] But the support of the Polish people did not spell support of the party as such: it was a kind of social contract with Gomułka to last only as long as he defended Poland's internal autonomy as well as the basic freedoms. Gomułka was backed by the Poles because he represented for them the only hope of returning to a system which would be somewhat nearer to democratic socialism than to Soviet communism, and of regaining at least a margin of independence from the Soviet Union.

One of the secrets of the successful October revolution was the fact that the party had in reserve a team of genuinely popular lead-ers, not only untarnished by the excesses of Stalinism but even victims of the "personality cult," and that it restored these leaders promptly, in time to prevent a civil war with all possible inter-national complications. Under the leadership of the new team the party did stand up for national sovereignty and a greater inde-pendence within the framwork of the Soviet bloc. Gomułka was lucky that the well-entrenched Stalinist leader, Bierut, had died just in time to make room for him, and that Ochab quietly stepped down and even helped in smoothly transferring power to Gomułka. Another secret was Gomułka's leadership, his cool head and strong nerves; unlike Imre Nagy in Hungary, while carried away by the patriotic sentiments, Gomułka never lost control of the wave of anti-Soviet feelings, and had behind him the bulk of the party — the party which had absorbed much of the rising tide of nationalism and was, therefore, closer to the masses than was the Hungarian party. In both countries the struggle for democratic freedom merged with the striving for national independence, but in Poland the party managed to avert the catastrophe by giving in to the popular demands in time and eventually even becoming the spokes-man of the masses in their resistance to the Soviet encroachments.

As a result of the October upheaval, the party, until 1956 an outwardly monolithic structure, was considerably weakened, and now became a grouping of several factions united more by common interest than by a common doctrine. Moreover, the party, although still a dominant force of the country, had to take into consideration the views of the amorphous but potentially powerful Catholic movement and others, once depleted but now reviving political groups like the United Peasant Party, and the Democratic Party.[21] Both these parties had been regarded as mere "transmission belts." Now they became reactivated and insisted on being treated not as stooges but as allies, and the hard-pressed and internally divided UPWP could not entirely refuse these demands. This in itself considerably altered the balance of political forces in Poland and blunted somewhat the authoritarian character of the regime.

The ERA
of GOMUŁKA,
1956-1970

The October revolution in Poland had deep repercussions in the Eastern bloc, especially in Hungary, where the news of Gomułka's victory triggered a mighty revolt. To the mounting ferment among the satellites Moscow replied with the declaration of October 30, 1956, concerning relations among the countries of the "socialist camp." The statement promised that henceforth the Soviet government would stick to the Leninist principle of equality in political and economic relations with other socialist states. Moscow would renegotiate the problem of the Soviet garrisons and bases situated on the territories of the members of the bloc. The declaration was outwardly accepted by the Polish leadership at its face value.[1]

The Soviet military intervention in Hungary profoundly shocked Polish public opinion and even the party.[2] Frank, bitter statements were published even in the Communist papers on the subject; the Marxist *Po prostu* was especially outspoken. This made the party re-tighten its censorship over the press and radio in order to control the new outbursts of anti-Soviet feelings. The official appeal of the Central Committee addressed to the Hungarian people while disapproving of the Soviet intervention warned the Polish people not to follow in the footsteps of the Magyars because "the Eighth Plenum enabled us to shape relations between the Soviet Union and Poland, both on the party and state level, relations based on the principle of sovereignty, equal rights, and friendship." The appeal further stated that the stationing of Soviet troops on Polish soil was necessary to protect the country's frontiers against "the schemes of German militarism."

It is known that so far only one of the four great Powers, the Soviet Union, has recognized and guaranteed our Western boundaries. This is not a time for demonstrations and meetings. Calm discipline, responsibility, consolidation around the party leadership . . . are the main demands of the hour. . . . This is demanded by the interests of Socialism in Poland and by Polish *raison d'état*.[3]

This sort of warning, appealing to political common sense, was repeatedly issued not only by the party but also by the released Cardinal Wyszyński. As a result, despite the deep sympathy that the people of Poland felt for the fighting Magyars, calm and discipline were preserved. A considerable quantity of clothing and medicines, including blood plasma, were collected by the Polish Red Cross and contributed to the Hungarians with the approval of the party under the overwhelming pressure of public opinion.

On November 15, when the fate of Hungary had already been decided, a Polish delegation led by Gomułka spent three days in Moscow negotiating a new agreement with the powerful eastern neighbor. The delegation obtained considerable economic concessions, including the canceling of debts amounting to 500 million dollars, and abolition of the ruinous deliveries of Polish coal to the Soviet Union, for which Moscow had paid prices well below those of the world market. Moreover, during 1957 Poland was to be supplied with 1,400,000 tons of Soviet grain on credit, and provided with a long-term loan to the amount of 700 million roubles for the purchase of goods in the USSR. Finally, a new modus vivendi was reached as far as the Soviet troops in Poland were concerned.

The temporary stationing of Soviet forces in Poland can in no way affect the sovereignty of the Polish state and cannot lead to interference in the internal affairs of the Polish People's Republic.

The agreement went so far as to state that any movement of Soviet troops "outside the place of their deployment will in every case require the consent of the Polish Government." [4]

Thus, the October upheaval was outwardly accepted by the Kremlin on the condition of Poland's remaining within the "socialist camp." The Moscow agreement consolidated Gomułka's position in Poland, and Poland's position within the Eastern bloc. The agreement was hailed by the party press as a great triumph for Gomułka and his middle line between the Hungarian rebellion and the Czechoslovak or Rumanian unconditional acceptance of reduced sovereignty.

Following the Eighth Plenum the armed forces underwent their shake-up. On October 29, it was announced that the minister of national defense, Marshal Rokossovsky had gone home "on leave"; meanwhile he was quietly replaced by Spychalski; thirty-two high

ranking general officers of Soviet origin were also "thanked for
their services to Poland," given high decorations, and sent packing.
The polonization of the armed forces was paralleled by a shake-up
in the Communist youth organizations and reorganization of the
trade-unions. During the October days, the Union of Polish Youth
had disintegrated. Out of the remnants of the Union a Socialist
and a Peasant youth group were formed. In the conditions of near-
competitive coexistence in which the Polish youth found itself during the turbulent period of the "thaw," the Communist forces were
melted down to the size of one of the other numerous political cur-
rents. Thus the October upheaval revealed that the mask of unity
arbitrarily imposed on the Polish youth at the peak of the Stalinist
period could be maintained only by force. Once the terror disappeared the multiplicity of views automatically reappeared.

Meanwhile the party, which had shrivelled to the size of its own
apparatus, was undergoing a feverish reappraisal of its ways and
means. Since the Warsaw party organization had been pro-Gomułka from the start, the reorganization affected mainly the provincial centers where the local apparatus was still largely Stalinist.
Soon after the October revolution, eleven out of nineteen Provincial
Committees were compelled to resign, not so much because of orders
from Gomułka as because of the spontaneous pressure from the
rank and file.[5] But Gomułka was initially reluctant to try the
traditional Communist method of the wholesale purge. In his speech
of November 4, delivered to the National Conference of Party
Activists, the new First Secretary warned his followers not to push
the cleansing too far.

I doubt whether it would be possible to find activists and workers holding
various responsible posts who cannot be accused of doing something wrong
if their past work is now evaluated.[6]

Simultaneously with the reshaping of the party, the reorganization of the country's economy, especially its agriculture, continued.
In his speech of October 20, Gomułka had suggested that only the
inefficient "producers' cooperatives" should be dissolved. But in
practice, the opposite took place: the most efficient dissolved while
the backward ones remained hoping that the state would continue
to support them one way or another. Thus, during the last two or
three months of 1956 the entire structure of Polish agriculture
underwent a profound transformation. During October, November,
and December, over 80 per cent of the collective farms, numbering
about 10,000, collapsed. Even many of the remaining ones trans-

formed themselves into loose associations resembling prewar rural cooperatives more than Soviet collective farms. This virtual revolution in the countryside was accompanied by a fair amount of looting and destruction of collective property.

At the beginning of December, the Central Committee of the United Polish Workers' Party and the Executive Committee of the United Peasant Party issued a joint statement which foreshadowed a new agrarian policy.[7] The statement, besides condemning the previous practices of treating the UPP as a mere satellite of the UPWP, promised a "clear definition of property law," an early removal of existing restrictions on the sale and purchase of land, extension of credits to "all groups of farms," even to the kulaks, and reduction of compulsory grain deliveries by one-third, while prices paid by the state were to be doubled. Moreover, the communal machine stations were to be disbanded and their equipment sold to individual farmers. The new agrarian policy was to be implemented by Ochab, who was given the tricky job of minister of agriculture.

The Five Year Plan, with its continued emphasis on heavy industry, was not to be scrapped altogether but gradually reshaped in the process of its implementation from year to year, to provide more consumer goods and housing.[8] State planning was to guide the national economy rather than to prescribe in detail every step of every single enterprise. Experimental profit-sharing plants were organized. Efforts have been made to re-orient somewhat the trade from the East to the West, and to lessen the dependence of Poland's economy on the Soviet Union.

One of the most interesting measures introduced by the Gomułka regime has been the establishment of workers' councils.[9] In reality this was a legalization and systematization of the process that had taken place before the October events. Workers' councils were to be established, if the majority of workers employed in a given enterprise so desired, in all industrial and construction enterprises, and on all state farms, "to implement the working-class initiative with regard to its direct participation in the administration of enterprises." [10] Unlike their Yugoslavia counterparts, the Polish councils were not allowed to elect factory managers.

THE ELECTIONS

One of the main concessions of the party toward public opinion was the promise of a new electoral law.[11] "The election law must enable people to elect and not merely to vote," said Gomułka in his speech of October 20, 1956. And indeed on January 20, 1957, the regime treated Poland to a national election that, although not democratic by Western standards, was not a mere plebiscite of the Soviet type. Candidates were proposed to local commissions by social, economic, and cultural organizations, and by the two political parties so far merely tolerated by the UPWP: the United Peasant Party and the Democratic Party.[12] Approximately 60,000 candidates were thus proposed; the local commissions approved about 10,000 names and passed them to the Central Electoral Commission which selected 722 candidates from among whom the voters were to elect 459 Sejm deputies. Thus, there were approximately seven candidates for every four seats in the Chamber. Besides the candidates of the three political parties many prominent Catholics and other non-Communists were put on the ballot. The electoral campaign was entirely overshadowed by the national issues of paramount importance: for or against the Gomułka regime, for or against the newly gained measure of autonomy within the Soviet bloc. "Sovereignty and independence," and "Socialism free from the Stalinist distortions" became the electoral slogans of the party. The significance of the election was dramatized by Gomułka himself, who, on the eve of the polling warned his countrymen that a failure to support him would result in Poland's disappearance from the map of the world.

The change of political atmosphere brought about by the October upheaval was deep and Gomułka's popularity genuine. The Polish-Chinese declaration of January 16, which ended Poland's growing isolation within the "socialist camp" increased his prestige because, while paying lip service to "proletarian internationalism" the declaration qualified the formula in a way that was bound to flatter the proud Poles: the relations between socialist countries, as independent and sovereign countries, should be based on principles of respect for their sovereignty, noninterference in their internal affairs, and mutual benefit.[13]

The electoral campaign was quiet; there was no terror and no administrative pressure. A large majority of the government-supported candidates were elected. In the new Sejm the UPWP had 237 deputies, the United Peasant Party 119, and the Democratic Party 39; there were also 63 deputies belonging to no party; among them there were 12 Catholics. Many nonparty candidates won more votes than the leading Communists, with the notable exceptions of Gomułka and Spychalski; generally speaking the members of the "Natolin" fared much worse than the "Liberals."

In the elections, which were a sort of national referendum, the Polish people gave a conditional approval to Gomulka's October program. The elections represented more of a personal triumph of the First Secretary than that of his party.

SEARCH FOR A MIDDLE WAY

Having won the October 1956 gamble, Gomulka began to reassess the precarious situation in which he found himself. The party intensified its effort to link the cause of Poland's independence to the regime's continuance in power. It warned, furthermore, that only Soviet protection restrained a remilitarized and aggressive Germany from attempting to destroy Poland once again.

Gomulka must have borne in mind Marshal N. A. Bulganin's grim warning, made in one of the speeches delivered in Poland in July 1956, when the Soviet leader was touring the country on behalf of Khrushchev: "We cannot close our eyes to the attempts at weakening the international bonds of the socialist camp under the label of so-called 'national peculiarity,' or to the attempts at undermining the power of people's democratic countries under the label of an alleged broadening of democracy." [14]

Since the elections, Gomulka was caught between the criticism of the Stalinists, who denounced him for his alleged betrayal of Communism, and "Titoist" proclivities; the demands of most people for further decompression; and the necessity of placating the powerful Eastern neighbor. Various groups that had supported him in 1956 now interpreted the implications of the October program in different ways. Gomulka obviously understood it as a maximum achievable, the freezing of the October revolution being his actual objective. He considered the great expectations aroused in various quarters as far too dangerous for Poland in her precarious geopolitical situation. The sullen hostility not only of Soviet Russia, but also of the rest of the Communist camp, especially East Germany and Czechoslovakia, made it inevitable that the program would be modified in many respects.

While making appeasing gestures toward his comrades from other Communist countries, Gomulka was aiming at a stablization of his position within his own party, by striking a balance between the "revisionists" and the Stalinists or "dogmatists." [15] In his speech at the Tenth Plenum of the Central Committee in October 1957, he sharply attacked the call of the "revisionists" for a "second stage of the Polish October." He called his opponents politically dangerous, because they were acting as if the country were an isolated island, and not a segment of a system of Communist world. He chided them for being ready to sacrifice Poland's survival for the sake of such liberal trifles as freedom of the press. Gomułka compared the revisionists to tuberculosis, and the Stalinists to mere influenza: "Influenza, even in its most serious form, cannot be cured by contracting tuberculosis. Dogmatism cannot be cured by revisionism. Revisionist tuberculosis can only strengthen the dogmatic influenza. . . . The revisionist wing must be out of the party. We shall destroy with equal firmness all organized or individual forms of anti-party activity launched from a position of dogmatism." [16]

His weighted medical metaphor was a fair reflection of his feelings. He obviously calculated that the "dogmatists," while constituting a nuisance, could not be dangerous because they worked within the system. The "revisionists," on the other hand, with their insistence on a second stage for the "Polish October," were a menace to the stability of Soviet-Polish relations, consequently to the very existence of Communism in Poland.

As long as he was in opposition to the Stalinists, he naturally had attracted the support of the younger, brighter, progressive intellectuals like Jerzy Andrzejewski, Leszek Kołakowski, Jan Kott, and Adam Ważyk. All of them were associated with the outspoken weekly, *Po prostu.* Its stringent, sarcastic criticism, which often challenged the basic Communist axioms and asked tactless questions, became a thorn in Gomułka's side. Once Gomułka was entrenched in power, the ideological unorthodoxy of these intellectuals came to be an obstacle to the process of reestablishing good relations with Moscow. The final provocation was an article reporting a trip to the West, which contained the following passage: "The first thing which strikes everyone coming from Poland is the prosperity of capitalist Europe. . . . How did it happen that in spite of [Communist] expectations the capitalist countries have been able to avoid an economic crisis?" [17] The closing of *Po prostu* in October 1957 was the first major signal of Gomułka's intentions for the future.

Gomułka's accommodating attitude toward the Soviet Union was given official expression during his visit to Russia the same month to celebrate the fortieth anniversary of the Bolshevik revolution. At the Kremlin the Polish leader emphasized the necessity of unity, solidarity, and cohesion in the Soviet camp. In the name of this solidarity Gomułka condoned the execution of Imre Nagy and his associates as an internal affair of Hungary. The fate of Nagy must have served as a grim warning not to extend the "Polish October" beyond the limits acceptable to Moscow.

But the closing of the *Po prostu* did not end the intellectual ferment. In September 1957, the Warsaw weekly *Nowa kultura* (New Culture) published a series of essays by the young philosopher, Leszek Kołakowski, editor of the bi-monthly *Studia filozoficzne* (Philosophic Studies), under the overall title "Responsibility and History." In his articles he dealt critically with some of the philosophic foundations of Marxism, and by implication, challenged the official line of the party. Among the basic Marxist principles challenged by Kołakowski were historical determinism and the view that "History" is the final judge of human action. He also insisted that the moral judgment of the autonomous individual is superior to any socio-economic forces that supposedly shaped the individual. No one, he argued, is exempted from the duty of forming such judgments.

Kołakowski's challenging of the deterministic Communist concept of historic necessity became the subject of widespread and passionate criticism by Gomułka as well as by Professor Adam Schaff, who was at that time the party's chief ideological spokesman, and director of the Institute of Philosophy and Sociology of the Polish Academy of Sciences. In his speech at the ninth plenary session of the Central Committee, Gomułka thundered: "By his revisionist longing, Comrade Kołakowski has won the attention of the bourgeois and Trotskyite press. . . . All revisionist theories are similar to one another, for they come from the same source: from the same bourgeois ideology under whose influence social democratic ideology was formed." [18]

In spite of these attacks Kołakowski continued his revisionist offensive. In the March-April 1959 issue of *Studia filozoficzne* he published a lecture he had delivered at the University of Tuebingen (West Germany), entitled "On Karl Marx and the Classical Definition of Truth." In his exposition Kołakowski compared the works of Marx's younger and later years and pointed out that certain "liberal" positions of the young Marx had been ignored, or even scorned, by most Communist interpreters. Following the publication of the essay, Kołakowski was dismissed from the position of editor-in-chief of *Studia filozoficzne,* and was attacked by Adam Schaff, who condemned Kołakowski's stand as openly "revisionist," and ignorant of the real Marx. [19]

The publication of the lecture on Marx was followed by another essay entitled "The Priest and the Jester," in which Kołakowski went on to criticize the official interpretation of Marxism treated by its "priests" as "the established dogma." In the struggle against the priests he operated in the spirit of critical inquiry characteristic of a jester, for whom there are neither untouchable authorities nor sacred doctrines.[20]

With the publication of his critical essays Kołakowski emerged as the most prominent and outspoken leader of the Polish, and indeed East European, "revisionist" school of Marxism.[21] One of the most important aspects of his writings was the fact that he was not satisfied with critical analysis of only Communist practice, but dealt with the essence of the officially sponsored theories of history, epistemology, and ethics.

In July 1959, Gomułka further mended Polish-Soviet relations by cordially welcoming Khruschev in Warsaw. Gomułka ended his warm speech with the shout "Long live our dear Soviet guest!" The visit and the conversation that followed opened a period of close cooperation between the two men, a partnership that was to last for some five years. Gomułka came to rely more and more on his good personal relations with Khrushchev, and came to regard them as an added safeguard of Poland's growing position as a Soviet ally, as well as of his own status within the Communist camp.[22]

The year 1959 also marked a turning point in the field of culture, and the tightening of the limitations on freedom. In October 1959, Bieńkowski, a moderate, was dismissed from the Ministry of Higher Education. In December, due to party pressure, Antoni Słonimski, the liberal and outspoken chairman of the Polish Writers' Union, was replaced in that capacity by the subservient Jarosław Iwaszkiewicz, who had been deputy chairman in the days of Stalinism. The changes on "the cultural front" were paralleled by those in the economic sector: the old Stalinist guard, Eugeniusz Szyr, Julian Tokarski, and Tadeusz Gede, returned to important posts.[23]

If a definite confirmation of Gomułka's new course was needed it came in May 1960, when he named General Witaszewski as head of the administrative department of PUWP. As head of party administration, Witaszewski was now in charge of party personnel — nominations and dismissals of officials in the State and party posts, the national councils, health service, and military and security forces. The department had been liquidated in the 1956 "thaw." [24]

THE EMERGENCE OF THE "PARTISANS"

The early sixties were a turning point in the history of the PUWP, because they saw a reshaping of the balance of power within the Central Committee as a result of the emergence of a new faction. The head of this faction was the ruthless and resourceful General Mieczysław Moczar, a former leader of Communist underground detachments under the German occupation. Moczar, who served after the war as chief of the Secret Police in Łódź and had been a member of the Central Committee since 1945, became Minister of the Interior in 1964. Since that time he adopted a clever tactical line of courting not only nationalistically inclined groups of party members, but also the broad, non-Communist masses. For that purpose he exchanged the traditional Communist slogan, "He who is not with us is against us," for the formula of the Kadar regime in Hungary: "He who is not against us is with us." The faction was called colloquially the "Partisans," because many of its members had been members of the Communist guerilla units during World War II. By skillfully manipulating nationalistic slogans, the Partisans penetrated the Citizens' Militia, as well as other security organs, including the Secret Police, which Moczar had controlled since 1964 in his capacity as Minister of the Interior. Moczar also tried to place many of his supporters in the provincial administration, and to infiltrate the armed forces, especially their Main Political Administration. At the same time, though he himself was a man of limited formal education, Moczar carefully cultivated certain intellectual circles; during the 1960's he had his spokesmen in such Warsaw weeklies as *Żołnierz Wolności*, *Kultura*, and *Stolica*.

One of the main instruments of the "Partisans" was the Union of Fighters for Freedom and Democracy, known from its Polish initials as ZBOWID. This previously largely Communist and small organization was turned by Moczar into a body uniting all those who had fought for Poland, irrespective of their political conviction or former affiliations, including some of the former members of the Home Army. By the early 1960's, ZBOWID had about a quarter million members, and chapters all over the country. Soon it became quite popular because of three factors. First of all, it had large funds at its disposal and made generous use of them to help its needy members. Secondly, it exercised a right of patronage: its members could get first chance at various jobs and housing, as well as education for their children and licenses to operate private stores and shops; ZBOWID even provided free medical coverage to thousands of small farmers and craftsmen who, at that time, were not eligible for state benefits. The third reason for ZBOWID's popularity was the lavish distribution of all sorts of decorations that it awarded to the veterans for wartime service. This was vital because those who had received them were entitled to higher pensions at retirement.[25]

The rise of the "Partisans" with their nationalistic slogans corresponded to a decrease in the influence of the Puławy faction, which, after October 1956, took a middle position between the "dogmatists" and the "revisionists." During the initial stages of the drive against the "revisionists," the Puławy group, led by Zambrowski, Albrecht, Matwin, and Morawski, supported Gomułka. But during the 1960's, as Gomułka began to rely more and more on the "Partisans," the Puławians became increasingly critical of his alliance with a group suspected of anti-Semitism, and often sided instead with the revisionists. The removal of Albrecht, Matwin, and Morawski from the Secretariat left Zambrowski, the oldest member of the Politburo, as the only representative of the Puławy group in the party's top leadership. The resignation of Zambrowski on July 3, 1963, from the Secretariat of the Central Committee on the avowed grounds of "poor health," was interpreted by some as a protest against the mounting influence of the "Partisans."

Thus the 1960's witnessed the emergence of Moczar as an active and resourceful contender for party leadership. Although not a member of the Politburo, the more dramatic and mercurial Moczar seemed to overshadow the other two strong men of the party, Ryszard Strzelecki, the leader of the former Natolinists, and Edward Gierek, the Silesian party boss. While Strzelecki was actively involved in intraparty affairs at the center of power, Gierek remained aloof from party intrigues and bickerings in Warsaw, and tried to create the image of an able organizer and administrator by running his Silesian bailiwick efficiently. In this he was largely successful, and by the late 1960's the people of Silesia enjoyed a much higher standard of living than the rest of the country.

RETREAT FROM OCTOBER

While analyzing Gomułka's retreat from "the gains of October," one must first take into consideration the balance of forces within the Communist camp. By 1957, after the suppression of the Hungarian uprising, Gomułka found himself isolated. Except for Yugoslavia, the remaining East European countries were either suspicious of him because of his ideological unorthodoxy, or jealous of his autonomy. Soon it became obvious that Poland could not outdistance to any great extent other East European countries, either in domestic liberalization or in cultivation of her Western connections. As a British observer of the Polish scene, Richard Hiscocks, put it: "Gomułka could scarcely become more revisionist without ceasing to be Communist." Had the extreme revisionists prevailed, the Party would have been exposed progressively to open controversy with other parties, and in the end Poland might have suffered the fate of Hungary in 1956, or of Czechoslovakia in 1968.

Another reason for Gomułka's growing rigidity was economic. Despite the improved situation in the conutryside, where the peasants began to produce more, the economic situation was still rather shaky. The Poznań uprising, the strikes and stoppages of work connected with the October coup — all this further dislocated the normal functioning of the Polish economy. Throughout the close of 1956 and most of 1957 sporadic strikes were taking place in the country. Moreover, while liberalizing the hitherto nearly totalitarian system, Gomułka also loosened labor discipline. He thus weakened the bond of compulsion that had kept the old economic system together, before revived individual initiative and the effects of material and moral labor incentives had a chance to stimulate the economy. During the late 1950's he began to reverse this course, and labor discipline was tightened. At the same time, he began to champion a greater integration of the Council of Mutual Economic Assistance, or CEMA.

From 1958–59 the hardening of the Gomułka regime was quite striking. Many explanations have been advanced as to why he lost his early gregariousness and turned into a rigid, narrow-minded, authoritarian, petty tyrant. Some were of domestic nature, some were motivated by the rapidly changing international scene, some may be attributed to his failing health and deterioration of his mental capacities. As Gomułka grew older, he lost his receptivity to new ideas. He became more and more suspicious and withdrawn, and relied on a restricted inner circle of trusted comrades to keep him advised and informed. Such sycophantic friends soon discovered that their survival depended on keeping their leader satisfied. Like most authoritarian rulers, he fell victim to the obligatory mood of official optimism, and came to distrust those advisers who brought bad news. He developed fits of rage, became moody, capricious, and morbidly preoccupied with his prestige. He could stand no criticism, and demanded blind obedience from his associates. Every indication of independent thinking in others produced an outburst of wrath from him. By throwing ever more frequent fits of anger, Gomułka terrorized his coworkers and forced them into silent submission and witlessness.

His attitude toward nonparty experts was one of suspicion; toward independent intellectuals he was full of spite. He and his closest co-worker, Kliszko, tended to treat the more outspoken writers as "the enemy within," as saboteurs of their efforts to unite the nation behind the Party's leadership. In 1963 the two most popular weeklies, *Nowa Kultura* (New Culture) and *Przeglad Kulturalny* (Cultural Review), were discontinued, and a new paper, *Kultura,* was founded. The restrictive cultural policies of Gomułka precipitated a series of protests among Polish intellectuals.[26]

Gomułka's autocratic and intolerant behavior, as well as his political rigidity and economic incompetence, caused also a great deal of dissatisfaction among the more outspoken party rank and file. In the summer of 1964 two young Communists, Jacek Kuroń and Karol Modzelewski, both instructors of economics at Warsaw University, published their ninety-page-long *Open Letter to the Party*. The letter submitted the situation in the PUWP and the country as a whole to a close scrutiny from a Marxist point of view. The main thesis of the letter was that in Poland, like in other Communist states, power was not being held by the party as a whole, but was instead concentrated in the hands of a small group, a party elite, which the authors called "the central political bureaucracy." The rank and file membership were denied any meaningful influence on party decisions. The bureaucracy, which identifies its interests with those of the state, determines all important issues: the allocation of resources, the level of wages, the conditions of employment. In consequence, argued the authors, while the productivity of workers has grown considerably since 1956, their standard of living has remained at the subsistence level. The letter concluded that the Gomułka regime was increasingly stale, bureaucratic, and ineffective. The manifesto also contained recommendations as to how to remodel Poland into what the authors considered a "true socialist" state.[27] In November 1964 both authors were expelled from the Party for "dishonesty" and "immorality."

The gap between the few who were "in" and the millions who were "out," which was exposed in the Kuroń-Modzelewski letter, was further explored in a book entitled *Motory i hamulce Socializmu* (The Driving Forces and the Inhibiting Factors of Socialism) written by a Communist veteran and old friend of Gomułka, Bieńkowski. The author, after analyzing both the positive and the negative factors of the Communist system, concluded that there was no communication between the party leadership and the people; the secret police, through its system of misinformation, kept the two apart. The vaunted dialogue to which top Communists are fond of referring from time to time remains a onesided affair — a simple transmission of fiats from the ruling elite to the masses. This alienation of the party from the masses the party is supposed to represent is one of the crippling handicaps of the system, inhibiting its effectiveness. Like the *Open Letter to the Party*, the book was banned in Poland and had to be published abroad.[28]

On October 20, 1966, on the tenth anniversary of Gomułka's return to power, Kołakowski drew up a balance sheet of the past decade at a student meeting at Warsaw University. He condemned Gomułka's record as characterized by increasing repressions, the lack of democracy, intolerance of opposition, and excessive bureaucratic rigidity. Kołakowski's analysis was stormily applauded by the students. In reprisal for the criticism, he was expelled from the party. Twenty-two writers, all members of the PUWP, signed a protest against his expulsion; by mid-1967, sixteen of the protesters had themselves been ousted from the party. Thus in the late 1960's there started an exodus of the most literate and outspoken elements of the PUWP, a brain drain that resulted in a marked lowering of the party's never too high intellectual caliber.

Besides fighting the detested intellectuals (the people "who produce neither bread nor steel, but only chit-chat"), Gomułka soon reopened the struggle against the Catholic Church. Already in September 1958 the government issued a directive which forbade members of religious orders from giving instruction in schools unless they were fully qualified as teachers, and laid down that, since schools were lay institutions, no religious emblems were to be allowed in them. The two grave issues that have divided the Roman Catholic Church and the State since 1956 have been taxation and religious education. Early in 1959, the government decreed that the clergy, churches, and such religious institutions as monasteries, convents, and seminaries were no longer to enjoy their customary exemption from taxation on their income and premises. In 1961 a law was adopted that abolished all religious instruction in schools, though the Church was able to continue with religious instruction through its own network of catechism centers.

It is quite probable that Gomułka's rigidity had a source in his perception of the German danger, and his increasing awareness of Poland's dependence on Soviet Russia. After his return to power, Gomułka made an effort to identify independence with adherence to the "socialist camp." He argued that Moscow was the sole power both willing and able to assure Poland's possession of the Western provinces, and that the country's good standing within the "socialist camp" was a precondition of Poland's survival. His calculations were shattered when a possibility of a Russo-German rapprochement at Poland's expense was dramatized by Adzhubey's planned trip to Bonn in the summer of 1964.[29] Gomułka regarded Adzhubey's mission as a possible first step toward German reunification before Poland's Western frontiers were recognized by the Federal Republic. The memories of the Stalin-Hitler pact must have been quite vivid in Gomułka's mind throughout the 1960's. His trust in Khrushchev's friendship also received a severe blow.

THE "ZIONIST PROBLEM" IN ITS POLITICAL CONTEXT

The issue which linked Gomułka's struggle against the "revisionists" to his conflict with the intellectuals was the "Zionist" problem. The anti-Zionist campaign of 1967–68 has to be analyzed against a broad background of the role of the Jews in the Communist movement in Poland, and the spread of official anti-semitism in Soviet Russia.

In order to set the problem in a historic perspective, one has to remember that in 1939 the country's population of some 35 million people included around 10 percent Jews. These, in turn, were overwhelmingly concentrated in urban centers and engaged in trade, handicraft, industry and liberal professions. In the 1920's the percentage of Jews in the CPP was very high, well over 50 percent. In the early 1930's it diminished somewhat but was still considerable.[30] A large percentage of Polish Jews saw in Communism an ideology of universal brotherhood and looked upon the Communist movement as an instrument of transplanting to their adopted country the highly idealized Soviet patterns. Although the Jewish component of the CPP constituted merely a fraction of the total Jewish population of interwar Poland, in a passionately anti-Russian and anti-Communist country the pro-Soviet sentiments of many Jews were sometimes heavily exploited. Native anti-Semites tried to make the terms Jew and Communist synonymous. Thus the conspicuously prominent role of the Jews in the Communist movement became another point of friction between Poles and Jews, and only further intensified the already existing ethnic, economic, and religious tensions.

Following the Soviet annexation of Eastern Poland in 1939, many Communist Jews who found themselves in that part of the country eagerly offered their services to Moscow. Since the spring of 1943, after the battle of Stalingrad, when Stalin apparently made up his mind to extend Soviet power Eastern Europe, they participated in the activities of the Union of Polish Patriots in Russia, as well as in the Central Bureau of Polish Communists in the USSR. Meanwhile, under the German occupation, over six million Polish citizens were exterminated in Nazi concentration camps; half of the victims were Jews, half ethnic Poles. As a result of the "final solution" only a small percentage of Polish Jews survived the war.[31]

Among the "Muscovites," as opposed to the "Natives," the Jews formed a large group, and, owing to their superior educational background and their close ties with some Soviet bureaucrats, their actual influence went far beyond their numerical strength. After 1945 Jews like Berman, Minc, and Zambrowski formed a closely knit team in the Polish Workers' Party, and they vied with the "Natives" like Gomułka, Kliszko, or Bieńkowski in influence on the official party boss, Bierut. According to the American historian Richard V. Burke, the Jews tended to concentrate in certain ministries and functions:

> They congregated in the foreign trade, because they were almost the only ones whom the party could trust who had the requisite knowledge of foreign languages and high finance. They also flooded into the central committee and the security police, perhaps because they felt safer near the centers of decision making. In Bucharest, Budapest and Warsaw virtually every important police official was Jewish. . . . Often these police officials were survivors of Nazi extermination camps, and they did not let mercy or other humanitarian considerations stand in their way when it came to dealing with the class enemy.[32]

Meanwhile Stalin, who used Jewish Communists belonging to various East European parties as his instruments of imperial conquest and control, was brutally purging the Soviet apparatus of "Zionists," as "rootless cosmopolitans" who constituted grave security risks. Thus, during the immediate postwar period the East European Jews were not unlike the Greek *phanariotes,* an oppressed minority of the Ottoman Empire who were used as a tool of the imperial system.

By the late 1940's Stalin's thinly disguised anti-Semitic policy had filtered down to East European countries like Hungary, Rumania, and Czechoslovakia, but not yet to Poland. As R. V. Burke pointed out:

Early in 1949, the Hungarian and Rumanian governments, on whose territories 90% of surviving East European Jewry was domiciled, outlawed Zionist organizations and deported Zionist missions. Local Zionist leaders were secretly tried and given long prison terms. Israeli diplomats were accused of espionage and expelled. In September 1940, on the occasion of the trial of Laszlo Rajk, the leader of the nationalist wing in the Hungarian party, almost the entire body of Hungarian Jewish Communists who had spent the war years in Switzerland was executed. In the summer of 1952, three top drawer Rumanian Communists of Jewish origin — Pauker, Georgescu, and Luca — were purged. In December 1952, the *eminence grise* of the Czech party, Rudolf Slansky, was placed in the dock, along with a dozen other Jewish leading cadres. Slansky and his fellow accused were condemned in December 1952.[33]

After Stalin's death a significant realignment of political forces took place within the PUWP. Many of the "Muscovites" of Jewish extraction, the "Puławy" faction, which originally held most of the Politburo posts during the crucial period 1945–1956, sought alliance with the more moderate faction of the party, and supported democratization of the Communist system in Poland. After the Poznań uprising of June 1956, the "Puławy faction" threw their support to the forces favoring the return of Gomułka to power, and the limitation of the Soviet controls over Poland.[34]

Thus, up to 1967–68 the record of Gomułka as far as anti-Semitism was concerned had been rather better than that of most East European parties. His wife was of Jewish origin and throughout his career he had had many close Jewish co-workers and supporters. In 1956, when Moscow suggested that the Polish Party try Minc and Berman as scapegoats responsible for the sorry state of the Polish economy, Gomułka refused to do so. The PUWP did not have in its annals either a cruel suppression of the Jewish cultural elite, like that conducted in the USSR in 1948–49, or, like its Czechoslavak counterpart, the Slansky trial — nor the slaughtering of many Hungarian Communists of Jewish extraction in 1949, or the brutal liquidation of the overwhelmingly Jewish Pauker-Georgescu-Luka faction in Rumania. The Polish state maintained many Jewish institutions, including the Jewish Historical Institute, and the excellent Yiddish Theater of Warsaw.

The first stimulus to harmonize Poland's cadres policy with that of the USSR came from Moscow. During the late 1950's Khrushchev repeatedly objected to the fact that there were many Jews in leading positions in the PUWP; he termed them "a virus." As a former party member testified, a secretary of the Soviet Embassy in Warsaw criticized the PUWP for "Judaization of the Polish press," and urged creation of a national cadre of the party, free of Jewish influence. Yet despite the strong Soviet pressure, there was no purge of the Jews in Poland until 1967, and the Jewish members of the party were relatively better off than in most other East European ruling groups.[35]

THE ARAB-ISRAELI WAR AND ITS CONSEQUENCES

The Arab-Israeli war of June 1967 and the Israeli victories were warmly greeted by many Poles. As the *New York Times* correspondent in Warsaw, Henry Kamm, put it on June 13, 1967, the sentiments of the Polish people as a whole were "running strongly in favor of Israel," and the Israeli Embassy in Warsaw was receiving numerous telegrams "overflowing with emotions and sentiments" and including congratulations and best wishes.[36]

The sympathetic reaction in Poland to the Israeli victory over the Arabs provoked a Soviet protest. The reaction was most embarrassing to Gomułka, who for over a decade had been trying to cement Poland's position as a staunch ally of Moscow. Acting on Moscow's insistence, Warsaw broke off diplomatic relations with Israel on June 12. This was followed by an anti-Zionist drive, which was to last for about a year. In his reminiscences Gomułka insisted that the anti-Zionist campaign was organized on the initiative of Moscow; the Soviet Government required of Warsaw that it curb the pro-Israeli manifestations in Poland, as these were harmful to Soviet-Polish friendship.[37]

In a speech of June 19, Gomułka violently condemned all those who "applauded the Israeli aggression" and warned that the party would not tolerate a "fifth column among its midst." [38] Soon similar speeches were made by other leaders, including Defense Minister Marshal Spychalski. By December 1967, the campaign came to include a purge of high officials who had been compromised by their pro-Israeli stand, or were regarded as security risks. Some of them were ethnic Poles sympathetic to Israel, but most of them were Jews.

On March 19, 1968, Gomułka, seeing that the drive was getting out of hand, urged party activists to tone it down. Addressing the Trade Union Congress in Warsaw, he stressed that the anti-Zionist campaign "may have been misunderstood by some in the past," and condemned anti-Semitism as well as Zionism. On the other hand he attacked the "Zionist circles" of Polish Jews who had "applauded" Israeli aggression against the Arabs. "We cannot remain indifferent to people who, in the face of a threat to world peace . . . and the peaceful work of our nation, come out in favor of the aggressor," he said. "We have made no difficulties for Polish citizens of Jewish nationality who wanted to move to Israel," but if they wish to remain in Poland, he stated, they must be loyal. "We hold the position that every Polish citizen should have only one country." Gomułka divided the Jews in Poland into three groups: the Zionists with open allegiance to Israel; the "cosmopolitans" with split allegiance between Israel and Poland; and the most numerous group, the "true native sons." He suggested that the first group should feel free to leave the country; the second category he advised to "avoid the fields of work in which national affirmation is crucial." The third group he praised for their loyalty to Poland.[39]

Gomułka's speech had far from a calming effect; it gave a further stimulus to the purge of people of Jewish extraction from many top-level jobs. A mass exodus of Jews from Poland followed. Meanwhile, the purge developed a dynamic force of its own: it engulfed some 9,000 people, both Jews and those who sided or sympathized with them.[40]

Gomułka's anti-Zionist campaign of 1967–68 cannot be fully comprehended unless it is placed in the framework of Polish-Soviet relations, in conjunction with the anti-Semitism affecting the Soviet orbit, and by analyzing the balance of forces within the party. One must bear in mind not only Gomułka's increasing subservience to Moscow and the filtering down of Soviet anti-Semitism to Poland, but also the factional feuds within the PUWP. Besides the previously discussed struggle between the "Muscovites" and the "Natives," one should also stress that the majority of the Jewish party activists, irrespective of their individual political past, had been since 1957–59 the focus of the liberal opposition to Gomułka. Threatened by the "revisionist" offensive, Gomułka sought a measure of support among the "Partisans."

The factional feud was also intertwined with the generational conflict between the younger and older members of the party machine. By the late 1960's the pressure of the dynamic, impatient, and intolerant young activists, who were largely of proletarian origin, was formidable. The road to advancement was barred by a host of older men, many of them of Jewish bourgeois background. The appetites of the young activists for fast promotion grew more rapidly than the party's ability to satisfy them. There was much less room at the top than there was number of candidates for high positions. Only a shake-up which would fundamentally alter the existing power structure could open new possibilities to the young members of the party *aparat*.

Gomułka obviously calculated that, in order to stay in power, he would have to satisfy the demands of the young; partly and temporarily he adopted the platform of the "Partisans," thus depriving them of their most popular battle cries, and thereby probably prevented his overthrow.[41]

THE "PRAGUE SPRING" AND THE SINO-SOVIET SPLIT

The Zionist affair was followed by the student riots of February and March 1968, and by the Czechoslovak crisis of the following summer. The revolt of the students, partly influenced by the "Prague Spring," was precipitated by the official ban of the Warsaw production of Adam Mickiewicz's classic drama, *The Forefathers' Eve* (*Dziady*). The play, which contains some sharp criticism of the tsarist administration in Poland, was demonstratively applauded by the audience, largely young people. This was condemned by the authorities as an act of provocation toward the Russians. Some 30 students were arrested and the play was discontinued.

The banning of the respected classic generated sporadic protests by numerous writers and riots amongst the students. The storm of indignation in Warsaw provoked a series of sit-ins and street manifestations in other academic centers. All the demonstrations were ruthlessly suppressed by police. The most violent and brutal reprisals were launched against the Warsaw students at the beginning of March. The "March events," as the incidents came to be called, were followed by numerous administrative measures against other dissenting students and intellectuals, writers as well as professors, many of them of Jewish extraction.

The mass media immediately pointed out that among the leaders of the demonstrations, the Jews, as it happened, were rather nu-

merous, and that many of the fathers of the most prominent demonstrators held important state as well as party posts. These facts were
seized to point to the existence of a widespread "Zionist-Revisionist
plot" within the party. The official propaganda stressed that the con-
spirators were eager to push Poland towards an "irresponsible, anti-
Soviet adventure" at the time of the Middle Eastern crisis in order
to help the state of Israel. The purge of the Jewish element in
Poland's political, economic, and cultural life was intensified.[42]

The "March events" of 1968 were followed by the Polish participation in the Soviet-led intervention in Czechoslovakia. Poland's
attitude toward the "Prague Spring" must be viewed in the light
of Gomułka's strategy of further consolidation of the Polish-Soviet
alliance. Despite Czech and West German protestations, the economic rapprochement between Prague and Bonn was not regarded as
a harmless matter. All the Czech assurances of loyalty to the WTO
and the CEMA notwithstanding, Gomułka, brought up on the Marxist school of economic interpretation of history, interpreted Prague's
"economic opening to the West" as the first step toward a more
intimate cooperation between Czechoslovakia and the strongest of
the European NATO countries.[43]

Polish participation in the Soviet military intervention was regarded by Gomułka as another step in the process of further consolidation of Poland's position within the Soviet camp. Like Brezhnev,
Gomułka must have viewed Czechoslovakia's evolution as representing not only a danger of a "revisionist" infection, but also a
potential threat to the existence of the East European Communist
system of states. By supporting the Soviet-sponsored military intervention, and acting consistently along parallel lines with Brezhnev,
Gomułka tried to impress upon Moscow that the Poles were trust-
worthy allies of Soviet Russia. This was a continuation of the policy
initiated in October 1956, when he pacified the country, reasserted
the leading role of the party, and reassured Khrushchev about Poland's loyalty toward the Center. Even since that time Gomułka
had stuck to the bargain, limiting Poland's domestic autonomy
and guaranteeing her reliability by strengthening her ties with the
CEMA and the Warsaw Treaty Organization. The second precedent
was established in August 1968, when, against the overwhelmingly
pro-Dubcek sentiments of his people, he ordered Polish troops to
march along with other Warsaw Pact partners.

The Sino-Soviet conflict had greatly enhanced the country's status
within the camp, while making Gomułka's personal position much

more prestigious. Albania's desertion, followed by the defiant line taken by Rumania, and the "Prague Spring," had all made Warsaw's loyalty so much more important to Moscow. Gomułka's policy of Polish-Russian solidarity in the Sino-Soviet conflict had its ideological as well as its geopolitical motivation. The latter was not without historical precedents. Only one generation ago, Roman Dmowski bluntly warned his countrymen against "the yellow peril" and anticipated that "The time may come when those who are now dreaming about partitioning Russia will anxiously ask whether she is strong enough to withstand the pressure of China . . . this moment may not be very far away." [44] Thus the unreliability of Czechoslovakia and the Sino-Soviet dispute catapulted Poland to a new position of prestige; after China's defection, Poland became the largest and most important ally of Moscow. [45]

Soviet gratitude for Gomułka's loyal behavior during the Sino-Soviet dispute, the Middle East, and the Czechoslovak crises was shown at the Fifth Congress of the PUWP, held in Warsaw in November 1968. Faced by a provincial party *aparat* that was penetrated by Moczar's "Partisans," Gomułka was able to win reelection as First Secretary of the Central Committee only due to Brezhnev's support. Once firmly in the saddle, Gomułka proceeded to reshape the top party organs to his liking. While his main economic adviser, Bolesław Jaszczuk, was made full member of the Politburo, Moczar became only its alternate member, and was shifted from the Ministry of the Interior to the post of Secretary of CC in charge of public security. After the Fifth Party Congress, the Politburo was composed of the following, who served as full members: Gomułka, Jaszczuk, Kliszko, Loga-Sowiński, Spychalski, Strzelecki, Cyrankiewicz, Gierek, Jedrychowski, Kociołek, Kruczek, and Tejchman. Deputy members were: Jagielski, Jaroszewicz, Moczar, and Szydlak. Of the full members the first five belonged to the inner leadership, while Cyrankiewicz was a man expected to vote always with the powerholder; Kociołek, Kruczek, and Tejchman were expected to be grateful for the elevation to the Politburo, and thus to support Gomułka. Thus, after the Congress, Gomułka's party position was stronger than ever: for the first time he had a clear and firm majority of the Politburo. [46]

The apogee of Gomułka's career was reached on December 7, 1970. It was on that day that the Chancellor of the Federal Republic of Germany, Willy Brandt, following his Moscow visit in September, came to Warsaw to sign the Warsaw-Bonn treaty acknowledging the

Oder-Neisse line as Poland's western frontier. The treaty, despite its shortcomings, must have appeared to Gomułka, as well as to many observers of the Polish scene, as a climax of his political career of nearly half a century. He could now rightly claim a large share of the credit for the normalization of relations between Warsaw and Bonn, and for the acceptance of the Oder-Neisse line by the Federal Republic of Germany.[47]

By then Gomułka's position appeared solidly secure. For a decade or so he had been recognized as an elder statesman of the Communist camp. His contributions to the Communist cause found their recognition in February 1970, when he was awarded the Order of Lenin on his 65th birthday by the Supreme Soviet of the USSR. The accompanying citation stressed Gomułka's "outstanding services to the development of fraternal friendship and cooperation between the peoples of the Soviet Union and the Polish People's Republic, for strengthening of peace and Socialism, and for many years of active participation in the world Communist movement." As his rival-supporter Moczar had to admit, Gomułka was the "patriarch of the Polish party."

Having sailed safely through the events of 1967 and 1968, the anti-Zionist campaign, the student revolt, the Czechoslovak intervention, having obtained Bonn's approval of the new Western frontiers of Poland, Gomułka probably thought that he could relax, and looked forward to a "small stabilization." Yet his extreme incompetence in economic matters, as well as his isolation from the people, made him commit the most costly mistake of his career.

THE MOUNTING CRISIS

The events of mid-December 1970 must be examined against the background of Poland's worsening economic situation and the attempt to modernize the country's economy. While Gomułka was muddling through a series of more or less acute political problems, the economic condition of the country was steadily worsening. Already by the early 1960's, the symptoms of serious economic difficulties were manifest: planned industrial growth had to be curtailed, and investment program revised. Early in 1962 Gomułka announced a series of austerity measures, and by 1963 prices of gas, coal, and other categories of fuel were drastically increased.

Gomułka's inability to cope with the mounting problems was compounded by his bad judgment in selecting his economic advisers, especially Jaszczuk, a man of erratic temperament and limited horizons. But even a statesman with a broader experience and sounder judgment would have been staggered by the variety of problems facing the country's economy. One of them was of a demographic nature. In the immediate postwar years Poland had had a very high birthrate, probably the highest in Europe at the time. The population shot up from an end of the war level of about 24 million to around 33 million in 1970. The postwar crop of babies was just hitting the labor market during the late 1960's. Employment had not increased fast enough to provide a sufficient number of jobs.

Another problem facing the Polish economy was the excessive centralization inherited from the Stalinist period. Here one must stress that various comprehensive schemes of modernization were outlined in 1957–58 by some leading economists, like Oscar Lange, as well as by other experts. All these efforts at reform were thwarted by the party hardliners, who warned Gomułka that decentralization of planning and control over individual enterprises would result in undermining of his political power. Taking a middle road he undertook numerous piecemeal changes, while avoiding a fundamental overhauling of the rigid, centrally controlled economic system. Thus, with some modifications, he returned to the policy of pursuing rapid industrial growth, regardless of obstacles and human sacrifices.[48]

The anti-Zionist campaign also contributed to the stiffening of Gomułka's economic policy. Among the victims of the campaign were many leading economists (such as Włodzimierz Brus), who had advocated various projects of economic reform. They were too closely associated with the group that had fallen victim to the witch hunt, and had considered plans too similar to the blueprints discussed during the "Prague Spring." The reform sponsored by the "revisionist" economists was centered around regulated use of the market mechanism, including an introduction of increased material incentives, application of cost accounting, and profit motive. In the post-March 1968 days, the suggestions were condemned by the "Partisans" as attempting to graft bourgeois ideas on the Polish economy, and, ultimately, threatening the party's control of the national economy, and hence undermining a foundation of the Socialist system.[49]

While the issue of economic reform was a kind of political football in endless factional feuds, the situation of the Polish economy was rapidly deteriorating. During the 1960's, the percentage of the na-

tional income devoted to consumption was gradually dropping, while
the accumulation of capital was increasing from 24.2 percent in
1960, to 28.8 percent in 1968, and 29.7 percent in 1969. These
increases were larger than the corresponding figures in Czechoslovakia, Hungary, or East Germany. Meanwhile, the housing, retail,
and service sectors of the economy were being overlooked.

The rapid growth of investments required a substantial increase
in imports of machinery and other industrial equipment. This, in
turn, resulted in a growing trade deficit, despite the stepped up export of food, especially ham. Most of the food export was conducted
at the expense of the home market. At the same time a mistaken
policy of low prices paid by the State to breeders of cattle, poultry,
and hogs as well as high prices for animal feed resulted in a dramatic drop of meat output. This had an adverse effect on the market
equilibrium, and together with the shortage of consumer goods in
general, further increased the inflationary pressures.

Combining the behavior of an ostrich with that of a hen, Gomułka
ignored the numerous warnings about a mounting crisis, and persisted in his short-sighted policy of reducing further the already low
standard of living. When some economic experts urged Gomułka to
import some consumer goods to channel the growing popular dissatisfaction, he retorted angrily that the nation was "living beyond
its means," and could not afford it. Instead, he urged tightening of
the belt. A price raise, decreed in November 1968, further depressed
the standard of living. During 1969–70, there was no growth at all.
This increased the mounting discontent, which was bound to find
an outlet sooner or later.

THE DECEMBER REVOLT AND GOMUŁKA'S FALL

The event that precipitated the outburst was another dramatic
increase in food prices decreed on December 13, 1970, on the eve
of Christmas. In some cases the prices were to rise by as much as
30 percent. The price increases were to be paralleled by the introduction of a new industrial wage scale. Thus, besides the price
increases for food, fuel, and other essentials, the workers were also
upset by proposals to alter the complex regulations governing their
wages. They feared that the wage changes would lower their weekly
earnings. The sheer fact that the party had imposed such drastic
measures which deeply affected every citizen, and the timing of these
steps revealed the dramatic alienation of the party's leadership from
the masses of the people. In consequence, there was an immediate

popular reaction in the form of bloody mass demonstrations in the three Baltic coast cities of Gdańsk, Gdynia, and Szczecin.[50]

The Decembrist revolt was more than a series of bread riots. It was neither a tinderbox flareup against the Communist system, as in Hungary in 1956, nor a peaceful protest and demonstration for political and social change as in Czechoslovakia in 1968. The revolt in the Baltic cities was a much more elemental expression of dissatisfaction with the quality of everyday life in Poland, with corruption of the "new class" and its arbitrary, high-handed ways. The tidal wave of discontent was no hopeless protest of the downtrodden poor, the "dark people," but of relatively well-paid dock workers. The Baltic seacoast workers could look across their Western frontier, and see higher wages and better living standards in East Germany, Denmark, and Sweden. They were restless, dissatisfied, and determined to express that dissatisfaction.[51] The destruction of party headquarters, governmental offices, as well as looting of shops seemed to confirm the saying of Poland's foremost satirist, S. J. Lec: "Where a harsh law rules, people yearn for lawlessness."

The massive outburst which lasted for five days (December 14–19), by spreading to other cities of Poland, threatened to turn into a civil war. Regular army detachments, including tanks, had to be used to fight the insurgents.

At the crucial moment, torn between *raison d'etat* and *raison de parti*, Gomułka decided to defend the regime at all costs and asked Brezhnev for help. It is noteworthy that Brezhnev did not oblige, and urged peaceful solution of the crisis. The reasons for the Soviet nonintervention are unknown. Moscow's fear of upsetting the germinating detente with the U.S. might have played a role; a second Soviet armed invasion, some two years after the Czechoslovak venture, would have certainly further tarnished the international image of the USSR. Another reason for Soviet neutrality in the Polish struggle for power might have been a reflection of Brezhnev's dissatisfaction with Gomułka's performance.

The uprising was suppressed only with the massive aid of the armed forces. According to the official communiqué, there were 45 killed and 1,165 wounded. In spite of the fact that the revolt was crushed, the rebels won a series of impressive economic as well as political concessions. First of all, they gained immediate relief from the worst abuses: withdrawal of the new wage system; toleration by the authorities of the genuine workers' committees, and, temporarily, of the workers' militia. Last but not least, the workers' revolt forced a major crisis within the party leadership.

On December 18, while defending his policy of armed repression of the revolt to a meeting of the Politburo, Gomułka suffered a cerebral hemorrhage, lost his eyesight, and was taken to the hospital. The next day, after seven hours of bitter debate, his previously solid majority crumbled: some of his former supporters abandoned him and sided with his critics, who were centering around Gierek, Moczar, and Jaroszewicz. Now a majority of the Politburo asked Gomułka for his resignation from his post as First Secretary, but not from the Central Committee, from which he was merely suspended. While making this relatively lenient decision the plenum took into consideration his "former services to the party and the country," as well as the state of his health. On December 20, after another protracted meeting, the Central Committee nominated Edward Gierek as its First Secretary.

Gierek promptly reconstructed the Politburo and the Secretariat to suit his purposes. Among the full members of the Politburo there were seven old-timers (Gierek, Cyrankiewicz, Jedrychowski, Kociołek, Kruczek, Loga-Sowinski, and Tejchman); three were promoted from among the non-voting members (Moczar, Jaroszewicz and Szydlak) and two were newcomers (Olszowski and Babiuch). Among deputy members the most striking person was the youthful Commander-in-Chief of the Armed Forces, General Wojciech Jaruzelski. Cyrankiewicz's place as Prime Minister was taken by Piotr Jaroszewicz.

Thus, for the second time in the history of post-war Poland, a workers' revolt forced a change of the top party leadership, and subsequently of the government of the country.[52]

THE ERA OF GOMUŁKA IN PERSPECTIVE

The post-mortem of Gomułka's rule took place at the February 1971 plenary meeting of the Central Committee. The seven-hour-long debate was not limited to the analysis of the causes and course of the Baltic coast riots of the previous December which, as one of the speakers pointed out, threatened the country with "incalculable consequences," but was extended to the entire span of the fourteen years of Gomułka's ascendancy. The criticism ran along three lines: Gomułka's mishandling of the workers' revolt, his abuse of power, and his gross incompetence in several fields, especially in economic matters. The deposed Secretary was bitterly condemned for his jealous and arbitrary exercise of power and for forming a clique within the party. The existence of this inner leadership, the core of which was formed by Kliszko, who had been responsible for ideology and cadres, and Jaszuk, a "virtual dictator" of the economic front, was denounced as a gross violation of the Leninist principle of collective leadership. Both men were expelled from the CC and censured for their numerous mistakes and shortcomings, including "limitless ambition."[53]

The balance sheet of Gomułka's rule is difficult to draw from a perspective of half a decade later. In his capacity as First Secretary of the General Committee he exercised a semi-dictatorial rule over the entire life of the country for over fourteen years. Some positive achievements are tightly intertwined with many negative actions. Gomułka was personally an honest and selfless man, in the sense that he did not abuse his power for personal aims. In comparison with other party leaders he lived in Puritan austerity, and was strongly critical of his comrades who enjoyed luxury. For instance, after his return from Belgrade, Gomułka was indignant at the Byzantine splendor that had been displayed by Tito, and threw away with anger a gold cigarette case studded with diamonds which his host had given him as a personal gift.[54]

Himself the victim of a purge in 1948–49, Gomułka never really purged his main party opponents: even people responsible for his downfall in 1948–49 like Berman or Minc, were never really punished but simply shifted to less important posts. His was an autocratic personality; he seldom summoned the Politburo, ran the Secretariat with an iron hand, and suffered no criticism. Until 1968 he did not try to build up systematically his own faction, but relied more on his personal authority and on his skill in maneuvering between various factions, playing one against the other, while trying to follow a middle course. His vigilance failed him conspicuously during the middle 1960's when he allowed his potential rivals, Moczar and his group, to become too strong for his own safety. It was, most probably, the lack of his own faction that compelled him to lean too heavily on Moczar's support during the critical days of 1967–68.

Gomułka's personal integrity and skill at manipulating intraparty feuds were not matched by political wisdom and foresight. The problem of how the exceptionally strong position which he held at the close of 1956 and the beginning of 1957 came to be squandered is worthy of a separate monograph. Here it is enough to note that his return to the party's highest post aroused great expectations which he was neither able nor willing to satisfy. The program of the party's democratization was not realized: the PUWP was ruled autocratically, arbitrarily, and rather erratically. His choice of close co-workers was far from judicious. Kliszko, Loga-Sowinski, and Jaszczuk were striking examples of incompetence and syceophancy. Always mistrustful of educated people, in 1968 Gomułka closed the Higher Party School of Social Sciences, as a hot bed of "revisionism."

While October 1956 constituted Comułka's finest hour, the years 1967–70 were the most controversial of his career. The crushing of the youth manifestations in defense of academic rights and cultural freedoms, his anti-Zionist campaign, as well as Poland's participation in the invasion of Czechoslovakia, tarnished his image. Thus, by the late 1960's, Gomułka, who came to power as a man of conciliation, was now engaged in a bitter struggle on many fronts: against the "revisionists," the intellectuals, the youth, and the Church. All this was compounded by mounting economic difficulties.

Economics constituted his Achilles' heel. The numerous attempts at economic reform by competent economists were frustrated. The initial promises notwithstanding, the workers' councils were reduced to the role of debating circles, preoccupied with marginal issues. Private initiative in economic and social matters was discouraged and even penalized. The pledge of improving the lot of the common people was subordinated to forced capital accumulation, largely at the expense of the working class. After the initial improvement in the standard of living during the late 1950's and the early 1960's, the last period of Gomułka's rule brought not only the end of the progress, but even considerable regression.

On the other hand, the plight of the Polish economy during the later period of Gomułka's rule should not obscure the fact that, during the late 1950's, the Polish economists spearheaded the movement for revision of the Stalinist patterns of centralized planning and management. During the years 1956–58 Poland provided a significant contribution to the reform of the Marxist political practice and pioneered in the attempts at humanizing the Soviet patterns. The political and social objectives of the Stalinist system were courageously criticized, its economic priorities reversed, and new alternatives outlined. Thus the Poles, like the Yugoslavs before them, repudiated the principle of the universality of Soviet experience, now part and parcel of most Communist movements, especially in the West.[55]

The most important gains of the Gomułka era, however, were psychological. After the gruesome years of Stalinism the country could enjoy during the late 1950's a brief breathing spell. At that time it had more internal autonomy than any other member of the Soviet orbit. This was perhaps best felt in the field of culture; socialist realism was solf-pedalled, if not abandoned altogether; East-West cultural exchanges were cultivated, and many Polish scholars and writers visited the West, while their Western colleagues travelled to Poland. Despite subsequent recompression, cultural exchange with the West, although often hampered, was never completely interrupted. The semi-colonial exploitation of the country by Russia was considerably reduced. Also, since the peasants were allowed to retain most of the land, the overall progress of Polish agriculture was significant. In addition, limited religious instruction was preserved, occasional administrative harassment notwithstanding. Most important, the Stalinist mass terror never returned to Poland.

Thus, despite Gomułka's retreat from the "gains of October," not all of them were abandoned, and the most significant ones, even if only in vestigial form, survived until the end of his rule and beyond it.

EPILOGUE: UNDER
17 GIEREK'S LEADERSHIP

The December 1970 revolt catapulted into power a new party team led by Edward Gierek, whose lifepath, more varied and Western oriented, was quite different from Gomułka's.

Gierek was born on January 6, 1913, in the district of Będzin in Russian Poland; the son of a miner who perished in a mining accident. Soon after his father's death the family moved to Northern France where young Gierek started work in a mine at the age of thirteen. According to his official biography, he joined the Communist Party of France in 1931. As an organizer of a miners' strike in Pas de Calais, he was arrested and expelled in 1934 from France to Poland, where he was drafted to serve in the army. In 1937 Gierek emigrated to Limburg, in Northern Belgium, where for eleven years he worked again as a miner, at the same time being active in the local Communist Party cell through World War II. As a consequence, he speaks better French than Russian.[1]

Gierek returned to Poland only in 1948. In May 1956 he was appointed Secretary of the Central Committee, entered the Politburo after Gomułka's return, and from 1957 to 1970 was party secretary in Upper Silesia, the industrial heartland of the country; meanwhile, in 1954, he obtained a diploma of a mining engineer by correspondence at the Cracow Mining Academy. He made of Upper Silesia a region which enjoyed a standard of living much higher than the rest of the country, and which was better provided with goods and services. As a result, Gierek became known as the Tsombe of the Polish Katanga. Gierek's Marxism is of a pragmatic variety, and in Silesia he sought the advice of non-party experts: economists, professors, and engineers. From the middle 1960's on he was generally regarded as one of Gomułka's possible successors.

The situation which Gierek inherited from his predecessor after the December events of 1970 was far from easy: the mood of the country was restless and rebellious, the economy in shambles. The shock produced by the revolt of the Baltic seacoast continued to spread tremors throughout the country. The smouldering unrest found its expression in a wave of scattered protests, slowdowns, and strikes lasting through most of 1971.[2] Consequently Gierek's primary task was to pacify the country. Just how difficult the task actually was may be seen from the incidents that took place on Sunday, January 24, 1971 in Szczecin, after the uprising had been crushed. The local Workers' Committees summoned a group of top party and governmental leaders to come in person from Warsaw to discuss the workers' grievances. And indeed the new First Secretary, Gierek, the Prime Minister, Jaroszewicz, accompanied by the Minister of the Interior and the Commander-in-Chief of the Armed Forces, obliged. The dignitaries not only spent some ten hours engaging with the workers in a free dialogue, but, what was more significant, they also gave in to most of the workers' demands. These included punishment and dismissal of some party bosses involved in the December tragedy, like the party secretary of the Szczecin province, and the head of the National Trade Union Council. This was a significant victory for the workers over the regime. No history of any other Communist Party knows a comparable phenomenon. Similar dialogues took place in several other industrial centers, including Gdańsk, Łódź, and Białystok.

Meanwhile Gierek made a new year address over the radio and television. Hitherto this privilege had been restricted to the Chairman of the Council of State, or the nominal President of the Republic. In his speech Gierek admitted that the party had made some serious mistakes by losing contact with the masses, but played down the systemic aspects of the events of December 1970. He solemnly promised to make an investigation into the causes of the tragedy. While pledging to remedy the political and economic mistakes, mostly attributed to Gomułka's character, and "draw the necessary conclusions" from the past, he stressed that the party and the government had already taken the necessary decisions "to meet the most burning social needs." A man with a pragmatic mind, he saw the roots of the workers' rebellion in the isolation of the party from the broad masses of the people, and in the neglect of their everyday basic needs, as well as in the lack of adequate rewards for work performed. Admitting previous mistakes, he promised to break with the idolatry of conspicuous production. He also declared that from then on the government policy would be "clear and understandable to everybody." [3]

Following Gierek's speech, on January 8, it was decreed that the prices of nondurable goods, including food, were to remain stable for the next two years, while prices of industrial goods were to be lowered as production costs decreased; an increased supply of inexpensive goods on the market was promised, together with correction of price abuses. The original Five-Year Plan for 1971–75 was to be redrafted to stress agriculture, consumer goods, and housing. It was also announced that manufacturers rather than the planning commissions, would set prices, on the basis of large scale consumer research. This was soon followed by the boosting of the minimum pay rates, family allowances, and pensions.[4] Moreover, the people were pleasantly surprised by the decision to rebuild the Royal Castle in Warsaw.

Later on, a small car was promised to Polish consumers, as well as more prefabricated houses. The hitherto rather punitive taxation of some 200,000 private enterprises in retail, trade, and service was somewhat alleviated. Gierek's intervention in Moscow produced some changes in the terms of trade between the two countries, and granted to Warsaw a loan of $100,000,000 mainly to purchase grain in the USSR. Gierek also obtained Moscow's approval for Poland's broadened economic contacts with the West. Already in 1971 and 1972 Poland's trade with the USSR and other Communist countries was decreasing, while it was increasing considerably with the Western capitalistic countries, as well as with those of the Third World. The Polish plan for 1971–75 provided for expansion of foreign trade by 11 percent per year, a tempo faster than the rate of growth of the economy as a whole. The large-scale purchase of foreign licenses and the massive import of consumer goods from abroad has resulted in considerable indebtedness.[5]

Soon after pacifying the workers, Gierek embarked on a new agricultural policy. Some ten million peasants who lived on 3.6 million private farms were granted significant concessions: compulsory delivery quotas, which the peasants had had to supply at artificially low prices fixed by the government, were now abolished as of January 1, 1972; indivisibility of small farms was established, and private ownership of land consolidated. At the same time, social security and an all-inclusive, free health service were extended to private farmers and their families. This policy, besides increasing income, gave individual peasants a greater sense of economic security.

While creating conditions favorable for a rapid growth of individual agricultural production, Gierek did not lose sight of the fundamental issues of ownership and long-time production relations in the villages. One of the resolutions of the Sixth Party Congress called for "the creation of conditions for the gradual socialist transformation of the countryside." It seems that "the socialist transformation" is to be pressed at a future time when the demographic situation becomes favorable and reserves of agricultural machinery as well as trained personnel will be available for the party's ultimate objectives in the countryside.[6]

While mending his fences with the workers and peasants, Gierek also made efforts to improve relations with the intellectuals and the academic community: censorship was relaxed somewhat, foreign travel made easier, and salaries of professors bolstered. Scholars have since been invited to advise the party and the government on various matters, including educational reform. Also, funds allotted to research were increased: by 1975 they are expected to comprise 2.5 percent of the GNP, and 4 percent by 1980. However, the initial loosening of control over freedom of expression was soon followed by a tightening of censorship which has affected especially writings on contemporary history, and by repeated warnings that the party was determined not to tolerate any meaningful cultural plurality.

POTENTIAL PROBLEMS

Gierek's emphasis on modernization through rationality and efficiency has produced some striking successes, and the years 1970–1974 registered considerable growth of the GNP, and a substantial rise in the standard of living, especially in the countryside. On the other hand, while investing heavily in new branches of industry, Gierek has neglected modernization of the old ones, as well as fundamental reform of the overly centralized system of management and planning. Consequently, his short-term successes may create long-term problems for him and for the country.

Although since December 1970 there have been noteworthy gains in industrial and agricultural production, labor productivity, real wages, and national income, considerable imbalances could be observed between import and export, the tempo with which investments are completed, as well as the earned and distributed income. In 1973, for instance, produced national income rose by 10 percent, while distributed income increased by 13 percent. Moreover, in spite of its price freeze on basic food products, the government has not been able to prevent a considerable rise in the overall prices of consumer goods and services. The inflationary trend is especially visible in the private market.

There are three critical points in the Polish economic situation. The first, and perhaps the most dangerous, is the excessive amount of money chasing an inadequate supply of goods. This is largely the result of the initial package of economic concessions made by Gierek at the beginning of 1971, to pacify the restless country. These concessions, which affected some 6–7 million people, had a cumulative effect of expanding the amount of money beyond the limits of the Polish economy's ability to absorb it, which is connected with the inability of the economy to supply the consumers with the quantity and quality of the products that they desire. This creates a serious market disequilibrium and also increases inflationary pressures. This inability to supply the fluctuating demands of Polish consumers has been the result of the second critical aspect of the country's industry, the overly long investment cycle, especially in the field of consumer goods. The third neuralgic point has been a steady growth of deficit in the balance of trade, which has been again largely a result of Gierek's desire to appease the restless population with a quick supply of foreign consumer goods.

From the point of view of the party Gierek's policy represents another potential danger: the rising standard of living is likely to stimulate political demands which, in the long run, may give rise to further instabilities, due to frustration of hopes for political concessions. Gierek's idea of a limited participatory partocracy may not satisfy the Polish masses.

In the long run, Poland's economic future depends on the ability of her leadership to cut down excess import and utilize foreign credit responsibly by applying it rigidly to productive investments. Only in this way can her industries be made more capable of satisfying the growing demands of a more and more sophisticated market.[7]

Gierek's scheme of doubling his country's potential and launching Poland into the technotronic age by means of automating and computerizing her economy has a strong visionary tinge. To achieve this he will have to overcome not only the ballast of history, including the grave mistakes of his predecessor, but also the inertia and skepticism of the Polish masses. In addition, he must cope with the doctrinal as well as structural limitations of the hegemonial sphere in which Poland has been encapsulated since the end of World War II.

CHURCH-STATE RELATIONS

The son of devout parents, Gierek has been more aware than Gomułka of the strength of religious belief and practice among the people. Consequently, almost immediately after taking power, he made attempts to placate the Catholic Church by offering concessions in return for support. Premier Jaroszewicz expressed this policy in his inaugural address to the Sejm:

We shall try to ensure full normalization of state and church relations, expecting at the same time that the government's efforts will be adequately understood by the ecclesiastic and secular forces.[8]

The hierarchy replied to this offer with a series of demands: the lifting of censorship on church publications, freedom of expression and conscience, the removal of the Pax group from publishing activities, title to the lands of German Poland, and easing of building restrictions so that 1,000 new churches could be built.

On March 3, 1971, Cardinal Wyszynski met the Prime Minister, Jaroszewicz. It was the first such meeting in ten years.[9] As a result of this new attempt at a church-state *modus vivendi,* the party promised to restore to church ownership 7,000 of the church buildings, chapels, monasteries, and parish halls in the Western territories, hitherto sequestered by the state authorities. Some 130 new churches were allowed to be constructed in several new localities, including the industrial town of Nowa Huta, near Cracow — an urgent and long denied request. On the other hand, similar permission was refused in other localities in almost equal need of appropriate places of worship, and demolition of churches built without permission continued. Furthermore, the problem of educational reform planned by the regime has continued to this time as a major focus of discord. The appointment of the head of the Pax, Bolesław Piasecki, as member of the Council of State, was also regarded as a slap in the hierarchy's face.

Negotiations have since been opened with the hierarchy to settle other outstanding problems of the state-church relationship, but they have made little progress, the main stumbling block being the educational reform. The party has continued to harass the remaining courses in religious instruction, and to insist on Marxist indoctrination of children. On June 18, 1973, the Roman Catholic bishops formally protested the national educational reform, as "including elements hostile to religious upbringings," and accused the country's state-run schools of teaching "atheistic principles" and undermining the "religious motivation" of children.[10]

Repeated attempts at drafting Catholic students of theological seminaries for military service, contrary to the church-state agreement of 1950, have also embittered the atmosphere, somewhat improved by the settlement of many outstanding problems in the Western territories. A protest against the regime's discrimination against the Catholics was boldly raised by the vice-chairman of the Catholic parliamentary group "ZNAK," Janusz Zabłocki, in his speech of December 17, 1973.

One of the major stumbling blocks to establishing normal diplomatic relations with the Vatican was Warsaw's insistence that Rome officially recognize the Oder-Neisse line. The Vatican had been unwilling to take this step before the signing of a formal peace treaty. The ratification by the Federal Parliament in Bonn of the Polish-West German treaty of December 1970, which terminated the territorial dispute between the two countries was followed on June 28, 1972, by the appointment of six Polish bishops to the Western dioceses. This step by the Vatican finally legitimized the ecclesiastical control of the Polish Church over the lands acquired by Poland after World War II, and thus implicitly recognized her Western boundaries. A significant symptom of the detente between Warsaw and the Vatican was the visit which the Polish Foreign Minister, Stefan Olszowski, paid to Pope Paul VI on November 12, 1973.[11] In 1974 a working group of diplomats was attached to the Polish Embassy in Rome to continue the confidential contact aiming at a legal *modus vivendi,* perhaps eventually a concordate, between the Polish People's Republic and the Vatican.

GIEREK CONSOLIDATES HIS POWER BASE

Parallel with these political and economic changes, efforts at altering the style of the party work have been undertaken by Gierek. Frightened by the events of December 1970, he has made several attempts to break the wall of mistrust between the party and the masses, to establish and initiate a dialogue with the people. A new daily television program called "Citizen's Tribune" has been established, on which different officials appear to answer questions that are telephoned by the audience. Unlike his predecessor, Gierek has traveled widely throughout Poland: during 1971 alone he set up 187 various grassroots meetings, held conferences with factory committees, listened to workers' grievances, and made himself available for questioning and debate. In his speeches, he has avoided the dry, dogmatic verbosity of style so characteristic of Gomułka, and used instead a more colloquial and often patriotic vocabulary and a more palatable phraseology. For instance, in the proclamation exhorting people to help rebuild the Royal Castle in Warsaw, the emphasis was on patriotic motivation. There was no mention of Communist ideology.

One of the most striking features of Gierek's policy has been his persistent effort to legitimize the position of the party as a product of native radical tradition and a permanent feature of the Polish political landscape. This was exemplified by a striking article published in 1971, significantly enough not in the official *Trybuna ludu*, but in a more widely read daily *Zycie Warszawy*. Wojna, a leading party publicist, made an ambitious attempt to draw a rather risky parallel between the elected kings of Poland in the sixteenth, seventeenth, and eighteenth centuries and the party.

The leading role of the party is the same privilege of the Socialist nation, as had been for the ruling group the privileges of the nobility, confirmed by the elective kings at the time of their coronation. This [confirmation of privileges] was an expression of the nobility's right to determine the fate of the country. Today the leading role of the party expresses the right of the whole nation, the party and non-party people, the believers and the non-believers, to decide about our common fate.[12]

The author's reasoning suggests the existence of a social contract similar to the old *pacta conventa* that had been traditionally negotiated between the Polish nobility and the freely elected king, about to be crowned. This strangely un-Marxist and historically rather shaky parallel is an expression of Gierek's anxiety to root the party in the consciousness of the people as a legitimate instrument of government, an heir to the past.

One of the crucial problems facing Gierek was how to strengthen his newly acquired power and reduce the influence of his former ally, and now the main rival, Moczar, the "kingmaker" of the December crisis. Supported by his "Partisans," Moczar was still in command of many important posts in the local administration, and in May 1971, he apparently made a behind-the-scene bid to oust Gierek. To this move Gierek replied in a characteristically undramatic way. A series of dismissals of Moczar's supporters from various key positions, including most provincial party secretaries, prepared the ground. On June 22, Moczar was appointed Chairman of the Supreme Control Council. By December 1971, only six of nineteen provincial secretaries had held their posts before December 1970. Prior to the 1971 Congress, over 100,000 out of some 2,300,000 card-carrying CP members were purged for "slackness, corruption, and various other shortcomings." [13]

Gierek's victory over Moczar was sanctioned by the Sixth PUWP Congress, deliberating between December 6 and 11, 1971, in Warsaw. The congress was characterized by a large turnover of the delegates, as well as of the elected dignitaries. Of the 1,815 delegates, 70 percent attended for the first time. The Secretariat was expanded from seven to eleven members. Approximately half of the new 115 member Central Committee were freshmen with a substantial number of the remainder having been elected within the year. This was called the party "renewal," and this expression became from then on one of Gierek's chief slogans.

Among the most significant changes, besides the removal of Moczar, from the Politburo, was the dismissal from this top policy-making body of two key people of the Gomułka era: the Minister of Foreign Affairs, Stefan Jędrychowski, and Józef Cyrankiewicz, who had been Prime Minister almost without interruption from 1948 to 1970. The departure of Cyrankiewicz was especially welcomed by many of his countrymen. Although he was a highly skillful politician, who, like a cat with nine lives, managed to survive the regimes of Bierut and Gomułka, Cyrankiewicz, had incurred the wrath of the Baltic shipyard workers during the 1970 upheavals when he delivered a bloodthirsty anti-strike speech, similar to the one he had made against the Poznań workers in June 1956. Cyrankiewicz was now removed not only from the Politburo, but also from Chairmanship of the State Council, and was replaced by a scholar, Professor Henryk Jabłonski of the University of Warsaw, a former Socialist.

The deposed leaders were replaced in the new 11-member Politburo (one more than the previous body) by people who had been brought to the fore after the Decembrist revolt. The new Politburo members were: Mieczysław Jagielski, head of the Economic Planning Commission; Henryk Jabłonski, Minister of Education; General Wojciech Jaruzelski, Defense Minister; and a former member of the now profoundly shattered "Partisan" faction, General Franciszek Szlachcic, Interior Minister. All but Szlachcic had been candidate, or alternate, Politburo members.

Thus, at the Congress Gierek consolidated his power by introducing a large number of his people to the top party organs. From the voting membership of the Gomułka Politburo, only Gierek, Kruczek, and Tajchman remained, while all of Gomułka's associates — Kliszko, Spychalski, Cyrankiewicz, and Loga-Sowinski — were dropped from the Politburo. Moreover, those 67 of the new Central Committee, who were elected for the first time, were apparently his supporters.

Thus, within a year after the December 1970 rebellion that catapulted him to power, Gierek emerged as undisputed leader of the party. The changes in the top leadership following Gierek's ascendancy were more thorough than those brought about after Gomułka's return to power in 1956. Gierek's close associates are mostly younger men who, like himself, have a technical education, come mainly from Western Poland, and are more attuned to the ways and policies of the First Secretary. Five of the full and candidate members of the Politburo were born between 1909 and 1920, and ten between 1924 and 1931. The average age of full Politburo members has dropped to 46. This makes the Polish ruling elite the youngest in the Soviet camp. Moreover, the new Polish leadership is better educated than the old one: of the 20 top leaders, five have Ph.D.'s, eight have M.A.'s, and three hold various other academic degrees.

RESHAPING THE PARTY

The period of party history since the Sixth Congress has been dominated by Gierek. Since the removal of Moczar he had no visible rival. His only remaining strong and ambitious associate, Szlachcic, was removed from the crucial post of Minister of the Interior on May 29, 1974, and shifted to the post of Deputy Prime Minister, probably a stepping stone toward eventual elimination from the top party organs. Szlachcic had been closely identified with Gierek since the new party leader gave him the crucial post of Minister of Interior soon after the Baltic sea coast revolt.[14] The reasons for downgrading this former "Partisan" are not yet fully known: it might have been caused by his "lack of vigilance" concerning the machinations of Moczar in the spring of 1971, or by financial scandals at the Ministry of the Interior.

Since his new year address of December 31, 1970, given in lieu of the President of the Republic, Gierek has been acting more and more like the actual head of state, and not merely the First Secretary of the PUWP. During his foreign visits (including one to the United States in October 1974) he was received with all the honors due to a head of state. By this means he stressed the primacy of the party over the state, and reasserted his position as the unquestioned "first man" in Poland. Although subject to apparently strong behind-the-scene pressures on the part of Moscow, he has managed to retain the confidence of the center.

One of the possible reasons why Gierek has enjoyed Moscow's confidence is the fact that his pragmatic approach to social and economic problems, with emphasis on modernization, has been paralleled by a vigorous drive to reassert the leading role of the party, to reinvigorate its discipline and ideological motivation. This has been regarded as particularly necessary because of his outgoing foreign policy of detente with the West, which has resulted in significant multiplication of contacts with the capitalistic world.

In the era of detente, which is interpreted by the Communist world as that of "ideological confrontation" with Western capitalistic ideas, Gierek, mindful of Lenin's dictum that "the cadres decide everything," has made a systematic effort to expand and tighten ideological training of his party cadres. In 1971, the Higher School of Social Sciences, abolished by Gomułka in 1968, was reestablished and expanded. After the Sixth Party Congress of 1971, a new three-step system of general party training, mandatory for every PUWP member, was given special attention. One of the symptoms of Gierek's preoccupation with extension of ideological control over the younger generation was the merger of the country's five youth organizations into a new Federation of the Socialist Unions of Polish Youth. The Federation, proclaimed in April 1973, is to facilitate party supervision of the hitherto quite separate and partly apolitical youth organizations, and thus facilitate recruitment of ideologically better trained potential candidates for membership in the PUWP. Also the reform of Poland's rural administration, which entered into force on January 1, 1973, has, as one of its purposes, to strengthen the party's control in the countryside.

In February 1974 Gierek ordered the establishment of the Institute of Basic Problems of Marxism-Leninism, to be headed by Andrzej Werblan, a party Secretary. Werblan is also a chairman of the editorial committee working on a new "history of the party and of the working class movement." Among the tasks of the Institute will be the "development of work on the theory of Marxism-Leninism, which is the basis of ideological activity of the party." [15]

OPENING WINDOWS TO THE WEST

The party has also been trying hard to improve its image, badly tarnished in Western eyes by the "anti-Zionist" campaign. The thirtieth anniversary of the heroic fight of the Jews of the Warsaw ghetto who rose in arms against the German exterminators in the Warsaw ghetto, was solemnly celebrated on April 18 and 19, 1973, by "an evening of speeches, music and poetry" and "a wreath-laying ceremony at the monument inside the ghetto." Party, government, and army delegations participated in both ceremonies.[16]

The crucial geopolitical position of his country, while restricting Gierek's freedom of maneuver in the sphere of international relations, has also provided him in the era of detente with a certain leverage, and a freer access to Western markets. The spring of 1971 marked a considerable improvement in Polish relations with the United States. The turning point was President Nixon's visit to Warsaw, on May 31–June 1, 1972, the first such event in the history of the two countries. The correct but not too demonstrative official reception was counterbalanced by a tumultous reception on the part of the people.[17] The visit was followed by a series of political, economic, and cultural agreements intended to bring the two countries closer together. Air and sea routes, as well as Polish-American cultural exchanges, have been expanded, and a consular agreement concluded. Finally, reciprocating President Nixon's visit to Warsaw, Gierek visited the United States between October 7–13, 1974.

The energy crisis has meanwhile markedly contributed to enhancement of Polish trade relations with the United States. The return to coal as a major source of energy in the United States provides a market for Polish hard coal with its low sulfuric content. Since 1974, Poland has become a major exporter of hard coal to the United States. As a result of this, the trade between the two countries has more than doubled: in 1973, it passed the $500,000 mark. According to the joint communique signed by President Gerald Ford and Gierck in Washington, both countries anticipate the American-Polish trade column to reach $2 billion by 1978.[18]

Years of imposed isolation from the West have widened the technological gap between the countries of Eastern Europe and the more advanced capitalistic countries. Until 1974 about 60 percent of Poland's trade has been with Cema countries. On the other hand, since 1971, Poland's trade with the Western countries has been developing steadily, with the Federal Republic of Germany playing here a leading role. Taking advantage of the new Soviet *Westpolitik*, Poland has tried to emulate Moscow as well as other members of the Cema in obtaining Western credits and technology. The opening of branches of various Western companies and banks in Poland, including First National Bank of Chicago, has had a symbolic value in this respect. Establishment of diplomatic relations with Bonn in September 1972 has also created new vistas for economic exchanges with the West.

The effort to improve relations with the non-Communist countries made Gierek pay more attention to some 10 million Polish emigrés living in the West, mainly in the United States, Brazil, Canada, Great Britain, France, and West Germany. Until 1956, the emigrés had been either ignored, or bitterly criticized as representing reactionary elements opposed to People's Poland. Gomułka's reluctant attempts to establish some sort of contact with the Polish diaspora have been replaced by Gierek by a vigorous offensive. Since 1971–72 considerable sums of money have been earmarked for the purpose of winning the emigrés over to the side of the new Poland.

A CONTEMPORARY PROFILE OF THE PARTY

The system created in Poland after the war, and its quintessence, the PUWP, have not remained static: in its size, social and ethnic structure, its more accommodating attitudes toward the Poles, as well as its relations toward the great eastern neighbor, the party underwent considerable changes.

If one looks at the party from a perspective of well over three decades, perhaps the most striking feature is its dramatic growth in size. From a few thousand members at its foundation in 1942, the party expanded in 1973 to 2,322,500 in a country of 33,500,000 people. This means that every sixth or seventh adult individual is a card-carrying party member.[19] There are about 72,000 civilian and some 3,500 military primary party cells.

As far as its social structure is concerned its changes are illustrated by the following chart.

In 1945, the party had the following make-up: 61 percent of its members were workers, 28.1 percent peasants, and 10.7 percent white collar workers. By 1950, after the merger with the Polish Socialist Party, the proportions had become quite radically altered: only 54.7 percent now were workers, only 14.1 percent were peasants, while the white collar membership had gone up dramatically to 28.9 percent. The trend of the evolution has continued ever since. On the eve of Gomułka's downfall, in 1970, only 40.3 percent of those holding party cards were workers, only 11.5 percent were peasants, while the white collar membership numbered 42.3 percent.

Social Composition of the Polish Workers' Party (PPR) and Polish United Workers' Party (PZPR) *

	Workers	Peasants	White Collar	Other
PPR				
1945	61.0	28.1	10.7	0.2
1946	64.7	23.2	9.3	2.8
1947	57.7	21.6	14.1	6.6
1948	58.8	21.3	17.6	2.3
PZPR				
1949	55.9	14.7	26.7	2.7
1950	54.7	14.1	28.9	2.3
1951	49.3	13.3	35.2	2.2
1952	48.2	13.4	36.2	2.2
1953	47.7	13.0	37.1	2.2
1954	48.1	13.8	36.2	2.0
1955	45.1	13.0	39.2	2.6
1956	44.6	12.8	39.5	3.1
1958	41.8	12.2	42.1	3.9
1959	40.0	11.5	43.5	5.0
1960	40.3	11.8	42.9	5.0
1961	40.1	12.0	42.9	5.0
1962	39.8	11.5	43.7	5.0
1963	39.7	11.2	43.9	5.2
1964	40.2	11.4	43.0	5.4
1965	40.1	11.7	42.7	5.5
1967	39.7	11.5	missing	missing
1968	40.2	11.4	43.0	5.4
1969	40.2	11.4	42.8	5.6
1970	40.3	11.5	42.3	5.9
1971	39.7	10.6	43.6	6.1
June 1973	39.6	10.1	43.9	6.4

* The table was prepared by David S. Mason, a Ph.D. candidate at the Department of Political Science, Indiana University, as a part of his thesis, "Elite Change and Policy in Communist Poland." Data missing for 1957, 1966, and 1972.

Sources: PZPR, Komitet Centralny, Zakład Historii Partii, *PPR: Resolucje, Odezwy, Instrukcje i Okólniki K. C., I.1946–I.1947* and *I.1947–XII.1948* (Warsaw, 1961 and 1973); A. Alster and J. Andrzejewski, "W Sprawie Składu Socjalnego PZPR," *Nowe Drogi*, January-February 1951, p. 239; "Liczby dotyczące składu partii," *Nowe Drogi*, July 1957, pp. 125–127; *Rocznik Polityczny i Gospodarczy* (Warsaw, 1959–1973); Theodor Palimaka, "Nasza Partia," *Życie partii*, October 1968; for the latest data available see the article on the party's dynamics in *Życie partii*, No. 8 (267), 1974.

In June 1973 the corresponding figures were: 39.6 percent, 10.12
percent, and 43.9 percent. On the other hand, one must remember
that a large percentage of the white collar workers are first generation sons of workers and peasants.

For several years party organizers have waged a recruiting campaign to make the PUWP once again "the party of the working
class," but this effort has evidently still not borne sufficient fruit.
The party leadership is reportedly concerned that intellectuals,
administrative leaders, and white collar workers outnumber the blue
collar membership, and has called for intensifying the drive to re-
cruit new members among industrial workers, especially from the
younger generation. The breakdown of party membership by social
class is in a way misleading because the statistics go by the status
of individuals at the time they join the party and in most cases do
not change as the people change social status through education and
advancement. The result is that the working class membership is
probably statistically overstated and the administrative and managerial share of the membership is probably understated. For example, most of the leadership of the party is said to be listed still
as worker or peasant members of the party because this was their
category when they joined years ago.

While the number of urban workers in the ranks of the party has
been steadily diminishing, their educational level, self-confidence,
and hence political role in the country as a whole has been on the
increase. The urban working class, numbering now nearly half of the
country's population, is a force to be reckoned with. Twice in a
generation the workers have shown their mettle: during the 1956
crisis in June as well as in October, and in December 1970. In each
case they challenged the Communist authorities, fought stubbornly
for their rights, and in both cases they were partly victorious: they
forced significant changes in the top Party leadership, as well as in
its policies. This double triumph has shown their political maturity,
and has given them a new sense of importance and self-confidence.
The workers are aware that whatever gains they have achieved are
due largely to their determination to fight for their rights.

Parallel with the bureaucratization of the social structure of the
PUWP, the turnover of its members has been remarkably high. In
fewer than two years after Gomułka's return to power, more than
200,000 members did not get their party cards renewed. As the
campaign against "loosening of party discipline" and for "revolutionary vigilance" gained momentum after the Fourth Congress of

the PUWP in 1967, the rate of expulsion reached 100,000 a year. A purge of similar scope took place in 1971, before the Sixth Party Congress.

The structural evolution of the party should be viewed against the background of the profound socioeconomic changes going on in Poland since the end of World War II. One of the most important has been the process of urbanization to the cities. The restructuring of Polish society has been paralleled by the spread of education, and by conscious or subconscious absorption by the new intelligentsia of the traditional values of the old educated class. As a Polish-educated sociologist observed:

The Polish intelligentsia, although constituting only six per cent of the population before World War II, played a dominant social role. At present this stratum constitutes about one fifth of the whole nation and the lower social strata are now much more exposed to the patterns, values and the whole way of thinking typical for the [old] intelligentsia. It is the Party elite which holds all power but it is the intelligentsia which dominates the intellectual and spiritual superstructure.[20]

The ethnic composition of the party has also undergone a significant evolution. The old Communist Party of Poland was largely led by intellectuals of Jewish extraction and cosmopolitan leaning. Its successors, the PWP and the PUWP, were strongly influenced by the survivors of this prewar party apparatus. The extermination of Polish Jewry by Hitler destroyed the former important recruitment base of the Communist elite. Moreover, the postwar socioeconomic changes, the influx of large masses of peasants into the cities, further eroded the initially preponderant position of this small intellectual group. The events of 1967–68, that is the anti-Zionist campaign and the emigration of a large part of all Polish Jewry, have dealt the final blow to the vital role of the Jews in the party.[21] Since the resignation of Zambrowski from the Politburo in 1963, there has been no person of Jewish extraction in the top party organ. There are, to be sure, a few Jews in the Central Committee, but except for Eugeniusz Szyr who is also a vice-Prime Minister, they do not play such a decisive role.

The changes which took place in the PUWP in the 1960's were analogous to the purge of the old Bolshevik party apparatus carried out on the CPSU during the 1930's, when the younger activists replaced the prerevolutionary cadres. On the other hand, restructuring of the Polish cadres, unlike the Soviet operation, was more gradual and bloodless.

Another field where the evolution of the PUWP can be well observed is the succession to the top party post, that of the First Secretary of the Central Committee. The course of the successive ascensions to the post may be regarded as indicative of the changing relationship between Warsaw and Moscow. The post of First Secretary of the party has changed hands four times since the seizure of power by the Communists: Gomułka-Bierut in 1948, Bierut-Ochab in 1956, Ochab-Gomułka in March 1956, and Gomułka-Gierek in 1970. While the first two changes were most probably dictated by Moscow, the third one witnessed an abortive Soviet intervention, followed by an *ex post facto* reluctant approval by the Soviet Union of the choice of the Polish Central Committee. During the fourth succession crisis, in December 1970, Moscow did not interfere at all. It is worth remembering that in the third and fourth succession crises, the change of Polish leadership had been forced on the party by popular disturbances, strikes, riots, and even armed uprisings which in one instance, December 1970, threatened to turn into a civil war.

During the December 1970 disturbances in Poland, Moscow has tried very hard to preserve the semblance of complete neutrality and even disinterest. For instance, on December 21, *Pravda* reported merely that the Seventh Plenum of the PUWP had approved the resignation of its First Secretary, Gomułka, "due to his health." The notice commented that the new Polish leaders had analyzed the situation and made some "unavoidable decisions." The December 22 issue carried a complimentary letter of congratulation to the new Secretary, Gierek. The reserved Soviet behavior in December 1970 shows that Moscow would like to avoid appearance of interference in domestic affairs of its largest and most important ally in Eastern Europe, located on the strategically crucial Western border of the USSR, and a linchpin of the Soviet system of alliance.

It is thus possible to infer that over the last two decades or so, while overt Soviet influence on the changes in Polish leadership has declined, the effectiveness of popular pressure has grown. This has brought about a further domestication of Polish Communism, and deepened the tendency of the party leadership for accommodation with their countrymen while under pressure.

Comparing the problems of political succession in Poland and the USSR, a young American scholar pointed out the following:

Though there are some similarities between the characteristics of political succession in the Soviet Union, and those of Poland, the differences are probably more significant. While in the Soviet system, the changing of the guard "inevitably" produces a political crisis, in Poland a more general political crisis tends to precipitate a change in leadership. While in the Soviet Union the crisis is brought about by the fact that the ruler is gone, and occurs within the leadership, the political change in Poland is dictated by factors exogenous to the political leadership, i.e., the Soviet leadership of the Polish nation. The fact that these factors exogenous to the leadership necessitate a rapid and efficient change of political leadership may account for the more orderly transfer of political authority in Poland than in the Soviet Union. No political vacuum is allowed to last very long.[22]

Initially, the party, established in power in 1944–45 with the support of the Soviet Army, sought to create a new order which would be essentially a sub-system and mirror of its Soviet model. During the 1940's and early 1950's many overzealous, fanatical party leaders made attempts to copy uncritically the Soviet patterns. On the other hand some more realistic individuals, the most prominent among whom was Gomułka, came to the conclusion that the party had to modify somewhat its methods, if not its final objectives, to win over their countrymen to Communism. After a bitter struggle this program was accepted by the party. After October 1956, and especially after December 1970, the party had to adopt a more accommodating posture, by taking into consideration at least some of the deeply ingrained traditions, habits, and values that could not be removed overnight.

One of the peculiarities of the position of the PUWP is that it has carried on a Communist experiment in a Western-oriented and overwhelmingly Roman Catholic country, where the church provides the masses with an alternative system of values. Most students of contemporary Polish politics agree that more than thirty years of Communist rule has not undone the continuity of the country's national tradition.[23] Most of them are also in agreement that the Polish Communist regime has been, perhaps, less immune to environmental pressure than other similar post-World War II creations.

The factor which has been slowly reshaping not only the Polish party but the entire Communist movement has been the impact of nationalism. This polycentric tendency has increasingly pervaded the relations between Moscow and its East European dependencies, including Poland. The survival of independent, and even antagonistic Communist centers like Yugoslavia, China, and Albania has had its unspoken but visible effect also on Poland. Neither the mili-

tary interventions in Hungary and Czechoslovakia, nor the proclamation of the Brezhnev doctrine, have inhibited to any marked
degree the corollary growth of domestic perspective deepened by
the party's preoccupation with national objectives, at the expense
of broader, international goals.[24]

Thus, one may cite the old saying that political movements are
like old reusable bottles — the label may remain but the contents
change constantly. The present day PUWP has altered considerably
despite the retention of the old name.

The task of reconciling the party's desire for monopoly of power
with the mounting aspirations of a restless society craving for a
respite from the dictates of an alien ideology, is especially difficult.
Industrialization, pushed so hard by the party, has created a large
consumer-oriented middle class with a thirst for the Western style
of life and more participation in running the country. The deep,
erosive effect of the consumption ethic upon the Communist practice, an effect compounded by nationalism, has been visible in the
ranks of the PUWP itself perhaps more than in other parties of Soviet-controlled Eastern Europe.

Consequently, the position of Polish party leadership has been
marked by a sort of schizophrenia. For over three decades, but
especially since October 1956, it has been torn between conflicting
necessities: one is to appease its powerful sponsor, the other to keep
the latent domestic ferment from exploding, as in June 1956 or in
December 1970. By paying less attention to Marxist principles, and
by taking an increasingly pragmatic approach to current problems,
the party is trying to establish itself as a spokesman of the Polish
people, and defender of its historic heritage. This, however, makes
the party run the risk of arousing the suspicion of its sponsor.

The question as to what extent the PUWP has gained the support of the people, and to what extent its self-image has been accepted by non-Communist Poles, has never been squarely faced by
the party.[25] The fact that it enjoys a monopoly of political power
and control of all public media (except for the church pulpits and
a few church related periodicals) makes any precise answer subject
to doubt. The harsh and so often inefficient methods used by the
party to achieve its objectives have been often as much resented
as the objectives themselves. Agreeing with many basic objectives
of the "Socialist construction," in the sense of modernization of their
country, many Poles have been critical of the high-handed and

often arbitrary methods the party used to reshape the socioeconomic and cultural patterns of the country. The privileged position of party members and discrimination against non-Communists is another problem. In an open letter to the weekly *Polityka*, one nonparty man from Poznań complained: "Only one word — *but* — is necessary for my path to promotion to be closed off. I am praised for good work, but when a job in my factory becomes vacant, I am disqualified on the spot. It is taken by a party member. The party speaks of the equality of all citizens, but is this really the case? If I have to join the party to get a managerial position, it means there is no equality." [26]

Since 1955–56 the Polish party has been more in flux than other Eastern European Communist parties, and more affected by the virus of domesticity. Oscillations of the decompression and recompression seismograph have been caused by the shifting balance of power within the Soviet bloc, by the struggle for power between the rival factions in the Kremlin, and by the ever vivid aspirations of the Polish people for at least greater autonomy at home, if not full eventual state sovereignty.

Bibliography

Notes

Index

.

Selected
Bibliography

I. Primary Sources

Aufrufe des Exekutivkomitees der kommunistischen Internationale zur polnischen Frage. Berlin, 1920. Two proclamations of the Communist International of February 17, 1920 and of May 16, 1920.

Bieńkowski Władysław, *Nauka o Polsce współczesnej* (Contemporary Poland). Warsaw, 1948. An official handbook used in Polish high-schools until 1948.

Bierut, Bolesław, *O partii* (About the Party). Warsaw, 1952. A collection of articles and speeches.

Blueprint for World Conquest as Outlined by the Communist International. Washington-Chicago, 1946. A selection of important documents emphasizing the revolutionary imperialism of the Third International, edited by Wm. H. Chamberlin.

Bregman, Aleksander (ed.), *Faked Elections in Poland as Reported by Foreign Observers.* London, 1947. A selection of reports of foreign observers on the Polish elections of January 1947; compiled by an *émigré* publicist.

Broński, Mieczysław, *Propagandysta socjalistyczny* (A Socialist Propagandist). Petrograd, 1918. Published on behalf of the Executive Committee of the SDKPiL in Russia. A slightly modified translation of a pamphlet issued in 1916 by the Union of the Swiss Socialist Youth. A popular explanation of the history and of the theory of "revolutionary Marxism" as opposed to the "reformism."

Brun (Bronowicz), Julian, *Pisma wybrane* (Selected Works), Vols. I & II. Warsaw, 1955 and 1956. Published by the Historical Department of the Central Committee of the UPWP.

—— *Stefana Żeromskiego tragedia pomyłek* (Stefan Żeromski's Tragedy of Errors). Warsaw, 1924. A series of brilliant essays; an important statement of the so-called "National Bolshevism"; not included in his selected works.

Ciechońska, Maria, *Położenie klasy robotniczej w Polsce 1929–1939* (The Situation of the Working Class in Poland, 1929–1930), Warsaw, 1965.

Co dała rosyjska rewolucja robotnikom miast i wsi (What the Russian Revolution Gave to the Workers of Towns and Villages). Warsaw, 1919.

[Czeszejko-Sochacki, Jerzy] Bratkowski, Jerzy, *Poland on the Road to Revolutionary Crisis.* New York, [1933]. A propaganda booklet written by a leading member of the CPP.

―――― ed., *Uzlovye voprosy revolutsionnogo dvizhenia Polshi na XII plenumie ispolkoma kominterna* (The Key Problems of the Revolutionary Movement of Poland at the XII Plenum of the Executive Committee of the Comintern). Moscow, 1933.

Daszyński, Ignacy, *Pamiętniki* (Memoirs), Vols. I and II. Cracow, 1925. Well written and informative.

―――― *Polityka proletariatu — kilka uwag o taktyce rewolucyi w Polsce* (Policy of the Proletariat — Some Remarks on the Revolutionary Tactics in Poland). Warsaw, 1907. Written by the leader of the Polish Socialists of Galicia; the pamphlet supports basically the line of the PPS Revolutionary Faction.

Degras, Jane ed., *The Communist International 1919–1943: Documents*, 2 vols., New York, 1956–1960.

Deklaracja ideowa PZPR: statut PZPR (The Platform and the Rules of the United Polish Workers' Party). Warsaw, 1949.

Documents and Reports on Poland. The Provisional Constitution of February 20, 1947 and the Declaration of Rights. New York, 1949. Issued by the Polish Research and Information Service.

Dokumenty i materiały do stosunków Polsko-Radzieckich, Warsaw, 1962 ―. A heavily edited official selection of documents published jointly by the Polish and Soviet Academies of Sciences.

[Dzierzyński] Dzerzhinskii, Felix E., *Iz dznevnika* . . . (From the Diary . . .) Moscow, 1939. Aims at idealizing the man.

―――― *Izbrannye statii i rechy 1908–1926* (Collection of articles and speeches 1908–1926). [Moscow], 1947. Includes also a large part of Dzierżyński's diary.

Dziesiąty zjazd PPS — program — taktyka — organizacja (The Tenth Congress of the PPS — Program — Tactics — Organization). Cracow, 1908. The first congress of the PPS-Left, called "The Tenth" to stress the continuity of the party.

Dziewanowski, M. K. (ed.), *Poland To-Day as Seen by Foreign Observers*. London, 1946. A selection of American, British, French, and Swedish newspaper reports on Poland; covers the period of the second half of 1945 and the first half of 1946.

(The Eighteenth Congress of the All-Soviet Communist Party (Bolshevik) 10–21 March, 1939. Stenographic Report) *XVIII sezd vsesoyznoi kommunisticheskoi partii (b) 10–21 Marta 1939 g. Stenograficheskii otchet*. Moscow, 1939.

Fiedler, Franciszek, *Za waszą wolność i naszą*. Warsaw, 1946. A reprint of propaganda pamphlet written in 1936 for the Polish brigade fighting during the civil war in Spain on the side of the Republican forces.

Fifth Congress of the Communist International: Abridged Report of Meetings Held at Moscow, June 17th to July 8th, 1924. London, 1924.

(The Fifth Congress of the CPP — Resolutions and Materials) *V. zjazd KPP — uchwały — rezolucje — materiały*. Warsaw, 1930.

(The First Congress of the Communist International: Minutes of the Meeting held in Moscow from March 2nd to 19th, 1919) *Der I. Kongress der kommunistischen Internationale: Protokoll der Verhandlungen in Moscaw vom 2. bis zum 19. Marz 1919.* Warsaw, 1930.

Foreigners on Poland. Warsaw: Ministry of Foreign Affairs, 1946–1948. An official selection of articles written on Poland by American, British, French, and Soviet journalists. The selection does not contain any material on the electoral campaign and the election of 1947.

Fourth Congress of the Communist International. Abridged Report of Meetings Held at Petrograd and Moscow, November 7–December 3, 1922. London, 1923.

Gankin, Olga and Harold H. Fisher (eds.), *The Bolsheviks and the World War — The Origins of the Third International.* London-Stanford, 1940. A valuable collection of documents; it contains numerous documents concerning the Socialist movement of Poland. The well arranged bibliography includes a list of periodicals used, together with brief sketches on the history of these publications.

Gomułka-Wiesław, Władysław, *Przemówienia . . . 1956 . . . 1957 (Speeches, 1956–57)* [Warsaw], 1957.

—— *Przemówienia . . . 1957 . . . 1958* [Warsaw], 1959.

—— *Przemówienia, 1959* [Warsaw], 1960.

—— *Przemówienia, 1960* [Warsaw], 1962.

—— *Artykuły i Przemówienia* [Warsaw], 1962.

—— *Przemówienia,* Warsaw, 1969.

—— *W walce o demokrację ludową* (The Struggle for People's Democracy), Vols. I and II. Warsaw, 1947. A comprehensive collection of articles and speeches.

[Horwitz, Max] Walecki, Henryk, *O taktyce w stosunku do parlamentaryzmu* (On Tactics in Regard to Parliamentarism). Warsaw, 1921. A pamphlet written by a leading member of the Communist Party of Poland to criticize the boycott of the first *Sejm* election by the CPP.

—— *Przyczynek do programu PPS* (A Glossary to the Program of the PPS). Warsaw, 1906. Written by a leader of the PPS-Left.

Kamenev, L. B. (ed.), *Leninski sbornik* (Collection of Lenin's Writings), 3 Vols. Moscow-Leningrad, 1925.

Kautsky, Louise (ed.), *Rosa Luxemburg — Letters to Karl and Louise Kautsky from 1896 to 1918.* New York, 1925.

KPP: uchwały i rezolucje (CPP Statements and Resolutions), 3 Vols. Warsaw, 1954–1956. An official publication of the UPWP carefully edited. Some documents have been altered to suit the changing party line; this has been admitted as far as Vol. I is concerned; see J. Kowalski's article in *Nowe drogi,* May 1956; also *Trybuna ludu,* December 13, 1956 and February 15, 1957, and *Nowe drogi,* June 1956.

KPP w obronie niepodległości Polski: materiały i dokumenty (CPP in Defense of Poland's Independence: Materials and Documents). Warsaw, 1953. A set of strictly edited documents published by the Historical

Section of the United Polish Workers' Party to prove that the CPP was a patriotic party; some falsifications; see *Nowe drogi*, May 1956.

KPP w walce z wojną, faszyzmem i atakami kapitału: XIII plenum komitetu wykonawczego Międzynarodówki Komunistycznej (CPP in Struggle with War, Fascism and Attacks of Capitalism: XIII Plenum of the Executive Committee of the Communist International). Moscow, 1934. Reprinted speeches of J. Leński, E. Próchnik, and G. Henrykowski, held at the XIII Plenum of the Comintern. Valuable as a study of the initial phases of the united front tactics.

Krauz-Kelles, Stanisław, *Wybór pism politycznych* (A Selection of Political Writings). Cracow, 1907. Written by a leading theoretician of the PPS.

[Kravchinskii, Sergei, M.] Stepniak, *The Russian Storm-Cloud: Russia in Her Relations to Neighboring Countries*. London, 1886. Contains an interesting essay entitled "Young Poland and Russian Revolution."

Kridl, Manfred, Józef Wittlin, and Władysław Malinowski, *The Democratic Heritage of Poland*. London, 1944. An anthology of Polish democratic writing; contains several essential documents pertaining to the history of the working-class movement in Poland.

Księga pamiątkowa PPS (The Memorial Book of the PPS). Warsaw, [1923]. Collected reminiscences of numerous leading members of the Polish Socialist Party; covers the period 1892–1918.

Kun, Bela (ed.), *Kommunisticheskii Internatsional v dokumentakh 1919–1932* (The Communist International in Documents 1919–1932). Moscow, 1933. The platform, the resolutions, and the proclamations of the Communist international congresses as well as those of its executive committee, edited and annotated by the leading members of the organization. The book includes, i.a., the proclamation issued during the Second Congress on the subject of the Soviet-Polish war.

Lange, Oskar, and others, *We will join hands with Russia*. New York, 1944. A collection of speeches made by O. Lange, S. Orlemański, L. Krzycki, J. M. Tunnell, and C. Lamont at a meeting organized in New York on December 19, 1943, by the National Council of American Soviet Friendship.

Lapiński, Henryk M. and Horwitz-Walecki, Max G., *Russko-polskie otnosheniia v period Mirovoi Voiny* (Russia-Polish Relations During World War I). Moscow-Leningrad, 1926. A selection of documents from the archives of the tsarist government on the Polish problem; covers the period July 1914–February 1917.

Lenin, V. I., *Collected Works*. New York and London, 1927–1945.
Vol. IV, *The Iskra Period, 1900–1902, Parts I and II*
Vol. XIII, *Materialism and Empirocriticism*
Vol. XVIII, *The Imperialist War*
Vol. XIX, *The Imperialist War, 1916–1917*
Vol. XX, *The Revolution of 1917: From March Revolution to July Days, Parts I and II*

Vol. XXI, *Toward the Seizure of Power: From the July Days to October Revolution, Parts I and II*

Vol. XIII, *1917–1918*

—————— *Sochineniia* (Works), 35 Vols., 4th edition. Leningrad, 1941–1950.

Leński, Julian, *O front ludowy w Polsce, 1934–1937* (For the Popular Front in Poland, 1934–1937). Warsaw, 1956. A collection of articles and speeches, with a biographical introduction.

Livre rouge: recueil des documents diplomatiques relatifs aux relations entre la Russie et la Pologne 1918–1920, Moscow, 1920. exponent.

Londonskii sezd rossiskoi sotsial demokraticheskoi rabochei partii (sostoiavskiisia v 1907 g.): *polnoi tekst protokolov* (The London Congress of the RSDWP held in 1907: Complete Text of Protocols). Paris, 1909.

Luxemburg, Rosa, *Czego chcemy? Komentarz do programu SDKPiL* (What do We Want? A Commentary on the SDKPiL Program). Warsaw, 1906.

—————— *Gesammelte Werke, herausgegeben von Clara Zetkin und Adolf Warski.* Out of the projected six volumes of Rosa Luxemburg's collected works only three actually appeared in print. They include mainly the material of general theoretical value as well as her work pertaining to her activity in the German Social Democratic Party.

Vol. III, *Gegen den Reformismus: eingeleitet und bearbeitet von Paul Froelich.* Berlin, 1925.

Vol. IV, *Gewerkschaftskampf und Massenstreik: eingeleitet und bearbeitet von Paul Froelich.* Berlin, 1928.

Vol. VI, *Die Akkumulation des Kapitals.* Berlin, 1923.

—————— *Die industrielle Entwicklung Polens.* Leipzig, 1896. A key book of the Social Democratic movement in Poland.

[Luxemburg, Rosa] Chmura, Jan, *Kościół a socjalizm* (The Church and Socialism). Cracow, 1905. A popular anticlerical pamphlet.

—————— *Leninism or Marxism.* Glasgow, 1935. Published by the "Anti-Parliamentary Communist Federation of Great Britain." A reprint of two attacks of Luxemburg on the Leninist conception of Marxism.

[——————] Rózga, Maciej, *Niepodległość Polski a sprawa robotnicza* (Poland's Independence and the Workers' Cause). Paris, 1895. A fundamental formulation of the Social Democratic doctrine on the subject.

—————— *The Russian Revolution.* New York, 1940. With an introduction by Bertram D. Wolfe. The pamphlet was written in prison, in spring 1918. A critical appraisal of the Bolshevik policies following their seizure of power.

[Malinowski, Alexsander, ed.], *Materiały do historyi PPS i ruchu rewolucyjnego w zaborze rosyjskim . . . od r. 1893 do 1904* (Materials for the History of the PPS and the Revolutionary Movement in Russian Poland . . . from 1893 to 1904), Vol. I (1893–1897). Warsaw, 1907; Vol. II (1898–1901). Warsaw, 1908.

Marchlewski, Julian, *Iz istorii Polshi* (From Poland's History). Moscow, 1925. Two popular historical essays written in 1923 by a leading Polish Communist: one on the origins of the "dictatorship of the gentry" in Poland, another on the development of the country's capitalism.

——— *Pisma wybrane* (Selected Works), Vols. I and II. Warsaw, 1952 and 1956.

——— *Sostsialnye otnosheniya v Polshe* (Social Conditions in Poland). Moscow, 1920. A reprint of a lecture held in May 1920, at a meeting of the Moscow Council of Workers' and Soldiers' Delegates.

Marchlewski, Julian, J., *Rosja proletariacka a Polska burżuazyjna* (Proletarian Russia and Bourgeois Poland). Moscow, 1921. A propaganda pamphlet.

——— *Rozmowa Macieja z Jędrzejem* (A Talk Between Matthew and Andrew), n.p., 1921. A popular pamphlet issued by the Communist Workers' Party of Poland to explain its program to the peasants.

Markhlevskii, Julian, *Voina i mir mezhdu bourzhuaznoi Polshei i proletarskoi Rossiei* (War and Peace Between Bourgeois Poland and Proletarian Russia). Moscow, 1921. A popular pamphlet about the war 1919–1921.

Markhlevskii, Julian J., *Polsha i mirovaya revolutsia* (Poland and the World Revolution). Moscow, 1920. A reprint of two articles which appeared in Nos. 6 and 7 of the *Kommunisticheskii International* (Communist International), with an additional essay on "Poland in War Against Soviet Russia."

Marx, Karl and Friedrich Engels, *Gesammelte Schriften bis 1850*, 3 Vols., III: *Von Mai 1848 bis October 1850*. Stuttgart, 1902. The third volume contains the essential statements of Marx on Poland.

——— *Manifesto of the Communist Party.* London, 1946.

Materiały archiwalne do stosunków Polsko-Radzieckich (Archive Materials on Polish-Soviet Relations), ed. Natalia Gąsiorowska, Warsaw, 1957 —.

Materiały do programu KPP (Materials for the Program of the CPP). Moscow, 1933. The booklet consists chiefly of the minutes of the discussion held during the Sixth Congress of the CPP and the resulting project of the party's program with addition of amendments introduced by the Program Committee of the Central Committee.

Międzynarodówka komunistyczna — statut i rezolucje uchwalone na II kongresie Międzynarodówki Komunistycznej, 19 lipca–7 sierpnia 1920r. (The Communist International — its Statute and Resolutions passed at the Second Congress of the Communist International, July 19–August 7, 1920), Warsaw, 1921.

Minc, Hilary, *Poland's Economy, Present and Future.* New York: Polish Research Information Service, 1949. Minc's report made at the First Congress of the UPWP.

Narada informacyjna dziewięciu partii (The Information Conference of the Nine Parties). Warsaw, 1947. Minutes of the meeting of the Communist parties of Bulgaria, Rumania, Hungary, Poland, Soviet Union,

France, Czechoslovakia, France, and Italy, that set up the Cominform. Special issue of *Nowe drogi*.

O co walczymy? Deklaracja programowa Polskiej Partii Robotniczej (What are we Fighting for? A Programmatic Declaration of the Polish Workers' Party). Warsaw, November 1943.

Official Documents Concerning Polish-German and Polish-Soviet Relations, 1933–1939. London and Melbourne, n.d. The "Polish White Book" concerning the outbreak of World War II, published by the Polish Government.

[Perl, Feliks] Res, *Esdectwo w walce z socjalizmem naukowym* (Social Democrats in its Fight against Scientific Socialism). Warsaw, 1917. A polemical pamphlet written by a leading member of the PPS, directed against the SDKPiL.

Pierwszy zjazd Międzynarodówki Komunistycznej w Moskwie w marcu 1919r. (The First Congress of the Communist International in Moscow in March 1919). [Hamburg], 1919. A selection of documents pertaining to the foundation of the Communist International.

Piłsudski, Józef, *Memoirs of a Polish Revolutionary and Soldier*. London, 1931. An abbreviated version of Piłsudski's writings.

—— *Pisma zbiorowe* (Collected Works), Vols. I–IV. Warsaw, 1937.

Piłsudski, J., and others, *Z dziejów prasy socjalistycznej w Polsce* (From the History of the Socialist Press). Warsaw, 1919. A collective work composed of contributions written by several leading Socialists; covers the period from 1894 to the end of 1918.

Platforma Międzynarodówki Komunistycznej przyjęta na I kongresie III Międzynarodówki w Moskwie w marcu 1919r. (The Platform of the Communist International as Accepted at the First Congress of the Third International in Moscow in March 1919). [Hamburg], 1919.

Polish-Soviet Relations, 1918–1943: Official Documents. [Washington, D. C.], 1944. Issued by the Polish Embassy by the authority of the Government of the Republic of Poland.

Program of the Young Communist International. New York City, [1929].

Protokoll des Zweiten Weltcongresses der Kommunistischen Internationale, Hamburg, 1921.

Protokoll des Vierten Kongresses der Kommunistischen Internationale, Hamburg, 1923.

Protokoly obedinitelnogo sezda rossiskoi sotsial-demokraticheskoi rabochei partii sostoiavshegosia v Stokgolme v 1906 godu (The Protocols of the Unity Congress of the RSDWP held in Stockholm in 1906). Moscow-Leningrad, 1926.

The Provisional Constitution of February 20, 1947, and the Declaration of Rights. New York: Polish Research and Information Service, 1947.

Pyatyi vsemirnyi kongress kommunisticheskogo internationala . . . stenograficheskii otchet (The Fifth World Congress of the Communist International . . . Stenographic Report), Parts One and Two. Moscow-Leningrad, 1925.

Radek, Karol, *Rozwój socjalizmu od nauki do czynu — nauki rewolucji rosyjskiej* (The Development of Socialism from Theory to Practice — The Lessons of the Russian Revolution). [Hamburg], 1920. A propaganda pamphlet, written in September 1918, to explain the Soviet system to non-Russian workers.

——— *Voina polskikh bielogvardieycev protiv Sovietskoy Rossii* (The War of the Polish White Guards Against Soviet Russia). Moscow, 1920. A propaganda pamphlet.

Reale, Eugenio, *Nascita del Cominformo, Milano,* 1958.

——— *Raporty. Polska 1945–1946* (Reports. Poland, 1945–1946), Paris, 1968.

Rewolucja i wojna (The Revolution and the War). Warsaw, December 1917. The pamphlet published by the SDKPiL expresses solidarity of the SDKPiL with the Bolshevik revolution.

Rewolucja i wojna, No. 2, po gwałcie brzeskim (The Revolution and the War, No. 2. After the Violence of the Brest Treaty). Warsaw, March 1918. A protest of the SDKPiL against the Brest Treaty.

Rewolucja i wojna, No. 3, po gwałcie brzeskim. Warsaw, April 1918. The second pamphlet published by the SDKPiL against the Brest Treaty.

[Rotstadt, Józef] Krasny, Józef (ed.), *Łódzkie powstanie zbrojne — w 20-ą rocznicę* (The Armed Uprising of Łódź — On the Twentieth Anniversary). Moscow, 1925. A collection of documents and articles on the Łódź Uprising of June 1905.

——— *Materiały do dziejów ruchu socjalistycznego w Polsce. . . .* (Materterials for the History of the Socialist Movement in Poland), Part I, *SDKPiL.* The first part of a larger, unfinished work, continued and expanded by O. B. Szmidt.

——— *1905 Rok w Polsce — zbiór artykułow* (The Year 1905 in Poland — A Collection of Articles). Moscow, 1926. A collection of articles written in 1905–06 by R. Luxemburg, St. Pestkowski, J. Krasny, Z. Leder, G. Walecki, B. Grobelna, and A. Markowski. The articles cover various aspects of the Marxist movement in Poland.

Róża Luxemburg, Warsaw, 1920. A collection of articles in Polish translation, written by R. Luxemburg for the German Social Democratic press during the Russian Revolution of 1905. Published by the Communist Workers' Party of Poland.

The Second Congress of the Communist International as Reported and Interpreted by the Official Newspapers of the Soviet Russia, July 19–August 7, 1920. Washington, 1920. A selection of excerpts of the Soviet press, published by the U. S. Department of State.

Sontag, Raymond J. and James S. Beddie (eds.), *Nazi-Soviet Relations, 1939–1941. Documents from the Archives of the German Foreign Office,* U. S. Department of State Washington, D. C., 1948.

Sovjetrussland und Polen, Reden von Kamenew, Lenin, Trotski, Marchlewski, Sokolnikow, Radek und Martow in der vereinigten Sitzung des allrussishen zentral-exekutiv-Komitees des Mosckauer Rates der Arbeiter — und Bauerndelegierten, der Gewerkshaftsverbände und der Betriebsräte am 5 Mai 1920. Moscow, 1920.

Sovietskaya Rossiya i Polsha — offitsialnye dokumenty (Soviet Russia and Poland — Official Documents). Moscow, 1921. An official publication of the People's Commissariat for Foreign Affairs; covers the period 1917–1920.

Sprawozdania stenograficzne z posiedzeń Sejmu Rzplitej, 1921–1934 (Stenographic Records of the Polish Diet, 1921– 1934). Warsaw, 1921–1934.

Sprawozdanie z III konferencji KPRP (Record of the Third Party Conference of the Communist Workers' Party of Poland). Warsaw, 1922.

Sprawozdanie ze zjazdu organizacyjnego Komunistycznej Partii Robotniczej Polski — zjednoczonych SDKPiL i Lewicy PPS (Report from the Organizational Congress of the Communist Workers' Party of Poland — United SDKPiL and PPS-Left). Warsaw, 1919.

Strobel, G. W. ed., *Quellen zur Geschichte des Kommunismus in Polen, 1978–1918,* Cologne, 1968. A collection of primary sources preceded by a scholarly introduction.

Sukiennicki, Wiktor (ed.), *Biała księga. . . .* (A White Book), Paris, 1964. A selection of documents and facts pertaining to Polish-Soviet relations during World War I and World War II.

Swiatło, Józef, *Za kulisami Bezpieki i Partii* (Behind the Facade of the Ministry of Public Security and the Party). [New York, 1955]. A pamphlet containing revelations of a former high official of the Secret Police.

Szmidt, O. B. (ed.), *Socjaldemokracja Królestwa Polskiego i Litwy: materiały i dokumenty, 1893–1904* (Social Democracy of Poland and Lithuania. Materials and Documents, 1893–1904). Moscow, 1934. A very useful collection of materials and documents.

—— *Socjaldemokracja Królestwa Polskiego i Litwy: materiały i dokumenty, 1914–1918* (Social Democracy of the Kingdom of Poland and Lithuania. Materials and Documents, 1914–1918). Moscow, 1936. The third volume of the projected three volume-collection of historical materials; the second never appeared in print.

Ten Years of International Red Aid in Resolutions and Documents: 1922–1932. [Moscow, 1933]. An official Soviet publication.

Theses and Resolutions Adopted by the Second Congress of the Comintern. Chicago, 1928.

Theses and Resolutions Adopted at the Third World Congress of the Communist International (June 22–July 12, 1921). New York, 1921.

Thèses et Résolutions du VIe Congrès de l'Internationale Communiste. Paris, [1929].

Trotsky, Leon, *Sochineniia* (Works), various dates, incomplete.

Uchwały IV konferencji KPP (Resolutions of the IV Conference of the Meeting of the C.C. of the CPP, September 1926), *Wydanie zupełne* (Complete Edition). Warsaw, 1926.

Uchwały II zjazdu KPRP (Resolutions of the Second Congress of the Communist Workers' Party of Poland). Warsaw, 1923.

Uchwały III zjazdu KPP (Resolutions of the Third Congress of the Communist Party of Poland). Warsaw, 1925.

Uchwały IV konferencji KPP (Resolutions of the IV Conference of the CPP). Warsaw, 1926.

W dziesiątą rocznicę powstania Polskiej Partii Robotniczej: materiały i dokumenty, styczeń 1942r.–grudzień 1948r. (On the Tenth Anniversary of the Foundation of the Polish Workers' Party: Materials and Documents, January 1942–December 1948). Warsaw, 1952. A heavily edited selection of documents and articles, published by the United Polish Workers' Party.

W walce o ziemię, wolność i chleb (In the Struggle for Land, Liberty and Bread). Vienna, 1920. A valuable collection of proclamations issued by the Communist Workers' Party of Poland in the autumn of 1919 in connection with the strikes of agrarian and industrial workers proclaimed by the party.

Yulskii, B., *Panska Polsha — avanpost interventsii* (The Landlord Poland — The Vanguard of Intervention), [Kharkov], 1931. An accusation charging Poland with armed intervention against the Soviet Union. The pamphlet contains some interesting passages on the relations between the C.P. of Poland and the Communist parties of Western Ukraine and Western Byelorussia.

Z jaśniepanami przeciwko robotnikom czy z robotnikami przeciwko jaśniepanom (With the Lords Against the Workers or with the Workers Against the Lords), n.p., May 1920. A propaganda pamphlet published by the Propaganda Section of the Red Army during the campaign of 1920.

2. Secondary Sources

Alton, Thad, P., *Polish Postwar Economy*. New York, 1955.

Bełcikowska, Alicia, *Polityczne związki młodzieży w Polsce w 1925r.* (Political Youth Associations in Poland, 1925). Warsaw, 1925. Contains a chapter on Communist organizations and their origins.

―――― *Stronnictwa i związki polityczne w Polsce* (Political Parties and Associations in Poland). Warsaw, 1925. Contains some background information concerning the origins of the parties and associations in question.

Betts, Reginald R., *Central and Southeast Europe, 1945–1948*. London and New York, 1950. A collection of informative essays on Bulgaria, Rumania, Yugoslavia, Czechoslovakia, Hungary, and Poland, each written by a British expert on the subject.

Bicz, Henryk (ed.), *Proletarjat; pierwsza socjalno-rewolucyjna partja w Polsce* (Proletariat: the First Social Revolutionary Party in Poland). Moscow, 1934. A collection of documents and articles pertaining to the activities of the party, the Proletariat.

Bierut, Bolesław, *O konstytucji Polskiej Rzeczypospolitej Ludowej: konstytucja Polskiej Rzeczypospolitej Ludowej* (About the Constitution of the Polish People's Republic: The Constitution of the Polish People's Republic). [Warsaw], 1952.

Bliss Lane, Arthur, *I Saw Poland Betrayed*. New York, 1948. Memoirs of a former ambassador of the United States to Poland; covers the period 1944–1947, till after the elections of January 1947.

Borkenau, Franz, *The Communist International. London*, [1938].

Bór-Komorowski, Tadeusz, *The Secret Army*. London, 1951. Memoirs of the former commander in chief of the Polish Home Army.

Brand, Edward, and Henryk Walecki, *Der Communismus in Polen*. Hamburg, 1921. A pamphlet written by two Communist leaders; published by the Communist International. Contains some valuable material concerning the foundation of the Communist Workers' Party of Poland.

Brand, Edward, *Tło gospodarcze przewrotu majowego* (Economic Background of the May Upheaval). Warsaw, 1927.

Brzeziński, Zbigniew, *The Soviet Bloc: Unity and Conflict*, Cambridge, Mass., 1960.

Bukhbinder, Naum A., *Istorya yevreiskogo robochego dvizhenia v Rossii* (History of the Jewish Workers' Movement in Russia). Leningrad, 1925. A useful outline of the history of the Jewish working-class movement in Russia.

Byrnes, James F., *Speaking Frankly*. New York and London, 1947.

Ciechanowski, Jan M., *Powstanie Warszawskie. Zarys podłoża politycznego i dyplomatycznego* (The Warsaw Uprising. An Outline of Political and Diplomatic Background), London, 1971.

Ciołkosz, Adam, *The Expropriation of a Socialist Party: The Present Situation of the Socialist Movement in Poland*. New York, September-October 1946. A pamphlet written by a leading Polish Socialist in exile, denouncing the Communist-sponsored Polish Socialist Party in Poland.

Czapski, Józef, *Terre inhumaine*. Paris, 1949. Two years in the Soviet Union (1941–1943) described by an intelligent observer; a valuable contribution to the subjects of forced labor and deportations in Russia.

Dąbal, Tadeusz, *Powstanie Krakowskie* (The Cracow Uprising). Mińsk, 1926. A propagandistic account of the Cracow Uprising of 1923; written by a leading Polish Communist.

Daniszewski, Tadeusz, *Feliks Dzierżyński, jego życie, praca i walka* (Felix Dzierżyński, His Life, Work and Struggle). Warsaw, 1948. A propaganda booklet, written by leading Communist historian, a lecturer in history of the Marxist movement and the Central Party School of the Polish Workers' Party.

Daniszewski, Tadeusz and others (eds.), *Rewolucja 1905–1907 roku na ziemiach polskich: materiały i studia* (The Revolution of 1905–1907 in Poland: Materials and Studies). Warsaw, 1952. Propagandistic.

Daszyński, Ignacy, *Polityka proletaryatu — kilka uwag o taktyce rewolucyi w Polsce* (Policy of Proletariat — Some Remarks on the Tactics of Revolution in Poland). Warsaw, 1907. A pamphlet written in 1906 by the leader of Polish Socialists in Galicia; it analyzes the experiences of the revolutionary movement in Russian Poland.

Dominko, Józef, *Z minionych lat: wspomnienia działacza-spółdzielcy z okresu pracy na terenie Lublina* (From My Past Years: Reminiscences of a Cooperative Social Worker from the Lublin Region). [Warsaw], 1945. Contains interesting details concerning the career of B. Bierut.

Dziewanowski, M. K., *Joseph Piłsudski: A European Federalist, 1918–1922*, Stanford, Cal., 1969.

Fejtö, François, *Historie des Démocraties Populaires*. Paris, 1952. A popular attempt to sketch the origins and the development of people's democracies from 1944 till 1952.

Fisher, Ruth, *Stalin and German Communism: A Study in the Origins of the State Party*. Cambridge, Mass., 1948. Mainly the introductory part.

Froelich, Paul, *Rosa Luxemburg, Her Life and Work*. London, 1940. A useful and vivid biography written by a noncritical admirer.

Gójski, Józef, *Strajki i bunty chłopskie w Polsce* (Strikes and Peasant Mutinies in Poland). Warsaw, 1949. Popular; propagandistic.

Grabski, Stainsław, *Na nowej drodze dziejowej* (On a New Historical Road). Warsaw, 1946. A political last will of an elderly statesman advising his nation to have close cooperation with Russia and other Slavic nations, but not a straightforward reception of the Communist system.

Griffits, Stanton, *Lying in State*. New York, 1952. Memoirs of a United States ambassador; chiefly chapter: "The Iron Curtain and I descend on Poland."

Gross, Feliks, *The Polish Worker: A Study of a Social Stratum*. New York, 1944. Contains a great deal of factual and background information.

Gryziewicz, Stanisław and others (eds.), *Ramy życia w Polsce* (The Background of Life in Poland). Vols. I-V. Paris, 1952–53. Five special issues of the *émigré* monthly *Kultura*, devoted to a detailed analysis of Poland after World War II.

Gumplowicz, Władysław, *Kwestya Polska a socjalizm* (The Polish Question and Socialism). Warsaw, 1908. A collection of essays written by a prominent Polish scholar and leading Socialist between September 1905 and November 1907. Contains i.a. a polemic against Luxemburg and her theory of the "organic incorporation" of the Congress Kingdom into the Russian Empire.

Healey, Denis (ed.), *The Curtain Falls: The Story of the Socialists in Eastern Europe*. London, 1951. Mainly the factual and well documented essay by Adam Ciolkosz on the fate of Polish socialism.

Holzer, Jerzy, *Polska Partia Socjalistyczna w latach 1917–1919* (The Polish Socialist Party, 1917–1919), Warsaw, 1962.

Horwitz, Max H., *W kwestyi żydowskiej* (On the Jewish Question). Cracow, 1907. A criticism of the Jewish bourgeois groups by a Polish Socialist of Jewish origin.

Jabłoński, Tadeusz, *Za wolność i lud* (For Freedom and People). Warsaw,

1947. A short history of the Polish Socialist Party, written with the obvious purpose of stressing the necessity of a "united front" with the Communists.

Janta, Aleksander, *Wracam z Polski* (I Am Returning from Poland). Paris 1949. An interesting report of an independent Polish writer who was allowed to travel freely and publish his observations abroad.

Jordan, Zbigniew, *Oder-Neisse Line: A Study of the Political, Economic and European Significance of Poland's Western Frontiers*. London, 1952. A well documented booklet published by the Polish freedom movement "Independence and Democracy."

Józefowicz, J. S., *Wielka rewolucja październikowa i formowanie się państwa polskiego w 1918r.* (The Great October Revolution and the Formation of the Polish State in 1918). [Warsaw], 1948. A Polish translation of an article written by a Communist publicist and published in *Izviestia Akademii Nauk SSSR* (The Bulletin of the Academy of Science of the USSR) in its May-June 1948 issue.

Jóźwiak (Witold), Franciszek, *Polska Partia Robotnicza w walce a wyzwolenie narodowe i społeczne* (The Polish Workers' Party in the Struggle for a National and Social Liberation). Warsaw, 1952. A propagandistic account by a leading member of the PPR and PZPR.

Komarnicki, Tytus, *Rebirth of the Polish Republic*, London, 1957.

Kon, Feliks, *Felix Edmundovich Dzerhinskii — biografisheskii ocherk* (F. E. Dzierżyński — A Biographical Sketch). Moscow, 1929.

——— *Natsionalnyi vopros v Polshe* (The National Problem in Poland). Moscow, 1927. A popular pamphlet written to prove that the eastern provinces of Poland should be incorporated into the Soviet Union.

——— *Pod sztandarem rewolucji — wspomnienia proletariatczyka* (Under the Banner of Revolution — Reminiscences of a Member of the "Proletariat"). Moscow, 1923. Another version of the author's story of conspiratorial work with the "Proletariat." A popular biography.

[Kon Feliks] F. K., *Sądy wojenne w Królestwie Polskim* (Military Courts in Russian Poland). Cracow, 1909. A collection of statistical data and documents pertaining to the Russian Military Courts after the revolution of 1905.

Kon, Feliks, *Vospominaniia* (The Reminiscences). Moscow, 1921. An ininteresting essay on the conspiratorial work of the author in the party, the "Proletariat."

——— *Za pyatdesyat let* (During Fifty Years). Moscow, 1936, Vols. I-IV, 2nd edition. Interesting memoirs of one of the leading Polish Communists; covers the period up to World War I.

——— *Zapadnaya Belorussia, kolonia panskoi Polshi* (Western Byelorussia, a Colony of Feudal Poland). Moscow, 1928. A propagandistic pamphlet written on the occasion of a trial of members of the "Hromada," a revolutionary Byelorussian organization. A restatement of the Soviet policy toward nationality minorities of eastern Poland.

Korboński, Stefan, *W imieniu Kremla* (In the name of the Kremlin). Paris, 1956. The second volume of the memoirs.

—— *W imieniu Rzeczypospolitej* (In the name of the Polish Republic). Paris, 1954. Memoirs of a former leader of the Polish Underground.

—— *Fighting Warsaw. The Story of the Polish Underground State, 1939–1945* [New York], 1965.

Kormanowa, Zanna (ed.), *Historia Polski, 1864–1945* (A History of Poland, 1864–1945). Warsaw, 1952. A handbook of Polish history for the use of both teachers and students of high schools; thoroughly Stalinist.

—— *Materiały do bibliografii druków socjalistycznych na ziemiach polskich w latach 1866–1918*, z przedomową L. Krzywickiego (Materials for A Bibliography of Socialist Publications in Poland, 1866–1918, with an Introduction by L. Krzywicki). Warsaw, 1935. An incomplete but very useful guide in the labyrinth of the Socialist publications.

Korowicz, M. S., *Polska pod sowieckim jarzmem* (Poland under the Soviet yoke). London, 1955. Well written and informative memoirs of a professor of the Jagiellonian University.

Korsch, Rudolf, *Żydowskie ugrupowania wywrotowe w Polsce* (Jewish Revolutionary Groups in Poland). Warsaw, 1925. An interesting study written by a Jewish expert of the Polish government.

Koryniev, Józef, *Julian Marchlewski*. Moscow, 1930. A short biography of J. Marchlewski, written by a Communist; with a preface by Klara Zetkin.

Kowalczyk, Józef, Tadeusz Daniszewski and Felicja Kalicka (eds.), *KPP wspomnienia z pola walki* (Communist Party of Poland Reminiscences from the Battlefield). Warsaw, 1951. A collection of essays-reminiscences of members of the CPP and the left wing of the PPS.

Kowalski, Józef, *Zarys historii polskiego ruchu robotniczego w latach 1918–1928* (An Outline of History of the Polish Working Class Movement, 1918–1928), Warsaw, 1959.

—— *Trudne Lata. Problemy rozwoju polskiego ruchu robotniczego 1929–1935*, Warsaw, 1966. Both books were written by a leading Party historian and focus largely on the Communist fringe of the Polish working class movement.

Krivitsky, Walter G., *I Was Stalin's Agent*. London, 1940.

[Kulczycki, Ludwik] Mazowiecki, M., *Historya polskiego ruchu socjalistycznego w zaborze rosyjskim* (History of the Polish Socialist Movement in Russian Poland). Cracow, 1904. Supplements the book of Res-Perl (Feliks Perl).

Kuśnierz, Bolesław, *Stalin and the Poles: An Indictment of the Soviet Leaders*. London, 1949. A well documented book by a Polish politician in exile.

Kwapiński, Jan, *Organizacja bojowa — katorga — rewolucja rosyjska —*

1904–1919 (The Fighting Organization — the Deportation — The Russian Revolution, 1904–1919), 2nd edition. London, 1943. Written by a leader of the PPS.

Kwiatkowski, J. K. (Ren), *Komuniści w Polsce* (The Communists in Poland). Brussels, 1946. A collection of articles on the Polish Communist movement.

Łańcucki, Stanisław, *Moje wspomnienia* (My Reminiscences), Vol. I. Moscow, 1931. Memoirs of a leading Polish Communist from Galicia, with an introduction by F. Kon. The first volume covers the period from the end of the nineteenth century until 1921.

[Lausic, N.], *Procès 490 de la Hromade Bielorusse à Vilna*. Prague, 1928. A propaganda pamphlet written by a spokesman of the "Hromada," with an introduction by Professor Z. Neyedly.

Leinwand, Artur, *Polska Partia Socialistyczna wobec wojny polsko-radzieckiej 1919–1920* (The Polish Socialist Party and the Polish-Soviet War of 1919–1920), Warsaw, 1964.

Lerska, Hanka (ed.), *Druki Polski podziemej i wydawnictwa powstańcze* (Publications of the Underground Poland and the Warsaw Insurrection). n.p., n.d. A useful bibliography of the Polish resistance movement.

Malara, Jean and Lucienne Rey, *La Pologne: d'une occupation à l'autre, 1944–1952*. Paris, 1952. A factual and well documented account of the Communist take-over and consolidation of power in Poland.

Malinowski, Marian, *Geneza PPR* (The Origins of the PPR), Warsaw, 1972 (a recent attempt of a party historian to deal with the rebirth and the first moments of existence of organized Communist activity in Poland in 1939–1942).

Martov, Lev, and Theodor Dan, *Geschichte der russischen Sozialdemokratie mit einem Nachtrag von Th. Dan: die Sozialdemokraite Russlands nach dem Jahre 1908*. Berlin, 1926.

Martov, Lev and others (eds.), *Obshchestvennoe dvizhenie v Rossii v nachale XX-go veka* (The Social Movement in Russia at the Beginning of the Twentieth Century). St. Petersburg, 1909. Mainly Vol. I, chapter 3, "The National Movement"; Vol. II, Part I, "The Workers of the Borderland," in 1905; also Vol. IV, Part II, an article by K. Zalewski on the "National Movements."

Matuszewski, Stefan, *Na progu wolności* (On the Threshold of Freedom). Warsaw, 1945. A collection of speeches and articles, written by the Minister of Information of the Lublin Committee.

Mikołajczyk, Stanisław, *The Rape of Poland*. New York and Toronto, 1948. The memoirs of the leader of the Polish Peasant Party, minister of interior of the Polish government in London and its premier (July 1943–November 1944), and, later on, vice-prime minister of the Provisional Government of National Unity (June 1945–February 1947).

Miłosz, Czesław, *The Captive Mind*. Translated from the Polish by Jane
    Zielonka. New York, 1953. A brilliant analysis of some aspects of in-
    tellectual life in Stalinist Poland.
——— *Zdobycie władzy* (The Seizure of Power). Paris, 1955. A novel on
    the years 1944–1946 in Poland.
Minc, Hilary, *On People's Democracy in Eastern Europe and China*. Lon-
    don, 1951. A revealing essay by Poland's economic boss.
——— *Osiągnięcia i plany gospodarcze* (Economic Achievements and
    Plans). Warsaw, 1949. A selection of speeches.
Misko, M. V., *Oktiabrskaia revolutsia i vosstanovienie nezavisimosti Pol-
    ski* (The October Revolution and the Establishment of Poland's
    Independence), Moscow, 1957.
Monnerot, Jean, *Sociology and Psychology of Communism*. Boston, 1953.
Mysłakowski, Zygmunt, and Feliks Gross, *Robotnicy piszą: pamiętniki
    robotników. Studium wstępne* (Workers write: Memoirs of Workers.
    An Introductory Study). Cracow, 1938. Useful as background.
Naurois, Claude, *Dieu contre Dieu? Drame des Catoliques Progressistes
    dans une église de silence*. Paris, 1957.
Nevskij, Vladimir N. (ed.), *Deyateli revolutsionnogo dvizheniya v Rossii*
    (Participants of Revolutionary Movement in Russia), Moscow, 1931.
    Vol. V. Bio- as well as bibliographic dictionary of members of revolu-
    tionary movements in Russia, from 1880–1904; contains also data on
    Polish revolutionaries and their relations with the Russia parties.
Newman, Bernard, *Russia's Neighbor — the New Poland*. London, 1946.
    A vivid report by an experienced British writer; it covers the end of
    1945 and the beginning of 1946.
[Perl, Feliks] Res, *Dzieje ruchu socjalistycznego w zaborze rosyjskim*
    (History of the Socialist Movement in Russian Poland), Vol. I.
    Warsaw, 1910. Very helpful work written from the PPS viewpoint;
    covers the period until 1893.
Piasecki, Bolesław, *Zagadnienia Istotne . . .* (The Essential Problems . . .),
    Warsaw, 1954.
Piaskowski, Stanisław, *Zarys historii polskiego socjalizmu* (An Outline of
    the History of Polish Socialism). Breslau, 1946. Popular but factual.
Piłsudska, Aleksandra, *Memoirs . . .* London, 1940. The first part gives
    a vivid picture of conditions under which the Socialist movement of
    Russian Poland worked from 1892 until 1918.
Pogodin, Alexander L., *Glavnyia techeniia polskoi politicheskoi mysli
    (1863–1907)* (Main Currents of Polish Political Thought, 1863–
    1907). St. Petersburg, 1908. An objective work of a Russian scholar;
    the book is based on extensive and well selected material.
Polskie siły zbrojne w drugiej wojnie światowej (Polish Armed Forces Dur-
    ing World War II), Vol. III: *Armia Krajowa* (The Home Army).
    London, 1950. A detailed work based on primary sources; produced

by the Historical Commission of the General Staff of the Polish Armed Forces in Great Britain.

Próchnik, Adam, *Idee i ludzie: z dziejów ruchu rewolucyjnego w Polsce* (Idea and People: From the History of the Revolutionary Movement in Poland). Warsaw, 1946. A series of popular sketches on the history of the Socialist movement in Poland, from 1864 until 1918; written by a member of the PPS with the purpose of popularizing the glorious aspects of the party's history.

[Próchnik, Adam] H. Swoboda, *Pierwsze piętnastolecie Polski niepodległej.* Warsaw, 1934. A history of Poland 1918–1933 written by a prominent member of the PPS.

Radek, Karl, *Rosa Luxemburg — Karl Liebknecht — Leo Jogiches.* Hamburg, 1921. Three brilliant biographical essays written by a former party comrade and personal friend.

Rafes, Moisei G., *Ocherki po istorii Bunda* (Sketches of the History of the Bund). Moscow, 1923. An outline of history of the Jewish Bund, written by a former member who turned Communist in 1921.

Raina, Peter, *Gomułka—Politische Biographie,* Cologne, 1970. An outline of Gomułka's life by an Indian scholar educated in Poland and eyewitness of many events of the Gomułka era.

Reguła, Jan, Alfred, *Historia Komunistycznej Partii Polski* (A History of the Communist Party of Poland). Warsaw, 1934. An attempt to write a history of the Communist Party of Poland on the part of an investigating judge for political cases. In spite of its obvious bias, the book contains a wealth of valuable material in the form of long quotations from the underground Communist publications and from the minutes of the Central Committee's meetings some of them not published in the official selections.

Rewolucja 1905–1907 roku na ziemiach polskich: materiały i studia (The Revolution of 1905–1907 in Poland: Materials and Studies). Warsaw, 1955. A symposium prepared by twenty-one students of the Institute of Social Studies of the Central Committee of the UPWP.

Rose, William J., *Poland Old and New.* London, 1948. An expanded version of *The Rise of Polish Democracy.*

——— *The Rise of Polish Democracy.* London, 1944. Useful as background.

Rychliński, Stanisław, *Les syndicats professionnels des travailleurs en Pologne.* Warsaw, 1927. A concise factual essay on the development of Polish trade-unions from the end of the nineteenth century up to 1927.

Rzepecki, Jan, *Wspomnienia i przyczynki historyczne* (Reminiscences and Historical Contributions), Warsaw, 1956. Historical sketches of the former head of Information and Propaganda Office of Home Army.

Scaevola, *A Study in Forgery.* London, 1945. A story of the transformation of the Union of Polish Patriots in Moscow into the Polish Committee of National Liberation and, later on, into the Provisional Government of Poland.

Seton-Watson, Hugh, *The East European Revolution.* London, 1950. Scholarly and informative.

Sharp, Samuel L., *Poland, White Eagle on the Red Field.* Cambridge, Mass., 1953. Contains some interesting observations on Polish Communists.

———— *New Constitutions in the Soviet Sphere.* Washington, D.C., [1950]. A penetrating analysis.

Skarżynski, A., *Polityczne przyczyny powstania warszawskiego* (Political Causes of the Warsaw Uprising), Warsaw, 1964.

Sowińska (Barbara), S., *Lata walki* (The Years of Struggle). Warsaw, 1948. Vivid reminiscences of a Communist underground fighter, active during the German occupation.

Stapiński, A., *Wywrotowe partie polityczne* (The Subversive Political Parties). Warsaw, 1933. A handbook written for the use of a Polish police training center. Contains numerous valuable excerpts from various Communist publications.

Starr, Richard F., *Poland 1944–1962: The Sovietization of a Captive People,* New Orleans, 1962.

Stypułkowski, Zbigniew, *Invitation to Moscow.* London, 1952. Memoirs of a former underground leader, one of the sixteen arrested by the NKVD in March 1945.

Świetlikowa, Frańciszka, *Komunistyczna Partia Robotnicza Polski 1918–1923* (The Communist Workers' Party of Poland, 1918–1923), Warsaw, 1968. Written by a Party historian.

Syrop, Konrad, *Spring in October. The Story of the Polish Revolution 1956.* London, 1957.

Taylor, J. J., *The Economic Development of Poland.* New York, Ithaca, 1952.

Teslar, Tadeusz, *Propaganda bolszewicka podczas wojny polsko-rosyjskiej 1920 roku* (Bolshevik Propaganda During the Polish-Russian War of 1920). Warsaw, 1938. Contains numerous documents and large quotations of primary material.

Tuominen, Avro, *Kremlin Kellot* (The Bells of the Kremlin). Helsinki, 1956. Memoirs of a former leader of the Communist Party of Finland and member of the Presidium of the Comintern. The book covers the period 1933–1939 and contains some interesting material on the dissolution of the CPP.

Die ukrainische nationale Frage. Materialen zur Frage der sogenanten ukrainischen nationalen Abweichung ("Schumskismus") in der kommunistischen Partei der Urkaine und der kommunistischen Partei der West-Ukraine. Lemberg, 1928. A polemical pamphlet issued by the Communist Party of Western Ukraine.

Ulam, Adam, *Titoism and the Cominform.* Cambridge, Mass., 1952. Includes a penetrating account of the Gomułka affair.

Umiastowski, Roman, *Poland, Russia and Great Britain, 1941–1945*. London, 1946. A selection of annotated documents and quotations.

Unszlicht, Julian, *O program ludu polskiego: rola socjal-litwactwa w niedawnej rewolucji* (For a Program of the Polish People: The Role of the Social-Litwaks During the Recent Revolution). Cracow, 1913. A strongly anti-Semitic attack on the SDKPiL, especially on Luxemburg and Jogiches-Tyszko.

[Unszlicht, Julian] Sedecki, W., *Socjal-litwactwo w Polsce: z teorii i praktyki SDKPiL*. (Social-Litwaks in Poland: From the Theory and the Practice of the SDKPiL). Cracow, n.d. Another vitriolic attack on the SDKPiL.

Vonsovskii, B. and Rudomino, G., *Kuda Piłsudski vedet Polshu* (Where Piłsudski is Leading Poland). Mińsk, 1927. A popular propaganda pamphlet.

Warriner, Doreen, *Revolution in Eastern Europe*. London, 1950. A study of economic changes in Eastern Europe since 1944–45.

Warski, Adolf, *Rosa Luxemburgs Stellung zu den taktischen Problemen der Revolution*. Hamburg, 1922. The Communist interpretation of the pamphlet on the *Russian Revolution*.

Wasilewski, Leon, *Vzaimnyia otnoshenia polskikh i russkikh sotsialistov* (Mutual Relations Between the Polish and the Russian Socialists). London, 1902. Written from the PPS viewpoint.

——— *Zarys dziejów polskiej partii socjalistycznej w związku z historią socjalizmu polskiego w trzech zaborach i na emigracji* (An Outline of History of the PPS against the Background of the History of Polish Socialism in Three Parts of Poland and in the Emigration). Warsaw, n.d. Written from the PPS viewpoint.

Wilder, J. A., *The Polish Regained Provinces*. London, 1948. A short and concise survey of the achievement of the new Poland in the western territories during the years 1945–46.

Wołoszczowski, M., *O jednolity front proletariatu: o anty-faszystowski front ludowy (odprawa renegatowi Artuskiemu)* (For a United Front of the Proletariat: For an Anti-Fascist Popular Front (A Reply to the renegade Artuski). [Paris], 1936. An anti-Trotskyite polemical pamphlet.

Wood, William, *Poland: Eagle in the East. A Survey of Modern Times,* New York, 1968. A light but perceptive book on contemporary Poland.

Załuski, Zbigniew, *Czterdziesty Czwarty* (The Year 1944), Warsaw, 1968.

Zambrowski, Roman and Świątkowski, Henryk, *O statucie i zagadnieniach organizacyjnych PZPR* (On the Statute and Organization of the United Polish Workers' Party). Warsaw, 1949.

[Żarski, I.] Czerwiec, O., *Komitet 21 — z doświadczeń walk masowych proletariatu w Polsce* (The Committee of Twenty-One — From the Experience of Mass Struggle of the Proletariat of Poland). n.p., n.d. [1924].

Zetkin, Klara, *Um Rosa Luxemburgs Stellung zur russischen Revolution.* Hamburg, 1922. A defense of the Bolshevik viewpoint published by the Communist International.

Zetkin, Klara and others, *Rosa Luxemburg.* Moscow, 1921. A collection of articles written to commemorate the second anniversary of the death of R. Luxemburg.

Zinoviev, Grigori, *Le prolétariat européen devant la révolution. Discours prononcé au Congrès du Parti Social-Démocrate indépendent d'Allemagne à Halle, le 14 Octobre 1920.*

Zubov, Nikolai, I., *F. E. Dzerzhinskii: Biografiia* (F. E. Dzierżynski: A Biography), Moscow, 1965.

Zweig, Ferdynand, *Poland Between Two Wars.* London, 1944. A popular but useful background of Polish socioeconomic history.

3. Periodicals

Barykada wolności: tygodnik polityczny polskich socjalistów (The Barricade of Freedom: A Weekly of Polish Socialists). Warsaw, 1940–1944.

Biuletyn komisji organizacyjnej zjazdu rad delegatów robotniczych miast i wsi Polski (Bulletin of the Organizing Commission of the Congress of the Councils of Urban and Rural Workers Delegates of Poland). Warsaw, 1919. Irregular.

The Communist International, Kommunisticheskii Internatsional, and *Die Kommunistische Internationale.* Petrograd-Leningrad-Moscow, 1919–1938. The monthly organs of the Executive Committee of the Comintern.

Czerwony sztandar: organ socjaldemokracji królestwa Polskiego i Litwy (The Red Flag: The Organ of the Social Democracy of the Kingdom of Poland and Lithuania). 1902–1918; 1918–1935. Irregular, published at various places; legal in 1918, then published underground. The press organ of the Central Committee of the CPP.

Dąbrowszczak (The Soldier of Dąbrowski). Irregular, appeared at various places, 1937–1939. After 1938 the paper was turned into a Polish version of the *Volunteer of Freedom.*

Dzieje najnowsze (Recent History). Warsaw, 1947–1974. Quarterly.

Dziennik Polski i Dziennik Żołnierza (Polish Daily and Soldier's Daily). London, 1940–1974.

Dziennik ustaw Rzeczypospolitej Polskiej (The Journal of Laws of the Polish Republic). Warsaw, 1918–1939; Lublin and Warsaw, 1944–1974.

East Europe, New York, 1952–1974. Monthly published by the Free Europe Committee up to 1970; independent publication after that date; appearing irregularly after 1970.

Gazeta robotnicza: organ komitetu Warszawskiego SDKPiL (The Workers' Journal: The Organ of the Warsaw Committee of the SDKPiL). Warsaw, 1912. Irregular.

Głos komunisty (The Voice of a Communist). Kharkov, 1920. A daily for the Soviet soldiers of Polish nationality.

Głos ludu (The Voice of the People), 1944–1948. The main daily organ of the PPR.

Głos robotniczy (The Workers' Voice). Warsaw, 1916–1918. Weekly.

Gwardzista (The Guardsman); 1942–1944. Irregularly appearing underground organ of the People's Guard.

International Press Correspondence. Vienna-London, 1922–1938. An English language organ of the Comintern; changed its title into *World News and Views* in 1938.

Inter Catholic Press Agency. New York, 1950–1957.

Komunista: organ komitetu Zagłębia Dąbrowskiego Komunistycznej Partii Robotniczej Polski (The Communist: The Organ of the Communist Workers' Party of Poland in the Dąbrowa Basin). January-March, 1919. Irregular.

Krasnyi arkhiv (The Red Archive). Moscow, 1922–1941. Vol. 16, 1926; and Vol. 29, 1928. A historical journal of the Central Archive Department of the USSR.

Kultura (Culture), a monthly published in Paris, 1947–1974.

Monitor polski (The Polish Gazetter). Warsaw, 1918–1939.

Na Antenie (On the Antenna), a monthly published since 1962 by the Polish Section of Radio Free Europe.

Nasza trybuna: tygodnik socjaldemokratyczny (Our Tribune: A Social Democratic Weekly). Warsaw, 1917–1918.

Die Neue Zeit (The New Time). Stuttgart, 1896–1919. Weekly.

News from Behind the Iron Curtain. New York, 1952–1956. Monthly. Renamed *East Europe* in 1952. Published by the National Committee for a Free Europe.

News from Poland. New York, 1955–1958. A weekly information bulletin of the Free Europe Committee.

Niepodległość (Independence). Warsaw, 1929–1939. Quarterly.

Nowe drogi (New Roads). Warsaw, 1947–1974. The theoretical organ of the Central Committee of the PPR. Bi-monthly 1947–1951; monthly since 1952.

Nowy przegląd (New Review), 1930–1935. The main theoretical organ of the CPP; irregular, appearing at various places.

Oświata socjalistyczna (The Socialist Education). Moscow, 1918. A periodical appearing at irregular intervals in Moscow; published by the Polish Commission of the People's Commissariat of Nationalities.

Poland Today, a monthly issued by the Polish Government Information Center of New York, 1946–1950.

Po prostu (Speaking frankly). Warsaw, 1955–1957. A weekly organ of young Marxist intellectuals.

Przegląd socjalnodemokratyczny. Miesięcznik, organ socjaldemokracji Królestwa Polskiego i Litwy (The Social Democratic Review. Monthly, the organ of the Social Democracy of the Kingdom of Poland and Lithuania). 1902–1904 and 1908–1910.

Robotnik (The Worker). Warsaw, 1923–1938; 1945–1948. The daily organ of the PPS.

Robotnik polski (The Polish Worker). New York, 1950–1958. Biweekly.

Robotnik polski w Wielkiej Brytanii (Polish Worker in Great Britain). London, 1944–1954. Weekly.

Sprawa robotnicza (The Workers' Cause), July 1893-July 1896. Irregular.

Sztandar socjalizmu: organ Komunistycznej Partii Robotniczej Polski (Banner of Socialism: The Organ of the Communist Workers' Party of Poland), Nos. 1–24. Warsaw, December 1918–January 1919. Irregular. Later appeared as Sztandar komunizmu.

Trybuna: organ C.K.W. grupy SDKPiL w Rosji (The Tribune: The Organ of the Central Executive Committee of the SDKPiL group in Russia). Moscow, 1918. Daily.

Trybuna chłopska (The Peasant Tribune), 1942–1944. Irregularly appearing organ of the PPR.

Trybuna ludu (The Tribune of the People). Warsaw, 1948–1974. The daily organ of the United Polish Workers' Party.

Trybuna wolności (The Tribune of Freedom), 1942–1944. Irregularly appearing underground organ of the PPR.

Tygodnik powszechny (Catholic Weekly), Cracow, 1945–1953 and 1956 —.

Wiadomości (News). London, 1946–1974. Weekly.

Wiadomości komisariatu: organ urzędowy Komisariatu Polskiego przy komisariacie ludowym do spraw narodowościowych (The News of the Commissariat: The Official Organ of the Polish Commissariat at the People's Commissariat for Nationalities), Moscow, 1918. Bi-monthly.

Wiadomości rady delegatów robotniczych m. Warszawy (News of the Council of Workers' Delegates of Warsaw). Warsaw, 1918. Irregular.

Wiadomości rady delegatów robotniczych okręgu sosnowieckiego (News of the Council of Workers' Delegates of the Sosnowiec Region). Sosnowiec, 1918. Irregular.

Wiadomości robotnicze: organ polskich związków zawodowych (The Workers' News. The organ of the Polish Trade Unions). Warsaw, January 1918–December 1918. Irregular.

Z dokumentów chwili (From the Documents of the Moment). Warsaw, 1917–1918. A weekly digest of periodicals; many documents given in full.

Z pola walki (From the Battlefield). Moscow, 1926–1933. A quarterly organ of the Polish Commission of the Central Committee of the All-Soviet Communist Party (b); resumed in 1956 in Warsaw.

Zeszyty historyczne (Historic Folders), Paris, 1962–1974. A quarterly published by Literary Institute *Kultura*.

Zhizn natsionalnostiei: organ narodnogo komissariata po delam natsionalnostiei (Life of Nationalities. The Organ of the People's Commissariat of Nationalities). Moscow, 1918–1922. Weekly.

Notes

PART I: THE ORIGINS

CHAPTER I THE BEGINNINGS OF SOCIALISM IN POLAND, 1832–1892

1. Karl Marx and Friedrich Engels, *Manifesto of the Communist Party* (London, 1946), pp. 37–38. For early history of Polish Socialist movement see a comprehensive work in progress by Lidia and Adam Ciołkosz, *Zarys dziejów socializmu polskiego* (An Outline of History of Polish Socialism), Vol. I, London, 1966, Vol. II, 1972.

2. Res [Feliks Perl], *Dzieje ruchu socjalistycznego w zaborze rosyjskim* (History of the Socialist Movement in Russian Poland) (Warsaw, 1910), I, 11–12.

3. Marx and Engels, *Manifesto of the Communist Party*, p. 37.

4. Quoted by Paul Frœlich, *Rosa Luxemburg: Her Life and Work* (London, 1940), p. 38.

5. J. Grabiec [J. Dąbrowski], *Współczesna Polska w cyfrach i faktach* (Contemporary Poland in Figures and Facts) (Cracow, 1911), pp. 10–11.

6. *Ibid.*, pp. 157–158.

7. Stepniak [Kravchinskii], "The Young Poland and Russian Revolution," *The Russian Storm-Cloud: or, Russia in her Relations to Neighboring Countries* (London, 1886), pp. 145–146.

8. M. Mazowiecki [Ludwik Kulczycki], *Historya ruchu socjalistycznego w zaborze rosyjskim* (History of the Socialist Movement in Russian Poland) (Cracow, 1903), p. 12.

9. Rosa Luxemburg, *Die industrielle Entwicklung Polens* (Leipzig, 1898), pp. 10–14.

10. *Ibid.*, p. 17.

11. *Ibid.*, p. 28.

12. Aleksandra Piłsudska, *Memoirs* . . . (London, 1940), p. 98.

13. Some beneficial, though cautious, reforms were made between 1882 and 1886 under the auspices of Bunge, but they were soon nullified when he was dismissed on a charge of "socialism." Between 1890 and 1893 a series of laws permitted employment of children at night and relaxed factory inspection. A number of strikes which broke out in 1897 made the government limit the hours of work to eleven and one-half during the day and ten at night.

14. O. B. Szmidt, ed., *Socjaldemokracja Królestwa Polskiego i Litwy: materiały i dokumenty 1893–1904* (Moscow, [n.d.]), I, ii–iii.

15. Quoted by Feliks Gross, *The Polish Worker* . . . (New York, 1944), p. 111.

16. A popular saying described socialism as a wind blowing simultaneously from two directions: from the East and from the West, or "from the Neva and from Geneva" (*z Genewy i z nad Newy*).

17. For the text of the program of the "Proletariat," see Mazowiecki [Kulczycki], *Historya polskiego ruchu socjalistycznego w zaborze rosyjskim* (Cracow, 1904), pp. 54–61.

18. *Patriotyzm i socjalizm* (Patriotism and Socialism) (Geneva, 1881), *passim*.

19. Quoted by Res, *Dzieje ruchu socjalistycznego w zaborze rosyjskim*, p. 42.

20. *Ibid.*, pp. 168–181; also Feliks Kon, *Escape from the Gallows* (London, 1933), p. 6.

21. Waryński died there, three years later, in 1889.

22. Kon, *Escape from the Gallows*, pp. 5–6.

23. Res, *Dzieje ruchu socjalistycznego w zaborze rosyjskim*, p. 195; Kon, *Escape from the Gallows*, p. 6. Kon's *Pod sztandarem rewolucji-wspomnienia proletariatczyka* (Moscow, 1932), affords some valuable insight into the revolutionary psychology of the group. See also his memoirs *Za pyatdesyat let* (Moscow, 1926), Vol. I, Chapter V.

24. Quoted by Manfred Kridl, Józef Wittlin, Władysław Malinowski, *The Democratic Heritage of Poland* (London, 1944), p. 106.

25. Szmidt, *Socjaldemokracja . . . 1893–1904*, I, vi–vii.

26. *Ibid.*, pp. 12–14.

27. Res, *Dzieje ruchu socjalistycznego w zaborze rosyjskim*, pp. 265–266.

28. For the Polish text of the program, see: Res, *Dzieje ruchu socjalistycznego w zaborze rosyjskim*, pp. 385–400; Aleksander Malinowski, ed., *Materiały do historii PPS i ruchu rewolucyjnego w zaborze rosyjskim od r. 1893 do 1904*, I, 1893–1897 (Warsaw, 1907), 20–24. For the documents on the foundation of the PPS see L. Wasilewski's, ed., "Dokumenty do historii zjazdu paryskiego 1892" (Documents pertaining to the Paris Congress of 1892), *Niepodległość*, Vol. VIII, No. 1 (18). 1933, pp. 107–152.

29. Leon Wasilewski, *Zarys dziejów Polskiej Partii Socjalistycznej . . .* (Warsaw, n.d.), pp. 30 ff.

30. Informator, *Stronnictwa polityczne w królestwie Polskim*, p. 63.

CHAPTER 2   SOCIAL DEMOCRATS VERSUS "SOCIAL PATRIOTS"

1. All these documents are to be found in a collection of materials edited by Szmidt, *Socjaldemokracja . . . 1893–1904*, Vol. I.

2. *Ibid.*, pp. 55–60.

3. *Ibid.*, pp. 134–165.

4. *Ibid.*, pp. 177–188, 195–218 and 230–235.

5. *Ibid.*, pp. 11–112; Mazowiecki, *Historya polskiego ruchu socjalistycznego w zaborze rosyjskim*, p. 403.

6. *Bund* is an abbreviation which stands for *Algemeiner Yidysher Arbeiter Bund;* it was established in Lithuania in 1897, as a result of the merger of a number of Jewish Socialist circles.

7. For her biography, see Froelich, *Rosa Luxemburg, Her Life and Work*.

8. For her more essential writings, see Rosa Luxemburg, *Gesammelte Werke* (Clara Zetkin and Adolf Warszawski, eds.), Vol. III: *Gegen den Reformismus: eingeleitet und bearbeitet von Paul Froelich*, and Vol. VI: *Die Akkumulation des Kapitale*.

9. This pamphlet, published in Paris in 1895 under the pseudonym of Maciej Rózga, became one of the major propaganda publications of the party on the national problem.

10. In the German movement he was known under the pseudonym of Johannes

Kaempfer; for his work see J. Marchlewski, *Pisma wybrane,* Vol. I (Warsaw, 1952); Vol. II (Warsaw, 1956).

11. Szmidt, *Socjaldemokracja* . . . *1893–1904,* pp. 188–220.

12. *Ibid.,* pp. 14–15.

13. *Ibid.,* pp. 177–217.

14. *Ibid.,* pp. 349–402, 514–535; Mazowiecki, *Historya polskiego ruchu socjalistycznego w zaborze rosyjskim,* p. 373; *Protokoly obedinitelnego sezda rossiiskoi sotsialdemokraticheskoi robochei partii sostoiavshegosia v Stokgolme v 1906 godu* (Moscow-Leningrad, 1926), *passim.*

15. *Neue Zeit,* No. 42, 1903 and No. 43, 1904; these articles were also published in *Iskra,* No. 69, 1904, pp. 2–7, under the title "Organizatsionnye voprosy ruskoi sotsialdemokratii" (The Organizational Problems of the Russian Social Democracy).

16. The gist of Lenin's national doctrine may be found in the following statements and articles, all of which are included in Volume XIX of his *Collected Works* . . . *1916–1917* (New York, 1942): "Peace Without Annexations and the Independence of Poland as Slogans of the Day in Russia," "The Socialist Revolution and the Right of Nations to Self-Determination (Theses)," "The Pamphlet by Junius [R. Luxemburg]," and "The Discussion on Self-Determination Summed Up." Most of this material is conveniently collected in the work edited by Olga Gankin and Harold H. Fisher, *The Bolsheviks and the World War — The Origins of the Third International* (Stanford-London, 1950), pp. 507–532.

17. M. Rafes, *Ocherki po istorii Bunda* (Moscow, 1923), p. 45; Naum A. Bukhbinder, *Istorya yevreiskogo robochego dvizhenia v Rossii* (Leningrad, 1925), p. 87.

18. *Ibid.,* p. 94; Rafes, pp. 144–145.

CHAPTER 3   THE REVOLUTION OF 1904–05 AND ITS AFTERMATH

1. "Nacjonalistyczne manifestacje" (The Nationalist Manifestations), *Czerwony sztandar,* No. 18, July 1904.

2. Józef Piłsudski, *Memoirs of a Polish Revolutionary and a Soldier* (London, 1931), pp. 153–175.

3. For the attitude of the revolutionary parties in Russian Poland toward the events of 1904–05, see Szmidt, *Socjaldemokracja* . . . *1893–1904,* I, 443 ff; also Les Martov & Theodor Dan, *Geschichte der russischen Sozialdemokratie* . . . (Berlin, 1930), p. 105; Rafes, *Ocherki po istorii Bunda,* pp. 138–139; Alexandr L. Pogodin, *Glavnyia techeniia polskoi politicheskoi mysli, 1863–1907* (St. Petersburg, 1908), pp. 520 ff; Les J. Martov & others, eds., *Obshschestwennoe dvizhenie v Rossii v nachale XX-go vieka* (St. Petersburg, 1909); Vol. IV, Part II, the essay of K. Zalewski on the "National Movement"; also *Z pola walki,* Nos. 11–12, 1931, *passim;* see also *Rewolucja 1905–1907 roku na ziemiach polskich* . . . (Warsaw, 1955), *passim.*

4. The editorial entitled "Wojna" (The War), *Czerwony sztandar,* February 14, 1904; Adolf Warski [Warszawski], "Polska aporte!" (Here Poland!), *Przeglad socjaldemokratyczny,* February 1904.

5. Szmidt, *Socjaldemokracja* . . . *1893–1904,* I, 460–463; a similar slogan

was repeated in the appeals of conscripts in October and December 1904, *ibid.*,
pp. 554–557, 559–561, and 580–583.

6. *Ibid.*, pp. 568–575: see also P. Miliukov, *Natsionalny vopros* (The
Nationality Problem) (Berlin, 1935), pp. 163–183.

7. "Odezwa zarządu głównego SDKPiL; jak nie należy urządzać demonstracji"
(The Appeal of the Central Committee of the SDKPiL: How One Should Not
Organize Demonstrations), Szmidt, I, 562–567.

8. Martov & Dan, *Geschichte der russischen Sozialdemokratie,* p. 105.

9. "Odezwa zarządu głównego z powodu rzezi 1-go maja" (The Proclamation
of the Central Committee because of the Massacre of May 1st), *Czerwony
sztandar,* No. 26, May 1905.

10. So-called colloquially, after the initials of its Polish name, "Narodowa
demokracja"; an essentially middle-class, strongly nationalist, and conservative
party.

11. It was by means of this party that the National Democrats managed, during
the years preceding World War I, to gain some influence among the working
masses.

12. "Wybory pod osłoną bagnetów" (The Election Under the Protection of
Bayonets), *Czerwony sztandar,* No. 43, January 13, 1906; also, the appeals to
workers in No. 46, January 16, and No. 57, March 4, 1906.

13. "Koło Polskie" (The Polish Faction [in the Duma]), *Czerwony sztandar,*
No. 76, June 1906; also "Walka ideowa zamiast walki na pięści" (Ideological
Flight Instead of Fist Fight), No. 77, June 19, 1906; "Walka rewolucyjna czy
rewolucyjne awanturnictwo?" (Revolutionary Struggle or Revolutionary Ad-
ventures?), No. 100, August 20, 1906.

14. For martial law in the Congress Kingdom, see F. K. [Feliks Kon], *Sądy
wojenne w Królestwie Polskim* (Cracow, 1909), p. 65 ff.

15. This problem has been widely discussed in Socialist literature. See Leon
Wasilewski's, "Walka o postulat niepodległości . . . (Fight for the Postulate of
Independence . . .), Part III, *Niepodległość,* Vol. X, No. 3, 1934.

16. During 1914 and 1915, toward the end of his life, Kon became one of
the leaders of the PPS-Left and, later, one of the founders of the Polish Communist Party.

17. For SD criticism of the electoral system and methods, see the pamphlet
of J. Karski [J. Marchlewski], *Duma carska a bezprawie wyborcze* (The Tsarist
Duma and the Electoral Lawlessness) (Warsaw, 1906), *passim.* The October
Manifesto granted universal suffrage, but the electoral law of the Duma was so
devised as to give proportionately larger representation to landowners than to
the middle classes, workers, and peasants.

18. *Protokoly obedinitelnego sezda . . . 1906 godu,* pp. 338–358. See also V. I.
Lenin, *Sochineniia* (Moscow, 1947), X, 127–142; Szmidt, *Socjaldemokracja . . .
1893–1904,* I, 406–407.

19. "The Social Democracy of Russian Poland could join the Russian Social
Democratic Party so much more easily," wrote K. Radek in 1916. "Theses and
Resolution of the Editorial Board of *Gazeta robotnicza . . .*" in Gankin and
Fisher, pp. 515–518.

20. For the minutes, see *Londonskii sezd rossiskoi SDRP (sostoiavshiisia v
1907 g.): polnoi tekst protokolov* (Paris, 1909).

21. Gankin and Fisher, pp. 95–96.

22. "Przesilenie w partii" (The Party's Crisis), *Gazeta robotnicza,* July 16,

1912. See also "Antysemityzm pod rękę z bandytyzmen" (Antisemitism Hand in Hand with Banditry), *Czerwony sztandar,* No. 180, February 1911. For the vital role of the Polish group within the RSDWP see L. B. Kamenev, ed., *Leninskii sbornik,* Vol. III, Part 3.

PART II: THE COMMUNIST PARTY OF POLAND

Many of the periodicals used in these chapters are to be found in the Hoover Library, Stanford University.

CHAPTER 4   WORLD WAR I AND THE FOUNDATION OF THE PARTY

1. At the outbreak of the war Lenin was still in Poronin, in Galicia. His room was searched by the Austrian police and he was arrested as a potential spy but soon freed, thanks to the intervention of Austrian and Polish Socialists who, disregarding political differences, deemed it to be their duty to help a comrade. Lenin was permitted to leave Austria for Switzerland.

2. Szmidt, *Socjaldemokracja Królestwa Polskiego i Litwy: materiały i dokumenty, 1914–1918* (Moscow, 1936), III, 3–5.

3. For the full text, see Carl Grünberg, ed., *Die Internationale und der Weltkrieg; Materialen,* Part II in the *Archiv fur die Geschichte der Sozialismus und Arbeiter Bewegung* (Leipzig, 1916), VII, 120–135; Szmidt, *Socjaldemokracja . . . 1914–1918,* III, 6–7; see also Gankin and Fisher, pp. 150–156.

4. Szmidt, *Socjaldemokracja . . . 1914–1918,* III, 18–20.

5. *Gazeta robotnicza,* No. 24, February 1915.

6. Szmidt, *Socjaldemokracja . . . 1914–1918,* III, 22.

7. Horwitz-Walecki was one of the leaders of the PPS-Left, a member of its Executive Committee from 1906 until 1918 and, later, prominent member of the Communist Party of Poland.

8. Bronski and Krajewski were both leading members of the SDKPiL while living abroad; both became Communists.

9. For the attitude of the two parties during the Zimmerwald and Kiental conferences, see, Szmidt, *Socjaldemokracja . . . 1914–1918,* III, 333–337; also pp. 28–32, and 130–142.

10. For the text of the resolution, see Gankin and Fisher, pp. 507–518. The resolution was first issued in *Gazeta robotnicza,* No. 25, January 1916. The theses, the author of which was Radek, were published anonymously in the second (and last) issue of a paper issued by the Zimmerwald-Left: [K. Radek], "Thesen ueber Imperialismus und nationale Unterduckung," *Vorbote* (Bern), No. 2, April 1916. To these two statements should be added two articles, also written by Radek: Parabellum [K. Radek], "Annexionen und Sozialdemocratie," *Beilage zur Berner Tagewacht,* No. 252, October 28, 1915 and No. 253, October 29, 1915; and "Das Selbstbestimmungrecht der Voelker," *Lichtstrahlen* (Berlin), No. 1, October 3, 1915. All these pronouncements put together form a complete statement of the views of the SDKPiL on the subject.

11. Lenin, "The Theses," in Gankin and Fisher, pp. 518–530.

12. Lenin, *The Imperialist War: The Struggle Against Social-Chauvinism and Social-Pacifism, 1914–1915*, in *Collected Works*, (New York, 1930), XVIII, 373.

13. Lenin, *Itogi diskussii o samoopredelenii* (The Results of the Discussion on Self-Determination) in *Sochineniia* (4th Russian ed.; Moscow, 1948), XXII, 306–344.

14. *Z dokumentów chwili*, No. 57, Warsaw, September 6, 1917, p. 64.

15. Szmidt, *Socjaldemokracja . . . 1914–1918*, III, 163, the declaration "O akcie piatego listopada" (On the Act of November Fifth), *Głos robotniczy*, No. 15, December 9, 1916, in an article "Państwo i proletariat" (The State and the Proletariat) again declared that the aim of the class struggle should not be the restoration of a state, but social revolution.

16. "Krajowa konferencja zjednoczeniowa" (The Home Unification Conference), Szmidt, *Socjaldemokracja . . . 1914–1918*, III, 169–171.

17. *Czerwony sztandar*, No. 191, June 1917. pp. 7–8.

18. No. 10, March 24, 1917, No. 11, March 31, 1917 and No. 12, April 7, 1917; also the article "Socjaldemokracja i wojna" (Social Democracy and War), *Czerwony sztandar*, No. 91, June 1917, pp. 1–2. For the position of the PPS-Left, see its proclamation in *Z dokumentów chwili*, No. 41, June 12, 1917, pp. 47–50.

19. In this respect see the PPS organ in Russia, *Jedność robotnicza* (The Workers' Unity), No. 24, Petrograd, June 16, 1917; and the article "Co robi PPS w Rosji" (What the PPS is Doing in Russia), No. 26, June 30, 1917; also the article "Konstytucja niedemokratycane" (The Undemocratic Constitution), No. 32, August 11, 1918, strongly criticizing the Bolsheviks.

Julian Leszczyński [Leński], originally a member of the *Bund*, became a prominent member of that group of the SDKPiL which early sided with the Bolsheviks. He took an active part in the Bolshevik revolution; soon he became a leader of the CPP, member of its Central Committee and Political Bureau, and leader of its left wing. From 1929 Leszczyński was secretary-general of the CPP. He was liquidated during the Great Purge, together with other leading members of the party. For a more detailed biography of Leński see the introduction to the book: J. Leński, *O front ludowy w Polsce, 1934–1937* (Warsaw, 1956).

20. Szmidt, *Socjaldemokracja . . . 1914–1918*, III, 217–225 and 386–387. For the text of the resolution on the national question, *Ibid.*, pp. 386–387.

21. Lenin, "The Speech on the National Question," May 12, 1917, in *Collected Works . . . The Revolution of 1917* (New York and London, 1929), p. 311. The report at the Conference was delivered by Stalin and represented the Leninist school of thought; a co-report was made by G. L. Pjatakov, who sided with Dzierżyński, perhaps the fiercest opponent of the right of self-determination for his native country.

A certain analogy may be drawn between the national and the agrarian policies of Lenin. Both the offer of land to the peasants and the granting of the right of self-determination to all oppressed nations proved to be only short range, tactical moves, a kind of Indian giving.

22. "Proklamacja z powodu nominacji Tymczasowej Rady Stanu" (Proclamation on the Occasion of the Nomination of the Provisional Council of State), Szmidt, *Socjaldemokracja . . . 1914–1918*, III, 195. The PPS-Left denounced the council less violently.

23. "Pokój i rewolucja" (The Peace and the Revolution), *ibid.*, p. 246.

24. T. Żarski, "Ani kroku wstecz" (Not a Single Step Back), *Głos robotników*

i żołnierzy: organ CKW PPS w Rosji (The Voice of Workers and Soldiers: The Organ of the Central Executive Committee of the PPS in Russia), No. 12 (412).

25. *Na Barykady* (On the Barricades!), (Moscow, February 25, 1918), pp. 3–4.

26. *Z dokumentów chwili*, No. 119, April 20, 1918, p. 37.

27. *Nasza trybuna*, No. 2, November 9, 1918, pp. 6–8. After the Brest Treaty the SDKPiL supported the left-wing Bolsheviks and were in favor of revolutionary intervention abroad. A Polish Red Army, after receiving great publicity (*Gazeta robotnicza*, No. 1, July-August 1918, p. 4) never actually materialized.

28. See the proclamations entitled "Z rewolucją rosyjską" (With the Russian Revolution), and "Rewolucja listopadowa" (The November Revolution), both in Szmidt, *Socjaldemokracja . . . 1914–1918*, III, p. 249.

29. "Działalność SDKPiL w Rosji" (The Activities of the SDKPiL in Russia), *ibid.*, p. 303.

30. The proclamation of the SDKPiL, "Niech żyje strajk powszechny" (Long Live the General Strike), *ibid.*, p. 249.

31. "Odezwa PPS (Lewicy)" (The Proclamation of the PPS (Left)), *Z dokumentów chwili*, No. 106, March 2, 1918, pp. 36–39; see also a similar proclamation in No. 112, March 26, 1917.

32. "Ziemia dla chlopów" (Land for Peasants), *Nowiny socjalistyczne* (Socialist News), No. 3, July, 1918; also *Nasze hasła* (Our Slogans), No. 14, November, 1918, pp. 4–5.

33. The so-called *Spartacus Letters* appeared at irregular intervals, first from December 1914 to August 1915, and then from August 1915 to October 1918. They contained trenchant criticism of the policies supported by the majority and center of the German S.D.P. Luxemburg and Marchlewski (the latter known in Germany as Johannes Kaempfer) were among the chief contributors.

34. "Do ludu pracujacego miast i wsi" (To the Toiling People of Towns and Villages), in Szmidt, *Socjaldemokracja . . . 1914–1918*, III, 305–307.

35. *Ibid.*

36. "Demokracja i konstytuanta" (The Democracy and the Constituent Assembly), *Nasza trybuna*, No. 1, November 1, 1918.

37. For the program of the so-called "Lublin Government," see *Niepodległość*, XIV, No. 2 (1936), pp. 268–273; for the background and origins, see Ignacy Daszyński, *Pamiętniki* (Memoirs), II, 320–324.

38. The PPS-Left was invited by Piłsudski to join the coalition government of Moraczewski, but scornfully turned this proposal down: *Głos robotniczy*, November 14, 1918, p. i; for a Communist point of view of the relations between Piłsudski and the PPS see J. Brun, *Pisma wybrane*, I, 115–167.

39. *Głos Robotniczy*, No. 98, December 6, 1918.

40. "Do proletariatu Polski!" (To the Proletariat of Poland!), *Wiadomości rady delegatów robotniczych okręgu sosnowieckiego*, No. 1, December 6, 1918, p. 1; No. 2, December 23, 1918. It was admitted later by a Communist paper that the strike had to be abandoned because of apathy on the part of the masses.

41. *Głos robotniczy*, November 12, 1918, p. 1.

42. The proclamation "Przeciwko rozbiciu Rad Delegatów Robotniczych" (Against the Split of the Councils of Workers Delegates), Szmidt, *Socjaldemokracja . . . 1914–1918*, III, 318.

43. An editorial in the official Communist organ *Sztandar socjalizmu*, Decem-

ber 27, 1918, p. 1, stated *inter alia:* ". . . [T]he lack of a spontaneous, strong revolutionary movement caused the internal life of the Councils to die down, and the conscious efforts of the false Socialists managed to weaken and to paralyze their activities."

44. *Gromada,* No. 3, November-December 1918, pp. 4–6; the resolution of the November Conference of the SDKPiL on the agrarian question, Szmidt, *Socjaldemokracja . . . 1914–1918,* pp. 325–326; "Głód ziemi" (The Hunger of the Soil), *Gromada,* August, 1918. After some greatly exaggerated reports (*Gromada,* November-December 1918, p. 56 and February 1918, pp. 3–4) on revolutionary developments in villages of the Lublin district, there was almost complete silence in the Communist press on the subject.

45. *Nasza trybuna,* No. 4, December 6, 1918, and No. 5, December 13, 1918; both issues were largely devoted to the conference. See also the editorial of No. 1 "Ku zjednoczeniu" (Toward Unification) which pointed out that if the PPS-Left really favored the Social Democratic program, the existence of two proletarian organizations with the same platform would then be a piece of nonsense.

46. "Do zjednoczenia" (Toward Unification), *Głos robotniczy,* November 7, 1918; also "Najwyższy czas" (The Supreme Time), *ibid., November* 10, 1918.

47. At first the new organization bore the name Communist Workers' Party of Poland — The United SDKPiL and PPS-Left. The subtitle was dropped in February 1921.

48. "Do proletariatu Polski! Proklamacja zjazdu organizacyjnego Komunisty-cznej Partii Robotniczej Polski (Zjednoczonej SDKPiL i PPS-Lewicy)" (To the Proletariat of Poland! Proclamation of the Organization Congress of the Com-munist Party of Poland — The United SDKPiL and the PPS-Left), *Sztandar socjalizmu,* No. 1, December 19, 1918.

49. In October 1918, during a Moscow conference of the Communist and Communist-gravitating parties of neighboring countries, a representative of the SDKPiL made a report on the position of his party in Poland. This report ad-mitted that there were only seven Social Democratic groups in Warsaw (one of them Jewish), each numbering from twenty to thirty members. The number of sympathizers was two or three times larger. Consequently, according to the re-port which had no reason to be modest since the party was pushing the Bolshe-viks to an armed intervention, the stronghold of the SDKPiL numbered about 200 members and about 600 sympathizers. In Łódź, the second largest region of the party, the situation was no better, *Zhizn natsionalnostiei,* No. 1, November 9, 1918, p. 2.

50. This first large secession, that of Łódź, was led by Szczerkowski and took place as early as March 1918. Szczerkowski carried most active party members in the Łódź district with him. The Poznań district followed. See Antoni Szczer-kowski, "Opozycja niepodległościowa w PPS-Lewicy," *Księga pamiatkowa PPS.* (Warsaw [1923]); also *Jedność robotnicza,* June 2, 1918, p. 6; and the article "Dezorganizatorzy" (The Disorganizers) in *Głos robotniczy,* June 16, 1918.

51. For the text of the program, see *Sprawozdanie ze zjazdu organizacyjnego Komunistycznej Partii Robotniczej Polski . . . ,* (Warsaw, 1919); *Z pola walki,* Nos, 7–8. See also *KPP: uchwały i rezolucje,* I, 33–58.

52. The new party trusted that the resolution of the SDKPiL Party Confer-ence in November 1918, took proper care of the agrarian problem, *Nasza trybuna,* No. 5, December 13, 1918, p. 7.

53. In this respect see also "Z Gdańskiem czy bez Gdańska" (With or Without Danzig), *Nasza trybuna*, No. 210 (238), November 3, 1918. The article repeated with emphasis the old slogan, "Away with frontiers." They were of no concern to the party — only the dictatorship of the proletariat would create an "International State of Labor" (*Międzynarodowe państwo pracy*).

Besides a proclamation, "To the Proletariat of Poland," and an ideological as well as tactical platform, the congress passed a statute of organization for the party. At the head was a central committee, composed of nine members. For the management of current affairs the central committee was to designate a permanent secretariat. Matters of exceptional importance were to be decided by the party congress, summoned by the central committee. The party congress was to be composed (in addition to members of the central committee) of delegates from the regional organization; larger regions were to send two delegates and the smaller regions one representative each. The congress would elect the first central committee, the editorial board of the central press organ, *Sztandar socjalizmu*, and the members of the finance control board.

54. For a criticism of the party's mistakes on the national problem see J. Brun, *Pisma wybrane*, I, 180–201.

CHAPTER 5   THE YEARS OF HOPE

1. *Trybuna*, No. 218, November 16, 1918, p. 3, and No. 221, November 21, 1918.

2. Avenging of relatives who had been murdered by the Cheka in Russia during the revolution was given by the guards as their main reason for assassinating the Soviet delegates.

3. *Przełom* (Break), No. 1–2, February 9, 1919.

4. *Przełom* in its February 9, 1919 issue. The first party council which took place in February 1919 expected an almost automatic downfall of the capitalist system in Poland, *KPP: uchwały i rezolucje*, I, 63–68.

5. Edward Brand and Henryk Walecki, *Der Communismus in Polen . . .* (Hamburg, 1921), p. 154. For the attitude of the party toward the first *Sejm* elections, see the article "Strusia polityka" (The Policy of an Ostrich) in *Sztandar socjalizmu* of December 21, 1918, forecasting boycott, and an editorial in an issue of the same paper, dated January 19, 1919, which stated: "Not the election to the *Sejm*, but the struggle for power . . . is the way of the conscious proletariat . . ." ". . . [T]he boycott of the *Sejm* elections in 1919 by the CWP was justified" a Communist pamphlet as late as 1921 stated, "because there existed a possibility of shifting over to a direct struggle for power . . . Under these circumstances [the] participation in the election would mean predetermining the result of the struggle . . . ," quoted by J. A. Reguła, *Historia Komunistycznej Partii Polski* (Warsaw, 1934), p. 38; for a similar defense at a still later date, see "Poland" by "K" in *The Communist International*, No. 1, 1924; for the criticism of this attitude see H. Walecki [M. Horwitz], *O taktyce w stosunku do parlamentaryzmu* (Warsaw, 1921).

6. *Sztandar komunizmu*, No. 2 (Warsaw, 1921), pp. 3–4.

7. Quoted by *Przegląd komunistyczny*, No. 1, May 1921, pp. 3–4.

8. For the Communist side of the picture, see *Biuletyn komitetu organiza-*

cyjnego zjazdu delegatów robotniczych miast i wsi, Nos. 1 and 2, March 8 and May 20, 1919.

9. *Monitor polski,* No. 13, January 17, 1919, p. 1.

10. According to official sources of information, the party numbered up to 22,000 members by the spring of 1919. *Ibid.,* No. 160, July 19, 1919, p. 2. The Communist historians do not claim such a large following; according to *KPP: uchwały i rezolucje,* I, 62, the party numbered at that time around 6,350 members in 127 localities. It is difficult to estimate the number of sympathizers.

11. Szmidt, *Socjaldemokracja . . . 1914–1918,* III, 335–337; also Lenin, *Sochineniia, XXIX,* 152–153. For a professional revolutionary, Marchlewski had a strong fear of disorder; on several occasions he deplored the anarchy caused by the Bolshevik revolution, especially the way in which land was seized and divided by the peasants themselves, with tremendous losses in cattle, buildings, and implements.

12. *Pierwszy zjazd Międzynarodówki Komunistycznej w Moskwie w marcu 1919r.* (Hamburg, 1919), pp. 7–8. The invitations to the congress were signed by the "Foreign Bureau of the Communist Party of Poland." It is interesting to note that this Bureau failed to add the word "Workers' " to its name; also *Sztandar komunizmu,* No. 2, April-May, 1919, pp. 4–6.

13. F. Kon, "Polonia Militans," *Die Kommunistische Internationale,* No. 6, October 1919, and J. Marchlewski (Karski), "Polen und Weltrevolution," *ibid.,* No. 7–8, 1919.

14. F. Zweig, *Poland Between Two Wars* (London, 1944), p. 28.

15. For the Communist position, see "Strajk rolny" (The Land Strike), *Gromada,* April 20, 1919: also "Sejm o głodzie ziemi" (The Sejm on the Land Hunger), *Gromada,* April 1, 1919. Land reform was to be carried out by local councils of workers and peasants and individual farming was to be limited. Both issues of the paper indicated that the government measures produced some positive effects. For the PPS viewpoint, see *Niedola chlopska* (Peasant Misery), No. 6 (42), October 19, 1919; the newly created Land Workers' Trade Union (*Związek Zawodowy Robotników Rolnych*) was organized largely by radical peasant parties, such as the "Wyzwolenie" (*The Liberation*), but the PPS also had something to do with this step.

16. *Jahrbuch für Politik-Wirtschaft Arbeiterbewegung, 1923–1924* (Hamburg, 1924), pp. 914–923; also Stanisław Piaskowski, *Zarys historii polskiego socjalizmu* (Breslau, 1946), pp. 26–27.

17. J. Dominko, *Z minionych lat; wspomnienia działacza-spółdzielcy . . .* (Warsaw, 1945), *passim.*

18. This letter was conveniently dropped from the fourth complete Russian edition of Lenin's works and was not included in the current edition of Stalin's writings; it is to be found in the third edition of Lenin's *Sochineniia,* XXV, 624, as well as in the French and German translations of his works, published before the war.

19. This part of the history is largely based on material found in Tadeusz Teslar's *Propaganda bolszewicka podczas wojny polsko-rosyjskiej 1920 roku* (Warsaw, 1938); the work contains many pertinent documents either reprinted in full or in extensive quotation. For the Communist point of view see J. Marchlewski, *Pisma wybrane* I, 743–786; also J. Brun, *Pisma wybrane* I, 167ff, II, 364–375; also *KPP: uchwały i rezolucje,* I, 86–103.

20. "During the Russo-Polish war the Polish Communist Party worked hand

in hand with our department, and we prepared that party for action in cooperation with the Red Army. The Polish Communist Party obeyed all the commands of the advancing army of Tukhachevsky. Members of the Polish Communist Party aided us in organizing sabotage, in creating diversions, and in impeding the arrival of munitions from France." W. G. Krivitsky, *I Was Stalin's Agent* (New York, 1940), p. 30.

21. *Die Kommunistische Internationale,* No. 9, 1920, pp. 1463–68.

22. Teslar, pp. 39–41. Bibliography of Soviet propaganda during the war of 1919–20 comprises over 140 items printed in about 7 million copies, i.e., about one fourth of all Soviet propaganda publications of that period. *Ibid.,* p. 297.

23. *Ibid.,* pp. 238–239.

24. Karol Radek, *Voina polskihk bialogvardieicev protiv Sovietskoy Rossii* (Moscow, 1920).

25. For the text of the appeal, see Teslar, pp. 148–150.

26. Radek, "Die Polnische Frage und Die Internationale Revolution," *Die Kommunistische Internationale,* No. 12, 1920.

27. *Ibid.*

28. *Village Commune,* July 18, 1920, quoted in U. S. Department of State: *The Second Congress of the Communist International,* (Washington, 1920).

29. *Ibid.,* p. 33.

30. For the text of the appeal, see Bela Kun (ed.), *Kommunisticheskii Internatsional v dokumentakh . . . 1919–1932* (Moscow, 1933). Also *Die Kommunistische Internationale,* No. 13, 1920, the appeal of the Comintern: "An die Proletarier Aller Laendern."

31. Quoted in U. S. Department of State: *The Second Congress of the Communist International,* p. 38. The resolutions of the Second Congress have been reprinted in W. H. Chamberlin (ed.), *Blueprint for World Conquest* (Washington-Chicago, 1946).

32. *Ibid.,* p. 140.

33. J. Marchlewski (Karski), "Die Agrarfrage und die Weltrevolution," *Die Kommunistische Internationale,* No. 12 (Moscow, 1920).

34. One of the first actions of the Department of Security was to establish " 'Revolutionary Tribunals' for the combatting and the punishing of offenses against the revolutionary power of the toiling masses," Teslar, pp. 267–268.

35. *Ibid.,* p. 240; for the reminiscences of the leading member of the committee, see J. B. Marchlewski, *Rosja proletariacka a Polska burżuazyjna.* Marchlewski took a rather poor view of most of his officials; he considered them "one-sided, narrow-minded," and "not familiar enough with the obligations and duties of a revolutionary power," p. 30.

36. For the text of these appeals, see Teslar, pp. 248–268.

37. *Ibid.,* pp. 248–250; Markhlevskii, *Voina i mir mezhdu bourzhuaznoi Polshei i proletarskoi Rossiei* (Moscow, 1921), p. 22; Marchlewski, *Rosja proletariacka a Polska burżuazyjna,* p. 26.

38. "W kwestii żądań naszych wobec robotników wiejskich i włościan" (On the Problem of Our Duties Toward the Agricultural Workers and Peasants), *Przegląd socjaldemokratyczny,* 1908; see also J. Marchlewski, *Pisma wybrane,* I, 589–625; II, 556–668.

39. J. Marchlewski, *Wobec kwestii rolnej w Polsce* (Facing the Agrarian Problem of Poland) (Moscow, 1918).

40. *Rozmowa Macieja z Jędrzejem* (Wiedeń, 1920); also J. Marchlewski,

Komuniści a wiejski lud roboczy (Communists and the Village Toiling Masses) (Wieden, 1920).

41. During the whole campaign the Red Army took some 24,000 Polish prisoners; of these 239 volunteered to serve with Soviet forces and no more than 123 joined the Communist Party of Poland, Teslar, p. 116.

42. Kon, *Felix Edmundovich Dzerzhinskii* (Moscow, 1929), p. 76. For the texts of the appeals to peasants and agricultural workers, see Teslar, *Propaganda bolszewicka podczas wojny polskorosyjskiej 1920 roku*, pp. 287–289, and 283–285.

43. Teslar, pp. 240–241.

44. For the promises of freedom of conscience and religious tolerance, see *ibid.*, pp. 263–265.

45. The Congress of Trade Unions, which deliberated in Warsaw in July, produced a clear anti-Communist majority. This was at the height of the Red Army's successes, *Archiv fur Politish-Wirtschaft Arbetervegung, 1922–1923* (Hamburg, 1921), p. 920.

46. Marchlewski, in his pamphlet *Rosja proletariacka a Polska burżuazyjna*, reprinted in the second volume of his selected works, admitted that "The Red Army could not attract the peasants"; on the other hand, he consoled himself with the belief that in case of victory, despite the deep mistrust, the Committee could have coped with the situation successfully.

47. *Nowy przegląd*, No. 4 (34), July-August 1930, p. 20.

48. *Przegląd komunistyczny*, No. 1, May 1921, p. 12.

49. K., "Poland," *The Communist International*, No. 1 (Moscow, 1924).

CHAPTER 6 IN SEARCH OF A NEW BEARING

1. In the social sphere Poland became one of three countries in the world that provided against risks of sickness, old age, and unemployment, thus covering all three principal forms of social insecurity, Sir William Beveridge, *Social Insurances and Allied Service* (New York, 1942), Appendix F, p. 289.

2. "Materiały do strajku rolnego w Poznańskiem w 1921r" (Materials for the Agrarian Strike in Posnania in 1921), *Dzieje najnowsze*, Vol. I, No. 2, 1947.

3. Łańcucki, a self-educated railway worker from Galicia, quarrelled with the PPS leadership and joined the CWPP; arrested for subversive activities, he was exchanged to Russia. Jerzy Czeszejko-Sochacki, a lawyer by profession, underwent a strange ideological evolution from Roman Catholicism, through socialism, to communism. After a stormy career as one of the leaders of the CPP, he went to Russia.

4. The *Bund* was the largest and most influential socialist Jewish Labor party in Poland. There were, at the time, some pro-Soviet sympathizers among the Bund rank and file who insisted on joining the Third International.

5. Łańcucki, *Moje wspomnienia* (Moscow, 1931), pp. 197–198 and 201–206; *Przegląd komunistyczny*, No. 1, May 1921, pp. 96–101.

6. Dąbal started his political career as a radical peasant politician and an organizer of Piłsudski's military units in Galicia. Arrested in 1922 for subversive activities, he was exchanged a year later for some Poles arrested in Russia. He soon became a leader of the newly organized "Peasant International."

7. For the full text, see *Sprawozdanie z III konferencji KPRP* (Warsaw, 1922). See also *KPP: uchwały i rezolucje*, I, 127–178.

8. *Sprawozdanie z III konferencji* . . . , p. 16.

9. *KPP: uchwały i rezolucje*, I, 140.

10. At the Fourth Congress of the Comintern of November 1922, Zinoviev admonished the party for its deviations. "[T]here are . . ." he said, "important points on which the Executive of the Polish Party had certain differences of opinion, such as the agrarian question, the question of nationalities, and partly the question of the United Front . . . I must recall the stand that was taken by the II Congress upon this question. At that congress we adopted a platform wherein we proposed, in order to win over the peasantry, to include a statement of the problem of redistribution of land." *Fourth Congress of the Communist International* . . . (London, 1923), p. 24.

Wera Kostrzewa (Koszutska, Maria), originally a member of the PPS-Left, joined the CPP in 1918; soon she became its leading theoretician and a member of the Central Committee and the Political Bureau; author of numerous articles and pamphlets; liquidated during the Great Purge, together with other leading members of the CPP.

11. The PPS polled 911,000 votes, and the Bund 80,000; altogether the seven working-class parties received 1,614,000 votes and 61 mandates, while the parties of the Right drew 2,551,000 votes and 153 mandates. The Communists polled one and one-half per cent of the total vote.

12. *Sprawozdanie stenograficzne z 10 posiedzenia Sejmu Rzeczypospolitej z 23 stycznia 1923* (Stenographic Record of the Tenth Session of the Sejm of the Polish Republic of January 23, 1923), pp. 83–85. Also *Sprawozdanie . . . z 6 marca 1924*, pp. 43–44; *Sprawozdanie . . . z 26 kwietnia 1926*, p. 23, and many others. *Sprawozdanie . . . z dnia 16 stycznia 1923*, pp. 15–18; also *Sprawozdanie . . . z dnia 26 stycznia 1926*, pp. 9–12.

13. Anti-Semitism was a grave factor in the life of the country during the period from 1918 to 1939. The one-sided occupational and social structure of the Jewish population in Poland, an impoverished and overpopulated country, was one of the most common propaganda arguments put forward by various anti-Semitic groups. The large percentage of people of Jewish origin among CPP members, "the Jewish-Communist conspiracy" was also a standard slogan of the extremist groups. Thus, the racial conflict also embittered interparty strife.

14. *Polityka społeczna Państwa Polskiego* (Social Policy of the Polish State), an official publication of the Polish government (Warsaw, 1935), pp. 39–40.

15. *International Press Correspondence*, July 12, 1923, p. 501. The bulletin will, henceforth, be referred to as *IPC*.

16. O. Czerwiec [T. Żarski], *Komitet 21* . . . (The Committee of 21 . . .), n.p., n.d., p. 12ff.

17. For the full text of the resolutions, see *Uchwały II zjazdu partyjnego KPP* (Resolutions of the Second Party Congress of the CPP) (Warsaw, 1923); also *KPP: uchwały i rezolucje*, Vol. I, chapter three.

18. Quoted by J. Warski, "SDKPiL wobec II-go zjazdu SDPRR," *Z pola walki*, No. 5–6, 1929, p. 41.

19. Several weeks before the Second Party Congress in July, 1923, the Central Committee of the CPP sent a letter to PPS leaders suggesting a common fight for a workers' and peasants' government.

20. E. Brand, "Rise and Fall of Piłsudski," *The Communist International*, No. 28, 1923.

21. Within the Ukrainian Social Democratic Party the Communists soon won decisive influence. When Polish authorities dissolved the party, many of its members joined the newly created C.P. of Western Ukraine.

In March 1923, the Council of Ambassadors finally recognized the eastern frontiers of the Polish Republic. This brought about some appeasement of the eastern provinces of the state; to counteract this development, which helped to consolidate the Replublic, the radical (not necessarily Communist) elements organized guerilla detachments and, supported by the Soviet authorities, waged war on the Polish police and armed forces. The peak of this movement took place in 1924. The CPP, while encouraging this movement at the start, did not back it very energetically since it was not sure of the Soviet support. The internal struggle for power in Russia practically excluded any possibility of a "revolutionary intervention" abroad.

22. During the Trade Union Congress of May 1922, the PPS held the allegiance of 155 out of 225 delegates, while there were no more than 34 Communist and Communist-gravitating delegates.

23. This was admitted by T. Dąbal, *Powstanie Krakowskie* (Mińsk, 1926), pp. 32–33.

24. *Ibid.*, p. 39.

25. "Od strajków masowych do powstania zbrojnego" (From Mass Strikes to Armed Uprising), *Nowy przegląd*, December 1923.

When in March 1924, the C.C. of CPP analyzed the causes of the November 1923 defeat it concluded that: "Our party has been yet prepared to control great struggles . . . the idea of armed fight, the only means of destroying the bourgeoisie, has not been yet inculcated by the party to the masses . . ." Quoted by Reguła, *Historia KPP*, p. 92.

26. For the records of the congress, see: *Pyatyi vsemirnyi kongress kommunisticheskogo internationala . . .*, Parts One and Two (Moscow-Leningrad, 1925). For the English text, see *Fifth Congress of the Communist International* (London, 1924).

27. Quoted by Reguła, *Historia KPP*, p. 105.

28. *Ibid.*, p. 109.

29. *Fifth Congress of the Communist International . . .* (London, 1924), pp. 38–39.

30. His speech was reprinted by *Bolshevik*, September 20, 1924, under the title "O kompartii Polshi" (About the Communist Party of Poland); it is also to be found in Stalin's collected works: I. V. Stalin, *Sochineniia* (Moscow, 1947), VI, 264–272.

31. Under the law of 1924, unemployment insurance was extended to all persons over the age of 18 who were working for wages, including workers in state enterprises and white collar workers, as well as seasonal workers employed more than 6 months per year. Land and forestry workers and those employed less than 6 months in a given year did not benefit from the insurance.

32. For an account of Communist attempts to utilize the Upper Silesia crisis in order to set up revolutionary factory committees and to take over the factories, see O. Czerwiec, *Komitet 21*. The pamphlet is an expression of the anti-trade-union trend within the CPP, which aimed at replacement of trade-union organizations by the so-called "Committees of Action."

33. Article 3 of the School Act of July 30, 1924, provided that the local languages should be used in elementary schools in three ways: as the sole language of instruction; jointly with Polish; or as one of the subjects taught. The prevalent type of elementary school in the eastern provinces was one called "utraquist," in which Polish and the local language were used jointly as parallel media of instruction; this arrangement could not possibly satisfy leaders of irridentist movements.

34. Sylwester Wojewódzki was a former Intelligence officer of the Polish General Staff who, through peasant radicalism, evolved toward communism.

35. Among them was, for example, Tadeusz Wieniawa-Długoszowski, brother of one of the Marshal's favorite A.D.C.'s. At that time, 1923–1926, there existed a semi-conspiratorial group of so-called "Red Officers" in the army who staked their calculations on a *coup d'état* to be led by their retired commander in chief.

36. Julius Brun-Brunowicz, *Stefana Żeromskiego tragedia pomyłek* (Warsaw, 1924).

37. The book was not officially condemned by the party as heretical until September 1926, after Piłsudski's coup; *Uchwały plenum KC-KPP . . .* (Warsaw, 1926). Writing about Piłsudski's role during World War I, Brunowicz said: "Piłsudski's Legions were a beautiful symbolical gesture . . . Moral strength revealed in the activities of the legions were generated exclusively by the young intelligentsia, the young peasants and workers . . . " In 1923, the CPP members residing in Moscow celebrated the thirtieth anniversary of the foundation of the SDKPiL stressing that it had been set up five years earlier than the RSDWP. For this they were rebuked by the Soviet party; Reguła, p. 25.

38. *Sprawozdanie . . . z dnia 12 grudnia 1925,* p. 75. The same deputy offered a helping hand to all parties left of Center in the realization of radical social and economic reforms and an alliance with the Soviet Union.

39. For the full text of the resolutions, *Uchwały III zjazdu KPP* (Warsaw, 1925); also the official commentary in the form of a pamphlet, *Do walki o ziemię i władzę! Co III zjazd KPP powiedział chłopom?* (On the Struggle for Land and Power! What did the Third Congress of the CPP say to the Peasants?) (Warsaw, 1925); see also *KPP: uchwały i rezolucje,* Vol. II, chapter two.

40. The factory cells were destined to undermine the influence of trade-unions and, ultimately, eliminate them. This would prepare workers to gain control of industrial establishments, and run them under the control of the workers' committees; *KPP: uchwały i rezolucje,* II, 188–205.

41. The I.O.A.R., often referred to as M.O.P.R. from its Russian initials, was organized during 1923 and 1924 on the initiative of Marchlewski, who became its first chairman.

42. For the material concerning the Polish Commission see *KPP: materiały i rezolucje,* II, 52–60.

43. The bill provided for distribution of farms over 445 acres by means of a partly private, partly state-sponsored parcelling; priority was to be given to agricultural workers, the landless, and small peasants. The Communist proposal insisted on immediate and compulsory confiscation.

44. For the full text, see *Uchwały IV konferencji KPP* (Warsaw, 1926); the same idea also in a parliamentary speech; *Sprawozdanie . . . z dnia 2 marca 1926,* pp. 65–73. See also *KPP: uchwały i rezolucje,* Vol. II, chapter three.

45. "Session of the Enlarged Executive Committee of the Communist International," *IPC,* March 4, 1926, p. 254.

46. *IPC,* March 17, 1926, p. 306.

47. *Biuletyn polityczny,* No. 2–3, 1927, p. 341.

48. Radek's article "Piłsudski's Victory" (*IPC,* May 27, 1926), which was merely a reprint from *Pravda,* contained a very sober analysis of the situation and was conspicuous for any lack of criticism of the CPP. Only after Stalin's speech of June 8 (*IPC,* June 24, 1926, pp. 286–287), did the tone of the Soviet press undergo a change.

49. *Ibid.;* see also "Przewrót faszystowski w Polsce a KPP" (The Fascist Upheaval in Poland and the CPP), *Nowy przegląd,* August-September 1936, a reprint of the article from the *Kommunisticheskii Internatsional* of August 1936.

CHAPTER 7   UNDER PIŁSUDSKI

1. For an example see M. Fiedler, *Tło gospodarcze przewrotu majowego* (Economic Background of the May Upheaval) (Cracow, 1927).

2. Swoboda [Adam Próchnik], *Pierwszych piętnaście lat Polski niepodległej* (Warsaw, 1934), p. 234. The problem of the extent to which Piłsudski's agents managed to penetrate the CPP and other Communist-inclined parties, or the so-called "Wallenrodyzm," became a key question in CPP internal controversies; the term comes from the name of a Teutonic knight, Konrad Wallenrod, hero of a historical drama of Mickiewicz. Konrad, a Lithuanian by birth, had joined the Order of Teutonic Knights, became its Grand Master, and in this capacity sabotaged its anti-Lithuanian activity.

3. Eugene Varga, "Economics and Economic Policy in the Third Quarter of 1926," *IPC,* November 1926. "Polish economy has continued to improve . . . ," says Varga, in "Economics and Economic Policy in the Third Quarter of 1927," *IPC,* November 24, 1927.

4. In this respect, see Ruth Fischer, *Stalin and German Communism* (Cambridge, Mass., 1948), p. 639.

5. This is also the opinion expressed by L. D. Trotsky in his memorandum entitled "Pilsudchina, fashizm i kharakter nashei epoki," (The Regime of Piłsudski, Fascism and the Character of our Epoch), written in 1932, in Prinkipo, for his followers in Poland. Trotsky was a member of the Polish Commission set up to analyze the "May error," and, according to him, Warski was pardoned because he had promised beforehand to assume responsibility for the failure. The memorandum is to be found in the Trotsky Archive, Houghton Library, Harvard University.

6. *KPP: uchwały i rezolucje,* II, 360–366. "[T]he Party swept by the petty bourgeois wave lost its own identity, and found itself at the tail of the masses," said Bukharin at a meeting of the Enlarged Executive Committee of the Comintern, *IPC,* December 3, 1926, p. 1478.

7. Karol Radek, "Is the Soviet Union threatened by Intervention," *IPC,* February 10, 1927. J. Stalin, "Concerning Current Questions," *IPC,* August 4, 1927; B. Vonsovskii and G. Rudomino, *Kuda Piłsudski vedet Polshu* (Mińsk, 1927), pp. 95–97; M. H., "Will Piłsudski make War in May?," *IPC,* April 17, 1930.

8. J. Bratkowski [J. Czeszejko-Sochacki], "Poland — Instigator of Imperialist War and Intervention," *IPC,* August 1, 1934; also the speech of Leński at the Thirteenth Plenum of the Executive Committee of the Comintern, *IPC,* Feb-

ruary 5, 1934. In support of his thesis Leński did not hesitate to quote Trotsky; the original text of the speeches made by the CPP delegation at the Thirteenth Plenum was reprinted in a separate pamphlet entitled *KPP w walce z wojną, faszyzmem i atakami kapitału* (The CPP in its Struggle Against War, Fascism, and Attacks of Capitalism) (Moscow, 1934).

9. For the gist of the "Majority" viewpoint, see Wera Kostrzewa's article "K roli mielkoy burzhuazii v revolutsii" (On the Role of Petty Bourgeoisie in Revolution), *Bolshevik*, October 1926; for attacks on the author's theory, and her own as well as her friend's reply to them, see *Nowy przegląd,* January-February 1927; a summary of the views of the "Minority" may be found in the article by J. Ryng [Jerzy Heryng], "Jak szliśmy do programu KPP" How We Marched Toward the Program of the CPP), *Nowy przegląd,* No. 8 (71), 1935.

10. The CPP never published a full report of the Congress minutes. The present account has been based largely on one published in Reguła, *Historia KPP,* pp. 199–205, on fragments to be found in current issues of the *IPC,* and on *KPP: uchwały . . . ,* Vol. II, chapter four. The bitterness of the struggle may be judged from the fact that for years members of the warring factions refused to talk to their opponents living next door to them at the Lux Hotel in Moscow, A. Burmeister, "Syzyfowe prace," *Kultura,* November 1952, p. 123.

11. *IPC,* July 30, 1928, p. 739.

12. For the material concerning the Fourth Congress of the CPP see *KPP: uchwały i rezolucje,* Vol. II, chapter four. The previously cited pamphlet by Brand on the economic background of the 1926 coup also put forward the theory of "agrarization of Poland" resulting from her inevitable enslavement to Anglo-American capital; see also Vonsovskii and Rudomino, *Kuda Piłsudski vedet Polshu,* pp. 35–37.

13. Shumski, for some time, was Commissar of Education of the Soviet Ukraine; he tended to accept Lenin's nationality doctrine at its face value. Immediately after the Fourth Congress of the CPP the "shumskist" group of Wasilhiv, Maxymovich, and Turiansky seceded from the CPWU and set up a separate unit. A large group of CPWU members followed the secessionists. Similar developments took place within the Byelorussian pro-Communist groups and within the Communist-inclined "Selrob," which split into two separate parties.

14. In this respect see the "Open letter of the Executive of the Comintern to all members of the CPP," *KPP: uchwały i rezolucje,* Vol. II, chapter five.

15. Isaac Deutscher, *Stalin* (London, 1949), p. 396.

16. *IPC,* October 12, 1928, pp. 1291–92.

17. *Ibid.,* September 17, 1928.

18. "The White Terror in the Poland of Piłsudski," *IPC,* October 21, 1926. During the summer of 1926, Warski started to publish a legal periodical *Trybuna* (Tribune). Between 1925 and 1933 there was a lot of coming and going between Moscow and Warsaw, and Polish Communists were, generally speaking, not hindered in their trips to the Soviet Union and back. At the beginning of 1930, there were slightly over 2,700 political prisoners in Poland, while W. Rożek, a Communist deputy, claimed there were 6,000. *Sprawozdanie stenograficzne . . . z 6 lutego 1930,* p. 37. The period following the signature of the Polish-Soviet nonaggression pact, the years 1932–1933, brought even a note of cordiality into the mutual relations between the two countries with a great deal of cultural exchange and even occasional military visits.

19. See *IPC*, August 16, 1928, p. 890; also *Sprawozdanie stenograficzne z . . . posiedzenia sejmu z dnia 3 lutego 1930 roku*, pp. 85, 89.

20. "The membership of the CPP [including the CPWU and CPWB] never exceeded 20,000." Tadeusz Daniszewski in "Droga walki KPP" (The Fighting Path of the CPP), *Nowe drogi*, November-December 1948, p. 148.

21. When the Independent Peasant Party was dissolved in 1927, some of its former members founded the organization generally known as the "Peasant Self-help," a much more strongly pro-Communist group than the former one.

22. "Selrob" was the colloquial name for the Ukrainian Alliance of Peasants and Workers, the largest Marxist organization in Galicia. The party was founded in 1927; in the summer of 1927 a leftist group seceded and founded the "Selrob-Left." The fact that the CPP was the focal point of dissatisfied national minorities, largely contributed to the growth of xenophobia, especially anti-Semitism, in the country.

The party's attraction for the Slavic national minorities decreased only after 1930 in connection with the shifts of the Soviet nationality policy. By that time the Polish peasants became increasingly attracted to the CPP.

23. The group numbered several thousand members; it disintegrated in 1929 and its left wing joined the CPP.

24. A. Strapiński, *Wywrotowe partie polityczne* (Subversive Political Parties) (Warsaw, 1933), pp. 39–40.

25. *IPC*, August 16, 1928, p. 890; also *IPC*, August 18, 1928, pp. 918–925; see also *KPP: uchwały i rezolucje*, Vol. II, chapter five.

26. In this respect, see a frank statement in *Die Ukrainische nationale Frage. Materialen zur Frage der sogenantern ukrainischen nationalen Abweichung ("Schumskismus") in der komunistischen Partei der Ukraine und der Komunistischen Partei der West-Ukraine* (Lemberg, 1928), pp. 3–4; also B. Yulskii, *Panska Polsha — avanpost interventsii* (The Landlord Poland — a Vanguard of Intervention) (Kharkov, 1931), pp. 44–45.

27. See the speech by Adolf Warski in defense of "Hromada" in *Sprawozdanie stenograficzne z 327 posiedzehnia sejmu R.P. z dnia 22 marca 1927*, p. 15; "Against the Brutal Policy of Suppression of the Fascist Government in Poland," *IPC*, February 17, 1927; "The Fight in Defense of the Hromada," *IPC*, February 23, 1928; also, *Sprawozdanie stenograficzne . . . z dnia 13 marca 1929r.*, pp. 57–58; for the Soviet interpretation of the Byelorussian movement, see Felix Kon, *Zapadnaya Belorussia kolonia panskoi Polshi* (Western Byelorussia — a Colony of Landlord Poland) (Moscow, 1928), *passim*.

28. *Die ukrainische nationale Frage . . .* (Lemberg, 1928), *passim;* also J. Leński, "The CPP between the Sixth and the Seventh Congress of the Communist International," *The Communist International*, July 5, and 20, 1935.

29. *Die ukrainische national Frage . . .*, pp. 4–6, 32–4; Sixth World Congress of the Comintern . . . ," *IPC*, August 25, 1928, p. 964; also Yulskii, *Panska Polsha — avanpost interventsii*, p. 48.

30. "The leadership of the Communist Party of West Ukraine has not been up to its task, was not able to take up the counterattack at once, to expose the interventionist machinations regarding the Soviet Union and thus to strengthen confidence in the Soviet national policy among the masses. Opportunist vacillations and capitulatory tendencies appeared in the weakest link of the party. The fact that a certain part of the activists and the leaders gave way to the pressure of nationalism proved that the nationalist ideology of Vasilkov had not been

completely overcome and that not sufficient resistance was offered to the national opportunist conception of Skrypnik, as result of which hostile elements
were supported . . . For or against the Soviet Union and its national policy this
is the dividing line," Leński, "XIII Plenum of the Executive Committee of the
Comintern," *IPC*, February 5, 1934; see also *KPP: uchwały i rezolucje*, III,
348–354.

31. Resolution of the C.C. of the C.P. of Poland on the Situation in the Western Ukraine," *IPC*, October 16, 1930; "Against the reign of terror . . . Appeal
of the C.C. CPP and C.C. CPUW," *ibid.*, October 30, 1930; see also *KPP:
uchwały i rezolucje*, III, 209–239, and 333–340.

32. For the minutes: *V zjazd KPP — uchwały — rezolucje — materiały* (Warsaw, 1930); for an evaluation of the "leftist" leader, J. Leński, see "The V
Party Congress of the C.P. of Poland," *IPC*, October 23, 1930. See also *KPP:
uchwały i rezolucje*, Vol. III, chapter two; at the time of the congress the CPP
numbered about 14,000 members while the Union of Polish Communist Youth
had about 7,500 members. The social composition of the CPP was as follows:
industrial workers 30%; white collar workers, artisans, and people employed in
small establishments 45%; peasants 25%; *ibid.*, III, 104.

33. An article by S. Żbikowski (a Soviet general of Polish origin commanding
a Soviet military school for the CPP) in *Żołnierz rewolucji* (The Soldier of the
Revolution), November 1931, reads as follows (quoted by Reguła, p. 268):
"The worker and peasant masses must come out against the Polish bourgeoisie
in case of war, and collaborate with the Red Army . . . Therefore, wherever
the situation warrants, in case of a mass resistance of the population against
mobilization, they are to form partisan movements in the rear of the Polish army,
and to organize strikes in industry and transportation. The principal aim of these
orders is the active support of the Red Army; together with a general strike and
an armed insurrection which is to transform the imperialist war into a civil war."

34. The Comintern's support of German revisionist tendencies was gradually
withdrawn after Hitler's seizure of power; in 1933, K. Radek referred to Pomerania as an area "in which the majority of inhabitants are Polish"; K. R.,
"Poland and Danzig," *IPC*, August 25, 1933, p. 803.

35. Mirosław Zdziarski (M. Wojtkiewicz) attacked the Central Committee for
its tactics of splitting the trade-unions and establishing separate Communist unions; Halma, "The Question of T.U. Tactics in Poland," *The Communist International*, No. 9, 1930.

36. The platform, which was an adaptation of the Comintern program to local
Polish conditions, was finally voted by the CPP in the autumn of 1932, at its
sixth congress. For the text, see *Materiały do programu KPP;* also *KPP:
uchwały i rezolucje*, Vol. III, chapter four.

37. The CPP employed approximately two hundred full-time officials and a
much larger number of half-time employees. See Reguła, p. 227. A former prominent member of the CPP, describing the financial dependence of the smaller
parties on the Russian party writes: ". . . Moscow encouraged them to spend
on organization and propaganda beyond their means; and the more they did so
the bigger grew their bureaucratic establishments and their need for subsidies.
Accustomed to easy money they then tended to neglect the collection of their own
dues, which had a demoralizing effect on them . . ." Deutscher, *Stalin*, p. 397.

38. "The Brest trial is an epilogue of the disputes within the different factions
of Polish fascism . . . There stands in the dock the morally corrupt so-called

'Polish democracy,' which is eaten away by inner treachery," the Warsaw correspondent of the *IPC*, J. Najda, wrote on November 5, 1931; see also J. Bratkowski [Jerzy Czeszejko-Sochacki], *Poland on the Road to Revolutionary Crisis* (New York, 1933), pp. 61–62.

39. A February 1932 resolution of the Plenum of the CPP Central Committee declared that in 1931 "The general growth in the number of nuclei [cells] applies primarily to peasant nuclei," according to Bewer, in "Questions Relating to Factory Nuclei in the CPP," *IPC*, June 16, 1932, p. 559. See also Aronsky, "Questions Connected with the Growth of the CPP," *IPC*, June 9, 1932, in which the author writes, "In the CPP, excluding West Ukraine, the percentage of Jewish workers from small industry was reduced in one year from 30 to 23 per cent . . . this is the consequence of the rapid growth of the rural organizations . . ."

40. The number of industrial unemployed rose from 185,000 at the end of 1928 to 343,000 at the end of 1933, and to 466,000 by the close of 1936. The Labor Fund, created in March 1933, for the purpose of financing public works, only slightly alleviated the situation. Unemployment in the villages, an endemic feature even in times of prosperity, was still more aggravated. For criticism of the governmental policy on unemployment, see the *Sprawozdanie stenograficzne . . . z dnia 5 lutego 1931,* pp. 75–81; . . . *16 października 1931,* pp. 14–18; . . . *20 października 1931,* pp. 18–19; . . . *3 listopada 1932,* pp. 92–100; also the report of Lenski at the "IX Plenum of the Executive Committee of the Communist International . . . ," *IPC*, June 30, 1931; "The Next Task of the CPP," *IPC*, August 20, 1931; "The Experience of the Unemployment Movement of the Capitalist Countries," *IPC*, October 30, 1931; J. Bratkowski, *Poland on the Road to Revolutionary Crisis*, pp. 81–129.

41. The industrial strikes rose as follows: in 1930, there were 312 strikes; in 1931, 357; in 1932, 504; in 1933, 631; in 1934, 946; in 1935, 1,165; in 1936, 2,056, and in 1937, after the depression had ended, 2,078 strikes were recorded. See Feliks Gross, *The Polish Worker* (New York, 1944), p. 140. For a presentation of the peasant strikes, sympathetic to the CPP see J. Gójski, *Strajki i bunty chłopskie w Polsce* (Warsaw, 1949).

42. For the psychology of sit-down strikes, see Gross, *The Polish Worker*, p. 140.

43. Leński, "The Situation in Poland and the C.P.," *IPC*, December 22, 1932; also Leński's report in the issue of February 5, 1934. For a case study of Communist tactics during a strike, see the pamphlet published by the CPP, *Dziesięciodniowy strajk białostockich włókniarzy* (Białystok, 1932).

44. The problem of Trotskyism in the CPP has been discussed on the basis of material to be found at the Trotsky Archives, Houghton Library, Harvard University, supplemented by the depositions of Messrs. Isaac Deutscher and Paweł Minc, both former leaders of the Trotskyist faction of the CPP, and some notes of Mr. Jerzy Luxemburg, former prosecuting judge for cases of special importance at the Warsaw Court of Appeals. See also *KPP: uchwały i rezolucje,* II, 140–143; characteristically enough the selection contains little material on this vital issue.

45. For an attempt at identification of Luxemburgism and Trotskyism, see a speech by L. M. Kaganovich, *IPC*, December 24, 1931; this was not devoid of foundation since the Left Opposition used some of Luxemburg's arguments. For the CPP's attempts to repudiate both Luxemburgism and Trotskyism, see the historical periodical of the CPP, *Z pola walki*, No. 13, 1832, *passim.*

46. "Resolution of the C.C. of the C.P. of Poland Against the Right Danger in the C.P. of Germany," *IPC*, December 7, 1928; also "Against the Right Danger. The C.C. of the C.P. of the Soviet Union in the Fight Against the Right Danger," *IPC*, March 22, 1929.

47. *IPC*, February 25, 1928, p. 230.

48. In his writings, Deutscher developed the theory that Piłsudski's regime was not Fascist but merely a military-police dictatorship; this was not, however, the attitude of the whole opposition group of the CPP, most of whom followed Trotsky's viewpoint in this respect. Deutscher, for instance, quarrelled with Trotsky over his analysis of the Piłsudski regime, which Trotsky described as Fascist. Deutscher and his followers argued that under a Fascist regime there was little or no scope for class struggle and revolutionary activity, whereas the Piłsudski regime was a military and bureaucratic dictatorship, with no real mass basis and, therefore, too weak to suppress revolutionary activity. For Trotsky's view, see "Pilsudchina, fashizm and kharakter nashei epokki," Trotsky Archives, 1930, Houghton Library, Harvard.

49. See Trotsky's essay of August 31, 1932, "Privet Polskoi levoi oppozitsi" (Greetings to the Polish Left Opposition), Houghton Library, Harvard.

50. "Stalinisme est le syphilis du mouvement ouvrier," Trotsky's letter to Victore Serge of March 5, 1937, Trotsky Archives, Houghton Library, Harvard.

51. See Trotsky's essay "Evreiskii organ oppozitsii v Polshe" (The Jewish Organ of the Opposition in Poland), 1932, Houghton Library. The absence of trials of Trotsky's followers between 1932 and 1938, when such trials were rather frequent occurrences as far as regular members of the CPP were concerned, and the ephemeral character of Trotskyist periodicals in Poland, all seem to indicate that the faction was neither numerous nor very active. The Trotsky Archives at Houghton Library contain only scanty evidence of contacts between Trotsky and his followers in Poland.

CHAPTER 8   BACK TO THE UNITED FRONT —
DISSOLUTION OF THE PARTY

1. *IPC*, March 24, 1933. It is almost certain that the policy of the two parties was a result of Comintern instructions, since the Comintern wished to test united front tactics in those countries most exposed to German pressure. For a careful selection of documents concerning the united front tactics of the CPP see *KPP: uchwały i rezolucje*, Vol. III, chapter five.

2. G. Henrykowski [S. Amsterdam], "For the Class Unity of the Trade Union Movement in Poland," *IPC*, September 14, 1934; "Why the C.C. of the *Bund* has Broken Off United Front Negotiations. Communiqué of C.C. of the CPP," *IPC*, November 10, 1934; Leński, "The United Front Must Be Extended," *IPC*, December 1, 1934. For an explanation of the Communist approach to the united and popular fronts, see M. Wołoszczowski, *O jednolity front proletariatu . . .* [Paris], 1936, pp. 23ff. For a selection of carefully edited documents illustrating the party's efforts to bring about the "united front," see *KPP w obronie niepodległości Polski* (CPP in Defense of Poland's Independence) (Warsaw, 1953), pp. 225–413.

3. For a blunt reply from the PPS, see M. Niedziałkowski, "Złudzenia i

możliwości. Sprawa jednolitego frontu" (Illusions and Possibilities. The Problem of the United Front), *Robotnik*, March 27, 1934.

4. *Robotnik* of November 18, 1932, stated, "The PPS is faced with the task of giving the maturing mood definite organizational forms, of rallying them around a real workers' and peasants' government . . ."

5. N. Barlicki, "Mea culpa," *Robotnik*, Warsaw, January 1, 1933, and Naprzód (Cracow), January 3, 1933. This opinion was supported by several other left-wing PPS members — Dr. Adam Próchnik, Stanisław Dubois, and Andrzej Strug. Dr. Bolesław Drobner, the *enfant terrible* of the PPS, aso shared the leftist proclivities of these leaders and, at various times, was even inclined to go much further than his more balanced and responsible comrades.

6. W. Floriański, "Jedność akcji na frontach walki narodowej" (Unity of the Action on the National Front), *Nowy przegląd*, March-April 1935; G. Rwal, "O jednolity front proletariacki na Ukrainie Zachodniej" (For the United Front in Western Ukraine), *ibid.*; Leński, "Bardziej niż kiedykolwiek jednolity front" (The United Front More than Ever), *ibid.*; Leński, "The United Front — the Need of the Hour," *IPC*, April 13, 1935; W. Floriański, "The Fascist Constitution in Poland," *IPC*, April 20, 1935; G. Henrykowski, "The Political Strike Against the Fascist Constitution in Poland," *IPC*, July 13, 1935.

7. Leński, "Under the Banner of the People's Front in Poland," *IPC*, August 3, 1935; also Henrykowski, "Struggle for the Anti-Fascist People's Front in Poland," *IPC*, August 24, 1935; Leński, "Na drodze do antyfaszystowskiego frontu ludowego" (On the Way to the Anti-Fascist Popular Front), *Nowy przegląd*, August 1937; Leński, "Kongres jedności walki" (The Congress of the Unity of Action), *Nowy przegląd*, September-October 1937; Henrykowski, "Co dalej z jednolitym frontem" (What more is to be Done with the United Front), *Nowy przegląd*, December 1937.

8. *IPC*, October 12, 1935, p. 1329; also "Open Letter of the CPP," *IPC*, November 16, 1935.

9. K. Czapiński, "Manewry, Manewry bez końca . . ." (Maneuvers, Endless Maneuvers . . .), *Robotnik*, March 7, 1935.

10. *IPC*, August 17, 1935, p. 1935; and the last part of Leński's report in *IPC*, October 30, 1935, pp. 1407–1409; see also the issues of November 11, 1935, p. 1493 and of December 2, 1935, p. 1613; also Lenski's article "The CPP Between the Sixth and the Seventh Congress of the C.I.," *The Communist Internationale*, Nos. 13 and 20 of July 5 and 20, 1935. The years 1928–1935 were, according to Leński, "a period of big success on the road to the Bolshevization of our Party," which, however, was not yet "consistently" and "firmly" Bolshevik. See also *Kommunisticheskii internatsional pered VII vsemirnym kongressom* (The Communist International Before the Seventh World Congress) (Moscow, 1935), the chapter "Poland."

11. Quoted by Tadeusz Daniszewski, in "Droga walki KPP" (The Fighting Way of the CPP), *Nowe drogi*, November-December 1948, p. 144; for the story of the united front efforts of the CPP from 1934 to 1936, by a Polish Workers' Party publicist, see J. Kowalczyk, "Rok przełomu. Jak się tworzył jednolity front" (The Decisive Year. How the United Front was Being Created), *Głos ludu*, October 30, November 1 and 2, 1948; see also numerous articles on the subject of J. Brun (Brunowicz), collected in the second volume of his *Pisma wybrane*.

12. *Uchwała zasadnicza XXIV kongresu PPS* (The Platform of the XXIV Congress of the PPS) (mimeo., n.p., n.d.), p. 3. To these demands a CPP

publicist retorted: "The demand of a united front in the USSR or of freedom of action for the Trotskyites and the Mensheviks . . . is a treacherous attempt of sabotaging the united front in the capitalist countries . . . ," M. Wołoszczowski, *O jednolity front proletariatu* . . . , p. 25.

13. *Program Polskiej Partii Socjalistycznej* (Program of the PPS), a new edition with a foreword by Adam Ciołkosz (London, n.d.), p. 14.

14. In 1937 several prominent PPS writers and publicists, such as Barlicki, Próchnik, and Dubois, had joined the *Dziennik popularny* (The Popular Daily), which favored a united front; this took place with the party's permission.

15. The last plenary session of the Central Committee of the CPP again appealed to the democratic parties to form a united front, and declared that the C.P. would be prepared to support a government formed by the PPS and the Peasant Party. *IPC*, May 8, 1937, pp. 473–474.

16. M. Wołoszczowski, *O jednolity front proletariatu* . . . , p. 35.

17. Wiktor Alter, *Antysemityzm gospodarczy w świetle cyfr* (Economic Anti-Semitism in the Light of Statistics) (Warsaw, 1937), p. 140; see also J. Brun, *Pisma wybrane*, Vol. II, Part I, pp. 116–136 and Vol. II, Part II, pp. 16–21, 102–111 and 166–173.

18. *Robotnik*, November 4, 1923.

19. For the "Socialist" view of the Wilno Communist group, see the novel by Jerzy Putrament, *Rzeczywistość* (Warsaw, 1947); for the attempts at infiltration of various non-Communist groups see: *KPP: uchwały i rezolucje*, III, pp. 535–540, 584–588; in 1936 there were up to sixteen legal but crypto-Communist papers in Poland; *ibid.*, p. 22.

20. "For the Unity of the Working Class in Poland. From the Resolution of the Fifth Plenum of the C.C. of the CPP," *IPC*, March 3, 1937. For the CPP support of the Loyalist cause in Spain see *KPP: uchwały i rezolucje*, III, 589–591, 640–641.

21. "Each soldier of the Dąbrowski Brigade ought to propagate the policy of the United Front," *Dąbrowszczak*, April 3, 1937; often the paper simply reprinted appeals and communiqués of the CPP or only slightly rewritten passages from party publications; the appeal of the CPP to the Dąbrowski Brigade, *ibid.*, March 10, 1937, emphasizes ideological links between the brigade and the party. The link was also reflected in the following articles, to mention only a few: "Pierwszego Maja w Polsce" (The First of May in Poland), *ibid.*, May 17, 1937; "W jedenastą rocznice śmierci Dzierżyńskiego" (On the Eleventh Anniversary of the Death of Dzierżyński), *ibid.*, August 4, 1947; "Odezwa ochotników batalionu Dąbrowskiego do chłopów i robotników w Polsce" (Appeal of the Volunteers of the Dąbrowski Battalion to the Peasants and Workers of Poland), *ibid.*, September 27, 1937; "Pozdrowienia ze Związku Radzieckiego . . ." (Greetings from the Soviet Union . . .), *ibid.*, November 3, 1937; "Do Czerwonej Armii ZSSR" (To the Red Army of the USSR), *ibid.*, November 25, 1937.

22. Rada, "Polish Fascism Tries to Blackmail the T.U. Delegation," *IPC*, June 26, 1937; for the impressions of the "Bundist" delegates from Spain, see, J. Deutsch and W. Alter, *Hiszpania w ogniu* (Spain in Flames) (Warsaw, 1937). The pamphlet provoked vivid protests on the part of the CPP press because of its attack on terrorist and totalitarian methods applied by the Communists toward their opponents; "List otwarty w sprawie rewelacji tow. Altera" (Open Letter Concerning the Revelations of Comrade Alter), *Dąbrowszczak*, June 25,

1937; for a Communist point of view concerning the Spanish Civil War see J. Brun, *Pisma wybrane*, II, *passim*.

23. Karol Świerczewski was born in Warsaw, but left Poland for Russia during World War I. He took part in the Bolshevik revolution and in the Civil War. After graduating from the Soviet Military Academy he advanced rapidly, reached the rank of general, and was dispatched to Spain; there, for some time, he commanded the Polish Brigade, under the assumed name of "Walter." Until the end of 1937 the brigade published its own press organ, *Dąbrowszczak*. After 1938 the paper was turned into a Polish version of the central periodical called *The Volunteer of Freedom*. Altogether, some 8000 people served in the brigade. For a factual account of the brigade's story see, "Zapomniani ludzie" (The Forgotten People), *Robotnik polski w Wielkiej Brytanii*, January 1, 1944.

24. "O niekatorykh rezervach trotskistskich provocatorov . . ." (About Some Reserves of Trotskyite Provocateurs), *Kommunisticheskii Internatsional*, No. 3, 1937; I.A. Sventitskii [Święcicki], "Provocatory za rabotoi" (Provocateurs at Work), *ibid.*, No. 1; also T. S. Bobrovskaia, "Vraga nado znat" (Know your Enemy), *ibid.*, No. 1, 1938. From Święcicki's article we learn that "the leading figures of both factions, the 'Majority' and the 'Minority,' following the instructions of the [Polish] counter-intelligence, widely applied the policy of deceiving the Comintern"; see also *World News and Views* (formerly *International Press Correspondence*), April 6, 1939, p. 382.

25. The affair of Tomasz Dąbal did not attract so much attention. The first head of the *Krestintern*, or the Peasant International, was liquidated without much publicity for having associated too intimately with bourgeois circles (his wife came from that milieu) and with the Polish police.

26. W. Albert, "Pilsudchikovskaya sistema provokatsii" (Piłsudskite System of Provocation), *Kommunisticheskii internatsional*, October 1, 1934; and "W sprawie peowiackich prowokatorów," (Concerning the Case of the Provocateurs from the Polish Military Organization), *Nowy przegląd*, January 1935.

27. The story of Sochacki's alleged spying, as reported by Ypsilon in *Pattern for World Revolution*, (Chicago-New York, 1947), might very well be the version which the NKVD purposely circulated in Moscow. The Comintern failed to provide any convincing proof of Sochacki's guilt.

28. Stalin's suspicion of the Poles was reflected in a characteristic incident which took place in 1943, during General de Gaulle's visit to the Kremlin. When Gaston Palewski, chief of General de Gaulle's cabinet, was introduced to the Soviet leader, Stalin said: "You must be a Pole," to which Palewski replied that he was merely of Polish extraction. Stalin retorted: "Raz Poliak — vsiegda Poliak" (once a Pole — always a Pole).

29. For substantiation by a CPP member who apparently was in Moscow at that time, see A. Burmeister, "Tragedia polskich komunistów" (The Tragedy of Polish Communists), *Kultura*, January 1952; another source of evidence as to the course of the purge is the reluctant and cautious testimony of those who survived the tribulations of Soviet camps. According to the estimates of the author, no more than seventy or eighty of those who survived the war were released and returned to Poland after 1944.

30. "One of the most unsavory jobs assigned to this department is the luring to Moscow of foreign Communists suspected of disloyalty to Stalin. A Communist who believes himself in good standing with the Comintern will receive word from the executive committee that he is needed in Moscow. Flattered at

this recognition of his importance, he hastens to the Comintern capital. Upon his arrival, he is turned over to the OGPU and disappears. Many such catches are credited to the Cadres Section, which through its network of spies frequently receives 'information' not only false, but malicious, tending to show that the individual in question has not been toeing the Stalinist line. The number of foreign Communists who have been thus lured to their destruction will probably never be ascertained." W. G. Krivitsky, *I Was Stalin's Agent* (London, 1940), p. 82. See also the memoirs of the former Finnish Communist leader, A. Tuominen, *Kremlin Kellot* (Helsinki, 1956), pp. 250–253.

31. Burmeister, "Tragedia polskich komunistów," *Kultura*, January 1952; according to Tuominen, p. 250, the liquidation of the CPP took place in the spring of 1937; the evidence is conflicting in this respect.

32. Tadeusz Daniszewski, "Droga walki KPP" (The Way of Struggle of the CPP), *Nowe drogi*, November-December 1948. The exact date of the dissolution is not known; it took place sometime after May 1, 1938; on that day the party still distributed its customary May Day appeal; the last document published in Volume III of *KPP: uchwały i rezolucje*, bears the date June 1938.

33. *Kommunisticheskii Internatsional*, No. 4, April, 1939, p. 119.

34. "The Eighteenth Congress of the Communist Party of the Soviet Union (B). Report . . . given by Comrade D. Manuilsky," *World News and Views*, April 6, 1939, p. 382.

35. For the rehabilitation of the CPP see *Trybuna ludu*, of February 19, 1956; for Khrushchev's view see *Khrushchev Remembers*, Vol. I, Boston, 1970, p. 107.

PART III: THE POLISH WORKERS' PARTY

Many of the periodicals used in these chapters are to be found in the archives of the Polish Underground Study Trust, which is in process of publishing a multivolume collection entitled *Armia Krajowa w dokumentach* . . . (The Home Army in Documents . . .), 1970 —.

CHAPTER 9 THE UNION OF POLISH PATRIOTS AND THE POLISH WORKERS' PARTY

1. Quoted in *Official Documents Concerning Polish-German and Polish-Soviet Relations, 1933–1939* (London-Melbourne, n.d.), p. 189.

2. R. J. Sontag and J. S. Beddie, eds., *Nazi-Soviet Relations, 1939–1941. Documents from the Archives of the German Foreign Office*, U. S. Department of State (Washington, 1948), p. 89.

3. Quoted by *Soviet Peace Policy, Four Speeches by V. Molotov*, published for the *Anglo-Russian New Bulletin* (London, 1941), p. 101.

4. *The Dark Side of the Moon* [anonymous] (London, 1944), p. 213.

5. Wanda Wasilewska, daughter of a distinguished Polish Socialist who for some time had been a close friend and collaborator of Piłsudski, secretly embraced communism long before the war. In 1940 she married a Soviet-Ukrainian writer, Korneychuk, who, in 1944, became First Deputy Commissar of Foreign Affairs of the Ukrainian SSR.

Helen Usiyevich was a daughter of Feliks Kon. She spent period from 1920 to 1939 in Russia.

6. According to data collected by the Polish Ministry of Information in London, approximately 1,500,000 people were deported during the 1939–1941 period of Soviet rule in Eastern Poland.

7. Wiktor Sukiennicki, *Biała Księga* . . . , Paris, 1964, pp. 102–115.

8. *Ibid.*, pp. 116–142.

8. *Ibid.*, pp. 42–43.

9. The left wing of the PPS seceded in September 1941, and formed a separate group called Organization of Polish Socialists, or OPS. This secession was a protest against the policy of the party's leadership, which allegedly favored collaboration with remnants of the prewar regime; out of the OPS emerged the Workers' Party of Polish Socialists, which soon became an instrument of the Communists. "Organizational Reports of the Polish Underground Movement," Nos. 118 and 190; a complete set of these reports is available in the Archives of the Polish Underground Study Trust, hereafter referred to as A.P.U.S.T.

10. "In the German occupied zone," writes General Bór-Komorowski, "the Communists refrained from activity, thereby showing that the Soviets were prepared to stand by their agreement with Germany. In March 1940, my staff received information that an NKVD mission had come to Cracow to work out with the Gestapo the methods they were jointly to adopt against Polish military organizations." Tadeusz Bór-Komorowski, *The Secret Army* (London, 1951), p. 46.

11. "By the time Germany started her attack on Russia, there were no less than 168 underground periodicals being published in Poland. Among all these, however, there was not one single organ of the Communist Party. It was only in November 1941, that a modest paper appeared with the title *Miecz I Młot* (Sword and Hammer). And this was after twenty-six months of German occupation and five months after the beginning of the war between Russia and Germany." *Ibid.*, pp. 121–222. Report No. 15, on the internal situation from March 15 till April 2, 1940, transmitted to London by the Intelligence Service of the Polish Underground Movement, also confirms only limited Communist activity in the *General-Gouvernement*. Archives of the Polish Underground Study Trust in London. "Communist Activities in the *General-Gouvernement*," February, 1941, A.P.U.S.T.

12. The name was that of a Polish national hero, General Tadeusz Kościuszko, also known in the United States where he had taken part in the War of Independence.

13. Gomułka was born in 1905 in Krosno, Galicia, the son of a Socialist trade-unionist. He became a blacksmith's apprentice and a trade-union organizer at the age of 16. Gomułka started his political career during the twenties as a Communist in the Trade Union of Chemical Workers, in the oil district of Eastern Galicia. In 1932 he was arrested in Łódź, convicted, and sentenced to four years' detention, but soon released because of his poor health. Back in conspiratorial work in April 1936, Gomułka was again arrested and sentenced to seven years of imprisonment. This time he was not released until the outbreak of the war, in September 1939. He fought against the Germans in Warsaw. He openly disapproved of the Nazi-Soviet pact and urged the Comintern to create a Communist underground in Poland. In December 1942, Gomułka became secretary of the Warsaw branch of the PPR and, at the end of the year, a

member of the party's Central Committee. Gomułka strongly disapproved of the collaboration between the party and the Gestapo, collaboration that had been ordered by Moscow. In November 1943, Gomułka became secretary-general of the PPR, at a time when communications between the party and Moscow were temporarily broken. The Soviet party, therefore, had nothing to do with his nomination.

14. *W. dziesiątą rocznicę powstania PPR: materiały i dokumenty* (Warsaw, 1952), pp. 23–27. When the dissolution of the Comintern was decided upon on May 15, 1943, its organ *Kommunisticheskii Internatsional* in its last issue, Nos. 5–6, 1943, published resolutions of various Communist parties, including the PPR, approving the step taken by the Presidium of the Comintern.

15. *Trybuna wolności,* February 1, 1942.

16. *W dziesiątą rocznicę powstania PPR,* pp. 83–87.

17. "Głowy gorące ale mętne" (Foggy but Fiery Heads), *Biuletyn informacyjny* (Information Bulletin) (Warsaw), December 4, 1941.

18. "What is to be Done?" *Trybuna wolności,* January 15, 1943.

19. Reports No. 190 and 220, A.P.U.S.T., also Bór-Komorowski, *The Secret Army,* pp. 118–119.

20. "Organizational Report of the Polish Underground Movement No. 190," A.P.U.S.T.

21. Report of the Polish Ministry of Interior of March 11, 1943, A.P.U.S.T.; also Bór-Komorowski, *The Secret Army,* pp. 119–120; "List Otwarty" (An Open Letter), *Trybuna wolności,* January 25, 1943; the letter was written by W. Gomułka.

22. Later the agreement was repudiated by Moscow. Stanisław Mikołajczyk, *The Rape of Poland* (New York and Toronto, 1948), p. 42.

23. Reports on "The Organizing Activities and the Internal Situation Inside the Communist Camp" and "The Communist Problem in Poland Against the Background of War and Occupation," both in A.P.U.S.T.

"Despite its numerical insignificance," writes the commander in chief of the Home Army about the Communist underground, "its existence was a danger to us because of the anonymity of the underground movement. The people saw no difference between this small group and the organization to which the overwhelming majority of the fighters belonged. At the beginning, few people knew even the official name, Home Army. It was usually said in Poland that a man belonged to 'the organization.' In these circumstances, the deeds of PPR units (which, of course, were also anonymous) were identified with those of the Home Army." Bór-Komorowski, *The Secret Army,* p. 170.

24. Report on the Communist activities for the period November 1942–July 1943; also report of the Polish Ministry of Interior of March 11, 1943; both in A.P.U.S.T.

25. *Ibid.*

26. Organizational Report of the Polish Underground Movement No. 118, A.P.U.S.T.

27. A declaration of the Central Committee of the PPR of March 1, 1943, *W dziesiątą rocznicę powstania PPR,* pp. 138–140. Great emphasis was put on organizing a people's militia. In November 1943 the PPR published a more detailed platform, which is the first concrete plan of the Communist take-over. Political power, insisted the declaration, should be in the hands of the PPR "as the representative of popular masses." The PPR is, of course, "the vanguard

of the working class," the continuation of the traditions of the Social Democracy of Poland and Lithuania and of the Communist Party of Poland. After the liberation all governmental organs will be created by workers, peasants, and intelligentsia. All Polish lands must belong to Poland; in the West and on the Baltic Sea we have to reconquer "all lands which are ethnographically Polish or which were Germanized by force. . . ." In the East, the Ukrainian and the Byelorussian population should be granted the right of self-determination. Close friendship should be maintained with the Soviet Union. After the country's liberation all German nationals will be interned, all German loot seized by the Polish authorities, all war criminals arrested and punished. People's militia must be immediately organized; the the People's Guard will be the nucleus of the future Polish Armed Forces. Banking, large industries, transport and large estates will be confiscated without compensation. An eight-hour working day will be introduced immediately. Political liberties and basic rights of citizens will be guaranteed. A planned but democratic scheme of social and economic reconstruction will be undertaken by the new regime, "O co walczymy," November 1943, pp. 186–209.

28. At the Nuremberg Trial the Soviet Union included the Katyń massacre in its list of German war crimes. Since it was impossible to prove that the Germans committed this particular crime, the charge was finally dropped. The crime has been recently investigated by a special committee of the U. S. Congress. For a full treatment of the matter, see J. Mackiewicz, *The Katyń Wood Massacre* (London, 1951); also Dr. Bolesław Kuśnierz, *Stalin and the Poles* (London, 1949), pp. 88–126.

29. On May 4, 1943, Stalin answered two questions submitted to him by Moscow correspondents of the London *Times* and the *New York Times,* reaffirming his desire to see a "strong and independent Poland" allied with the Soviet Union.

30. Berling was a former regular officer in the Polish army who decided to side with the Communist cause when in Soviet captivity.

31. Documents concerning the official creation of the Union of Polish Patriots and its first congress are to be found in the already quoted *W dziesiątą rocznicę powstania PPR,* pp. 222–237.

32. "Report for the period March 16-May 17, 1943," A.P.U.S.T.; also the editorial of *Trybuna wolności,* May 1, 1943.

33. Bór-Komorowski, *The Secret Army,* p. 130.

34. "Field Report, No. 12 of June 7, 1943," A.P.U.S.T.

35. "Zdrada" (Treason), *Wolna Polska,* No. 8, April 24, 1943.

36. On May 22, 1943, the Communist International dissolved itself and issued a proclamation in which it called on all supporters to concentrate their efforts toward active participation in the war of liberation. According to secret reports of the Home Intelligence Service, dissolution of the Comintern was received critically by the PPR leadership, still composed largely of former CPP members, who viewed this step as a sign of weakness toward the West. Only after some hesitation and internal controversies was the decision accepted as a temporary shift of strategy. See *A History of the PPR (Its Origins, Organization and Development from November 1942 until August 1944 — Materials and Documents),* A.P.U.S.T., p. 15; for a Communist history of the party's origins see F. Jóźwiak (Witold), *Polska Partia Robotnicza w walce o wyzwolenie narodowe i społeczne,* chapters 2–7.

37. *A History of the PPR*, p. 13.

38. *Ibid.*, pp. 18–19. Bolesław Bierut, a Communist social worker in cooperative movements, soon became a Comintern agent in Berlin, Vienna, and Prague. In 1931 he returned to Poland as a special agent to smooth out difficulties which arose between the Communist Party of Poland and Moscow. Arrested in 1933 and sentenced to seven years' imprisonment, he was released in 1938 because of an amnesty. Until the middle of 1943 Bierut was in the Soviet Union.

39. *A History of the PPR*, pp. 22ff.

40. The first chairman of this body was the future head of the Communist-controlled Democratic Party, Wacław Barcikowski, then an ardent anti-Communist. At the end of January 1944, the N.K.L. merged with some leftist but non-Communist groups and set up the so-called C.K.L. (Centralny komitet ludowy — the Central People's Committee).

41. In the autumn of 1943, the left wing of the RPPS, led by Edward Osóbka (Morawski), revolted and drew nearer to the PPR; the formal split took place in January 1944. The new group, led by Osóbka and Stanisław Szwalbe, decided to join the K.R.N. Szwalbe was an old friend of Bierut, former go-between of the Communists and left-wing Socialists of the RPPS variety.

42. *Krajowa Rada Narodowa* literally means Home National Council or National Council of Poland.

43. In reply to the PPR proposal, the underground organ of the Peasant Party, *Przez walkę do zwycięstwa* (Through Struggle to Freedom), on November 28, 1943.

"The Polish peasantry will not let itself be deluded by the misleading program of 'radical reforms' in the style of state socialism modelled on that of Russia. They do not want to become manorial serfs in the barracks of the collective farms, or slave workers in the hands of state bureaucracy."

To the refusal, Gomułka, secretary-general of the PPR since November 1943, replied in an article entitled "New Ideas of the Leaders of the Peasant Party"; he denied the PPR's intention to collectivize the country's agriculture and, on behalf of his party, extended an offer of alliance to the Peasant Party; ". . . the natural place of the peasant masses . . . is beside the workers' movement and not in the camp of reaction. . . ." *Trybuna wolności*, March 15, 1944.

44. In 1948 Gomułka admitted: "The creation of the National Council, as a national, representative, political body — a kind of clandestine parliament — was brought about with a relatively slim participation of the other political and social groups outside our own party . . . It was the polish Workers' Party which was the actual decisive power in the National Council." *Nowe drogi,* September-October 1948, p. 45.

45. This signature meant that the PPR was determined to regard the left wing of the RPPS, led by Osóbka (Morawski), as representative of the whole party; as a matter of fact, at that time, Osóbka still formally belonged to the parent party, the split taking place in January, 1944.

46. Testimony by S. Mikołajczyk and S. Bańczyk. For official correspondence between the PPR and other political groups, see *W dziesiątą rocznicę powstania PPR* . . . , pp. 254–258; establishment of the K.R.N. pp. 259–280. According to the testimony of Mr. Tadeusz Zawadzki, the first attempts at negotiating with non-Communist groups were undertaken by Paweł Finder, the predecessor of Gomułka, as far back as January 1943. The negotiations failed. For a fairly accurate description of Gomułka's attempts to attract some left-wing Socialist

and peasant groups to the K.R.N. see *Nowe drogi,* September-October 1948, No. 11, pp. 40–47; also Gomułka's writings: "List otwarty do delegatury rządu londyńskiego," (An Open Letter to the Office of the Chief Delegate of the London Government in Poland), *Trybuna Wolności,* January 15, 1943; "O myśl polityczną polskiej demokracji" (For a Political Program of the Polish Democracy), *ibid.,* September 1, 1943; "O armię ludu" (For a People's Army), *ibid.,* November 22, 1943.

47. Repudiation of the 1935 Constitution, besides being an attempt to undercut the legal basis of the Polish government in London, was to serve another specific purpose. The Constitution of 1921 had provided that, in certain circumstances, presidential power could be transferred to the Speaker of the Sejm. Since the People's Council of Poland declared itself the supreme legislative body (corresponding to the Sejm), its speaker, Bierut, would consequently have a "legal" claim to be Poland's acting head of the state.

48. Special Report of the Home Army. No. 15, of June 20, 1944, A.P.U.S.T.

49. Report from Poland No. 19 of May 19, 1944, A.P.U.S.T.

50. In 1942 Żymierski [Rola] approached the Nationalist Armed Forces or N.S.Z. with the view of obtaining a post in that organization. This offer was rejected and, previously, General Sikorski had refused to admit him to the clandestine military group out of which the Home Army grew. Back in 1914 Żymierski had joined Piłsudski's legions and in 1917, when an oath of allegiance was demanded from the legionnaires, he was among the few who took the oath.

Żymierski took part in the Polish-Soviet War of 1920. After the war he was made deputy quartermaster-general of the Polish army and in that capacity he contracted with a firm for the supply of army gas masks. The price paid by the Ministry of War was found to be excessive, and Żymierski was tried, convicted for bribery, and sentenced to five years' imprisonment. After his release from prison, Żymierski left the country and went to Paris; during the Spanish Civil War he started a business supplying arms to the Republicans. His contact with the Communists dates from that time. From Poland Żymierski contacted the Communist underground in April 1943, S. Sowińska (Barbara), *Lata walki* (The Years of Struggle) (Warsaw, 1948), pp. 282.

51. For instance, "The Thieves of the Names," *Biuletyn informacyjny,* February 24, 1944.

52. For negotiations between these groups and details of the merger, see *W dziesiątą rocznicę powstania PPR* . . . , pp. 315–325 and 338–339.

53. See Gomułka's letter in *Trybuna wolności,* January 15, 1943; also "O myśl polityczną polskiej demokracji" (For a Political Line of the Polish Democracy), *ibid.,* September 1, 1943; "O armię ludu" ("For a People's Army"), *ibid.,* November 22, 1943; also "Nowe myśli wodzów stronnictwa ludowego" (New Ideas of the Peasant Party Leaders), *ibid.,* March 15, 1944.

54. For the Communist summary of the negotiations, see "Oświadczenie K.C. PPR" (A Statement of the Central Committee of the PPR), *Trybuna ludu,* February 20, 1944; see also Gomułka's lecture given in December 1944, "PPR w walce o niepodległość, Polski" (PPR in the Struggle for Poland's Independence), W. Gomułka-Wiesław, *W walce o demokrację ludową* (Warsaw, 1947), I, 89–90.

55. Bór-Komorowski, *The Secret Army,* pp. 196–197. The Polish government in London estimated that by the end of September 1944, more than 21,000 Home Army men had been arrested. Only those men and officers of the Home

Army were set free who, after a period of imprisonment, agreed to sign a declaration to the effect that they were ready to serve under General Żymierski. Scaevola, *A Study in Forgery* (London, 1945), p. 117.

56. Report of the Polish Armed Forces of January 30, 1944; A.P.U.S.T. The report also tells of numerous attacks by Communist squads and Soviet partisan detachments against army units and Polish underground leaders.

57. Bór-Komorowski, *The Secret Army*, p. 193.

58. "Appeal to the Polish Nation" in *Rada Narodowa* (The National Council) (Warsaw), March 25, 1944.

59. The full text in *Rada Narodowa*, July 26, 1944.

60. *Biuletyn Sovietskoi Pressy* (issued by the Soviet Legation in Stockholm), July 26, 1944, pp. 7–8.

61. The network was obviously very incomplete, if not largely fictitious. The first instruction issued by the PPR Central Committee was concerned with the expansion of this system of People's Council. The Central Committee ordered its party cells to delegate two members to each commune, with the purpose of encouraging further establishment of such Councils. *W dziesiątą rocznicę powstania PPR . . .* , pp. 304–310.

62. For the principal sources, see A. Pomian, *The Warsaw Rising: A Selection of Documents* (London, 1945). By the middle of 1944, Home Army units, scattered all over the country, numbered about 300,000 men. In Warsaw there were 35,000 frontline fighters and 7,000 auxiliary troops; of these some 20,000 were armed with rifles and light machine guns. See also Mikołajczyk, *The Rape of Poland*, p. 68.

63. Bór-Komorowski, *The Secret Army*, p. 202.

64. *Ibid.*, pp. 201 and 203.

65. Mikołajczyk, *The Rape of Poland*, p. 68.

66. *Ibid.*, pp. 71, 74, 86.

67. *Polskie siły zbrojne w drugiej wojnie światowej*, III, 119, 168, 810. Bór-Komorowski, *The Secret Army*, p. 242; Stypułkowski, *Invitation to Moscow* (London, 1952), pp. 159–160.

68. See the editorials of *Armia ludowa*, August 24, 28, and September 1944.

69. Quoted by Bór-Komorowski, *The Secret Army*, pp. 258–259.

70. Pomian, *The Warsaw Rising: A Selection of Documents*, p. 267. When, on August 9, 1944, Mikołajczyk begged Stalin to help Warsaw, the latter retorted that, according to information he had received from Warsaw, there was no uprising in the capital; S. Mikołajczyk, "Spotkania ze Stalinem" (Encounters with Stalin), *Jutro Polski*, Washington, D. C., April 5, 1953.

71. Bór-Komorowski, *The Secret Army*, pp. 346–347.

72. A. Bliss Lane, *I Saw Poland Betrayed* (New York, 1948), p. 177.

73. Quoted by Bliss Lane, *I Saw Poland Betrayed*, p. 304.

CHAPTER 10   SEIZURE AND CONSOLIDATION OF POWER

1. *Dziennik ustaw R. P.* (The Official Journal of the Polish Republic, hereafter referred to as Dz.U.R.P.), No. 5, 1944.

2. See Mikołajczyk, *The Rape of Poland*, p. 100.

3. See editorials of *Głos ludu*, November 11 and December 12, 1944; W. Go-

mułka-Wiesław, "Zadania Rządu tymczasowego" (The Tasks of the Provisional Government), *W walce o demokrację ludową* (Warsaw, 1947), I, 128–137.

4. "The Soviet Union," notes a former U. S. secretary of state, ". . . wanted to continue the Lublin government. Stalin was willing to add a few persons but he wanted to make certain that those who were added did not affect the Soviet Union's control of the government." J. F. Byrnes, *Speaking Frankly* (New York and London, 1947), p. 31.

5. For the Polish side of the story, see Z. Stypułkowski, *Invitation to Moscow*, pp. 211ff. For the Soviet view of the affair, see the official Soviet publication, *Trial of Polish Diversionists* (Moscow, 1951).

Anticipating another Soviet occupation of Poland, the London government, although it ordered dissolution of the Home Army, insisted on preserving the nucleus of a secret organization called *Niepodległość* (Independence). For the viewpoint of the new regime on the matter, see J. Mulak, *Wojsko podziemne, 1939–1945* (Warsaw, 1946), pp. 45–46, 76. For obvious reasons, there have been no comments on the matter on the part of the London government.

6. Three of the sixteen were pronounced innocent and were acquitted; one, owing to illness, was not tried; the other twelve were condemned to imprisonment ranging from four months to ten years.

7. On April 21, 1945, in order to strengthen the hand of his protégés, Stalin signed a twenty-year pact of alliance with Poland against any recurrence of German aggression. For the full text of the treaty, see an official Soviet poublication entitled, *Soviet-Polish Relations: A Collection of Official Documents, 1944–1946* (London, 1946).

8. B. Drobner, "Fałszywa polityka Zaremby i Żuławskiego" (The False Policy of Zaremba and Żuławski), *Naprzód* (Forward), March 11, 1947. In prewar Poland school teachers were known for their social radicalism and leftist tendencies.

9. "I zjazd PPR" (The First Congress of the PPR), *Głos ludu,* December 3, 1945; by the middle of 1944 there were 20,000 members, and 30,000 by January, 1945. In the second half of 1945 elections for factory councils took place throughout Poland, the PPR suffering humiliating defeats in numerous places; W. Gomułka-Wiesław, *W walce o demokrację* . . . , I, 317–318.

10. A. L. Strong, *I Saw the New Poland* (Boston, 1946), p. 59.

11. There were also some border-line cases, among them Franciszek Jóźwiak (Witold) who, although a "native" party member, tended to side mostly with the "Muscovites." Jóźwiak was born in 1895 in the Lublin province, the son of a peasant, and in 1921 he joined the Communist Party of Poland. Jóźwiak was arrested soon afterward and spent several years in prison. In 1942 he became a member of the PPR's Central Committee and later was chief of staff of the People's Guard. In 1945 Jóźwiak was appointed commander in chief of the Citizen's Militia. For his comments on the controversy between the "natives" and the "Muscovites," see his book, *Polska Partia Robotnicza w walce o wyzwolenie narodowe i społeczne* (Warsaw, 1952), p. 266.

12. For a reflection of this sort of ambition, see Gomułka-Wiesław, "O uchwałach Plenum K.C. PPR" (On the Resolutions of the Plenary Meeting of the Central Committee of the PPR), *W walce o demokrację* . . . , I, 148–165, also pp. 286–295.

13. The Communists calculated that 15,000 party members were killed between 1944 and 1948; over half of them lost their lives before the end of 1946.

A. Alster and J. Andrzejewski, "W sprawie składu socjalnego PZPR" (On the Social Composition of the Polish United Workers' Party), *Nowe drogi,* January 1951, p. 263.

14. The resolution of the First Congress, adopted on December 13, 1945, defines this sufficiently clearly: "The Congress affirms that the Polish Workers' Party is a new organization of the working class and the toiling masses of town and country, an organization born and created during the struggle against the Hitlerite invaders for the freedom and independence of Poland, for the rebirth of the country in a spirit of democracy." For material on the First PPR Congress, see *W dziesiątą rocznicę powstania PPR,* pp. 447–470; also *Głos ludu,* December 3–8, 1945; for Gomułka's speeches at the First Congress, omitted in the above-mentioned collection of documents, see his *W walce o demokrację* . . . , I, 215–332.

15. By the time of the Second Party Congress, in December, 1946, the PPR and 555,000 members; one year later this figure had already increased to 820,000.

16. "Zwycięstwo Polski w Poczdamie" (Poland's Victory in Potsdam), *Głos ludu,* August 5, 1945.

17. E. Ochab, "Uwagi o demokracji ludowej" (Remarks on the People's Democracy), *Trybuna wolności,* November 1, 1945.

18. For the standard set of arguments directed against Mikołajczyk, see Gomułka-Wiesław, *W walce o demokrację* . . . , I, 191–203.

19. Gomułka's speech in *Narada informacyjna dziewięciu partii.*

20. "Ustawa z dnia 27 kwietnia o głosowaniu ludowym," (The Law of April 27 on the Popular Referendum), *Dz.U.R.P.,* 1946; also *Głos ludu,* April 27, 1946.

21. For the final report of the U. S. Ambassador on the results of the referendum, see, Bliss Lane, *I Saw Poland Betrayed,* pp. 244–45; for a Communist comment, see Gomułka-Wiesław, *W walce o demokrację* . . . , II, 71–87.

22. Bliss Lane, p. 240.

23. For the program of the PPR, see "O co walczymy. Deklaracja programowa PPR" (What We Are Fighting For. The Platform of the PPR), *W dziesiątą rocznicę powstania PPR,* pp. 186–209.

24. During the period 1925–1939, this reform resulted in the distribution of nearly seven million acres of land. F. Zweig, *Poland Between Two Wars* (London, 1944), p. 133.

In 1938, land used for agricultural purposes amounted to about 77 million acres. There were slightly more than 3,000,000 farms, 82 per cent of which were owned by small farmers; only 14,700 farms were larger than 125 acres; some 2,611,000 farms had fewer than 25 acres. *Concise Statistical Yearbook of Poland 1938* (Warsaw, 1938), p. 67.

25. See the statement made by Professor Oskar Lange on June 7, 1944, upon his return to the United States from the Soviet Union, *Soviet Russia Today* (London, July 1944).

26. *Dekret PKWN z dnia 6 września 1944 o przeprowadzeniu reformy rolnej* (Decree of the Polish Committee of National Liberation of September 6, 1944, Concerning the Land Reform), *Dz.U.R.P.,* No. 3, 1945, item 13.

27. Originally, land belonging to religious groups was excluded from nationalization. This was a result of the new regime's cautious attitude toward the churches, but agrarian policy was reversed when the Sejm passed a law on March 20, 1950, providing that most ecclesiastical land also be nationalized.

28. E. J. Williams, *Christian Science Monitor*, November 1, 1945; see also *Rocznik statystyczny 1949* (The Statistical Yearbook 1949) (Warsaw, 1949), p. 53.

29. "Blaski i nędze akcji osadniczej" (Glories and Miseries of the Resettlement Action), *Gazeta ludowa*, November 26, 1945.

30. For a typical statement on the matter, see Gomułka-Wiesław, "Polska wobec nowych zagadnień" (Poland Facing New Tasks), *W walce o demokrację* . . . , I, 140–141.

31. For a detailed discussion of the problem, see J. K. Serafin, "Money and Banking," in the special issue of *Kultura*, No. 1, 1952. Although private wholesale trade was almost completely eliminated during 1947, when "the battle of trade" took place, petty retail commerce has lingered up to the present time.

32. For the text of the nationalization law, see *Dz.U.R.P.*, February 5, 1946. The law specified that newly created private enterprises "would not be transferred to the state, even if they were capable of employing more than 50 workers per shift"; the law also assured the owners ". . . of liberty to develop these undertakings" and of state support and assistance "within the framework of the national economic plan."

33. Hilary Minc, *Poland's Economy, Present and Future* (New York, June 1949), p. 5.

34. Minc, "The Polish Three Year Plan," speech delivered on September 21, 1946, to the K.R.N. (National Council of Poland) in the Debate on the Bill for a National Economic Plan and a Plan for Economic Reconstruction, in *Changing Epoch Series*, No. 2, London, 1946, p. 31.

35. As an intelligent observer of the East European scene remarked: ". . . it must be admitted that immense material progress was made. For this the main credit should go to the vitality and endurance of the workers and peasants." Hugh Seton-Watson, *The East European Revolution* (London, 1950), pp. 245–246.

36. The relation between industrial production and employment in industry during the Three Year Plan is illustrated by the following table:

Index of Industrial Production and Employment (1947–1949)
1938 = 100

Year	Industrial Production	Employment in Industry
1947	104	120
1948	135	136
1949	166	158

J. Taylor, *The Economic Development of Poland* (New York, Ithaca, 1952), p. 182.

37. In a memorandum presented by the Polish Peasant Party to Stalin on October 10, 1946, Mikołajczyk wrote: "The Polish Workers Party usurps for itself the right of monopolization of Polish-Soviet friendship. For this reason it views with displeasure and even hostility the genuine efforts of other parties to confirm the friendly relations between the Polish and Soviet nations. Cases have even occurred when Polish Peasant Party meetings dedicated to Polish-Soviet

friendship have been broken up." S. Mikołajczyk, *The Rape of Poland* . . . , p. 295.

38. "According to this embassy the Communists of the Polish government would fall if fair elections were held. In that event the Russians would march in and take over the country. The Polish Communists felt that they were justified in employing any means to keep the government in power." Bliss Lane, *I Saw Poland Betrayed,* p. 279; for the Communist comment on the electoral bloc, see Gomułka, *W walce o demokrację* . . . , II, 7–30, 51–6, 71–87, 179ff.

39. For Communist arguments on the matter, see *ibid.,* II, 151–246.

40. "On the other hand, independent sources held that the pogrom was prepared by the government to provoke difficulties for the opposition, especially among Jewish circles in the United States. The government, they claimed, figured that the falsifying of referendum returns would be overshadowed by the more spectacular and tragic event of the pogrom — with all those American and British correspondents in Poland!" Bliss Lane, *I Saw Poland Betrayed,* p. 249.

41. Commenting on cooperation between the PPS and PPR during the electoral campaign, Bierut said: "Thanks to this concentration of the democratic forces it was possible to demask and destroy definitely . . . the Polish Peasant Party." Bolesław Bierut, "Od 'Wielkiego Proletariatu' do PZPR" (From the "Great Proletariat" to the United Polish Workers' Party), *Trybuna ludu,* December 16, 1948.

42. For the text of the Electoral Law see *Dz.U.R.P.,* No. 48, 1946.

43. In his report of the press conference held on January 17, 1947, Sydney Gruson, the *New York Times* correspondent, wrote that M. Bzowski, the Chief Electoral Commissioner, said: ". . . only 200,000 persons, 1.6 per cent of the electorate of about 12,000,000 persons, had been stricken off the voting lists under article 2 of the electoral law. It deprives of the vote those who collaborated with the Germans or maintained contacts with the underground. The electorate of 12,000,000 is down a little more than 1,000,000 from the referendum level. But M. Bzowski could not account for the difference, except to say that it might have been caused by 'migration' from one part of the country to another. In reality the number of those disfranchised was even higher, for since the referendum in July 1946, the population of Poland had increased by some tens of thousands of repatriates."

44. Even accepting the number of inhabitants as the basis for allocation of seats, the new Electoral Law did not treat the various constituencies equally.

45. "Jednością silni" (Strong Through Unity), *Nowe drogi,* January-February 1947; see also Gomułka's collection of speeches and articles, *W walce o demokrację* . . . , II, pp. 154–158 and 160.

46. Mikołajczyk, *The Rape of Poland,* p. 205; for an electoral speech illustrated with biblical metaphors, see Gomułka, *W walce o demokrację,* II, 211.

47. See the report of Marguerite Higgins in the *New York Herald Tribune* of January 7, 1947.

48. According to Mikołajczyk's deposition Stalin ordered the Polish Communists to send him — secretly — the real results of the election. "I want to see," he told them, "how influential you actually are."

49. Quoted by Jean Malara and Lucienne Rey, *La Pologne: d'une occupation à l'autre (1944–1952)* (Paris, 1952), p. 143. For a triumphant official commentary, see "Pełne wyniki wyborów" (Complete Results of the Election), *Głos ludu,* January 21, 1947. The Warsaw Ministry of Foreign Affairs published a se-

lection of articles on Poland written by American, British, French, and Russian correspondents, entitled *Foreigners on Poland* (Warsaw, 1948); characteristically enough, the book contained no articles covering the election or the electoral campaign.

50. James F. Byrnes, *Speaking Frankly* (New York-London, 1947), p. 33.

51. *Dz.U.R.P.*, No. 9, 1947, item 43; *Dz.U.R.P.*, No. 18, 1947, item 71; also *Dz.U.R.P.*, No. 3, 1947, item 130. For the English text of the new charter, see *Documents and Reports on Poland. The Provisional Constitution of February 20, 1947 and the Declaration of Rights* (New York, 1949).

52. S. L. Sharp, *New Constitutions in the Soviet Sphere*, Washington, D. C. [1950], p. 31; see also the comments of Gomułka, *W walce o demokrację* . . . , I, 318.

53. See Sidney Gruson, "Poland Now Being Pressed Into the One-Party Mold . . . ," *New York Times,* November 2, 1947.

54. Z. K. Brzezinski, *The Soviet Bloc* . . . , Cambridge, Mass., 1960, pp. 28–29.

CHAPTER II PURGES AND MERGERS

1. For the first crucial phase of the Gomułka affair, see *Nowe drogi,* September-October 1948, *passim;* for a Stalinist evaluation see F. Jóźwiak (Witold), *Polska Partia Robotnicza* . . . , Ch. 10, and B. Bierut, *O partii,* pp. 117–184. For a penetrating analysis of the whole affair and its background, see the chapter on the crisis in the Polish Communist Party in Adam Ulam's *Titoism and the Cominform* (Cambridge, Mass., 1952); the present section of this chapter owes a great deal to Ulam's work.

2. For Gomułka's speech see *Narada informacyjna dziewięciu partii* (Warsaw, 1947).

3. At a meeting of the Central Committee in April 1947, Gomułka said: "Party organizers and the party as a whole can be trained in the Marxist spirit only through a close correlation of Marxism with our Polish realities, past as well as present . . . We must teach Marxism in reference to the example of our country's history. To simplify the problem, one might say that the proper thing is to teach our party Polish Marxism." *Nowe drogi,* May-June 1947, p. 34.

4. "Jaką jedność budujemy" (What Kind of Unity We Build), *Nowe drogi,* May–June 1948; see *Khrushchev Remembers,* Vol. II, pp. 170–182.

5. According to the testimony of the Polish-American journalist, Alexander Janta, who spoke to several members of the Central Committee shortly after the critical meeting, Gomułka broke down after beginning the first sentence of his *samokritika:* "Comrades, I have erred . . ." The rest of the recantation was read by Bierut, while the weeping Gomułka sat at a nearby table.

6. J. Kowalewski, "Międzynarodówka Don Kichotów" (The International of Don Quixotes, *Wiadomości,* January 1, 1950.

7. Testimony of S. Mikołajczyk; see also the pamphlet of J. Światło, *Za kulisami* . . . *Bezpieki* [New York, 1955], pp. 14–18.

8. Accusations against Spychalski were renewed during the trial of a group of high Polish officers (July 1951) who returned from the West. According to the testimony of Światło, the charges against Spychalski were as much invented as were those against Gomułka.

9. For the minutes of the Central Committee session of the United Polish Workers' Party which excluded Gomułka, Kliszko, and Spychalski from the Central Committee, and barred them from holding any party post, see a pamphlet issue of *Nowe drogi*, entitled *III Plenum Listopad 11–13, 1949* (Warsaw, 1949), *passim*. The same plenum "admitted" Marshal K. Rokossovsky as a member of the Central Committee; *ibid.*, p. 5.

10. Ulam, *Titoism and the Cominform*, p. 188.

11. "The fight against the right-wing elements of the Polish Socialist Party cannot be a fight against the Polish Socialist Party as such. The postwar, reborn Polish Socialist Party . . . has made and is making its positive contribution to the work of unifying the working-class movement, "Jaką jedność budujemy," *Nowe drogi*, May-June, 1948, p. 5.

12. *Nowe drogi*, September-October 1948, p. 144.

13. Jean Monnerot, *Sociology and Psychology of Communism* (Boston, 1953), pp. 61–62.

14. *Deklaracja ideowa PZPR i statut PZPR* (Warsaw, 1949), pp. 16 and 44–45.

15. An important source of study on the Socialist surrender as given here is an article signed "R" by a Polish Socialist, entitled, "The Fate of Polish Socialism"; it appeared in the October 1949 issue of *Foreign Affairs*.

16. *Trybuna ludu*, December 16, 1948.

17. In the spring of 1947 the PPR put forward a plan to nationalize all commercial establishments outright; this was opposed by the PPS so far as small enterprises were concerned. Thus intimidated, the Socialists had to yield. "The Fate of Polish Socialism," *Foreign Affairs*, October 1949.

18. *W dziesiątą rocznicę powstania PPR* . . . , pp. 495–7.

19. *Robotnik*, May 10, 1947.

20. *Głos ludu*, May 11, 1947.

21. "R," "The Fate of Polish Socialism," *Foreign Affairs*, October 1949.

22. Flagrant violation of the by-laws of the PPS was necessary to bring about the merger. This was later admitted by Świątkowski: "The purging of the party ranks was conducted by means not envisaged by the Rules of the Polish Socialist Party . . . ," Zambrowski and Świątkowski, *O statucie i zagadnieniach organizacyjnych PZPR* (Warsaw, 1949), p. 68.

23. For documents concerning the Unification Congress, see *W dziesiątą rocznicę powstania* . . . , pp. 592–610; *Nowe drogi*, January 1949; B. Bierut, *O partii*, pp. 7–53; Zambrowski and Świątkowski; also *Trybuna ludu*, December 21 and 22, 1948.

24. *Deklaracja ideowa PZPR* . . . , p. 35.

25. *Ibid.*, pp. 15, 17–18, 19; in this respect see also B. Bierut, *Podstawy ideologiczne PZPR* (Ideological Foundation of the UPWP) (Warsaw, 1952), pp. 52–3.

26. *Ibid.*, pp. 49–50.

27. The general nature and aims of this plan were described by Minc, minister of industry and commerce, in a speech made on December 9, 1948. *Poland Today*, New York, February 1949, pp. 16–19; also the *Nowe drogi* of July-August 1950, entirely devoted to the Six Year Plan.

28. For the full text of the rules see *Deklaracja ideowa P.Z.P.R.* . . . The text is also to be found as an annex to the pamphlet edition of the two speeches

by Zambrowski and Świątkowski already quoted. (Warsaw, 1949, 1950). For an authoritative interpretation of the by-laws, see R. Zambrowski, "Podstawowe założenia statutu zjednoczonej Polskiej partii robotniczej" (The Basic Premises of the Rules of the United Polish Workers' Party), *Głos ludu,* November 6, 1948.

29. Marshal Rokossovsky was originally a worker of Polish origin. After service in the tsarist forces, he joined the Red Army and by 1936 had reached the rank of commander of a military district. Purged in 1936, he was rehabilitated in 1941 and soon made a front commander. The Polish army of General Berling was under his orders. Rokossovsky was instrumental in letting the Warsaw uprising be destroyed by the Germans. In November 1949, he was commander in chief of the Polish armed forces, minister of national defense and member of the Council of State. His co-option to the Central Committee and to the Politbureau immediately made Rokossovsky a key-man of the regime, until October 1956.

30. See F. Jóźwiak-Witold, "Podstawowe zadania w centralnej komisji kontroli partyjnej," (Basic Problems of the Party Central Control Commission), *Nowe drogi,* No. 2, March-April 1950. The chairman of the Central Commission for Party Control emphasized the necessity for constant vigilance in the following terms: "We should not toy with liberal, internal-party discussions . . . such internal ideological struggle becomes factional struggle — it shatters the unity of the party . . . ," Jóźwiak-Witold, "O stalinowską linię w polityce kadr" (For the Stalinist Line in the Staff Policy), *Nowe arogi,* November-December 1949, p. 172.

31. Zambrowski i Świątkowski, p. 10.

32. A Juszkiewicz, "Umacniający front narodowy" (Let Us Strengthen the National Front), *Sprawy chłopskie* (Peasant Affairs), No. 1, January 1957, p. 42.

PART IV: THE UNITED POLISH WORKERS' PARTY

CHAPTER 12   THE PARTY, THE PLANS, AND THE PEASANTS

1. For an outline of the revised plan and a discussion of the Fifth Plenum, see *Nowe drogi,* July-August 1950.

2. J. Wszelaki, "The Rise of Industrial Middle Europe," *Foreign Affairs,* October 1951.

3. *Nowe drogi,* February 1951.

4. For the text of the law: "Ustawa z dnia 20 marca 1950r. o terenowych organach jednolitej władzy państwowej," (The Law of March 20, 1950, on the Unified Organs of the State Administration), *Dz.U.R.P.,* No. 14, April 13, 1950; for a detailed and penetrating analysis of the law, see Ralph A. Jones, "Polish Local Government on Soviet Model" in *The American Slavic and East European Review,* February 1951.

5. For the text of the new constitution and its authentic interpretation, see B. Bierut, *O Konstytucji Polskiej Rzeczypospolitej Ludowej: Konstytucja Polskiej Rzeczypospolitej Ludowej* ([Warsaw], 1952).

6. For the Eighth Plenum, see *Nowe drogi,* March 1953.

7. By the end of 1953 there were 8,054 "producers' cooperatives" with some 11,500,000 acres of land; *Chłopska droga*, January 31, 1954. The rate of collectivization for the past five years has been as follows:

Year	No. of rural cooperatives	Increase
December 31, 1949	243	
December 31, 1950	2,199	1,956
December 31, 1951	3,056	857
December 31, 1952	4,900	1,744
March 31, 1953	6,253	1,767
July 31, 1953	8,105	1,852
December 31, 1953	8,054	
December, 1954	10,000	2,446
		Decrease
September, 1955	9,500	500

According to the above information, all based on official announcements made in the Polish Communist press, more than 3,000 rural cooperatives were created in 1953. Bierut stated at the congress that there were "over 8,000 cooperatives" by the end of 1953. *Trybuna ludu* put the figure at 8,300 as of January 30, 1954; quoted in *Communist Party Congresses in the Soviet Sphere: II. Poland*, p. 34.

8. Producers' cooperatives and state farms have to pay 96 złotys for plowing one hectare (2.5 acres) with a tractor; small and medium farms pay 198 złotys; largest farms pay 242 złotys, *Chłopska droga*, January 24–31, 1954; also R. Zambrowski, *Niektóre zagadnienia pracy na wsi* (Some Problems of our Work in the Countryside) (Warsaw, 1951), *passim*.

9. *Nowe drogi*, September-October 1948, p. 160; also Zambrowski, "Aktualne zagadnienia partii na wsi" (Topical Problems of the Party in the Countryside), *Nowe drogi*, March-April 1949, pp. 100–101.

For a competent discussion of agricultural problems in present-day Poland, see S. Gryziewicz, "Rolnictwo" (Agriculture), special issue of *Kultura*, 1952, Vol. I, pp. 316–318.

10. *For a Lasting Peace*, September 14, 1951.

11. *Gospodarka planowa* (Planned Economy), December 1953.

12. *Trybuna ludu*, December 31, 1953.

13. For their speeches, see *Trybuna ludu*, March 11, 14, 16, 1954.

14. At the Fifth Plenum of the Central Committee in July 1950, Minc, extolling Bolshevik planning, said that the "theory of a declining rate of growth in industry" is essentially bourgeois.

15. *Inwestycje i budownictwo* (Investments and Building), February 1954, quoted by *Communist Party Congresses in the Soviet Sphere; II. Poland*, p. 25.

16. *Ibid.*

17. "Uchwała II zjazdu PZRP . . ." (The Resolution of the Second Congress of the UPWP . . .), *Trybuna ludu*, March 20, 1954.

18. For the list of amendments and their interpretations, see E. Ochab, "O niektórych zagadnieniach organizacyjnych i zmianach w Statucie Partii" (About Some Problems of Organization and Changes in the Party Rules), *Trybuna ludu*, March 17, 1954.

19. *Ibid.*

CHAPTER 13   THE PARTY AND THE CHURCH

1. During the years 1939–1945, the Germans murdered three bishops and almost two thousand priests, altogether about eighteen per cent of the Polish clergy. Szułdrzyński, Położenie Kościoła w Polsce . . .” (The Situation of the Church in Poland . . .), *Kultura*, 1953, Special issue, V.

2. For an example of such a debate, see the article “Can There Be Co-operation Between Catholics and Marxists?” *Dziennik Polski* (The Polish Daily) (Cracow), June 30, 1946. Reprinted by an official Polish publication, *Poland Today*, January 1947.

3. This was eagerly stressed by the official Communist daily *Głos ludu*, of April 2, 1947.

4. Czesław Miłosz, *The Captive Mind* (New York, 1953), pp. 207–208.

5. The Vatican has continued to recognize the Polish government in exile.

6. *New York Times*, August 7, 1949. For the text of the “Decree on Freedom of Conscience,” see *Dz.U.R.P.*, August 6, 1949. Technically, there was no Communist Party in Poland. There has been only the United Polish Workers’ Party. Thus, “theoretical loopholes provided for many Catholics a temporary refuge from making a decision until the Catholic hierarchy would point out the path it wants the faithful to follow,” *New York Times*, July 30, 1949.

7. *New York Times*, October 12, 1949; for an interesting Catholic interpretation of the “progessive Catholic” movement in Poland see Claude Naurois, *Dieu contre Dieu?*

8. *New York Times*, January, 1950.

9. *Poland Today*, April 1950.

10. For the full English text of the agreement, see *ibid.*, May 1950, and *New York Times*, May 4, 1950.

11. “Promemoria . . .” *Tygodnik powszechny*, No. 19 (321), Cracow, May 1951.

12. *Trybuna ludu*, December 13, 1951; see also “Antypolskie knowania Watykanu” (Anti-Polish Intrigues of the Vatican), in *Trybuna ludu*, January 15, 1951.

13. “Watykan popiera kampanię rewizjonistyczną . . .” (The Vatican supports the Revisionist Campaign . . .), *Trybuna ludu*, September 27, 1951; see also attacks against the Polish Episcopate and the Vatican in *Nowe drogi*, December 1952; January, April, May, and July 1953.

14. *Dz.U.R.P.* (Polish Official Law Journal), No. 10, 1953; see also *New York Times*, February 12, 1953.

15. *Trybuna ludu*, February 13, 1953.

16. For the text of the statement, see *Inter-Catholic Press Agency* (New York), October 7, 1953. For a penetrating analysis of the memorandum, see Rel, *Zakończona próba* (The Finished Experiment), *Kultura*, 1954.

17. *New York Times*, September 14, 1953.

18. *Ibid.*, September 23, 1953.

19. *Ibid.*, September 28, 1953.

CHAPTER 14   THE THAW

1. J. Tokarski, "Na marginesie pierwszych doświadczeń realizacji wytycz-nych IV Plenum" (On the Margin of the First Experiences of Fulfilling the Instructions of the Fourth Plenum of the Central Committee), *Nowe drogi*, May–June, 1950.

2. Social composition of the party (by percentage) is illustrated by the following table:

		Workers	Land Workers and Peasants	White Collar Workers	Others
December	1945	62.2	28.2	9.6	—
December	1948	53.6	26.5	17.6	2.3
November	1949	51.9	19.2	26.1	2.8
June	1952	60.0	17.0	20.0	3.0
February	1954	48.3	13.2	36.4	2.1

This table and the following calculations have been compiled on the basis of several studies: "Partia w liczbach" (The Party in Figures), *Nowe drogi*, June 1956; "W sprawie składu socjalnego PZPR" (On the Social Composition of the UPWP), *Nowe drogi*, January 1951; T. Zawadzki, "Strength of the Communist Party," *Polish Affairs*, London, November 1952; W. Zalewski's chapter in the special issue of *Kultura*, Vol. II, Paris, 1952; B. Bierut, "Sprawozdanie Komitetu Centralnego na II zjazd PZPR" (Report of the Central Committee on the Second Congress of the UPWP), *Trybuna ludu*, March 12, 1954.

3. B. Bierut, "Sprawozdanie K.C. na II zjazd PZPR" (Report of the Central Committee on the Second Congress of the UPWP), *Trybuna ludu*, March 12, 1954; for further evolution of the party see "Partia w liczbach" (The Party in Figures), *Nowe drogi*, June, 1956. While the number of white collar members has been growing within the UPWP, the party bureaucracy, or full time officials employed by the party, was expanding also; in 1945 they numbered about 4,000; in 1956 it exceeded 13,000 persons, W. Skulski, "W sprawie aparatczyków" (Concerning the Party Apparatus), *Trybuna ludu*, November 23, 1956; for self-criticism concerning the bureaucratization of the party see two articles on the subject in *Nowe drogi* of January 1955.

4. Milovan Djilas, *The New Class* (New York, 1957), p. 155. For a vivid description of the Polish "new class" see the pamphlet of Józef Światło, *Za kulisami Bezpieki i Partii* (Behind the Facade of the Ministry of Public Security and the Party); for the party self-criticism in this respect see *Nowe drogi*, January 1955. It is interesting to note that the term "the new class" was coined in Poland well ahead of the publication of Djilas' book: "This new class, if it had succeeded in perpetuating itself, would not have denational-ized the factories and the land. It would have known how, while preserving the formal characteristics of our system, to destroy its content. It would have been able to dispossess the working class without in any way restoring private ownership of the means of production; it would have known how to create privileges for itself, to divide itself from the rest of the nation by a wall of

isolating 'elite' institutions, by an alienating way of life, by another type of culture, of housing, of vacation, of love, all of it based on economic and political privilege," *Po prostu,* June 1, 1956; see also the article of Janusz Chudzyński: "Za żółtymi firankami" (Behind the Yellow Curtains), *Po prostu,* April 1, 1956.

5. Seweryn Bialer, "The Origins of Gomulkaism," *The New Leader,* January 6, 1958. According to the author the UPWP wrote several letters to the CPSU urging it to rehabilitate the CPP. For a penetrating analysis of the mounting crisis within the UPWP see Seweryn Bialer, *Wybrałem wolność* (I Chose Freedom) (New York, 1956), mainly chapter II.

6. For his revelations see the already mentioned pamphlet of Światło: *Za kulisami Bezpieki i Partii;* for self-criticism of one of the men responsible for the terror see Berman's speech in *Nowe drogi,* October 1956; also the resolution of the Ninth Plenum in *Nowe drogi,* June 1957.

7. S. Bialer, *passim;* see also the December 1954 and January 1955 issues of the *Nowe drogi.*

8. In this respect see Berman's speech at the Eighth Plenum, *Nowe drogi,* October 1956.

9. For the English text of the communiqué see P. E. Zinner (ed.), *National Communist and Popular Revolt in Eastern Europe* (New York, 1956), pp. 37–39; this selection of documents contains numerous basic sources on the popular revolt in Poland in 1956; see especially Part II.

10. In 1946 he was elected a member of the Central Committee of the Polish Workers' Party and in 1948 put in charge of the Trade Unions. Next year we see him already as vice-minister of national defense, chief of the political administration of the army and deputy member of the Politbureau. In 1950, Ochab resigned this army post and became secretary of the party's Central Committee. In 1951 he was elected full member of the Politbureau. According to Józef Światło his rapid rise was due to a personal recommendation of Stalin who called him "a Bolshevik with sharp teeth" (*zubastyi Bolshevik*).

11. *Trybuna ludu,* April 7, 1956; see also the article of Jerzy Morawski on the congress in the same paper of March 27, 1956; the parliamentary speech of Cyrankiewicz, *ibid.,* April 27, 1956; also the ideological commentary to the congress by Adam Shaff in *Nowe drogi* of April 1956, stressing the need for collective leadership, democratic centralism, and control going from the bottom to the top.

12. See *Przegląd kulturalny* for the second half of 1955, and Chałasiński's article in *Nauka polska,* No. 2, 1955.

13. As translated by Lucian Blit, *Twentieth Century,* London, December 1955; for the Poem's analysis see Bernard Ziffer, "A Poem for Adults," *The Polish Review,* Winter 1956.

14. "For the Restoration of the Citizen's Rights," report by Antoni Słonimski, before the Nineteenth Session of the Council of Culture and Arts, March 24–25, 1956, quoted by *News from Behind the Iron Curtain,* No. 6, 1956; Jan Kott, "Mitologia a prawda" (Mythology and Truth), *Przegląd kulturalny,* April 5, 1956, and J. Putrament's article, *ibid.*

15. For a competent analysis of the problem see Magnus J. Kryński, "Poland's Literary 'Thaw': Dialectical Phases of Genuine Freedom" in *Polish*

Review, Autumn 1956; Czesław Miłosz, "Voices of Disillusion," in *Problems of Communism,* May–June 1956; also many articles in *East Europe* and *Kultura,* of 1956 and 1957.

16. For a brilliant discussion of the paper, see K. Jeleński's "The Rise and Fall of *Po prostu,*" in *The New Leader,* December 2, 1957; for the role of the clubs, Z. Jordan's article in *Kultura,* April 1957.

17. Jan Stanisławski, "Czy jestem chorągiewką?" (Am I a Weathercock?), *Po prostu,* March 25, 1956.

18. *Po prostu,* April 8, 1956; see also the statement of Helena Jaworska in *Sztandar młodych* (Banner of Youth), April 11, 1956.

19. W. Godek and R. Turski, "Czyżby zmierzch Marxizmu?" (Is This the Twilight of Marxism?), *Po prostu,* June 24, 1956. The article suggested that the real reason for the lack of technical progress of Polish industry was patronage, protectionism, and the fear that such a progress may further increase the already existing but carefully camouflaged unemployment.

20. J. M. Montias, "Unbinding Polish Economy," *Foreign Affairs,* April 1957. The article represents a well-balanced analysis of both the Polish economy of the Stalinist period and the measures undertaken since the October upheaval.

21. The present account of the Poznań uprising has been compiled on the basis of Polish and foreign press reports, supplemented by interviews with several eye-witnesses of the events.

22. For the official communiqué and the speech of Cyrankiewicz see *Trybuna ludu,* June 29, 1956.

23. Roman Juryś, "Niektóre zagadnienia naszej partii" (Some Problems of our Party), *Nowe drogi,* February 1957.

24. Z. Brzeziński, "Communist Ideology and Power: From Unity to Diversity," *Journal of Politics,* November 1957.

CHAPTER 15   THE RETURN OF GOMUŁKA

1. For the resolutions of the Seventh Plenum see *Nowe drogi,* July–August 1956; also Ochab's article "Zacieśnić więzy z masami" (Let's Tighten Our Ties with the Masses), and that of Franciszek Mazur, "Kierownicza rola partii i wewnętrzno-partyjna demokracja" (The Leading Role of the Party and Inner Party Democracy), which pays lip service to democratic principles while using the numb language of the Stalinist era; for Ochab's speech see *Trybuna ludu,* July 20, 1956; for Bulganin's speech, *ibid.,* July 22, 1956.

2. Later on the resolution of the Eighth Plenum admitted that: "A major obstacle to the consistent implementation of the decisions of the Seventh Plenum was the lack of unanimity and consistency in the Politbureau of the Central Committee in solving the concrete problems of the process of socialist democratization in the life of the party and the country. In this situation the work of the party was in many cases paralyzed," *Nowe drogi,* October 1956.

3. Radio Warsaw of August 22, 1956, as quoted by *News from Behind the Iron Curtain,* October 1956, p. 25; see also *Sztandar młodych,* July 17, 1956; for the attempts of the party at taming the rebellious youth see *Trybuna ludu,* April 26 and May 3, 1956, and *Życie Warszawy* of May 5, 1956.

4. *Trybuna ludu,* August 22. At this moment some of the ablest young

Communist intellects began protesting against lack of intellectual freedom. The theoretical organ of the UPWP published the article of a leading young Communist writer, Leszek Kołakowski, demanding freedom of scientific inquiry and questioning the role of the party in the state: "The Communist Party does not need intellectuals in order that they admire the wisdom of its decisions but in order that its decisions be wise. They are therefore needed as free thinking people and dispensable as opportunists," *Nowe drogi,* September 1956.

5. *New York Times,* July 15, 1956.

6. *Głos pracy* (Labor's Voice), August 24, 1956.

7. *Trybuna ludu,* September 6, 1956.

8. *Życie gospodarcze* (Economic Life), September 2, 1956.

9. *Nowa kultura,* September 9, 1956.

10. *Trybuna ludu,* September 11, 1956.

11. *Po prostu,* September 30, 1956.

12. *Trybuna ludu,* August 15, 1956. Demands for democratization of party life and structure began to appear too; Jerzy Mahl, "W sprawie aparatu partyjnego," *Trybuna ludu,* September 21, 1956.

13. *Trybuna ludu,* August 5, 1956.

14. *Trybuna ludu,* August 25, 1956.

15. *Trybuna ludu,* October 20, 1956; the old Politbureau was composed of the following full members: Ochab, Cyrankiewicz, Zawadzki, Rokossovsky, Zenon Nowak, Roman Nowak, Mazur, Jóźwiak, Gierek, Zambrowski, Rapacki, and Dworakowski; Jędrychowski, Stawiński and Chełchowski were alternate members.

16. For the communiqué on the Polish-Soviet talks of October 19–20 see *Trybuna ludu,* October 20, 1956; for a comprehensive report of the crisis see Flora Lewis, "36 Hours that Shook the Communist World," *Collier's,* December 21, 1956; see also the article by Bolesław Piasecki, "Instynkt państwowy" (The state instinct), *Słowo powszechne* (The Catholic World), September 17, 1956.

17. For the speech of Gomułka see *Trybuna ludu* of October 21, 1956; also *Nowe drogi,* October 10, 1956; for the resolutions of the Eighth Plenum, *ibid.*; also *Trybuna ludu,* October 25, 1956.

18. The composition of the new Politbureau was as follows: Cyrankiewicz, Gomułka, Jędrychowski, Loga-Sowiński, Morawski, Ochab, Rapacki, Zambrowski, and Zawadzki, *Trybuna ludu,* October 22, 1956; also *Nowe drogi,* October 1956.

19. *Trybuna ludu,* December 10, 1956.

20. The line of reasoning was voiced in the article of a leading Catholic publicist who wrote: "Poland must be ruled by the party, because the engine should be repaired by the man who upset it . . . "; moreover, the Soviet Union would not tolerate anybody else in power; Stefan Kisielewski, "Czy istnieje front narodowy?" (Is There a National Front?), *Nowa kultura,* November 18, 1956.

21. The position of the party in the countryside has been especially difficult as has noted an American observer: "In Poland the party has almost vanished. It has no mass basis. Intellectuals and bureaucrats remain. Go to a Polish village and ask who belongs to the Communist party. The peasant will smile slyly and answer: 'There aren't any members here — any more.' " H. E. Salis-

bury, "East Europe Is Now Seeking a More Democratic Communism," *New York Times,* October 24, 1957.

CHAPTER 16   THE ERA OF GOMUŁKA, 1956–1970

1. The text of the Soviet declaration is in *Trybuna ludu,* October 31, 1956; for the Polish reaction see the editorial "Deklaracja radziecka a polska racja stanu" (The Soviet Declaration and the Polish Raison d'État), *ibid.,* November 1956.

2. For the official party appeal to the Poles see *Trybuna ludu* of November 2, 1956; also its editorial of October 28. *Trybuna Ludu* of December 7, 1956, went as far as to publish an open letter of the French singer Yves Montand, sharply criticizing the Soviet intervention in Hungary; see also Ważyk's poem "Qui tacent clamant," *Nowa kultura,* November 25, 1956.

3. *Trybuna ludu,* November 12, 1956; see also the editorial of the paper of November 1, striking the same note.

4. For the joint Soviet–Polish communiqué see *Trybuna ludu,* November 19, 1956; see also the editorial of November 21, "Odra Nyssa i realizm" (The Oder Neisse and Realism).

5. For the reports on the great debate going on in the provincial branches see the party chronicles in *Trybuna ludu* of October, November and December, especially "W ogniu krytyki" (In the Fire of Criticism), *ibid.,* October 31, 1956; "Aktyw partyjny wobec uchwały VIII Plenum (The Party Activists and the Resolutions of the Eighth Plenum), *ibid.,* November 2, 1956; L. Krasucki, "Aparat partyjny a przemiany w partii" (The Party Apparatus and the Changes Within the Party), *ibid.,* November 11, 1956; also *Życie partii* (Life of the Party) of November and December 1956.

6. *Trybuna ludu,* November 5, 1956. The party formulated its attitude towards the Stalinists in the leader of the *Trybuna ludu* of November 28, 1956; the hopelessly compromised members must go, but the party must retain all those who had erred together with the entire movement; the party should beware of those who would like to bury socialism together with Stalinism.

7. For the statement see *Chłopska droga* of December 17, 1956, and *Trybuna ludu* of December 12, 1956.

8. See Jędrychowski's speech at the Diet in *Trybuna ludu,* November 8, 1957.

9. *Dziennik Ustaw P. R. L.,* November 24, 1956; and *Trybuna ludu* of November 4, 1956; see also Kazimierz Grzybowski, "Polish Workers' Councils," *Journal of Central European Affairs,* October 1957; and J. Urban, "Magna Carta Laboratorum," *Po prostu,* September 30, 1956.

10. *Trybuna Ludu,* November 20, 1956.

11. For the text of the law see *Trybuna ludu,* November 23, 1956; see also *Nowe drogi* of January 1957, devoted to issues connected with the electoral campaign.

12. During the pre-election period the party press leaned backward to emphasize that Poland ceased to be a totalitarian state. While stressing the leading role of the UPWP the editorial of *Trybuna ludu* of December 2, 1956,

pointed out; "We enter the electoral campaign with a multi-party political system and not with a mono-party one."

The fiftieth anniversary of the foundation of the PPS-Left was loudly celebrated, and the notion that this group was merely "a Polish variety of Menshevism" was now officially disclaimed; in this respect see *Trybuna ludu*, November 25, 1956.

13. *Trybuna ludu*, January 17, 1957.

14. Quoted by Konrad Syrop, *Spring in October* . . . , (New York, 1957, pp. 61–64. That Poland in October 1956 was only half a step from an actual Soviet military intervention and that there were powerful groups favoring such a step was confirmed by the British ambassador to the USSR from 1956 to 1957, Sir William Hayter. In his memoirs he noted that Marshal Gregory Zhukov, while describing his October 1956 visit to Poland, said with an expressive gesture: "We could have crushed them [the Poles] like flies . . ." Sir William Hayter, *The Kremlin and the Embassy* (New York, 1966), p. 112.

15. The aftermath of the October upheaval caused a great deal of anxiety and protest among Polish Stalinists. Radio Warsaw, in its program of July 1957, broadcast from an old party member, Żabinski of Łódź, who thus voiced his complaints: "I have been a member of the Party since 1922. First I belonged to CP in Paris, then in Holland and Belgium, and in 1945, after my return to Poland, I joined the Polish Party, and am a member to this day. . . . Since the Twentieth Soviet Party Congress in February 1956 I have closely watched the course of the policy pursued by Khrushchev and Bulganin, the lies they cast upon Stalin, the struggle with Beria. Then came the Polish October. The breaking up of Party organizations in the districts. . . . Many interesting things were revealed. The contemptuous treatment of Party members. The release of all sorts of criminals from prison. The flourishing of the rich peasantry in the countryside: the poor peasants will once again have to serve the kulaks. Even the yapping radio stations of Free Europe and London have stopped spitting upon the present system of government! They so greatly like this Titoist form!" Quoted by *East Europe*, September 1957, p. 31.

16. *Trybuna Ludu*, October 26, 1957. For confirmation of this point of view made after his downfall, see Gomułka's reminiscences published in an Israeli Polish-language paper, *Nowiny-Kurier* (News-Courier), Tel Aviv, May 4, 1973.

17. *Po prostu*, September 30, 1957.

18. For typical attacks on Kołakowski see Jerzy Wiatr's article in *Polityka*, September 25, 1957. For printing of Kołakowski article, together with a series of cartoons critical of the Soviet Union, the editor of *Nowa kultura*, Wiktor Woroszylski, was dismissed on February 2, 1958. Woroszylski had been awarded the State Poetry Prize in 1950. He had spent several years in the USSR, and was pro-Stalinist; in 1956 he had published some of the more interesting articles in *Nowa kultura*, including a report from Poznań supporting the striking workers and "A Hungarian Notebook," written in Budapest during the revolt and sympathetic to the insurgents.

19. *Nowe drogi*, December 1959; see also Wiatr's article on "The Priest and the Jester," in *Polityka*, December 12, 1969.

20. *Twórczość* (Creativity), October 1959.

21. The Yugoslav writer, Milovan Djilas, has characterized Kołakowski as "most probably the most original philosophic phenomenon of 'socialist' Eastern

Europe." Milovan Djilas, "Beyond Dogma," *Survey*, Winter 1971. Kołakowski's selected essays were published in English under the title *Toward a Marxist Humanism* (New York, 1968).

22. For Khrushchev's view of relations with Gomułka see *Khrushchev Remembers*, I (Boston and Toronto, 1974), pp. 170–183 and 207–214.

23. *New York Times*, October 29, 1959.

24. *Trybuna ludu*, May 17, 1960. Witaszewski (nicknamed "General Gaspipe" after he threatened to use physical force against the workers in the 1956 Poznań riots) had been sent as military attaché to Prague after Gomułka's return to power.

25. For a detailed analysis of the intra-party struggle see Jerzy Ptakowski, "Gomułka and His Party," *East Europe*, May 1967, and Jan Nowak, "The Struggle for Party Control in Poland," *East Europe*, June 1968.

26. For a background article see A. Ross Johnson, "Warsaw: Politics and the Intellectuals," *East Europe*, July 1967.

27. *List otwarty do Partii* (An Open Letter to the Party) (Paris, 1966), translated into German and published as *Monopolsocialismus* (Hamburg, 1969).

28. W. Bieńkowski, *Motory i hamulce socjalizmu* (The Driving Forces and the Inhibiting Factors of Socialism) (Paris, 1969).

29. For an interpretation of Adzhubey's mission to Bonn and its possible impact on Poland see Nicholas Bethell, *Gomułka . . .* second edition (London, 1972), p. 240. Bethell's opinion has been confirmed by Gomułka's reminiscences published in *Nowiny-Kurier*, May 11, 1973.

30. R. V. Burke, *The Dynamics of Communism in Eastern Europe* (Princeton, 1961), p. 160. The same author also writes about the CPP: "The influence of Jews on party life, moreover, was generally greater than the percentages would suggest. Jewish activists were probably better educated than the average, and more likely to achieve the level of leading cadre." *Ibid.*, p. 161.

31. For the story of Polish Jews under the Nazi rule see Phillip Friedman (ed.), *Martyrs and Fighters* (New York, 1954); Phillip Friedman, *Their Brothers' Keepers* (New York, 1957); K. Iranek-Osmecki, *He Who Saves One Life . . .* (London, 1970), W. Bartoszewski and Z. Lewin, *The Samaritans—Heroes of the Holocaust* (New York, 1971); W. Bartoszewski, *The Blood Shed Unites Us* (Warsaw, 1970); Joseph Tennenbaum, *Underground, The Story of a People* (New York, 1952). See also a series of documented articles by W. Bartoszewski in *Tygodnik Powszechny* in 1963.

32. R. V. Burke, *Dynamics of Communism*, p. 166.

33. *Ibid.*, pp. 167–168.

34. For an interesting interpretation of the tug-of-war between the Jewish and the Polish members of the PUWP, see Witold Jedlicki, "Chamy i żydy" (The Bumpkins and the Jews), *Kultura* (Paris, 1962); the author was a former Communist close to the liberalizing "Puławy faction." The thesis that the "Polish October" was a product of conspiratorial activity of the "Puławy faction" to save the Communist regime has not been fully corroborated by the facts quoted by the author. Nevertheless, the article is stimulating because it stresses the role of the faction in arousing Polish public opinion, and attempting to manipulate it in an anti-Soviet direction.

35. For testimony on the Soviet pressure on the Polish Party concerning its allegedly excessive Jewish membership, see Georges Mond, "A Conversation

in Warsaw," *Problems of Communism*, May–June 1964. For Khrushchev's anti-Semitic view of the Jewish problem see his *Khrushchev Remembers*, II, pp. 178–183.

36. *The New York Times* reported on June 13 that the party leaders opened a major campaign to counter popular sympathy for Israel within the country's Jewish as well as Catholic circles. *Le Monde* reported on June 14 that a Catholic deputy, Konstanty Łubienski, had abstained from a resolution [officially reported unanimous] passed on June 10 by the Sejm Assembly of Seniors and the Sejm Affairs Committee strongly condemning Israeli aggression. The article also quoted an unnamed "Catholic political personality" as saying that Poland's severance of diplomatic relations with Israel had "widened the gulf dividing the population from the government." 'The Anti-Israel Campaign," *East Europe*, August 1967.

37. *Nowiny-Kurier*, May 18, 1973. The Polish leader's British biographer, Nicholas Bethell, shows sympathetic understanding of Gomułka's difficulties in 1967–68 without subscribing to his views or excusing some of his obnoxious methods. The author stresses that "Gomułka is no anti-Semite," that he "was dragged along by events, by a situation he did not control, and that he tried to limit the anti-Zionist campaign"; *Gomułka . . .* , p. 261.

38. For the English test of Gomułka's speech see *Radio Free Europe Situation Reports*, June 22, 1967.

39. *Trybuna ludu*, March 20, 1968.

40. "The Party Purge in Poland," *East Europe*, June 1968.

41. The question of who actually engendered the March 1968 events is still a controversial issue. In the March 24 issue of *Prawo i Zycie*, Kazimierz Kakol a mouthpiece of Moczar, published an article arguing that the party leadership had been faced with an attempted coup. According to the article, unnamed forces were trying to take advantage of the disintegration of the international Communist movement to push plans for "a political earthquake in 1968. . . . A conspiratorial group connected with the Zionist center was trying—under cover of patriotic and democratic slogans—to bring about an increase of demonstrations and street clashes which would raise the very question of the continuation of our rule and its present personnel. . . . We were faced with an attempt to strike at the leadership . . . with an attempt at—I believe this is the proper phrase—a coup d'etat." For a discussion of the problem from a different point of view see Jan Nowak's article in *East Europe*, June 1968; the author argues that it was Moczar who, by brandishing the danger of a "Zionist plot," tried to overthrow Gomułka. Strangely enough, the Stalinist faction of Polish Communists operating in Albania, while sharply critical of the Gomułka regime, interpreted the March crisis in a way similar to that of Kakol. "The March events in Poland in 1968 cannot be boiled down to the problem of Mickiewicz's *The Forefathers' Eve*, the students, or the intelligentsia: it was a political struggle for return to the leadership of the PUWP of the [formerly] eliminated 'Leftist Faction of the Polish October,' the faction which pressed for the 'second stage' of the counter-revolution in Poland;" *W walce o zwycięstwo* (In the Struggle for Victory) (Warsaw, July 1974), p. 12. The pamphlet was most certainly printed not in Warsaw, but in Albania, probably in Tirana, where the dissident group which calls itself the Communist Party of Poland

has operated a radio station and a printing press since 1966. The party was organized by three ex-members of the Central Committee of the PUWP, and leaders of the Natolin faction: Stanisław Łapot, Wiktor Kłosiewicz, and Kazimierz Mijal.

42. For a collection of documents see Zygmunt Baum (ed.), *Wypadki Marcowe, 1968* (The March Events, 1968) (Paris, 1969). For an analysis of the March 1968 events in Poland by an American observer, see A. Ross Johnson's article, "Poland: End of an Era?" in *Problems of Communism,* January-February 1970; Stanisław Staroń, "Political Developments in Poland: The Party Reacts to Challenge," *Orbis,* Winter 1970; and George H. Mond, "The Student Rebels in Poland," *East Europe,* July 1969. The author also consulted "Polish Intellectuals in Revolt Against Neostalinism, March 1968," a manuscript by an eyewitness to the March 1968 events, the Indian scholar Dr. Peter Raina, then a doctoral candidate at Warsaw University and now at the Free University of Berlin.

43. As a spokesman of the Warsaw regime, a columnist of the official *Trybuna ludu,* S. Krasucki, put it in a fortnightly review *Fakty i myśli* of November 19, 1968: "In politics nothing exists on its own and everything is interconnected. An economic opening to the West must bring with it repercussions in foreign policy, particularly since this opening includes a hand extended toward a richer partner. . . . Every international agreement has its own logic." For Gomułka's speech advocating further integration of the Soviet camp see his *Przemówienia, 1967* (Speeches 1967) (Warsaw, 1968), especially pp. 307–308.

44. Roman Dmowski, *Świat powojenny a Polska* (The Postwar World and Poland) (Warsaw, 1931), p. 186. For an attempt to draw a parallel between Dmowski's and Gomułka's politics of cooperation with Russia, see A. Bromke, *Poland's Politics . . .* (Cambridge, Mass., 1967).

45. For Gomułka's stand on the Sino-Soviet dispute see M. K. Dziewanowski, "Poland," in Adam Bromke (ed.), *The Communist States at the Crossroads Between Moscow and Peking* (New York, 1965), and Hansjakob Stehle, *Polish Communism and the Sino-Soviet Rift* (Cambridge, Mass., 1963).

46. For a detailed analysis of the intra-party struggle see Jerzy Ptakowski, "The Fifth Polish Party Congress," *East Europe,* January 1969.

47. For the English text of the treaty see the *New York Times,* November 2, 1970. For a Polish-German comment on the treaty of December 7, 1970, see Adam Bromke and Harold von Rickhoff, "The Polish-West Germany Treaty," *East Europe,* February 1971; for a semi-official Polish view: Ryszard Frelek, *Subject Europe* (Warsaw, 1971), pp. 132–141; see also Hansjakob Stehle, *Nachbarn in Osten* (Frankfurt a.M., 1971), p. 255ff.

48. For a discussion of the issue of restructuring the economy see Michael Gamarnikov's book *Economic Reform in Eastern Europe* (Detroit, Mich., 1968), especially chapter 2 and the epilogue; also his article "Poland Returns to Economic Reform," *East Europe,* November-December 1969. For a scholarly analysis of the issue of reform of Polish industry prior to 1971, see J. G. Zieliński, *Economic Reform in Polish Industry* (London, New York, Toronto, 1973).

49. For the most outspoken criticism of Gomułka's economy see W. Brus, *Ogólne problemy funkcjonowania gospodarki socjalistycznej* (About General

Problems of Socialist Economy) (Warsaw, 1961); for an analysis of interdependence between politics and economics, Bogdan Mieczkowski, "Poland: Politics vs. the Economy," *East Europe*, December 1968.

50. For a collection of documents pertaining to the December 1970 events, see *Dokumenty: Poznań 1956–Grudzień 1970* (Documents: Poznań 1956-December 1970) (Paris, 1971); see also Ewa Wacowska (ed.), *Rewolta szczeinńska i jej znaczenie* (The Szczecin Revolt and Its Significance) (Paris, 1971); for the smoldering discontent see *Głos szczeciński* (Voice of Szczecin, January 26, 1971; see also Z. A. Pełczyński, "The Downfall of Gomułka," *Canadian Slavonic Papers*, Nos. 1 & 2, 1973.

51. Analyzing the causes of discontent among the workers, and the reasons for their revolt in December 1970, a Polish sociologist concluded that the party was largely responsible, for: "The Communist establishment, by pushing toward industrialization, egalitarianism (at least in some fields), and by generating great expectations as regards the general improvement of working class conditions, prepared the ground for dissatisfaction. There is too great a discrepancy between the growing aspirations of workers and the reality of low wages, limited opportunity for promotion, poor working conditions, and ineffective management. What happened in December 1970 was the outcome of these growing contradictions." J. Matejko, "Why Polish Workers Are Restless," *East Europe*, July–August, 1972,

52. While the downfall of Gomułka was triggered by the workers' revolt on the Baltic coast, there are some indications that inner party plotting and machinations may have contributed to the way the resulting crisis was handled. The conspiratorial explanation of the December 1970 crisis has yet to be more fully documented. An article published in *Neue Züricher Zeitung* of January 21, 1971, reported that a conspiracy against Gomułka by Gierek and Moczar had developed in the fall of 1970. The article, discussed by several observers of Poland, is the basis for the conspiratorial theory of the December 1970 events. The primacy of the workers' revolt, however, has not been disproved by the theory.

53. For a thorough analysis of Gomułka's system by his comrades, see: "The Eighth Plenum of the Central Committee of the Polish United Workers' Party, 6–7 February, 1971," *Nowe drogi* (New Roads), May 1971, Special Issue, restricted to party members. For a sympathetic appraisal of Gomułka's rule, by a Polish-Canadian scholar, see Adam Bromke, "Beyond the Gomułka Era," *Foreign Affairs*, April 1971. For a critical evaluation of the Gomułka era by a Polish Marxist and his former close coworker, see Władysław Bieńkowski, *Socjologia klęski* (Sociology of Disaster) (Paris, 1971).

54. As for Gomułka's personal habits, see Władysław Tykocinski's testimony in *East Europe*, November 1966.

55. For a discussion of Poland's contribution to the restructuring of the Soviet camp, see Andrzej Brzeski, "Poland as a Catalyst of Change in the Communist Economic System," *The Polish Review*, Spring 1971; for a view that Gomułka's rule embodied stagnation see Frank Gibney, *The Frozen Revolution* . . . (New York, 1959); for a sympathetic view of the Gomułka regime before its final decline: Hansjakob Stehle, *The Independent Satellite* (New York, 1965).

CHAPTER 17   EPILOGUE: UNDER GIEREK'S LEADERSHIP

1. For Gierek's official biography, see *Krajowa Agencja Informacyjna* (Polish Information Agency), December 15–21, 1971. A former party member who knows Gierek fairly well characterizes him in the following way: "Edward Gierek is an old-fashioned Communist, but without fanaticism or zealousness. His Marxism is encumbered by few dogmas. It is almost pragmatic. He believes profoundly in the leading role that history conferred upon Communist parties and lives by the maxim that a government should be strong and rule unshakeably." Mieczysław Maneli, "Poland's New Artful Dodger," *The New York Times,* January 16, 1971.

2. For analysis of events in Poland since December 1970, see Adam Bromke and Michael Garmańkow, "Poland Under Gierek," *The Problems of Communism,* September-October 1972; Harold Laeuen, *Polen nach dem Sturz Gomułkas* (Stuttgart-Degerloch, 1972); a special issue of *Canadian Slavic — Revue Canadienne des Slavistes,* Nos. 1 and 2, 1973; also Richard Staar, "Poland: Old Wine in New Bottles," *Current History,* May 1973.

3. *New York Times,* January 1, 1971; for Gierek's initial plans see also Gierek's speech in *Trybuna ludu,* February 8, 1971.

4. *Życie Warszawy,* January 9, 1971, and *New York Times,* January 27, 1971.

5. The question of how much indebtedness Poland can actually afford is controversial, and hotly contested by her official spokesmen. "An incorrect opinion is that Poland's indebtedness abroad was excessive and dangerous for our economic balance. As regards to our indebtedness abroad, by the end of 1970, it amounted to 50% of the Polish export value, repaid by annual installments amounting to 12% of the export value. Our indebtedness is relatively small compared to other countries: Norway 66%, Denmark 63%, Great Britain 103%, and Japan 175%." Interview with Henryk Kisiel, Vice-Minister of Foreign Trade, in *Trybuna ludu,* September 16, 1971.

6. Symptomatic for the party's future plans in the countryside is a series of articles published in *Życie Gospodarcze* (Economic Life), between October 24, 1972 and February 18, 1973. See also two articles by a high functionary of the Ministry of Agriculture, Karol Gawłowski, about state farms as a factor of modernization in *Życie Partii,* Nos. 7 (266) and 12 (271), 1974.

7. For an analysis of Polish economic situation since 1971, see Michal Gamarnikow's essay in *Radio Free Europe Research,* November 2, 1973. As an American observer of Eastern Europe pointed out: "Last year, Poland kept price increases of food to 8 per cent on the official market, but in doing so, created shortages. Poles were faced with a choice between empty shelves and long lines at government markets, or going to the private market (not quite a black market). They could generally get what they needed at the private market, but there, price increases last year were about 35 per cent." Malcolm W. Brown "East's Common Market Also Feels the Pinch," *New York Times,* February, 9, 1975.

8. *Trybuna ludu,* January 1, 1971.

9. *New York Times,* March 6, 1971.

10. *Radio Free Europe Research,* May 11 and June 22, 1973. For an analysis

of the program of educational reform (to come into effect in 1978) as a decisive factor in the party's youth policy, see *ibid.*, November 13, 1973; according to the R. F. E. analyst the hierarchy has repeatedly protested against the reform because long hours and consolidated parish schools will curtail parental influences over children and make it more difficult to organize religious educational classes.

11. *The New York Times*, November 13, 1973.

12. Jan Wojna, *"Pacta Conventa* Partii z Narodem"* (For a Social Contract of the Party with the Nation), *Życie Warszawy*, September 11, 1971.

13. PZPR, *VI Zjazd Polskiej Zjednoczonej Partii Robotniczej: 6–11 Grudnia 1971* (Sixth Congress of the PUWP: December 6–11, 1971) (Warsaw, 1972), p. 68. Edward Babiuch, ""O niektórych problemach rozwoju i umocnienia partii," *Nowe Drogi*, September 1971, p. 8; *New York Times*, December 12, 1971. See also Adam Bromke, "A New Political Style," *Problems of Communism*, September-October 1972. For an official collection of congressional documents: *For Further Development of People's Poland . . . Basic Documents* (Warsaw, 1972).

14. Szlachcic, originally a career officer of the Militia, was a former coworker and protégé of Gierek in Upper Silesia; since 1968, Szlachcic was a member of the Central Committee.

15. Wiesław Klimczak's article in *Życie partii* (Party Life), September 1973; also Edward Babiuch's article in *Nowe Drogi*, September 1971. For an analysis of the party schools see *Radio Free Europe Research*, March 8, 1974. Also the intensity of the party work at the top level has been heightened. While under Gomułka the Politburo was convened rarely and the Secretariat not at all; according to a report to the April 16, 1971 plenum of the Central Committee, Secretary Edward Babiuch stressed that the Politburo had met 23 times in 16 weeks, and the Secretariat 12 times; *Yearbook of International Communism* (Stanford, Calif., 1972), p. 57.

16. *International Herald Tribune*, April 19 and 20, 1973. Similar ceremonies took place in 1974, in a dozen places outside Warsaw. Considerable funds were granted for a new building of the Jewish Theater in Warsaw and also for rebuilding of the ancient Jewish Temple there. Confidential negotiations were opened for resumption of the diplomatic relations with Israel, broken in 1967.

17. On the other hand, "there was evident pride in the comments of officials, and in the press commentaries," observed James Feron, *The New York Times*, June 5, 1972.

18. *The New York Times*, October 10, 1974.

19. Central Statistical Office, *Concise Statistical Yearbook of Poland* (Warsaw, 1974), pp. 11 and XXVIII.

20. Alexander Matejo, "The Executive in Present Day Poland," *Polish Review, Summer,* 1971. For a study of the top echelons of the party leadership (members of the Politburo and the Secretariat) see Donald Pienkos, "The Polish Party Elite," *East Europe*, July 1974.

21. While 8–9,000 Polish citizens of Jewish extraction left Poland in 1968, there are still some 5–10,000 Jews who remained. Some 3,000 are organized in 18 religious congregations, but they have not a single rabbi. The Jews in Poland have their Historical Institute, their periodicals, *Folks Sztyme*, which prints 3,000 copies, as well as their theater in Warsaw; James Feron, *The New*

York Times Magazine, April 15, 1973, and *News From Poland,* Radio Free Europe, May 16, 1973.

22. David S. Mason, "Political Succession in Poland," manuscript.

23. As a Yugoslav journalist, a former correspondent of a Belgrade daily put it: "A large majority of the Poles consider their Catholicism a patriotic affirmation." Velizar Savić, *Politika* (Belgrade), April 14, 1968.

24. For a discussion of the concept of "domestication": Z. Brzezinski, *The Soviet Bloc* . . . (Cambridge, Mass., 1960), p. 52.

25. According to a Polish sociologist (who serves as Chairman of the governmental Council of Science, Higher Education, and Technology) writing at the end of the 1960's, "the young generation of Poles . . . has been already educated in the order of things and takes it for granted. They would, of course, like to improve it, but not to replace it with another system." Jan Szczepanski, *The Polish Society,* pp. 74–75. One wonders to what extent the statement is correct in view of the experiences of 1956 and 1970. One of the factors that irritates nonparty people is the secrecy shrouding the expenses involved in maintaining the huge party bureaucracy; see Ewa Wacowska's article in *Kultura, Paris,* No. 3 (313), 1973.

26. An interview with a nonparty worker by James Feron, *New York Times,* July 21, 1971.

INDEX OF SUBJECTS

In this index an effort has been made to list only those items which are significant. The bibliography and the notes have not been covered.

INDEX OF NAMES

Russian Research Center Studies

* Out of print.
† Publications of the Harvard Project on the Soviet Social System.